United Nations Interventionism, 1991–2004

After years of paralysis, the 1990s saw an explosion in the number of United Nations (UN) field operations around the world. In terms of scope and level of ambition, these interventions went beyond the tried and tested principles of classical UN peacekeeping. Indeed, in some cases – such as Cambodia, Kosovo and East Timor – the UN presence assumed the form of quasi-protectorates designed to steer warn-torn and deeply divided societies towards lasting peace. This book examines the UN's performance and assesses the wider impact on 'new interventionism' on international order and the study of international relations. Featuring eight case studies of major UN interventions and an introductory chapter outlining the most important theoretical and political features of the international system which have led to the increased interventionary practices of the United Nations, this book will appeal to students and researchers in international relations and international organisations.

MATS BERDAL is Professor of Security and Development in the Department of War Studies at King's College, London. He was formerly the Director of Studies at the International Institute for Strategic Studies in London.

SPYROS ECONOMIDES is Senior Lecturer in the European Institute of the London School of Economics. He was a Research Associate of the International Institute for Strategic Studies and has served as Specialist Adviser to the EU Committee of the House of Lords.

LSE Monographs in International Studies

Published for The Centre for International Studies,
London School of Economics and Political Science

Editorial board
John Kent (Chair)
Christopher Coker
Frederick Halliday
Dominic Lieven
Karen E. Smith

The Centre for International Studies at the London School of
Economics and Political Science was established in 1967. Its aim is
to promote research on a multi-disciplinary basis in the general field of
international studies.

To this end the Centre offers visiting fellowships, sponsors research
projects and seminars and endeavours to secure the publication of
manuscripts arising out of them.

*Whilst the Editorial Board accepts responsibility for recommending the
inclusion of a volume in the series, the author is alone responsible for views
and opinions expressed.*

United Nations Interventionism, 1991–2004

Edited by

Mats Berdal and Spyros Economides

CAMBRIDGE UNIVERSITY PRESS
Cambridge, New York, Melbourne, Madrid, Cape Town, Singapore, São Paulo

Cambridge University Press
The Edinburgh Building, Cambridge CB2 2RU, UK

Published in the United States of America by Cambridge University Press,
New York

www.cambridge.org
Information on this title: www.cambridge.org/9780521547673

First published 1996 as *The New Interventionism, 1991–1994: United Nations
Experience in Cambodia, Former Yugoslavia and Somalia* edited by James Mayall;
updated with new title 2007.

Printed in the United Kingdom at the University Press, Cambridge

A catalogue record for this publication is available from the British Library

Library of Congress Cataloguing in Publication data

United Nations interventionism, 1991–2004 / edited by Mats Berdal and Spyros
Economides. – [Rev. and updated ed.].
p. cm. – (LSE monographs in international studies)
Originally published: The new interventionism, 1991–1994 / edited by
James Mayall, 1996.
Includes bibliographical references and index.

ISBN-13: 978-0-521-83897-9 (hardback: alk. paper)
ISBN-10: 0-521-83897-5 (hardback: alk. paper)
ISBN-13: 978-0-521-54767-3 (pbk.: alk. paper)
ISBN-10: 0-521-54767-9 (pbk.: alk. paper)

1. Peacekeeping forces – Case studies. 2. Diplomatic negotiations in international
disputes – Case studies. 3. United Nations. 4. Intervention (International law)
5. World politics – 1989– I. Berdal, Mats R., 1965– II. Economides, Spyros.
III. New interventionism, 1991–1994.
JZ6374.U553 2007
341.5'84–dc22   2006036485

Contents

Contributors

ADEKEYE ADEBAJO is the Executive Director of the Centre for Conflict Resolution, University of Cape Town, South Africa. Before assuming this post, he was Director of the Africa Programme at the International Peace Academy and Adjunct Professor at Columbia University's School of International and Public Affairs in New York. He is the author of *West Africa's Security Challenges: Building Peace in A Troubled Region*, (2004).

MATS BERDAL is Professor of Security and Development in the Department of War Studies at King's College London. Prior to that, from 2000 to 2003, he was Director of Studies at the International Institute for Strategic Studies in London. He is the co-editor (with David Malone) of *Greed and Grievance: Economic Agendas in Civil Wars* (Lynne Rienner, 2000).

SIMON CHESTERMAN is Executive Director of the Institute for International Law and Justice at New York University School of Law. Prior to that he was a Senior Associate at the International Peace Academy and Director of UN Relations at the International Crisis Group in New York. He is the author of *You, The People: The United Nations, Transitional Administration, and State-Building* (2004).

SPYROS ECONOMIDES is Senior Lecturer in the European Institute of the London School of Economics and Deputy Director of the Hellenic Observatory. He has been a Research Associate of the IISS and has served as Specialist Adviser to the EU Committee of the House of Lords, UK. He is the co-author of *The Economic Factor in International Relations: A Brief Introduction* (2001).

SEBASTIAN VON EINSIEDEL is Special Assistant of the President at the International Peace Academy in New York. In 2004–05, he worked as a researcher with the UN Secretary-General's High-level Panel on Threats, Challenges, and Change. From 2002 to 2004, he served as

Senior Program Officer at IPA, focusing on State-building and Security Council diplomacy.

BRUCE JONES is Co-Director of the Center on International Cooperation at New York University. In 2003–04, Dr Jones served as Deputy Research Director for the High-level Panel on Threats, Challenges and Change. He is the author of *Peacemaking in Rwanda: The Dynamics of Failure* (2001).

DAVID KEEN is Reader in Complex Emergencies at the London School of Economics. His most recent publications include *Endless War?: Hidden Functions of the 'War on Terror'* (2006), and *Conflict and Collusion in Sierra Leone* (2005).

MICHAEL LEIFER was Emeritus Professor of International Relations and Pro-Director of the London School of Economics. He was also the founder of the Asia Research Centre at the LSE. He authored among others *Singapore's Foreign Policy: Coping with Vulnerability* (2000) and the *Dictionary of Modern Politics of South-East Asia* (3d Ed, 2000).

IOAN M. LEWIS is Emeritus Professor of Anthropology at the London School of Economics. He is the author of *Arguments with Ethnography: Comparative Approaches to History, Politics and Religion* (1999).

DAVID MALONE is High Commissioner of Canada to India. He is a former Ambassador of Canada to the UN in New York and from 1998–2004 served as President of the International Peace Academy. He is the author of several books, the most recent of the latter being *The International Stuggle for Iraq: Politics in the UN Security Council, 1980–2005.*

JAMES MAYALL is Emeritus Professor at the University of Cambridge. From 1997 to 2004 he was Sir Patrick Sheehy Professor of International Relations in the University of Cambridge and Director of the Centre of International Studies. He is the author of *World Politics: Progress and its Limits* (2000) and he edited *The New Interventionism 1991–1994: United Nations Experience in Cambodia, former Yugoslavia and Somalia* (1996).

PAUL TAYLOR is Emeritus Professor of International Relations, and, until July 2004, was Director of the European Institute, at the London School of Economics. Most recently he has published *International Organization in the Age of Globalization* (2003).

To Dominique

Preface

The original edition of this volume, *The New Interventionism, 1991–1994*, published in 1996 and edited by James Mayall, offered an initial assessment of the United Nation's (UN) interventions in the immediate post-Cold War. The volume concentrated on three case studies; Cambodia, former Yugoslavia and Somalia and included extensive chronologies, and the relevant Security Council Resolutions for each case, in several appendices.

In this volume we develop the debates on UN intervention post-1990 by updating the original three case studies and adding to them five more: Rwanda, Haiti, East Timor, Kosovo and Sierra Leone. In each case, the causes and consequences of UN intervention are examined in the context of the history of each specific crisis, as well as against the backdrop of wider changes – of both a normative and geopolitical kind – in international relations. The case selection is primarily driven by the extent of UN intervention and the significance of the UN experience in these crises for the functioning of the organisation and its international standing, as well as by their chronological and geographical scope.

As stated by James Mayall in the Introduction, this volume concentrates on the 'prospects for international cooperation, the preconditions for success, the causes of failure, and the constraints that must be overcome if the UN Charter is to act as a constitution for international society, rather than as a mere list of lofty but unattainable principles'. These themes were just as evident in the original volume, but that volume was published with the immediate post-Cold War context in mind; with the background of the much touted 'New World Order' which would allow for a significant UN interventionary role in a revamped international political system. We have moved on quite markedly from that prospect and the international context has developed in such a manner that a series of new factors have influenced attitudes towards the UN and its own ability to fulfil its Charter obligations.

This volume not only revisits the themes developed in the 1996 edition but also addresses a novel set of concerns in relation to the UN and its role in international interventions. As shown in the new case studies, and with the experience of Cambodia, former Yugoslavia and Somalia in mind, UN interventions rapidly moved on from their more traditional peacekeeping functions throughout the 1990s. Growing out of, but also partly in response to, the experiences of the early 1990s, the UN has assumed responsibilities well beyond traditional peacekeeping, with a much stronger emphasis on *justice*-related goals, democracy promotion, post-conflict peacebuilding, and even economic development. In some of the new cases examined, notably East Timor and Kosovo, the UN assumed governance functions that were unprecedented in scope and authority.

Financial and logistical issues continue to permeate all debates on UN policy and its effectiveness both in the broadest possible terms and within the specific discussions on UN interventions. As in the original volume, contributors have sought to assess the degree to which the UN has 'learned lessons' from previous operations or whether it has proved unable to do so because of bureaucratic inadequacies and external pressures from the sovereign member states from which it gains its legitimacy and upon which it relies for direction and support. But what the new cases also show is that the role of the UN in an evolving international system is determined just as much by the debates on what it should be doing as well as what it can or has been enabled to do. The issues outlined above have come to the fore because of a range of crises which sparked off demands for international intervention. Thus the lessons learned – or those that should have been learned – stray far beyond operational and resource-based issues, and heavily into wider questions about the changing roles, and the constraints on them, of the UN in the field of international peace and security.

Since the first edition was published, Professor Michael Leifer, a contributor and driving force behind the initial project, has passed away. The intellectual rigour, kindness and enthusiasm he displayed were a source of inspiration to the other contributors, just as they have been to countless students over the years.

MATS BERDAL AND SPYROS ECONOMIDES
London, December 2006.

Acknowledgements

The editors are much indebted to David Ucko and Eleni Xiarchogian-nopoulou for their help in the final stages of preparation of this book. Their research assistance, editorial work and technical skills proved invaluable.

1 Introduction

James Mayall

The nations and peoples of the United Nations are fortunate in a way that those of the League of Nations were not. We have been given a second chance to create the world of our Charter that they were denied. With the cold war ended we have drawn back from the brink of a confrontation that threatened the world, and, too often, paralysed our organisation.[1]

Boutros Boutros-Ghali (1992)

Historians may look back on the first years of the twenty-first century as a decisive moment in human history. The different societies that make up the human family are today inter-connected as never before. They face threats that no nation can hope to master by acting alone – and opportunities that can be much more hopefully exploited if all nations work together.[2]

Kofi A. Annan (2004)

The first edition of this book attempted to assess the chances that an international society would be able to respond positively to the second chance identified by Boutros Boutros-Ghali, the then United Nations (UN) secretary-general. It did so by examining three major international interventions of the early post-Cold War period in Cambodia, former Yugoslavia and Somalia. Well before the book went to press, it was already clear that the answer was not a foregone conclusion. Partly in reaction to failures on the ground and partly due to the escalating demands for UN intervention around the world, optimism gave way to pessimism as the prevailing mood surrounding UN peacekeeping. Evidence accumulated, particularly but not only in the United States, – the leading if notoriously reluctant paymaster of the UN – that

---

[1] Boutros Boutros-Ghali, *Agenda for Peace: Preventive Diplomacy, Peacemaking and Peacekeeping. Report of the Secretary-General Pursuant to the Statement Adopted by the Summit Meeting of the Security Council on 31 January 1992* (New York: United Nations, 1992), para. 75.

[2] Kofi A. Annan, 'Foreword by the United Nations Secretary-General', *A More Secure World: Our Shared Responsibility. Report of the Secretary-General's High-Level Panel on Threats, Challenges and Change* (New York, United Nations, 2004), p. vii.

the governments of the major powers were more interested in limiting than extending their international commitments. But, would they be able to?

A major rationale for our study rested on the conviction that the major powers would find it difficult to reverse the trend of internationally coordinated efforts at crisis management, even if they wished to do so. That trend had started during the closing stages of the Iran–Iraq war, when Mikhail Gorbachev's rise to power in the Soviet Union ended the paralysis of the Security Council. With the threat of the veto removed, a period of close cooperation among the five permanent members (P5) was inaugurated. The world is now so interdependent and Western governments so vulnerable to public opinion mobilised through the media, that there can be no guarantee that they will not repeatedly be drawn into international crises, even where their own instincts and the balance of professional advice are in favour of non-intervention. The five additional interventions – in Rwanda, Haiti, East Timor, Kosovo and Sierra Leone – that we analyse in this expanded second edition, suggest that this judgement was correct.

The sentiments underlying the two quotes from successive secretary-generals at the head of this Introduction are remarkably similar. Both men raise two perennial questions – what is to be the basis of international order and how is it to be upheld? In broad terms, their own answers – a revitalised world system of collective security, reformed to meet new challenges – are also comparable.

In other respects the contrast between the two statements could not be sharper. The main reason for the contrast is the sequence of dramatic events that separates the two documents. The terrorist attacks on the United States in September 2001 occasioned an unprecedented but sadly all too brief show of international solidarity. The divisions caused by the Iraq war unfortunately went deeper. Boutros Boutros-Ghali's *Agenda for Peace* was published when the reputation of the UN stood at an all time high. It was written at the request of the Security Council, whose members had endorsed the American president's call for a New World Order, in which global security would be underwritten by the UN and would provide protection not merely to states threatened by aggression but to the victims of large-scale human rights abuse, even where necessary from their own governments. Kofi Anan's statement is taken from his Foreword to a report – *A More Secure World: Our Shared Responsibility* – that he commissioned in an attempt to repair the damage inflicted on the organisation by the Iraq war.

It would perhaps be overly melodramatic to argue that by commissioning the report, the secretary-general was acknowledging that the UN was fighting for its life. But there can be little doubt that the current crisis of multilateral diplomacy is more severe than any that has preceded it. The report attempted to chart a reform programme that would both command the support of the United States, as the UN's main critic, and without whose support it could not function and more generally restore its credibility. Since the alternative to a reformed multilateral order – presumably some kind of world empire under which the will of the United States will be unrestrained – is both dangerous to the United States itself and deeply unattractive to the rest of the world, its resolution could hardly be more urgent.

That it will not be easy will be clear from the chapters of this book. As with the earlier edition, it is intended as a contribution to the debate about how the questions posed by the last two secretary-generals should be answered and for which Kofi Annan has specifically called. Our aim is to see what an examination of some of the major interventions that have been carried out by the UN since 1991 can tell us about the prospects for international cooperation, the preconditions for success, the causes of failure, and the constraints that must be overcome if the UN Charter is to act as a constitution for international society, rather than as a mere list of lofty but unattainable principles. The purpose of this Introduction is first to sketch the historical background out of which the 'new interventionism' emerged, and second to identify common issues that have been raised by the eight crises we examine, and the lessons that can be derived from the experience of the UN in its attempt to facilitate an appropriate international response to them.

The problem of intervention – or rather whether it can ever be justified, and if so, under what circumstances – lies at the heart of all debates about international order. Before turning to the immediate historical background of the eight case studies, it may be helpful therefore to outline the contending positions.[3] Apart from those un-reconstructed

---

[3] There have been a number of attempts to classify international thought according to the positions adopted by theorists and statesmen on such issues as sovereignty, the use of force, intervention and international cooperation. The most influential are Martin Wight, *International Theory: The Three Traditions*, Gabrielle Wight and Brian Porter (eds.) (Leicester: Leicester University Press, for the Royal Institute of International Affairs, 1992); Hedley Bull, *The Anarchical Society* (London: Macmillan, 1977); and Michael Donelan, *Elements of International Theory* (Oxford: Oxford University Press, 1991). Wight and Bull offer a triad of positions – realist, rationalist and revolutionist – while Donelan identifies five – realist, rationalist, historicist, fideist and natural law. In this Introduction, I have reduced the positions to two – pluralist or solidarist – on the grounds that it was the compromise between these two positions, and the various

realists who deny the possibility of international society, there is a broad consensus that it exists, but as a society of sovereign states, not peoples. On this view, while states are primarily concerned with defending their own interests, they also combine to uphold the institutions of international society: international law, diplomacy and, more contentiously, the balance of power and the special responsibility of the great powers for international order. However, the consensus breaks down at this point. On one side stand the pluralists: those who maintain that sovereignty demands minimal rules of coexistence, above all that of non-interference in the domestic affairs of other states. Opposing them are the solidarists: those who hold that sovereignty is conditional and that the existence of an international society requires us to determine both the ends to which, in principle, all states, nations and peoples should be committed, and the means by which international order should be upheld.

Those who hold to the pluralist position – that is of an international society defined by the law of coexistence – do not deny that intervention occurs. On occasion, they may even consider it justified, for example, to maintain the balance of power or to counter an intervention by a hostile state. They also allow one exception to the ethic of self-help, namely to permit alliances to deter or resist aggression. But they would be unlikely to accept the notion of a disinterested collective intervention to uphold an abstract conception of international order. This is because they believe that coexistence between sovereign powers rules out the possibility of developing a genuine community of mankind. To quote a recent American formulation, pluralists might concede that intervention is justified where 'there is an international community of *interest* for dealing with [a] problem on a multilateral basis',[4] but they would reject any suggestion that it could be justified merely in defence of a common humanity, or by reference to an organic theory of society under which a surgical intervention might be deemed necessary to cut out a cancerous growth before it spread, more or less the position advocated by the current US doctrine of pre-emption.

It is probably fair to say that, left to themselves, the governments of the major powers would have continued to favour a pluralist interpretation of international society. But they have not been left alone. The experiences of the twentieth century, two world wars, the ideological confrontation between capitalism and communism, the relentless pressures of an expanding world market and, above all, the repeated

---

combinations of rationalist and realist assumptions on which they rest, that shaped the UN Charter, and hence frames the current debate on UN intervention.

[4] PDD 25, my italics.

experience of genocide from the Holocaust in the 1930s and 1940s, through Pol Pot's regime in Kampuchea during the 1970s, to the Rwandan tragedy of 1994–1995, have led them to flirt with various forms of internationalism and/or cosmopolitanism, without ever carrying through the fundamental restructuring that would be required to put them into practice. Thus, after both the First World War and the Second World War, it was the victorious great powers that were the primary architects of the League of Nations and the UN, organisations that faithfully reflected the confusion on the pluralist/solidarist divide that reigned in their own societies. The attack on the Twin Towers and the Pentagon in 2001 merely deepened the confusion. It brought to the fore a group of intellectuals within the Republican Party, the so-called neo-conservatives, who combine a Wilsonian enthusiasm for seeking peace through the export of democracy, if necessary by force, with a ruthless rejection of those solidarist projects such as the International Criminal Court (ICC) and the Kyoto Protocol on Global Warming that they deem to be hostile to US national interests.

The Charter of the UN represents an attempt to bridge the two conceptions of international society. Under Chapter VII, the Charter countenances collective action to deter manifest threats to international peace and security. This commitment is arguably consistent with pluralist beliefs, since it can be represented as a global extension of the right to form alliances, with the same objective. Indeed, from this point of view, collective security is in effect an alliance of the whole, under the responsible leadership of the UN Security Council. But the Charter also binds its signatories to respect certain fundamental human rights, including the right of all peoples to self-determination. These latter commitments rest on solidarist assumptions. They therefore beg the question: how should international society respond when peoples' allegedly fundamental rights are systematically abused not by other states but by their own governments?

Since the end of the Cold War, the UN has been struggling with this question. It is our contention that, while the new interventionism raises important conceptual, even philosophical questions about the basis and extent of international obligation, answers cannot usefully be constructed *a priori*. This is essentially because while international society rests on the law, and while its current interpretation often shapes policy – for example, allowing 'the right of all peoples to self-determination' to apply to East Timor but not to Chechnya or Tibet – international society is neither synonymous with international law nor is the law itself static. We shall only know whether a measure of 'progress' is possible in international affairs, therefore, by examining on the one hand the experience of the UN in responding to individual crisis, and on the other the impact of this experience on member states themselves.

The impact of the Cold War and its aftermath

The Cold War silenced the debate between pluralists and solidarists. The use of the veto, primarily until 1966 by the Soviet Union and thereafter, by the West, also ensured that even pluralist conceptions of legitimate intervention were seldom put to the test. By the same token, the stand-off between the two superpowers ensured that there was little room for contesting the political vocabulary of international affairs. Thus, state sovereignty was the principle that not only took priority over all others – except of course when it stood in the way of state or alliance interests – but was also regarded as self-evident: either you had it or you did not. By entrenching sovereignty on either side of the ideological divide, other awkward questions were put safely out of reach. Eventually, virtually all states signed the Universal Declaration of Human Rights and the majority also ratified the two supporting conventions,[5] but it was governments alone which decided how they should implement their commitments. With the exception of South Africa, whose apartheid policy was singled out for international criticism from 1960 onwards, governments were not held to account for their human rights record. And even South Africa, which fell prey to an alliance between the ex-colonial states and the Soviet bloc, and which made the mistake of violating the professed values of the Western democracies, was nonetheless protected by the West from effective international sanctions.

Respect for sovereignty not only prevented humanitarian intervention but entailed respect for the territorial integrity of existing states. The merits of claims for national self-determination were never considered. Despite the right of all peoples to self-determination contained in the Charter, the exercisex of this right came to be identified only with European decolonisation. Subsequent secessions and/or irredentist enlargements were ruled out. This meant that the criteria for state creation and recognition, other than in the context of decolonisation, were never examined. The transfer of power generally followed a test of local opinion, but in many cases the independence election was the last to be held during the Cold War period. Authoritarian regimes replaced democratically elected ones, without it affecting in any way their membership of the international society. Article 2 (7) of the Charter

---

[5] The International Covenant on Civil and Political Rights and the International Covenant on Economic and Social Rights.

did not discriminate in the protection it provided to regimes from interference in their domestic affairs.

Finally, the combination of paralysis in the Security Council, caused by the virtually automatic use of the veto by one or the other side, and the conventional, static and unreflective interpretation given to the principle of state sovereignty marginalised the UN in what had been intended as its central role – the provision of a credible system of international peace and security. It is, of course, by no means certain that the outcome would have been any different in the absence of the Cold War. Indeed, a counterfactual analysis reinforces some of the negative evidence reviewed in this book. On this view, it is the ungoverned nature of the state system and the deep attachment to the principle of state sovereignty, however chimerical it may prove to be, that explains the resistance of international society to improvement of a solidarist kind, rather than any particular configuration of power. However, what seems likely is that, without the Cold War, the issue would have been settled one way or the other long before now.

The Cold War left two other legacies which cast a long and ambiguous shadow over subsequent attempts at reform. The first was the introduction of a distinction between the humanitarian and the political, and security dimensions of the international society. Since there was little prospect of forcing states to honour their obligations with respect to human rights, non-governmental organisations became adept at working to relieve suffering, with the tacit consent of state authorities and without confronting, let alone challenging, their sovereignty. So did UN agencies such as the UNHCR and UNICEF. This practice, while hardly ideal, worked well enough so long as the states in question were propped up by one or the other side in the Cold War, or indeed by their own efforts. But the idea that there could be an international humanitarian order, somehow divorced from political or strategic considerations, was an illusion, as we shall see, became abundantly clear when the state collapsed in Yugoslavia and Somalia. The point was driven home when Rwanda was abandoned to its genocide in 1994 and when the Indonesian military was left in charge of security in the run up to the referendum in East Timor in 1999, thus triggering the humanitarian catastrophe with which the UN then had to deal.

The second legacy of the Cold War to international society was the theory and practice of peacekeeping. The Charter had envisioned international action to repel or deter aggression under Chapter VII and measures, falling short of enforcement, to facilitate the pacific settlement of disputes under Chapter VI. It has generally been assumed that peacekeeping falls under Chapter VI, although it was an improvisation, largely developed by the second secretary-general, Dag Hammarskjöld, as a way of insulating areas of conflict from the Cold War. Peacekeeping operations depended on a mandate from the Security Council, and could therefore be mounted only where there was no objection from one or the other of the superpowers. These operations also depended on the consent of the conflicting parties and circumstances where a ceasefire had been agreed, and there was, therefore, a peace to keep.

Since the ceasefire agreements that the UN was called upon to police were generally precarious, success depended on the peacekeeping forces being trusted by both sides. This in turn required strict impartiality. The expertise developed by the UN during the Cold War stands as one of the organisation's major achievements. The legacy is ambiguous only to the extent that peacekeeping techniques were developed within the constraints imposed by the Cold War, thus making a virtue out of necessity. Once it was over, the organisation found itself drawn into conflicts with different characteristics and for different reasons. For a time it became fashionable to talk of peace enforcement by the UN in situations which, it was claimed, fell halfway between Chapter VI and Chapter VII. As we shall see, in entertaining the possibility of a Chapter Six-and-a-half solution, the UN ran serious risks of becoming part of the problem, rather than part of the solution. Much the same conclusion was reached by Boutros Boutros-Ghali himself in the Supplement to *Agenda for Peace*, which he published in 1995.[6]

The three UN interventions examined in the first edition of this book, and reprinted here, all bear the imprint of the Cold War and the structure it imposed on international relations. The Vietnamese invasion of Cambodia in 1978 was never accepted by the majority of UN member states, despite the fact that the government installed by Vietnam replaced the genocidal Khmer Rouge. Throughout the second phase of the Cold War, Vietnam was protected by the Soviet Union largely for power and for political reasons stemming from its rivalry with China and the United States. After 1985, when the Soviets progressively withdrew their support, possibilities for a political resolution of the conflict emerged. Even then, so strong was the regional interest in favour of sovereignty and against the recognition of regimes imposed from outside, that it was possible to involve the Vietnamese-imposed government only by creating a Supreme National Council, on which all

---

[6] *Supplement to an Agenda for Peace: Position Paper of the Secretary-General on the Occasion of the Fiftieth Anniversary of the United Nations*, A/50/60, S/1995/1, 3 January 1995, paras. 33–46.

Cambodian factions including the Khmer Rouge were represented. It was this council that was held to embody national sovereignty and which occupied the Cambodian seat at the UN.[7] Simultaneously, the UN Transitional Authority in Cambodia (UNTAC) was established with the unenviable, and ultimately impossible, task of creating a neutral political environment.

If the Cambodian intervention drew the UN into a complicated internal conflict concerning the legitimacy of the incumbent regime and its right to international recognition, its involvement in former Yugoslavia arose from the failure of international society to address two other issues: legitimate secession and the protection of minority rights. Although communist, Yugoslavia occupied a kind of ideological no-man's land during the Cold War. Indeed, after the rift with Stalin in 1948, Tito was able to exploit this status to extract tacit guarantees of the country's independence. After his death the structure he had created disintegrated; and since economically Yugoslavia had little to offer, the outside world lost interest in it.

The major powers appear to have given little thought to secession and the problems of recognition that it might pose. The working definition of self-determination as decolonisation had been tested several times during the Cold War, but only Bangladesh had fought itself successfully to independence, and then only after the decisive intervention of the Indian army. When the Yugoslav federation fell apart, the Western powers supported the restoration of democracy in the national republics, but paid little attention to the fears of minorities that would predictably arise. The Charter does not recognise minorities as having rights, vesting these entirely with the sovereign state on the one hand and the individual on the other. The collapse of communism led to an exaggerated optimism about the possibility of basing the international order on democratic foundations and about the utility of elections as a technique for conflict resolution. When, in multicultural societies such as Yugoslavia, they had the opposite effect, the UN was called upon to relieve the ensuing humanitarian catastrophe, without any clear understanding of what it could or should do.

Humanitarian disaster was the sole reason for the UN's third major post-Cold War intervention in Somalia. In this case there was no unresolved international problem deriving from the Cold War, since Somali irredentism had been finally abandoned after the country's defeat in the battle for the Ogaden in 1978. Nonetheless, the Cold War had largely shaped the crisis that led to eventual UN intervention in 1992.

---

[7] See chapter 2, pp. 33–5.

Somalia, a desperately poor country, had one saleable asset, namely its strategic coastline on the Red Sea. Under its dictatorial president, Siyad Barre, this asset was traded first to the Soviet Union and then to the United States, primarily in return for military hardware. This was in turn used to fuel inter-clan competition – the traditional pattern of politics in a society where the state was an exotic import – and to establish a dangerously unstable clan hegemony, unprecedented in Somali history.[8] The end of the Cold War left Siyad Barre without any international cards to play, and exposed him to attack by rival clan alliances, that had been put together to break his hegemonic control of the state. The aftermath of the battle left Somalia without a state of any kind, and so confronted the UN with an unfamiliar problem: how to deal with a country without a government.

In a variety of ways, the Cold War thus bequeathed to the UN the three major crises in which the capacity of its members to forge a new order would be tested. Even then, it is by no means certain that the Security Council would have mounted these operations – or at least those in former Yugoslavia and Somalia, where military intervention preceded rather than followed the implementation of a serious ceasefire – had it not been for the dramatic success of Operation Desert Storm in driving Iraq out of Kuwait in February 1991. With hindsight, it is clear that the Gulf War was atypical of the crises that the UN would be called upon to deal with in the post-Cold War world. It arose out of a straight-forward attack by one member of the UN on another. Iraq not only violated an internationally recognised political boundary, ostensibly in pursuit of an irredentist claim, but proceeded to annex Kuwait. As a result, it proved relatively easy to put together a wide-ranging alliance, including the majority of states in the immediate region, and, on the basis of unanimity among the P5, to repel the invasion. It was, more or less, the Charter working as originally intended.

The subsequent involvement in Iraq's internal affairs – to impose from the air safe havens for the Kurds in the north and Shiites in the south – was far more controversial[9] even though they were apparently accepted by Saddam Hussein in a series of memoranda of

---

[8] See chapter 4, pp. 102–7.

[9] This was because the legal rather than the moral basis on which these actions were taken was questionable. While some writers have seen it as the first move in the evolution of a new doctrine of humanitarian intervention, it was greeted with suspicion by several members of the Security Council who saw it as evidence of weakening Western resolve to uphold Article 2 (7). See Adam Roberts and Benedict Kingsbury, 'The UN's Role in International Society', in Adam Roberts and Benedict Kingsbury (eds.), *United Nations, Divided World: The UN's Role in International Relations* (Oxford: Clarendon Press, 1988), pp. 35–6.

understanding. The circumstances that made it possible – and indeed morally necessary – arose directly out of Iraq's defeat in the war and the proximity of Turkish airfields to northern Iraq. They were not likely to be repeated elsewhere; yet it was this aspect of the operation that led those who favoured a more active UN role in international security to see it as a precedent for a new doctrine of humanitarian intervention. This enthusiasm even communicated itself to governments. As Anthony Parsons, a former British permanent representative to the UN, observed:

When the Security Council met at the level of heads of government in January 1992, all speakers expressed confidence regarding the peace-making and peacekeeping capability of the Organisation in the post cold war climate, and many undertook to strengthen its capacity to act pre-emptively before disputes degenerated into conflict. There was no hint from any delegation that the UN was anything but a major asset in terms of national interest, let alone global peace – a far cry from the equivocations of the mid-1980s.[10]

It was against this background of hope tinged with euphoria that the UN embarked on three operations of a scale and complexity never previously attempted.

The post-Cold War context

The Cold War was less obviously a major influence in this second wave of crises, although even here, particularly in Kosovo and East Timor, trace elements of Cold War structures can be detected amongst their underlying causes. In these cases, however, it was the early efforts of the UN itself to put in place a new security framework – and most notably the failures that accompanied some of these efforts – rather than the Cold War that provided the international background against which the drama was enacted. The UN was soon aware that it was sailing into largely uncharted seas and that it needed to learn lessons from its exposure in the new world of expanded peacekeeping and building, if its performance was to improve. As we shall see, the gap between perceiving the need to learn from experience, and actually learning from it, proved harder to bridge.

What were widely represented as UN failures in Bosnia and Somalia initially had a negative impact on the Rwandan and Kosovo crises. The international response to the Rwandan genocide is rightly seen as the lowest point in the UN's post-Cold War history. Most of the blame

---

[10] Anthony Parsons, 'The UN and the National Interests of States', in Adam Roberts and Benedict Kingsbury (eds.), *United Nations, Divided World: The UN's Role in International Relations*, (Oxford: Clarendon Press, 1988), p. 117.

attaches to the members of the Security Council, but the organisation itself and its secretariat do not emerge unscathed. Essentially, when faced with the worst humanitarian catastrophe of the post-Cold War era, the international community did nothing. The crisis blew up in the immediate aftermath of the American withdrawal from Somalia. The Security Council first sounded a retreat from Chapter VII to Chapter VI, reluctantly agreeing to an inadequately resourced peacekeeping mission, and repeatedly ignoring evidence that the Arusha power-sharing agreement that it was meant to underwrite, was under threat from Hutu extremists. Then, when the genocide started in April 1994, even this force was reduced to a size that was barely capable of defending itself, let alone intervening to stop the slaughter, for which, in any case, it had no mandate. All the major powers avoided doing anything that might have encouraged reference to the 1948 Genocide Convention, and the United States refused to provide logistical support to the Nigerian government when it offered to lead a force for stopping the killing and enforcing a cease-fire.

If the Rwandan crisis was the UN's unfinest hour in Africa, the Kosovo crisis saw it ignored altogether in Europe. The reasons were different, although in both cases they hinged on American policy. In Rwanda, the United States was unwilling to take any action within the United Nations or outside it. In Kosovo, they were prepared to act but not under the auspices of the UN. Their reluctance to use the UN was a reflection of the frustration that had led them to abandon it in seeking an end to the wars of the Yugoslav succession. American diplomatic efforts finally led to the convening of a peace conference on Bosnia-Herzegovina, at a US Air Force base in Dayton, Ohio. This conference led to a comprehensive peace agreement that was formally signed in Paris on 14 December 1995. Under it, the UN handed over peacekeeping responsibility to NATO, a move that had become politically necessary after the Somali crisis if US ground troops were to participate. At Dayton, the Americans had decided against pressing the Kosovo issue in order to secure the agreement of Serbian leader, Slobodan Milošević. From the American point of view, therefore, NATO rather than the UN was already the organisation of choice once it was no longer possible for the Western powers to ignore the plight of the Kosovar Albanians.

There were also both legal and political reasons that stood in the way of using the UN to force a resolution of the Kosovo crisis. Neither the break up of the Soviet Union nor of Yugoslavia had been welcomed with enthusiasm by the international community. In the former, a loose analogy with post-1945 European decolonisation, plus the fact that Stalin's nationality policy had led to the creation of Soviet Republics along ethnic lines, allowed the UN to accommodate the successor states without altering its position on secession. By the same token the aspirations of the Chechnyans for self-determination were ignored because Chechnya was part of the Russian Federation and not a Republic in its own right. In the latter case, the same end was achieved by treating the internal boundaries between the national states of the former Yugoslav Federation as international boundaries. As with Chechnya, Kosovo was excluded from this accommodation, since it was an integral part of Serbia, albeit, theoretically with a special status.

There was no difference between the United States and the rest of the Security Council on the issue of secession. Indeed, at Dayton, the United States expended huge diplomatic and financial resources to ensure an outcome that maintained the fiction that the boundaries on the ground had not been changed by force. As it stands at present international law denies a right of unilateral secession in pursuit of self-determination. This was most recently confirmed in an Advisory opinion sought by the Supreme Court of Canada in relation to Quebec, although it is true that the opinion also stated that there was some evidence that in cases of sustained and large-scale human rights abuse of a minority population, a customary right *might be* evolving. Whether this will eventually be proved in Kosovo remains to be seen. Meanwhile, six years after its 'liberation', the unwillingness of international society to sanction the dismemberment of even an unpopular member state remains a formidable obstacle to achieving a final status for the territory.

Despite the damage done to its reputation by its failure to act effectively in Rwanda, and its initial marginalisation in Kosovo, the UN also derived some longer-term benefits from its experience in these conflicts. As Bruce Jones demonstrates in chapter 5, the Rwandan crisis delivered some necessary shock therapy to an institution that from the beginning has been a dumping ground for some of the world's most intractable problems. In 2001, President Clinton declared in Kigali that a similar tragedy must never be allowed to recur. The path to hell is paved with good intentions and sadly little has been done since to give one much confidence that world leaders will be able to deliver on Clinton's commitment. Indeed, the vacillating and ineffective response to the Darfur crisis in western Sudan, when it forced its way into public consciousness in 2004, as well as the totally inadequate international response to the prolonged and murderous, yet largely invisible, crisis in the Democratic Republic of the Congo, suggest that they will not. Nonetheless, since the Rwandan debacle, whenever the authority of the UN has been directly challenged in a crisis in which it is already involved, as in East Timor and Sierra Leone, both the Secretariat and the Security Council have reacted more robustly than they did in Rwanda.

Similarly, as Spyros Economides argues in chapter 8, while NATO had been able to initiate the intervention outside the UN, it could not end the crisis without bringing it back in. The political reason was that Russia supported Serbia for both cultural and geopolitical reasons. The NATO powers could not seek Security Council authorisation for fear of a Russian veto. On the other hand, they could not transform their military victory into a diplomatic and political settlement without Russian cooperation. The end result was the creation of a *de facto* UN trusteeship over Kosovo. This was itself problematic, and faced the UN with a new set of challenges, not all of which have been successfully overcome, but at least it established that the world body could not simply be dispensed with, and that it was the most obviously legitimate lead agency in post-conflict reconstruction.

Two of the remaining three interventions that we examine – East Timor and Sierra Leone – were in different ways directly influenced by the UN's cathartic failure to respond to the Rwandan genocide and its exclusion from the military campaign but subsequent involvement in the post-conflict reconstruction of Kosovo. In other respects, all three built on and were continuous with the first wave of UN interventions during the period of post-Cold War activism. Haiti arguably stands alone, in that the intervention was driven by the US interest in stemming the flow of sea-borne refugees following the overthrow of the Aristide government. But, like Somalia, Haiti demonstrated that when the Security Council has a will to act, the traditional interpretation of a threat to international peace and security as an actual or threatened aggression across a recognised international border, need not necessarily inhibit action under Chapter VII of the Charter. As in former Yugoslavia, the international reaction to the Haitian crisis also reflected the complex division of labour and the evolving relationship between regional organisations and the UN. In Central America, the Organisation of American States (OAS) had been instrumental in persuading the UN to view democratisation as an instrument of conflict resolution; and Haiti was the first case where the overthrow of a democratically elected government was interpreted by the Security Council as a threat to international peace and security.

From a legal point of view, East Timor was the least complicated and most successful of the second wave of UN interventions. In these respects it had much in common with Cambodia. In both cases the UN was brought in to help resolve a long-standing international dispute, along lines that had been previously agreed. East Timor was also relatively uncomplicated politically because it was unfinished business from the Cold War era. By rights, it should have become an independent state under the convention that equated the Charter right of self-determination with European decolonisation. By the mid-1960s, it had been accepted that colonies had a right to independence in accordance with the principle of *uti possidetis juris*, that is within the boundaries established by the outgoing colonial power. Portugal's African colonies – Angola, Guinea Bissau and Mozambique – had achieved independence following the 1974 Portuguese Revolution under this formula. In East Timor, Indonesia had pre-empted this possibility by annexing the territory in 1975, justifying its action on ethnic grounds, despite the fact that the Indonesian nationalist movement had never previously claimed ethnicity as the basis of the nation.

The annexation took place in the aftermath of the Vietnam war and the forced US withdrawal from Indochina, so it was perhaps not surprising that the West acquiesced in the annexation, since it removed the danger of another post-colonial Marxist regime. Nonetheless, with the exception of Australia, no Western country recognised Indonesia's takeover. The end of the Cold War had no immediate impact on Indonesia's determination to hold onto the territory, but the velvet revolution in Eastern Europe and the spread of democracy in Africa and Latin America, inevitably raised expectations in other parts of the world, including East Timor. As Boutros Boutros-Ghali had been careful to point out in his *Agenda for Peace*, not every dissatisfied group could expect to have its claims to statehood recognised. But for East Timor, like Eritrea before it, the cards were stacked in its favour. The Asian financial crisis of 1997 and the downfall of President Suharto opened a window of opportunity. Coming hard on the heels of the establishment of its administration in Kosovo, the UN again found itself called upon to set up an administration, in this case to prepare East Timor for independence in 2002.

The intervention in Sierra Leone was at times threatened with disaster but in the end finished up by doing more to restore the UN's tarnished reputation than any other operation. As Adekeye Adebajo and David Keen show in their contribution to this volume there was a major element of luck – or at least *fortuna* – in this outcome. It could certainly have gone the other way. The problem for the UN in Sierra Leone was not the mandate: Haiti had established that the restoration of an elected government could be interpreted as a legitimate reason for invoking Chapter VII; operations in both Somalia and former Yugoslavia had been justified by the need to halt a humanitarian catastrophe; and the Yugoslav and Haitian operations had been carried out in close cooperation with regional organisations. Rather the problem in Sierra Leone was how to generate both the resources and the political will to act in a crisis that lay beyond the spotlight of world affairs. Although potentially much richer, unlike the Horn of Africa, West Africa had never been a major zone of super-power confrontation. Moreover, given Nigeria's periodic aspirations to act as a regional hegemon, it was both convenient and relatively easy for the P5 to look the other way when first Liberia and then Sierra Leone collapsed into civil war and anarchy.

Curiously, the Economic Community of West African States (ECOWAS) has always worked better as a security organisation than as a mechanism for promoting economic integration. The most probable explanation is that in the latter area, a lack of complementarity between regional economies and fear of Nigerian dominance inhibit serious cooperation, whereas in the former, joint action addresses the shared fear of regional governments of insurgencies spreading from state to state. It also allows Nigeria to exercise legitimate leadership and the smaller states to protect their interests with its help. Nonetheless, by largely ignoring the humanitarian consequences of state collapse in Liberia and Sierra Leone, the Western members of the Security Council, and particularly Britain, found themselves caught in a contradiction.

Following the drawing up of the Harare Declaration at the Commonwealth summit in 1991, those who took power by force were suspended from Commonwealth membership. Nigeria itself was suspended in 1995 after its military dictator, Sani Abacha, had ignored Commonwealth pressure and executed the writer, Ken Sara Wiwa, and nine other Ngoni activists, as was Sierra Leone following the overthrow of the elected government of Ahmad Kabbah by Major Johnny Paul Koroma in 1997. Governments, which were preaching democratisation, not merely as an instrument of conflict resolution but as the basis of the post-Cold War international order, found themselves in the invidious position of depending on an odious military dictator to restore to power the elected government in Freetown. The death of Abacha in June 1998 paved the way for Nigeria's return to civilian rule, but the newly elected President Obansanjo quickly called the international community's bluff, making the perfectly reasonable argument that he could not be expected to address the manifold problems that had to be tackled at home in order to entrench democracy and simultaneously carry the main burden of policing the West African region. The stage was set for the UN, helped at a critical point by the United Kingdom acting unilaterally but in support of UN objectives, to both secure the Sierra Leone government against any recurrence of the insurgency and to oversee the country's reconstruction.

So much for the international and diplomatic background to the eight UN interventions that are the subject of this study. The countries involved were on four different continents, and apart from having been marked by the Cold War in the ways just described, and in the case of the second wave by ambiguous legacy of earlier UN interventions, the conflicts in which they were caught up had widely different origins. Nonetheless, we shall be able to assess how the organisation coped with the challenge only if we can identify common themes which united these operations, despite the contrasts.

Peacekeeping and peacemaking in the post-Cold War climate

Every UN operation rests on two supports, the objects pursued by the member states, and in the final analysis authorised by the Security Council, and their implementation by the Secretariat and/or the various UN agencies to which responsibility is delegated in the field. Any serious critique of the new interventionism must address both aspects, and how they interact. At the same time, if the UN is to expand its prerogatives, the ultimate responsibility must fall on governments, not the Secretariat. As Simon Jenkins has pointed out, blaming the UN, – that is the organisation, – when things go wrong is very often an easy way of deflecting attention away from those who are really responsible, – that is the permanent members of the Security Council.[11] What, then, are the lessons that can be derived from the eight case studies examined in this book?

The bases for UN intervention

Before the UN can intervene, the Security Council must draw up a mandate specifying the objectives of the operation and the means to be employed. Except in cases of unambiguous aggression, such as Saddam Hussein's attack on Kuwait in August 1990, the construction of a mandate presents formidable problems at the best of times. On the one hand it must be sufficiently flexible to allow for inevitable changes in the situation on the ground; on the other it must be sufficiently precise to prevent the UN from becoming embroiled in the conflict and hence unable to fulfil its role as an impartial umpire. The penalties for not getting the mandate right can be high, as the UN discovered during the

---

[11] Simon Jenkins, 'Out of the Valley of Death', *The Times*, 20 April 1994.

Congo crisis between 1960 and 1964. On that occasion, the interpretation of the mandate soon divided the permanent members of the Security Council, who had drawn it up. Was the UN required to stand between the warring factions or to support the government on whose invitation the operation had been mounted? As a result of this dispute both the Soviet Union and France withdrew their support and refused to pay their assessed contributions, thus saddling the UN with a financial debt which took years to pay off.

The major powers might have been better advised to have taken the Congo operation as their model – and warning – than to have allowed public opinion to lure them into the belief that the success of Operation Desert Storm, and enforcement action under Chapter VII, could be repeated in quite different circumstances. With the exception of East Timor, where the political objective was settled in advance by the referendum, and to a more limited extent Haiti, where the task was theoretically limited to restoring an elected government, all the operations under review involved the organisation in attempting to broker political settlements to civil conflicts in societies deeply divided along ethnic, factional, ideological or religious lines.[12] The conflicts thus had more in common with post-colonial struggles over state succession than traditional inter-state conflicts over territory. In circumstances where the line between the international and the domestic is blurred, three issues complicate the task of devising a workable mandate. The first is sovereignty: who holds it, and on what grounds is it to be either upheld or superseded? The second is the strategic objective the mandate is designed to serve: that is, what is the intervention intended to accomplish? and the third is resources: assuming the first two issues can be satisfactorily resolved, are the requisite manpower, money and material likely to be available?

Sovereign constraints on UN mandates

It is perhaps significant that of the eight operations, the three that, when all qualifications have been entered, can be judged the most successful were also those in which there was no attempt to challenge the prevailing norms of international society. As we note at the beginning of chapter 3, the UN operation in Cambodia had no bearing on the international status of the country, which had been a fact of international political life

---

[12] 'Of the five peace-keeping operations that existed in early 1988, four related to inter-state wars ... Of the 21 operations established since then, only 8 have related to inter-state wars ... Of the 11 operations established since January 1992, all but 2 (82 per cent) related to intra-state conflicts': *Supplement to an Agenda for Peace*, para. 11.

since its admission to the UN in 1955.[13] Sovereignty was not, therefore, an issue, even though the disputed legitimacy of the government in Phnom Penh was at the heart of the political problem to which the UN sought a solution. This distinction may seem academic, but it is not. The fact that Cambodian statehood was not in question ensured that any UN intervention would have to be framed under Chapter VI – the pacific settlement of disputes – and would have to follow, not precede, a negotiated ceasefire and settlement plan. The fact that all parties broke the Paris Agreement, that prior to the elections Cambodian sovereignty was largely symbolic and that UNTAC was unable to fulfil many parts of its mandate does not detract from the fact that the UN is better placed as a peacemaker when it is acting under the authority of the conflicting parties than when it is trying to impose its will from outside.

With minor qualifications, the same could be said of the East Timor, Sierra Leone and Haiti interventions. In East Timor, the UN was authorised to prepare the country for independence following a referendum to which Indonesia had agreed with Portugal as the former colonial power. Then, following the violence that followed a vote in which – in a 98 per cent turn-out – 75.5 per cent opted for independence, the Security Council passed a Chapter VII resolution empowering a peacekeeping force led by Australia to take 'all necessary measures' to restore security to the island. As will be clear from chapter 9 the story of the UN's involvement in Sierra Leone is more ambivalent. Nonetheless, its serious peacekeeping deployment in 2000 followed the restoration of the Kabbah government and had its full support. The case of Haiti was less obviously in conformity with prevailing internal norms and practice since it was the first time the UN had acted to restore a deposed government. Traditionally, while individual governments might withhold recognition from regimes of which they disapproved, the general convention was to recognise those in *de facto* control of a state. On this occasion, however, the operation not only had the necessary support in the Security Council but had been urged on the Council by the OAS, which had taken the lead in persuading successive secretary-generals, and through them the General Assembly, that support for democratisation was legitimate under the Charter.

The Yugoslav and Somali operations lacked these advantages from the start. The former arose out of the failure of the then European Community (EC) to accompany its recognition of Croatia and Bosnia-Herzegovina with credible conditions that would have reassured the minorities and deterred the various groups of Serbs from pressing their

---

[13] See chapter 2, p. 26.

claim for a united Serbia. The distinguished international lawyer, Rosalyn Higgins, has argued that the rights and wrongs of the recognition policy are beside the point, that once the secessionist Yugoslav republics had been recognised they were entitled to the full protection of the UN Charter, that is, including measures under Chapter VII, if they were subjected to aggression. Instead, she noted of the UN in Bosnia 'we have chosen to respond to major unlawful violence, not by stopping that violence, but by trying to provide relief to the suffering. But our choice of policy allows the suffering to continue'.[14]

The difficulty with this approach is that it assumes that providing juridical sovereignty has been conferred from outside, it need not have any empirical content at all. It is true – as Robert Jackson has demonstrated – that many Third World states are essentially wards of international society and thus heavily dependent on international recognition.[15] But it is one thing to prop up former colonies once power has been transferred, quite another to confer sovereignty from outside in the middle of a war over state succession and when the legality and moral authority of the new boundaries are repudiated by many who will have to live within them.[16] As we have already observed, the issue of sovereignty continues to stand in the way of agreement on a final status for Kosovo.

Much of the confusion surrounding the UN's role in former Yugoslavia arose from the fact that the organisation was drawn into a series of overlapping civil wars, in which none of the antagonists was prepared to abandon the hope that they could either win militarily or at least improve their position before agreeing to a political settlement. This meant that their consent to the UN's presence was strictly conditional. None of the ceasefires or settlement plans, negotiated first by the EC and then by the UN and European Union (EU) in harness, bore fruit. Meanwhile, the UN peacekeepers, whose presence was intended initially to protect relief convoys to besieged minorities from being highjacked by the warring factions, had their mandate changed from Chapter VI to Chapter VII, to allow them to 'take all necessary measures' in discharging it. Without a commensurate commitment of resources, and will, this change was largely symbolic.

Both the US-led Unified Task Force (UNITAF), which landed in Mogadishu in December 1992, and the UN Operation in Somalia

---

[14] Rosalyn Higgins, 'The New United Nations and Former Yugoslavia', *International Affairs*, vol. 69 no. 3, July, (1993), p. 469.

[15] Robert Jackson, *Quasi-States: Sovereignty, International Relations and the Third World* (Cambridge: Cambridge University Press, 1991).

[16] See chapter 3, pp. 59–63.

(UNOSOM II), which took over in May 1993, operated from the start with a peace-enforcement mandate drawn up under Chapter VII. Since the motive for UN intervention was humanitarian, rather than to deter or repel a threat to international peace and security, in a sense, these mandates demonstrated that where the Security Council is so minded sovereignty need not present an obstacle to action, and that the Charter will allow them to do pretty much what they want. The Council subsequently demonstrated similar creativity in relation to Haiti.

In the Somali case, the crisis that the UN attempted to address was a humanitarian catastrophe caused by the collapse of all authority – Somalia had in effect forfeited both its juridical and its empirical sovereignty. Yet empowering the UN to take all necessary measures to provide a secure environment in which Somalis themselves could reconstruct their polity was at best problematic, and at worst deeply flawed. The state had collapsed because Somalis had elevated their clan and sub-clan loyalties above even a minimal commitment to public order. Against whom then was the mandate to be enforced? The fact that UNOSOM II failed to find an answer to this question fed into the refusal of the Security Council to invoke Chapter VII in Rwanda, and indeed to get seriously involved in the Rwandan crisis until it was too late.

Goals and resources

If the issue of sovereignty imposed constraints upon the UN's ability to act decisively, the absence of a peace to which the conflicting parties were seriously committed undermined the organisation's ability to achieve its stated objectives. This held true in all three of the original cases. In the second set of interventions it also held at different times for Rwanda and Sierra Leone. Moreover, in Kosovo, the UN Mission in Kosovo (UNMIK)'s task was constantly undermined by the Kosovo Liberation Army (KLA), which did not support the ideal of reconstruction on a multi-ethnic basis. In Haiti, the restored democracy also failed dramatically to resolve the social and political crisis that had occasioned the UN's intervention in the first place. It was in the first half of the 1990s, however, that the major problems of goal setting and inadequate resourcing, in an unstable and competitive environment, first emerged. Since the problem for the UN is how to differentiate between what considerations are unique to a particular situation and what are common to all, it will be helpful to briefly revisit the circumstances in which it arose, before considering whether the lessons learned from its painful baptism by fire helped the UN to respond more effectively in the second wave of interventions.

Even in Cambodia, the ceasefire did not hold; the Khmer Rouge repudiated the agreement it had signed in Paris, and several of the leading factions engaged in violence prior to the elections.[17] But at least in this case the UN had been given the clear task of holding the political ring and preparing the country for 'free and fair' elections, which it would both organise and oversee. Its control of all administrative agencies in the fields of foreign affairs, defence, public security and information was considered necessary to ensure strict neutrality. This it singularly failed to achieve for reasons examined in chapter 3, but it promoted sufficient order, nonetheless, to preside over an election in which, despite intimidation, over 89 per cent of those on the electoral roll cast their ballot. In neither former Yugoslavia nor Somalia was the UN able to extricate itself with anything like so much credit. Indeed, in the first case, the UN was still deeply embroiled in mid-1995 with very little chance of being able to implement the stated objectives of its mandates, when the United States decided to take matters into its own hands. In the second, UNOSOM II was finally withdrawn at the end of 1994, leaving the country still without a government and as divided as when it had arrived.

For those who wanted to craft a new order on the basis of cooperation amongst the major powers, it was unfortunate that the major part of the UN's initial test should have been in two such unpromising environments. Cosmopolitan solidarity had little value in either society. The break-up of Yugoslavia challenged the most basic rule of post-1945 international society – that boundaries should not be changed by force – for which, ostensibly, the Gulf War had so recently been fought. The total collapse of the Somali state, was partly caused by the failure of repeated Somali efforts to challenge this same rule, in pursuit of their irredentist aims. Yet the Security Council could not command either the resources or the will to frustrate the challenge in the first case or repair the damage in the second.

From the time of their original involvement in 1991 in former Yugoslavia, both the EC and the UN had focused their peacemaking efforts on trying to find a political settlement within existing and internationally recognised boundaries. UN peacekeepers were employed on the ostensibly humanitarian mission of ensuring that relief reached the victims of inter-ethnic violence in the besieged cities and those who had been 'ethnically cleansed'. But the provision of relief in the middle of a civil war is always contentious. Where the relief agencies see only

---

[17] See chapter 2, pp. 54–5.

innocent victims, the conflicting parties regard intervention as an attempt to alter the status quo. They may welcome it or resist it, depending on their fortunes in the war, but will not in practice accept its disinterested neutrality. For those who put a city under siege, those inside the city are the enemy, not victims. Indeed, there can be no more telling illustration of the futility of confining intervention in a civil war to humanitarian objectives than the siege: the purpose of this ancient technique of warfare is, after all, precisely to starve the enemy into submission.

By the spring of 1993, the contradiction in UN policies had been recognised by the Security Council. It now concentrated on trying to find a face-saving formula that would first create a loose ethnic confederation and then allow it to split up peacefully. But for even this scheme to have a chance of success, it was vital that there should be no further ethnic cleansing: hence the policy of declaring Muslim safe areas in towns like Srebrenica and Gorazde. This policy did not require an army of occupation, but to be credible it would have still needed a massive increase in the number of ground troops serving with the UN. The problem was no longer one of the mandate, but of the resources to carry it through. UN convoys had the authority to take 'all necessary measures' to ensure the delivery of relief aid. If they failed to force their way against Serb opposition, it was because they knew they could not call up the reinforcements that were necessary to face down the stiffer resistance that they would be likely to meet on the next occasion. Shortly before he resigned as UN commander in Bosnia-Herzegovina in January 1994, Lieutenant-General Francis Briquemont complained publicly of the 'fantastic gap between the resolutions of the Security Council, the will to execute these resolutions, and the means available to commanders in the field'.[18]

The situation in Somalia was in some respects similar to that in Bosnia, and in others strikingly different. It was similar in that the UN was drawn into the crisis as the result of domestic pressure on governments in Western countries to do something to relieve a humanitarian tragedy. It was also similar in that any solution to the humanitarian problem would require the UN to address the political and security crisis at source. It was different, at least prior to the US, French, Belgian and Italian withdrawals from UNOSOM II in the spring of 1994, in that the basic problem of the Somali operation was not inadequate resources

---

[18] 'UN Bosnian Commander Wants More Troops, Fewer Resolutions', *New York Times*, 31 December 1993, p. A3.

but their inappropriateness and the manner in which they were deployed.[19]

Unlike the British and French, the Americans, who continued to dominate the UN forces even after they had formally handed over the operation to the UN secretary-general, instructed their patrols to 'employ maximum controlled violence' when they encountered opposition rather than 'minimum necessary force'. Had this policy been accompanied by an even-handed and sustained effort to marginalise all the rival warlords, and to take control of their heavy weapons, it might have been justified. But after the killing of over twenty Pakistanis in June 1993, allegedly by Somali National Alliance militia, any pretence at impartiality was abandoned. Both the failure and the lack of proportionality, of the US-led UN hunt for General Aideed, brought the whole operation into disrepute and led to the premature withdrawal of all the major Western contingents. In his final report to the Security Council in January 1994, the UN secretary-general proposed a modest follow-on scheme UNOSOM II. It would oversee voluntary disarmament and require 'the deployment of about 16,000 troops to protect ports, convoys and refugees'. He also warned that its success would be crucially dependent on the improbable cooperation of the Somalis themselves. The acknowledgement of failure in advance was barely concealed.

There is little that the UN, or any other intervening force, can do without the cooperation of the local population. Even empires, as the United States may soon discover, need the implicit support of the people to sustain their rule. When it is withdrawn, even the strongest power is likely to find the cost of holding on to be beyond their means. At first sight, it may seem that Somalia and former Yugoslavia provided an unhelpfully rebarbative environment in which to test the operating principles of a new world order. But on closer inspection why should one expect to find a friendlier reception in any failed or failing state where the UN is called upon to intervene. Certainly, as the analysis in

[19] The confusion surrounding the engagement in October 1993 in which 18 Americans were killed and 75 wounded was revealed by the two senior US military commanders when they testified before the Senate Armed Services Committee on 12 May 1994. Major-General Thomas Montgomery, the former deputy UN commander, confirmed that the administration had refused to meet his requests for tanks and other armoured vehicles, and Major-General William Garrison, who commanded the task force of Delta Force commandos and army rangers which suffered the casualties, disclosed that he had been refused AC 130 gunships. However, the generals disagreed on what difference the additional armour would have made. Montgomery believed that it would have reduced the number of casualties, but Garrison was sceptical: 'If we had put one more ounce of lead on South Mogadishu on the night of 3 and 4 October, I believe it would have sunk', *Washington Post*, 13 May 1994.

chapter 6 demonstrates the failure of the restored democracy in Haiti to resolve the social and political crisis of that troubled society was the primary responsibility of the Haitians themselves, not the international community.

Similarly, the early efforts at peacemaking in Sierra Leone were marred by UN complicity with the culture of impunity that had already spread from Monrovia to Freetown. One might have hoped that the lesson that insurgents must be defeated before they will be prepared to cooperate in peace-building would have been learned from the long series of meaningless cease-fires and peace agreements that the UN had helped to broker in former Yugoslavia and Somalia. It was not. The reason was the tactic of attempting to make peace by persuading the chief poacher to turn game keeper – first Charles Taylor and then Fodoy Sankoh – had been developed by ECOWAS Monitoring Group (ECOMOG) for understandable if wrong-headed reasons: they were operating with very limited resources and both men had allies amongst the Economic Community of West African States ECOWAS governments. The policy was inherited by the UN, when it became involved in 1995 and was kept going through the period when its own main resource effort was directed at establishing the administrations in Kosovo and East Timor. Only when Sankoh captured 100 ill-equipped peacekeepers was the challenge to the UN's authority sufficient to shock the Security Council into appropriate, and in the end effective, action. In this case at least it seemed that the UN was condemned to reinvent the wheel.

After the debacle in Bosnia, it was increasingly argued that in humanitarian catastrophes, it is inappropriate to rely on the traditional peacekeeping doctrine of impartiality. This was certainly the US view in Bosnia and Kosovo, where they decided to resolve the crises outside the UN by going single-mindedly after the Serbs. But as we have seen abandoning impartiality in Somalia was one reason for the political failure of the mission. In Sierra Leone, because UN forces were deployed in support of an elected government they were able to identify the rebels as the enemy, even though in reality sections of the government's forces were responsible for many of the atrocities committed against the civilian population and were often also guilty of plundering the country in collusion with the rebels. In Rwanda, on the other hand, Western diplomats on the ground urged that the Arusha talks needed to be inclusive to have any chance of success, but when the Rwandese Patriotic Front (RPF) vetoed the inclusion of the Hutu extremists, the Security Council continued to insist that the UN peacekeeping force could only operate under a Chapter VI Resolution. These were the men who later engineered the genocide.

Behind such inconsistency lay not merely an inability to differentiate clearly between what was appropriate in one context but not in another, and, as several contributors to this volume argue, a failure of intelligence, but the problem of funding. How is the UN to fund its growing security commitments around the world, particularly when new crises occur simultaneously as, in the nature of the case they are apt to do? Member states are more willing to authorise funding when their own interests are involved, and when, therefore, UN operations are a means of burden-sharing, than when they are called on to contribute to an operation in which they have no direct interest. Since the major resources for each peacekeeping operation have to be raised on a case-by-case basis, it is almost inevitable that horse trading takes precedence over an accurate assessment of what is required. The funding of United Nations Assistance Mission for Rwanda (UNAMIR), for example, was only possible as the result of a deal brokered by France, in which it agreed to support the missions in Haiti and Georgia for which the United States and Russia were lobbying respectively.

It is not true that the UN has learned nothing from its experience over the 15 years since the end of the Cold War. There have been no more indefensible safe havens. As we have seen the UN responded more robustly to the crises in Sierra Leone and East Timor, no doubt partly due to the shock therapy administered by the Rwandan tragedy. The Brahimi Report, commissioned by the UN secretary-general in its wake, also reinforced the process of professionalisation within the Secretariat's major departments concerned with peacekeeping and humanitarian intervention, that was already in train. And action on the recommendations of the UN secretary-general's High-level Panel will hopefully carry the process still further.

In the immediate aftermath of the terrorist attacks of September 2001 the United States settled its outstanding debts, but action to put the UN's finances on a permanent and proper footing, recommended as long ago as 1993, nonetheless remains elusive. It is difficult to avoid the conclusion, therefore, that the financial and organisational problems of the UN mask a deeper uncertainty within the governments of the major powers about the kind of international order they wish to support.

A democratic world order?

The sad fact is that the end of the Cold War has not fundamentally altered the problem of power in international relations any more than did the end of the First World War or the Second World War. On the other hand, as on these occasions, the outcome of the conflict shaped subsequent efforts to construct a new order based on legal principles and international norms. From this point of view, international history since the First World War can be seen as a series of attempts to come to terms with the implications of popular sovereignty and the concept of democracy for international relations. The collapse of the European empires, and the rise of the United States to world power after 1918, ensured that from now on international society would ostensibly be based on the principle of self-determination and the attempt to pro-scribe the use of force as an instrument of foreign policy. The 'demo-cratisation' of international society was carried a step further after 1945 with the withdrawal of European imperial powers from Asia, Africa, the Caribbean and Oceania, but the Cold War – and the contested con-ception of democratic government that underlay it – ensured that it would be a democracy of states only, and that no attempt would be made to enforce even minimum standards of domestic political beha-viour. Only with the end of the Cold War was it possible to ask whether democratisation – in the fuller sense of an international society of peoples – was a feasible international objective at all.

In large measure the uncertainty of governments on this issue flows from the ambiguities inherent in the idea of a democratic world order itself. It has become fashionable to view the problem in terms of a clash between the United States and the rest. Its critics maintain that by invading Iraq without the authority of the Security Council, the United States has demonstrated that its ambitions are imperial rather than democratic. Whether this will turn out to be the case is impossible to know. But it is a simplification in that it both discounts the strength of the US commitment to democracy and implies that the problem is confined to relations between the United States and the Republican administration of George W. Bush. In reality, there is no dispute between the United States and the UN about the importance of democracy to world order. The argument is about how to achieve this goal and, as we have seen, it was Clinton not Bush who lost patience with the multilateral approach in Bosnia and Kosovo.

There is no denying that the doctrine of pre-emption favoured by the neo-conservative wing of the present administration has immensely complicated the problem of cooperation between the United States and the UN. It is clear from even a cursory reading of the report of the UN secretary-general's High Level Panel that the ability of the UN to address the escalating number of both new and old security challenges crucially depends on this cooperation. Yet, as the dispute over Iraq illustrated, the UN will not sign a blank cheque, permitting the United States to claim international backing for whatever it wants to do.

Under Clinton, the United States appeared to favour a division of labour, under which it handled enforcement in those areas where its own interests were directly involved, and left it to the UN to handle the protracted and inherently messy business of post-conflict reconstruction.

Something of this ethos has survived and the secretary-general has signalled that the UN will build on its role in the February 2005 Iraqi elections to provide both political and technical assistance in the framing of a new constitution that will provide the country with a stable and prosperous future. As he put it himself, 'that is the hope and the vision behind which the international community *must* (my emphasis) come together, from now on, supporting the Iraqi people in their great experiment.'[20] We must hope that his optimism is not misplaced although the odds must still be against it. In Haiti, the UN's attempt to restore democratic government – ironically at US request – failed, at least first time round. In Kosovo, the 'standards before status' policy has provided a cover for postponing the question of independence, but does not suggest that democracy has struck deep roots. In Sierra Leone, democracy survives, but continues to be dependent on external security. Why should it be different in Iraq?

Democracy is a good in and of itself, but it seems to have been adopted by the UN and the United States for largely instrumental reasons – on the unproven assumption that it will make for a more secure world. Democratic peace theory is attractive but even if it is valid, putting it into practice raises formidable obstacles. Let us consider four of these. The first concerns the tension between the requirements of diplomatic prudence and democratic internationalism. Should foreign policy be driven by an interpretation of the national interest, including a proper regard for the likely consequences of major decisions such as the recognition of a new state, or should such decisions be taken primarily with regard to the democratic right of national self-determination and in response to popular pressures?

The creation of new states was sufficiently rare during the Cold War for democratic governments seldom to have been faced with the necessity of confronting this dilemma. But when Yugoslavia broke apart, the major powers did not know which way to jump. In the end, the sympathy of the German government for Slovenia and Croatia almost certainly resulted in a premature recognition that had alarming humanitarian and political consequences for the entire region. Admittedly, they were under strong pressure – there was a sizeable and vocal

---

[20] Kofi A. Annan, Speech given at Banqueting House, Whitehall, London, 10 February 2005.

Croatian minority in Germany and the government was vulnerable to the argument that having just restored the right of self-determination to the people of East Germany, they had no grounds on which to deny this right to the peoples of former Yugoslavia. But it is precisely because democratically elected governments will be prey to a variety of regional and local pressures that there is a case for taking recognition away from national governments and subjecting it to a UN's procedure.[21] Such a major derogation from state sovereignty, as traditionally understood, would inevitably attract opposition from the General Assembly, and perhaps for that reason has never been seriously entertained. The recognition of East Timor, by contrast, raised no such problems since it conformed to the practice that had been followed in other cases of decolonisation.

The second obstacle concerns the role of public opinion in the international policies of the major powers. Public opinion is notoriously fickle. It is a curious fact that in many cases where the UN has brought force to bear to protect the innocent victims of civil conflict it is Western publics that have forced their generally reluctant governments to support international intervention. But it is also by reference to public opinion – above all by raising the spectre of returning 'body-bags' – that Western politicians have sought to limit their involvement. Even in Iraq, where the United States has sustained significant casualties in its own cause, the administration has gone to elaborate lengths to control the way these are reported, for fear of resurrecting the ghosts of Vietnam. However, the rapidity with which the United States announced its final withdrawal from Somalia after the incident in October 1993, when 18 US servicemen were killed, its refusal to commit ground troops to Bosnia-Herzegovina until a ceasefire had been concluded, and the lengths it went to in Kosovo to ensure that it was a casualty-free war so far as its own forces were concerned, supports the hypothesis that democratic politics constrains rather than encourages any major extension of the UN's peace and security role. So does the British decision to provide support to Sierra Leone, in support of but outside the UN peacekeeping operation.

Third, democratic uncertainty at home creates opportunities for the manipulation of the UN by undemocratic forces in the countries where it operates. In several of the cases examined in this book, there was a gap between the apparent strength of the mandate and the weakness of the will and/or capacity to carry it out, which was quickly perceived by unscrupulous politicians who sought to use the UN presence to their

---

[21] See chapter 3, pp. 90–2.

own advantage. Thus in Cambodia, UNTAC failed to get control of many key functions of the Vietnamese-imposed administration that had been assigned to it, was forced to rely on much of the apparatus of the incumbent government and as a consequence, was unable to prevent the physical harassment of opposition parties. In former Yugoslavia, the numerous ceasefires provided a cover under which, usually, but not only, the Serbs, could regroup and move their heavy weapons to a new site. In Somalia, none of the local warlords showed any serious commitment to political reconciliation and reconstruction. In Haiti, local opponents of the US-led force threatened to 'turn Haiti into another Somalia', leading the United States to withdraw without consulting the UN. At different times in both Rwanda and Sierra Leone, UN forces were targeted by the *genocidaires* and the RUF respectively. Only in Sierra Leone was the UN eventually in a position to enforce what is widely regarded as an essential prerequisite of successful peacemaking (as distinct from peacekeeping), namely the disarming and demobilisation of rival factions.

Finally, there is a contradiction between the desire to build an international order based on democratic principles and the requirement of humanitarian intervention and political reconstruction, in societies where the collapse of the state has led to the criminalisation of society, or when enforcing the peace by international action may itself contribute to this outcome. This contradiction manifests itself in three ways.

To take the last point first. Although the authors of chapter 9 argue convincingly that at a critical point, in Sierra Leone, strategically targeted sanctions played an important part in turning failure into success, the imposition of sanctions more often inflicts hardship on the very people the UN is seeking to help. Multilateral sanctions were taken over by the UN from the League of Nations Covenant. They had originally been conceived as an alternative to the use of force. The underlying assumption was that if the costs of non-compliance with legitimate international demands were raised, the target population would force its government to comply. In democratic societies this assumption is plausible; in tyrannies it is not. To take only the most dramatic of the examples considered in this volume, in Haiti, the World Bank estimated that the cost of UN sanctions was equivalent to 30 per cent of the country's GNP. The devastation caused not only impoverishes the population, it helps to create the perfect setting in which black markets and protection rackets can flourish.

Second, although the UN has increasingly found itself involved in running transitional governments, and in Kosovo is ruling over a *de facto* UN protectorate, for historical reasons in Asia and Africa, and for reasons of immediate self-interest on the part of the Western democracies, there is no support for the formal revival of a system of UN trusteeship. If there were, this would involve the organisation explicitly in nation-building, and its leading members in expensive and long-run commitments. The consequence is that whenever the UN establishes an administration, it is preoccupied from the outset with planning its exit. It is true that there are no objective criteria by which to measure the ideal time for holding elections and handing over the reins of government. On the other hand, as several authors note, the constant need to return to the Security Council for the renewal of mandates, and the anxiety about organizing an orderly withdrawal, introduces a bias towards premature elections, before the preconditions for a stable democratic order have been met.

Finally, if the UN cannot reasonably be expected to act like an empire, it must find itself handicapped whenever it becomes deeply embroiled in attempts to preside over the transformation or reconstruction of a political system. During the colonial period, the British, French and Italians employed administrators who developed a sophisticated knowledge of local languages and political cultures. The UN does not enjoy any of these advantages.[22] The evidence that we have reviewed in this volume shows that its impact was repeatedly weakened by having to rely on personnel with only a superficial understanding of the cultures in which they were operating. Given the reluctance of the major powers to enter into open-ended commitments, it seems unlikely that the UN will be in a position to develop this kind of expertise in the future. And since the world is culturally extremely diverse, this lack of administrative capability will continue to set limits to successful intervention in failed states. Moreover, the need to rely on highly paid but transient personnel on short-term contracts invariably has a distorting impact on the local economy, inflating the real estate market and creating a demand for services, which is likely to collapse once the internationals depart. Thus there are formidable practical, as well as philosophical, obstacles to any early development of a more solidarist conception of an international society.

---

[22] This is not to say that there is no room, even under existing circumstances, for an improvement in the UN selection and training practices for administrative personnel who are employed in peacekeeping operations. In the Somali case, in particular, many of those employed appeared to have been inadequately briefed. See *Report of the Commission of Inquiry Established Pursuant to Security Council Resolution 885 (1993) to Investigate Attacks on UNOSOM II Personnel which Led to Casualties among Them*, 24 February 1994 (New York: United Nations, 1994), para. 255.

2　Cambodia

Mats Berdal and Michael Leifer

The United Nations (UN) operation in Cambodia from 1992 to 1993 was, at the time, the most ambitious and expensive undertaking in the peacekeeping experience of the organisation. At a cost of around US $1.7 billion, 22,000 military and civilian personnel were deployed to implement the Comprehensive Political Settlement of the Cambodia Conflict, the Paris Agreement, which had been concluded at an international conference in Paris on 23 October 1991.[1] That settlement made provision for a UN Transitional Authority in Cambodia (UNTAC) charged with holding the ring politically, so that elections under its aegis could determine the future governance of a country long afflicted by violent upheaval and human suffering.

UNTAC was provided with exceptional resources but its mandate was restricted to peacekeeping. Peace enforcement, which had been demonstrated early in 1991 in Operation Desert Storm, was not part of UNTAC's remit, which was confined, in essence, to a quasi-administrative role. The critical problem confronted by UNTAC virtually from the outset of its deployment was how to discharge its responsibility for filling a political vacuum in the face of obstructive violence by contending Cambodian parties.

The notorious Khmer Rouge refused totally to cooperate in implementing the Paris Agreement, which it had signed, while the incumbent administration in Phnom Penh used violence to force the outcome of the elections. In the event, UNTAC took a calculated risk in embarking on elections, which were conducted without serious disruption. No single party secured an overall majority, which paved the way for a coalition government which excluded the Khmer Rouge. The Khmer Rouge had repudiated the electoral process but failed to disrupt it with an effective military challenge. To that extent, the UN operation was an undoubted

---

[1] *Agreement on a Comprehensive Political Settlement of the Cambodia Conflict*, 23 October 1991 (London: HMSO, 1991, Cm. 1786).

success. More problematic has been the viability of the political order in place at the completion of UNTAC's mission.

This chapter addresses the experience of UN intervention in Cambodia after more than two decades of conflict. The organisation was involved throughout that period, but physically it intervened only once the Cold War had ended, by which time global rivalries had ceased to be relevant to the Cambodian issue. The regional dimension of the conflict had also diminished, leaving the UN to address domestic disorder among contending parties that had been incapable of reaching a compromise over power-sharing. To conventional peacekeeping was added the responsibility of democratic elections as a vehicle for conflict resolution, as well as a paradoxical reliance on the charismatic figure of Prince Norodom Sihanouk.[2]

First encounters

The UN operation in Cambodia has not had any bearing on the international status of the country, which was a French protectorate for nearly a century. Independence was conceded in November 1953, with international endorsement confirmed in July 1954 by the Geneva Conference on Indochina, which had not been convened under the auspices of the UN. Cambodia has been an established fact of international political life ever since it was admitted to the UN in 1955. The legitimacy of its governments has been subject to challenge at various times, and this issue engaged the attention and resources of the UN in the two decades leading up to the Paris Agreement of October 1991.[3]

---

[2] For the role of the UN in Cambodia, see in particular Steven Ratner, 'The United Nations in Cambodia: A Model for Resolution of Internal Conflicts?', in Lori F. Damrosch (ed.), *Enforcing Restraint: Collective Intervention in Internal Conflicts* (New York: Council on Foreign Relations Press, 1993), pp. 241–73; Michael Doyle and Nishtala Suntharalingam, 'The UN in Cambodia: Lessons for Complex Peacekeeping', *International Peacekeeping*, vol. 1, no. 2 (summer 1994), pp. 117–47; William Shawcross, *Cambodia's New Deal* (Washington, DC: Carnegie Endowment for International Peace, 1994); and Michael Doyle, Ian Johnstone and Robert Orr (eds.), *Keeping the Peace: Multidimensional UN Operations in Cambodia and El Salvador* (Cambridge: Cambridge University Press, 1997). For some of the operational lessons learned, see also Hugh Smith (ed.), *International Peacekeeping: Building on the Cambodian Experience* (Canberra: Australian Defence Studies Centre, 1994); and Trevor Findlay, *Cambodia: The Legacy and Lessons of UNTAC*, SIPRI Research Report, no. 9 (Oxford: Oxford University Press, 1995).

[3] For a discussion of the issue of international representation in the first decade of conflict, see Michael Leifer, 'The International Representation of Kampuchea', in *Southeast Asian Affairs 1982* (Singapore: Heinemann Asia for the Institute of Southeast Asian Studies, 1982), pp. 47–59.

The UN first became involved in the internal affairs of Cambodia following the coup that deposed Prince Sihanouk as head of state on 18 March 1970, when he was out of the country. The incumbent administration – led by the prime minister, General Lon Nol – mounted the coup, and succeeded to the Cambodian seat in the UN. That seat was retained when the name of the state was changed in October 1970, from the Kingdom of Cambodia to the Khmer Republic. With Vietnamese communist support, an armed challenge to the Phnom Penh administration was mounted by a Cambodian revolutionary movement, ostensibly on behalf of a government in exile in Beijing, headed by Prince Sihanouk. Abortive challenges to the credentials of the Phnom Penh delegation on behalf of that government were posed in the UN General Assembly in December 1973 and November 1974. In the event, the issue of the international representation of Cambodia was decided by force majeure.

On 17 April 1975, the armed forces of the revolutionary movement labelled by Prince Sihanouk as the Khmer Rouge took over the Cambodian capital. This internal transfer of power inaugurated a murderous era, but did not arouse controversy over legitimacy in Phnom Penh and representation in New York. One reason for the ready international acceptance of the new regime was its close identification with Prince Sihanouk, who had come to personify Cambodia to the outside world. Indeed, his domestic and international standing was to be an important factor in the calculations of permanent members of the UN Security Council when they assumed responsibility for restoring political order within the tormented country during the following decade. Although Prince Sihanouk was obliged to relinquish the office of head of state in April 1976, when the country was given a new constitution and renamed Democratic Kampuchea, the issue of the legitimacy and international representation of its government was not contested. It was only revived within the UN with Vietnam's invasion of Cambodia in December 1978, the forcible removal of the government of Democratic Kampuchea, and its replacement in January 1979 by a government of the People's Republic of Kampuchea.

Close engagement

From that juncture, the UN became continually involved in conflict in Cambodia. In principle, Vietnam's invasion had violated Article 2 (4) of the UN Charter. The Security Council was constrained by Soviet veto but the General Assembly passed recurrent resolutions against Vietnam, calling for its military withdrawal. It also upheld the right of the ousted government of Democratic Kampuchea to occupy the Cambodian seat despite revelations of its gruesome rule.

Although cloaked in principle, the Cambodian conflict was, in essence, about the balance of power in Indochina, with global as well as regional significance. At issue with the invasion of Cambodia was whether or not Vietnam was to become the dominant state in the peninsula. That matter primarily involved a test of will between Vietnam and China.[4] Vietnam's ruling Communist Party had long claimed a special geopolitical relationship with Laos and Cambodia arising from the experience of the liberation struggle against France and the United States. China's objection to this assertion of entitlement had been expressed openly in the wake of Vietnam's unification in 1975. Sino-Vietnamese alienation in the context of Sino-Soviet antagonism and a countervailing Soviet–Vietnamese association was brought to a head by the xenophobic impulses of the government in Phnom Penh led by Pol Pot. The economic failings of Cambodia's political salvationism led to a paranoid search for enemies, judged to be the Vietnamese and their internal agents. An open alignment between Cambodia and China in late 1977 concurrent with murderous attacks against civilian settlements across the border in southern Vietnam brought retribution in the form of invasion in December 1978.

That invasion was made possible through the Treaty of Friendship and Cooperation between the Soviet Union and Vietnam agreed in November 1978. This protective alliance was concluded at a time when Soviet–American detente had broken down and Sino-Vietnamese relations were deteriorating further. The attendant invasion of Cambodia was interpreted in both Washington and Beijing as clear evidence of Soviet expansionist intent through political proxy. China responded with a punitive military intervention in northern Vietnam in February 1979. The Soviet invasion of Afghanistan at the end of 1979 served to confirm Sino-American apprehensions. Vietnam's invasion of Cambodia also provoked a sharp diplomatic response from the Association of South-East Asian Nations (ASEAN) in support of Thailand, which faced with an unprecedented deployment of Vietnamese military power along its eastern border.

---

[4] For accounts of the origins and nature of the Cambodian conflict, see David W. P. Elliot (ed.), *The Third Indochina Conflict* (Boulder, CO: Westview Press, 1981); Grant Evans and Kevin Rowley, *Red Brotherhood at War* (London: Verso Books, 1984); Nayan Chanda, *Brother Enemy: The War after the War* (San Diego, CA: Harcourt Brace Jovanovich, 1986); and Michael Leifer, 'The Indochina Problem', in Thomas Bruce Millar and James Walter (eds.), *Asian-Pacific Security after the Cold War* (Canberra: Allen and Unwin, 1993), pp. 56–68.

A diverse anti-Vietnamese coalition materialised, which sought to exert extreme pressure on the country's society and government in order to influence the outcome of the conflict in Cambodia. The UN served as the arena for the diplomatic dimension of this strategy, with the leading role being assumed by ASEAN, whose regional credentials were employed to mobilise a recurrent voting challenge to Vietnam. Its spokesmen also pressed with success for the right of the ousted government of Democratic Kampuchea to retain the Cambodian seat.

The nature of the conflict

Central to the argument over Cambodia that raged within the UN was a fundamental disagreement over the nature of the conflict. Vietnam and its Soviet bloc supporters claimed that the government of Democratic Kampuchea had been overthrown by a so-called National United Front for National Salvation comprising dissident Cambodians determined to remove a genocidal regime. As civil war had been the agent of political change, the new government was entitled to occupy the Cambodian seat at the UN; it exercised effective power and control within the country, thus fulfilling the conventional criteria for international recognition. Vietnam's adversaries rejected the representation of the conflict as a civil war, maintaining that the change of government in Phnom Penh had been effected by a blatant and illegal act of external military intervention that needed to be reversed. At issue, therefore, was not only the withdrawal of Vietnamese forces from Cambodia but also the removal of the government that had ridden to power on their backs.

The ability to shape international understanding of the nature of the Cambodian conflict was seen by contending sides as directly relevant to the terms of its ultimate resolution. Contention over this matter had a direct bearing on the outcome of the next stage of the UN's involvement, which took the form of an international conference convened in New York in July 1981 under the auspices of its secretary-general, Kurt Waldheim. That conference had been sought by an ASEAN-sponsored resolution of the General Assembly passed the previous October. In the event, the conference did not provide an opportunity for conflict resolution. Vietnam and its supporters boycotted the conference, both because Vietnam considered the conference likely to condemn it as an aggressor, and because the government in Phnom Penh had been excluded while the representatives of the ousted regime were accredited because of its retention of the Cambodian seat. The conference generated more heat than light, while a proposal by ASEAN designed to accommodate the security interests of Vietnam was obstructed both by China and the United States.

That proposal merits a mention because of its partial reappearance a decade later, when a formal settlement of the Cambodian conflict was concluded. It was suggested that in the event of Vietnam's military withdrawal from Cambodia, all warring Khmer factions should be dis-armed and an interim administration set up before free elections were held under UN auspices. China's representative argued strongly against such an interim administration, maintaining that Democratic Kampuchea was a legitimate member of the UN and that the UN did not have the right to establish a trusteeship over the country. The involvement of the UN at that juncture was clearly not intended to promote a negotiated settlement of the Cambodian conflict. The organisation was being employed as an instrument of diplomatic pressure on the part of Viet-nam's adversaries, who commanded an overwhelming majority in the General Assembly.

With the failure of the UN conference of 1981 to produce a full meeting of minds among the anti-Vietnamese coalition, the coalition's members turned their attention to reinforcing pressure on Vietnam. A prime concern was to ensure that the Cambodian seat at the UN was retained, despite the murderous nature of the Khmer Rouge regime. Political embarrassment was partially overcome in June 1982 by forging a tripartite coalition between the Khmer Rouge and two non-communist factions. This so-called Coalition Government of Democratic Kampu-chea, presided over by Prince Sihanouk, assumed the Cambodian seat at the UN. Joining the Khmer Rouge was the United National Front for an Independent, Peaceful and Cooperative Cambodia (Funcinpec in its French acronym), led by Prince Sihanouk, and the Khmer People's National Liberation Front, led by former prime minister, Son Sann. This coalition contained the three main contending streams in Cam-bodian politics after the end of the Pacific War (1941–1945): the roy-alist, the republican and the social revolutionary. They were united up to a point in their anti-Vietnamese endeavour, but were more of an incipient civil war than a government in waiting.

The UN continued its feeble initiative for resolving the Cambodian conflict, with its secretary-general making a number of fruitless attempts at mediation. In the main, it reverted to its role as an arena in which an annual diplomatic ritual was played out with support mobilised for and against a resolution calling for Vietnamese troop withdrawals. The struggle for Cambodia then became a test of military resolve within the country, with a disparate insurgency operating with the benefit of ter-ritorial sanctuary in Thailand, as well as attracting military assistance from China and military training from some ASEAN states and the United Kingdom. Vietnam demonstrated a countervailing ability to underpin the government it had implanted in Phnom Penh despite growing economic distress arising from its diplomatic isolation and attendant sanctions.

A changing international context

The key to Vietnam's Indochina strategy was continuing material support from the Soviet Union. That support began to waver after the assumption of power in March 1985 by Mikhail Gorbachev, whose government set out to end its involvement in regional conflicts in order to improve its global relationships. Accordingly, the balance of advantage in the conflict began to change, prompting a radical response by Hanoi. In December 1986, the Sixth National Congress of Vietnam's Communist Party committed itself to a fundamental economic reform based on market principles, matching Soviet *perestroika*. This policy of *Doi Moi*, or renovation, was designed to safeguard regime security, but the required access to the international economy was obstructed by the Cambodian conflict. Vietnam addressed this obstacle by seizing the diplomatic initiative.

Vietnam was encouraged by Prince Sihanouk breaking ranks with his coalition partners during 1987 and entering into negotiations with Prime Minister Hun Sen of the Phnom Penh government. Indonesian and subsequently ASEAN support was then secured for an exclusive southeast Asian approach to a political settlement, involving all Cambodian factions as well as regional states. Vietnam attempted to trade off the withdrawal of its forces from Cambodia in return for regional endorsement of the government implanted in Phnom Penh. Talks between puinee Sihanouk and Hun Sen, and then multilateral negotiations which ensued in Indonesia from July 1988 onwards proved to be inconclusive. The tripartite Coalition Government of Democratic Kampuchea was internally divided, but was of one mind in insisting on the dismantling of the Phnom Penh government and its succession by an interim quadripartite coalition, which would conduct elections under international supervision. This proposal was rejected by the Phnom Penh government. Despite joining in negotiations with the Khmer Rouge, Prime Minister Hun Sen refused to accept their participation as an equal party to a political settlement and any provision for international peacekeeping. The failure of the regional approach to conflict resolution provided an opening for the permanent members of the Security Council to take up the diplomatic initiative, despite their mixed interests.

From Paris to Paris

In April 1989, faced with mounting economic difficulty and external pressure, Vietnam offered an unconditional withdrawal of its forces from Cambodia by the following September. This concession provided the opportunity for convening an international conference in Paris at the end of July, under the auspices of the secretary-general of the UN, Perez de Cuellar, chaired jointly by the foreign ministers of France and Indonesia. The anti-Vietnamese coalition reiterated their insistence on a comprehensive political settlement involving not only Vietnamese military withdrawal but also provision for an interim coalition to replace the Phnom Penh administration before national elections. The problem of interim power-sharing among Cambodian factions proved to be as intractable as ever, reinforced by the added objection from the Phnom Penh government, supported by Vietnam, to a UN role unless the Cambodian seat at the organisation were declared vacant. The conference suspended its deliberations at the end of August.

The UN's initiative did not lapse, however, aided by a continuing linked improvement in Sino-Soviet and Sino-Vietnamese relations which served to change the structure of the conflict by diminishing its international dimension. At the end of the year, the Australian government began to explore and flesh out a proposal by US Congressman Stephen Solarz for a direct UN role intended to overcome the impasse over power-sharing. The Australian government envisaged the establishment of an interim UN administration in Cambodia, which would conduct elections to determine the political future of the country. The Australian plan was discussed and taken up in January 1990 at a meeting in Paris of senior officials from the five permanent members of the Security Council; the meeting endorsed 'an enhanced role' for the UN, but without indicating explicit provision for administration by the organisation.

This initiative carried the germ of the ultimate peace settlement by identifying a symbolic device which might be employed to overcome the long-standing stumbling block to a political settlement. A Supreme National Council, on which all Cambodian factions would be represented, would embody national sovereignty and assume the Cambodian seat in the UN. Power-sharing would be circumvented between the onset and completion of a political settlement by that Council, delegating executive responsibilities to a UN administration which would run key ministries and also organise elections for a constituent assembly as well as supervising a ceasefire, the disarmament and demobilisation of contending forces and the withdrawal of foreign troops. The permanent members of the Security Council reached a framework agreement at the end of August 1990 in which original provision for a UN administration was diluted in the face of objections from the Phnom Penh government in particular. That agreement was then endorsed by the Security Council in September and by the General Assembly in October.

The Cambodian factions accepted this agreement as the basis for settling their conflict at a meeting in Jakarta in September 1990, including the general terms of reference of the 12-member Supreme National Council to include the Khmer Rouge. The early implementation of the Security Council agreement was frustrated, however, because the Phnom Penh government with Vietnamese support persisted in standing out against its virtual dissolution through UN's control as well as seeking a specific provision barring the return to power of the Khmer Rouge. It took another year of political wrangling among the Cambodian factions before the Paris conference could reconvene to conclude a political settlement.

The momentum of accommodation was accelerated by Sino-Vietnamese rapprochement whereby a weakened Vietnam signalled a willingness to accept that its invasion of Cambodia had been a grievous mistake. The Supreme National Council (SNC) overcame its deadlock at a meeting held in Beijing in July 1991, agreeing to a ceasefire and the despatch of a single delegation to the UN. Prince Sihanouk assumed the office of chairman, stepping down as leader of Funcinpec in favour of his son Prince Ranariddh. Terms of reference for the peacekeeping mandate were progressively worked out, but they stopped well short of interim administration and therefore did not challenge the nominal constitutional position of the Phnom Penh government, whose status had been at the heart of the conflict. By this juncture, the People's Republic of Kampuchea had changed its title to that of the more innocuous State of Cambodia. Correspondingly, shortly before the Paris Agreement was concluded, the ruling People's Revolutionary Party of Kampuchea changed its name to the Cambodian People's Party (CPP). These cosmetic changes were an attempt to make a virtue of political necessity in order to uphold the status quo established through Vietnam's military intervention.

To that extent, the term 'comprehensive' as applied to the ultimate settlement, was less than exact. The term had been employed by the anti-Vietnamese coalition as a code to indicate that a settlement required not only a withdrawal of Vietnamese forces, but also a change in the political status quo through the participation of all Cambodian factions, including the murderous Khmer Rouge. China's willingness to support a political

settlement depended on such participation, viewed by the other permanent members of the Security Council as a necessary evil to avoid a
continuing civil war. The attendant dismantling of the Phnom Penh
administration did not take place, however. The UN plan was implemented with that administration still in place, despite its having been
established as a direct consequence of Vietnam's invasion, which had
drawn the organisation into the conflict from the outset. China tolerated
this concession because Vietnam, bereft of Soviet support, was no longer
seen as a potential regional hegemon; the Khmer Rouge leadership almost
certainly miscalculated that the Phnom Penh administration would fall
apart with UN's intervention. In the event, the intervening presence of
the UN Transitional Authority served to bolster the position of the
incumbent administration to the fury of the Khmer Rouge.

The nature of the Paris Agreement

The Paris Agreement on Cambodia that concluded on 23 October 1991
envisaged a transitional period during which a constituent assembly
would be elected through free and fair elections organised and certified
by the UN. That assembly would be charged with drafting and
approving a liberal democratic constitution; the constituent assembly
would transform itself into a legislative assembly and create a new
government, which would mark the end of the transitional period and
the UN's mission. The intractable problem of power-sharing was to be
bypassed through the SNC delegating to the UN all powers necessary to
ensure the implementation of the agreement. To that end, the Security
Council was invited to establish a UN Transitional Authority in
Cambodia (UNTAC), with civilian and military components under the
direct responsibility of the secretary-general. Apart from law-and-order
peacekeeping duties relating to military arrangements and verification of
withdrawal of foreign forces, UNTAC was given the direct responsibility
for ensuring 'a neutral political environment' conducive to free and fair
elections. Under the terms of its mandate, all administrative agencies,
bodies and offices acting in the field of foreign affairs, national defence,
finance, public security and information were to be placed 'under the
direct control of UNTAC', which would be exercised as necessary to
ensure strict neutrality. This provision was intended to serve as an
alternative to dismantling the Phnom Penh administration, which the
UN did not have the resources to replace. Its degree of implementation
proved to be highly controversial from early in UNTAC's tenure. The
underlying problem was that the Cambodian factions to the agreement
were bitter adversaries who had accepted the Paris Agreement with

private reservations, because to abide strictly by their terms could lead to undoubted political disadvantage.

UNTAC's mandate and the problem of implementation

On 28 February 1992, the Security Council established UNTAC, whose powers and responsibilities on paper exceeded those of all previous UN peacekeeping operations. By its Resolution 745 (1992), the Council committed the organisation to the single most ambitious field operation in its history, aimed at producing a 'just and durable settlement to the Cambodia conflict' on the basis of free and fair elections in a neutral political environment within 'a period not to exceed eighteen months'.[5]

The UN operation was a success in its post-electoral outcome. A new constitution and government were created, while political violence had been reduced to a minimal level. Nonetheless, UNTAC had not been able to fulfil many of the terms of its mandate. For example, it had been unable to demilitarise and demobilise the armed factions, to protect human rights and to create a genuine 'neutral political environment' before conducting elections. It may be argued therefore that the Cambodian patient lived, but that the UN operation failed in a number of its responsibilities. Moreover, the political prognosis for the patient remains most uncertain. A structural problem of power-sharing has been only mitigated, and not resolved, through the intervening charismatic role of an ageing and infirm Prince Sihanouk. The Khmer Rouge, who have been outlawed by the coalition government, continue to pose a military and political challenge.

UNTAC's shortcomings may be examined and explained on two levels. First, the non-cooperation of parties to the October 1991 Paris Agreement – principally the Khmer Rouge and the State of Cambodia – made key provisions of the peace plan virtually impossible to implement. Although the power-sharing problem in the transitional period was only set aside by enshrining the 'sovereignty, independence and unity of Cambodia' in the SNC, UNTAC's timetable was still predicated on the assumption that all four factions would be committed to the peace process. The UNTAC operation was thus based firmly on traditional principles of peacekeeping without provision being made for enforcing any aspect of the plan submitted by Secretary-General Boutros Boutros-Ghali for approval by the Security Council on 19 February 1992. As the secretary-general himself put it

[5] Resolution 745, 28 February 1992.

shortly before the elections, UNTAC could only solve problems 'through dialogue, persuasion, negotiation and diplomacy'.[6]

Further complicating the UN's task of bringing stability to Cambodia was the erratic attitude and behaviour of Prince Sihanouk throughout the transitional period. Although he was in poor health and domiciled much of the time in Beijing, UNTAC could not risk alienating the hugely popular leader who had long been revered by peasants as a 'God-king' and who had enjoyed a pivotal position both domestically and internationally as chairman of the SNC. Second, in terms of resources, planning and execution, the UN operation suffered from major limitations which were not conducive to a lasting settlement. With the notable exceptions of its electoral and repatriation components, as well as that part of the civil administration responsible for information, the UN operation in Cambodia demonstrated that the organisation was ill-equipped to initiate and sustain large-scale multicomponent missions. UNTAC's operational efficiency was adversely affected by weakness in areas of logistics organisation and of command, control and communications. The quality of some of the troops and civilian personnel serving with the authority was also open to question.

The interaction of these two adverse factors, non-cooperation by the parties concerned and structural weaknesses in the UN peacekeeping machinery, resulted in a situation which, by the time the operation was completed in September 1993, differed markedly from that envisaged by the eighteen signatories to the Paris Agreement in October 1991.

The plan for implementing the Paris mandate, approved by Resolution 745 (1992), set out the structure and functions of UNTAC.[7] It contained detailed provisions outlining the functions of seven distinctive components: electoral, civil administration, human rights, civilian police, repatriation, rehabilitation and military. The electoral component was charged with formulating, in consultation with the SNC, a legal framework for the impending elections, consisting of an electoral law, regulations and codes of conduct. Additionally, it was to conduct civic education programmes, voter registration and the polling itself. The basis for the elections was to be proportional representation by province.

In order to facilitate the transition to a popularly elected government, the Paris Agreement emphasised that 'a neutral political environment

---

[6] Press Conference of the Secretary-General and Prince Norodom Sihanouk at the Royal Palace in Phnom Penh, 7 April 1993.

[7] Report of the Secretary-General on Cambodia, S/23613, 19 February 1992.

conducive to free and fair general elections' had to be created. To this end, UNTAC's civil administration would exercise 'direct control as necessary to ensure strict neutrality' over all 'agencies, bodies and offices acting in the field of foreign affairs, national defence, finance, public security and information'. Moreover, 'direct supervision or control' would also be exercised over those administrative structures that 'could directly influence the outcome of elections'.[8]

To promote a climate conducive to free and fair elections, UNTAC's human rights component was also given a role through education programmes, monitoring and investigation in fostering 'an environment in which respect for human rights and fundamental freedoms ensued'. Allied responsibility for ensuring that law and order was 'maintained effectively and impartially' in all twenty-one provinces was allocated to UNTAC's civilian police. Its strength was 3,600 officers from more than thirty police forces world-wide. The repatriation component was given the task of ensuring that some 360,000 refugees from camps along the Thai-Cambodian border were resettled within a nine-month period, while the rebuilding of basic infrastructure, public utilities and essential services was entrusted to the rehabilitation component.

By far the largest of UNTAC's components was the military one. The original tasks entrusted to it were both far-reaching and unprecedented in UN peacekeeping history. Its responsibilities covered four major areas: (1) verification of the withdrawal of foreign troops and their arms and equipment; (2) supervision of the ceasefire and the regroupment, cantonment and disarming of armed factions; (3) weapons control, including measures to locate and destroy caches throughout the country; and (4) a mine-clearing and education programme. According to UNTAC's timetable, 70 per cent of the existing armies of all four factions were to be cantoned and disarmed by September 1992. In addition, the military component was given important support tasks for other mission components relating, in particular, to security at reception centres for Cambodian refugees and the rebuilding of the country's basic infrastructure.

To achieve these objectives, UNTAC was allocated twelve enlarged infantry battalions (each supposedly with integral first-line and second-line support), responsible for establishing and manning regroupment and cantonment areas. At the same time, 485 military observers – posted at fixed locations or working as mobile Verification teams' – were given responsibility for physically verifying adherence to the provisions

[8] *Agreement on a Comprehensive Political Settlement of the Cambodia Conflict*, Annex 1, Section B, paras.

relating to the regroupment, cantonment and demobilisation processes.[9] To assist these operations, an air-support group with ten fixed-wing aircraft and twenty-six helicopters was attached to UNTAC. Because of the collapse of much of the country's existing infrastructure, an engineering unit of more than 2,000 soldiers was given responsibility for providing support to infantry battalions with water-purification systems, site preparation and track and road maintenance. Additional logistics support was provided by a logistics battalion charged also with supporting the civilian component 'as required'. Assistance to the civilian elements was to be provided by UNTAC's signals units whose primary task was to establish and maintain the force communications net.

It is clear in retrospect that the implementation plan, unprecedented in scope and complexity, contained some major weaknesses. In the first place, as will be discussed more fully later, it was not based on a coherent logistical estimate of the situation on the ground. Furthermore, it did not take sufficient account of the political and practical difficulties inherent in trying to assume a quasi-administrative role with existing government structures still in place. Most importantly, the extremely compressed timetable for elections came to act as a straitjacket on the activities of all the other components regardless of the difficulties encountered. Although one of the principal reasons for sticking so rigidly to the electoral schedule was financial, a systematic process of pre-deployment planning would have made it clear that UNTAC's mandate as set out in the Paris Agreement could not possibly be implemented responsibly within the space of eighteen months, even had the parties to the agreement been cooperative. After initial surveys by Australian and UN technical survey teams, it was decided that elections could only be held during the dry season in the first half of the year. This meant that any postponement would have generated particularly acute financial difficulties, a fact which undoubtedly added to the sense of urgency that characterised UNTAC's concept of implementation. As one report accurately noted, the timetable presented by the secretary-general in February 1992 would have required 'almost perfect efficiency to succeed'.[10] This was clearly too much to ask of the UN.

There is a further consideration to be addressed. Under the Paris Agreement, the SNC would offer 'advice to UNTAC' provided there

---

[9] To verify the withdrawal and non-return of foreign forces UNTAC originally planned to post forces at twenty-four fixed locations or 'ingress/egress points': seven along the border with Thailand, nine along the border with Vietnam and two along the border with Laos. See S/23613, para. 58.

[10] *The Lost Agenda: Human Rights and UN Field Operations* (New York: Human Rights Watch, June 1993), p. 44.

was consensus among its members. Failing to reach such consensus, however, Prince Sihanouk, president of the SNC and the 'legitimate representative of Cambodian sovereignty', who was declared head of state in November 1992 upon his return from exile, would be 'entitled to make decisions on what advice to offer UNTAC'. Although the SNC was in many ways a legal fiction, the standing of Prince Sihanouk among ordinary Cambodians made it necessary for the UN to ensure his continuing support for the operation. His volatile moods, absences from Phnom Penh and frequently contradictory statements complicated his relationship with the special representative of the secretary-general and head of UNTAC, Yasushi Akashi.[11] For example, although the Paris accords made no mention of a presidential poll, Prince Sihanouk at one stage 'persuaded' the UN to accept the idea. He did so by withdrawing his cooperation from the UN and by refusing to sign agreements in his capacity as president of the SNC for loans from the World Bank. He subsequently abandoned the idea for presidential elections after the adoption of a new monarchical constitution by the constituent assembly.[12]

The Khmer Rouge and the abandonment of the military provisions

Given the exceptionally ambitious nature of UNTAC's mission and the compressed schedule for the elections, it was hardly surprising that the implementation plan emphasised that the military component had to be 'assured that all the Cambodian parties will scrupulously fulfil the commitments that have been made in signing the agreements and will extend full cooperation to UNTAC at all times'.[13] In fact, throughout the entire period of the UN operation in Cambodia, fighting continued within the country. Moreover, UN forces were themselves subject to deliberate attack and sustained fifty-six fatalities. The kidnapping of UN personnel and the theft of their equipment was another frequent occurrence throughout the transitional period. The ceasefire, supposedly

---

[11] At a joint press conference with Boutros Boutros-Ghali, Prince Sihanouk himself noted how journalists referred to him as the 'changing prince or the mercurial prince': Press Conference of the Secretary-General and Prince Norodom Sihanouk at the Royal Palace in Phnom Penh, 7 April 1993.

[12] *Report of the Secretary-General on the Implementation of Security Council Resolution 792* (1992), S/25289, 13 February 1993, para. 49. Similarly, to the dismay of UNTAC and diplomats in the capital, during a critical and violent stage in the run-up to the elections, Prince Sihanouk left for North Korea to attend the birthday celebrations of Kim Il-Sung.

[13] S/23613, para. 81.

in effect from the signing of the Paris Agreement, only resulted in a reduction in the level of fighting which followed a cyclical pattern of dry-season government offensives succeeded by wet-season attacks by the Khmer Rouge.[14] Before the election, Khmer Rouge military operations against the Cambodian People's Armed Forces (CPAF) were often at battalion level and were accompanied by systematic acts of terror directed in particular against ethnic Vietnamese settlers.

Even before UNTAC began its deployment, the Khmer Rouge had launched a series of 'unusually well-coordinated offensives' in the countryside in an attempt to enlarge their base areas in the north of the country and secure strategic roads (National Highways 6 and 12) before the arrival of UN troops.[15] In provinces such as Battambang in the north-west, the Khmer Rouge successfully expanded its area of operations into State of Cambodia (SOC)-controlled territory beyond the agreed ceasefire line. Government forces in turn responded by counteroffensives and showed an increased determination not to relinquish administrative and government control. Throughout March and April 1992, large-scale fighting in Kompong Thom Province between the Khmer Rouge and government forces delayed the deployment of Indonesian peacekeeping units.[16]

In spite of an inauspicious start, when UNTAC became operational on 15 March 1992 it was still hoped that all four factions would abide by the military provisions of the implementation plan. Khmer Rouge offensives against the CPAF were dismissed by UN officials as 'tactical manoeuvring' before the disarmament process. This optimism resulted from the Khmer Rouge's willingness to permit UNHCR-directed repatriation of refugees from three camps under its control and also for some limited inspection by UN observers of its base areas. The repatriation process, which began on 30 March, was an inter-agency effort headed and organised by the UNHCR in the field. By April 1993, more than 96 per cent of the 360,000 targeted refugees had been repatriated. This achievement, while praiseworthy, serves to highlight the fact that continuous cooperation from all contending parties is the basic

[14] See 'Renewed Fighting in Cambodia Places UN Truce in Peril', *International Herald Tribune*, 17 June 1992; 'Khmer Rouge Widens Its Attacks...Ceasefire at Risk Nationwide', *International Herald Tribune*, 16 July 1992; and 'Phnom Penh Offensive Threatens Peace Plan', *Independent*, 2 February 1993.

[15] 'Khmer Rouge Reported to Grab for Territory', *International Herald Tribune*, 14–15 March 1992; 'UN Representative Sounds Cambodia Warning', *Financial Times*, 16 March 1992.

[16] An estimated 18,000 people were driven from their villages in the province of Kompong Thom between January and May and many of these have been unable to return because of the mines which have since been planted in the area.

condition for successful peacekeeping. When it came to implementing the military provisions of the Paris Agreement, such cooperation was not forthcoming.

On 9 May 1992, UNTAC formally announced that Phase I of the ceasefire would be followed on 13 June by Phase II, under which regroupment and cantonment of all four factions' military forces would take place. Reporting in July 1992 on the progress of the UNTAC operation, Boutros Boutros-Ghali observed that it was 'becoming increasingly clear' that the Party of Democratic Kampuchea (Khmer Rouge) would not honour the assurances it had originally given. Indeed, by this time the Khmer Rouge had already refused UNTAC entry to the areas under its control and had failed to provide figures on the number of troops and material there, as required by the Paris Agreement. Although various measures were taken to bring the Khmer Rouge into the process – including an informal proposal for discussion drawn up at a Ministerial Conference on the Rehabilitation and Reconstruction of Cambodia on 22 June in Tokyo, designed to meet some of the specific concerns set out by the Khmer Rouge – Khieu Sampan, its nominal leader and principal representative on the SNC, refused to rejoin the peace process. It is worth noting that the option of enforcement – briefly advocated by the French deputy force commander, Michel Loridon, who urged that UNTAC 'should call the Khmer Rouge's bluff' – was quickly rejected by the UN because troop-contributing countries (notably Australia, Japan and Indonesia) made it clear that they were not prepared to consider the use of force, except in self-defence.[17]

The immediate result was that UNTAC was denied entry to some 15 per cent of the country, specifically in Pailin close to the Thai border and in parts of north-western Siem Reap, northern Preah Vihear and central Kompong Thom. More seriously, the Khmer Rouge's attitude derailed the process of demilitarisation, gradually forcing the UN to abandon completely its demobilisation programme in the summer and autumn of 1992.[18] By mid-November, only some 55,000 troops of the three cooperating parties had been cantoned. The collapse of the military provisions of the agreement meant that less than 5 per cent of the estimated 200,000 troops had been cantoned by the target date. Those who did register in the regroupment areas were thought by UN officials to be untrained teenagers with old, often useless weapons, while superior

[17] Private discussion with UNHCR and DPKO officials. Lieutenant-General Sanderson was also keenly aware of the importance of not being drawn into enforcement-type operations within what was essentially a peacekeeping mission. See John M. Sanderson, 'UNTAC: Successes and Failures', in Smith, *International Peacekeeping*, pp. 29–30.
[18] 'UN to Halt Cambodian Disarmament', *International Herald Tribune*, 22 October 1992.

forces and caches of weapons remained in the field. Nonetheless, in late 1992, the Security Council decided, despite the incomplete application of the Paris accords, to authorise preparations for elections in all areas to which UNTAC would have access as of 31 January 1993.

The reasons given by the Khmer Rouge for not participating were twofold. First, it argued persistently that Vietnamese forces had not been fully withdrawn from the country. UNTAC, anxious to keep the 'door open for full and constructive participation by the PDK in the peace process', took the charge extremely seriously and intensified efforts to 'uncover' Vietnamese forces in hiding but found little basis for the charge.[19] By 'Vietnamese forces', the Khmer Rouge meant all ethnic Vietnamese inside Cambodia, including second-generation immigrants and those attracted temporarily by the boom created by the massive foreign presence, especially in Phnom Penh. The second reason advanced by the Khmer Rouge carried more force: namely, that 'real' power had not been transferred from the Phnom Penh government and that the UN's exercise of so-called direct control had not prevented the SOC from using the state apparatus, and especially the secret police, for party political ends.

The failure of the UN 'direct control' and SOC intimidation

It had been agreed in Paris that for a 'neutral political environment' to emerge before elections, some form of UN control had to be exercised over the SOC administration. The formula chosen was that of 'direct control' in the areas of foreign affairs, national defence, finance, public security and information. Conscious of the fluid nature of bureaucratic and administrative boundaries, UNTAC hoped that a 'functional ana-lysis would yield an identification of existing administrative structures concerned'.[20] By definition, this task required intimate knowledge of and sensitivity to the host culture. Yet both were in short supply and UNTAC's attempts to control the administration with any effect were wholly unsuccessful.

This failure of control obtained in part because SOC ministries and officials deliberately obstructed UNTAC. It was made impossible, for example, for it to 'work as a partner with all existing admini-strative structures charged with public security' as stipulated in the implementation plan. The failure of direct control, however, was also the result of inadequate preparation on the part of UNTAC's civil administration component, whose lack of qualified staff and knowledge

---

[19] Interviews with UNTAC officials.   [20] S/23613, para. 94.

of the nature of the SOC bureaucracy and the Khmer language hampered its activities from the outset. Many civilian administration positions simply remained empty. Moreover, even when appropriate personnel were available, a study by Asia Watch found that UNTAC administrators did not always carry out their duties when actually stationed in the ministries to which they had been assigned.[21]

The most serious failure of the civil administration component was its inability to monitor, let alone control, the activities of 'agencies, bodies and offices dealing with public security at the highest levels'.[22] Indeed, throughout the transitional period, the SOC secret police operated much as it had done before. The UN assigned two administrators to the Ministry of National Security who 'relied on periodic briefings by the Ministry itself to learn of its activities'. Moreover, the UN never specified standards of accountability, something which made control difficult to effect. As a result, the government was able to use the state apparatus against political opponents. A particularly bloody campaign of assassinations was directed against Funcinpec functionaries when the political popularity of the party of Prince Norodom Sihanouk's son, Prince Norodom Ranariddh, increased dramatically in late 1992.

To counter this breakdown in law and order, the UN could have employed its 3,600-strong police force whose mandate included the continuous monitoring of the internal security forces and local police forces at all levels. With a few isolated exceptions, however, UNTAC's Civilian Police Component (CIVPOL) was the least successful of its components.[23] An important reason for this failing was the lack of pre-deployment planning and agreement on standard operational procedures and the lack of a working language among its officers: a multinational force drawn from more than thirty different police forces world-wide.

The most serious weakness of the civilian police operations, however, stemmed from the inability to prosecute. Following a significant increase in violence throughout the country in November and December 1992, UNTAC Directive 93/1 of 6 January 1993 established a Special Prosecutor's Office with 'powers to arrest, detain and prosecute persons accused of politically motivated criminal acts and human rights violations'.[24] For the first time in UN peacekeeping history, UN civil police forces were given powers of arrest. This provision marked a potentially significant departure from the principle of non-enforcement. The efficacy of the Prosecutor's Office turned out to be very limited, however. In the

---

[21] *Lost Agenda*, p. 51.   [22] S/23613, para. 101.   [23] Private interviews.
[24] S/25289. See also 'UN to Combat Political Murders in Cambodia', *Los Angeles Times*, 8 January 1993.

first place, the directive was strongly opposed by other UNTAC components, most prominently by the civil administration, which argued that it went beyond UNTAC's mandate. Similarly, UNTAC's military component was unwilling to use force when making arrests. A more serious obstacle was the failure to find any independent local court that could hear cases brought by the Prosecutor's Office. Added to this, the absence of any witness protection programme, proper defence council or criminal laws under which to prosecute suspects all served to undermine the value of this innovation in UN practice. While UNTAC was able to place a SOC policeman and a Khmer Rouge soldier in custody early in February 1993, their cases had not come to court by the end of 1994.

As indicated earlier, the failure to obtain cooperation from the parties to the Cambodian conflict was not the only factor impairing the effectiveness of the UN operation in Cambodia. Although preparations for a major UN commitment began before the Paris Agreement were signed, they did not prevent acute problems from developing in areas of logistics support, command, control and communications. Furthermore, financial problems, the lack of systematic procedures for collecting and processing intelligence (or 'information' to use UN terminology) and the highly uneven quality of the troops and civilian staff serving with UNTAC further weakened its effectiveness.

Planning, logistics preparations and initial deployment

The ambitious nature of UNTAC's mandate placed a premium on obtaining accurate data on which pre-deployment planning could be based. This task was severely complicated by Cambodia's long period of isolation from the outside world and, in particular, by the absence of reliable government records and statistics (most of which had been destroyed by the Khmer Rouge between 1975 and 1978). It was partly for this reason that the Security Council, even before the final agreements were signed in Paris, had authorised the deployment of several technical survey missions to reconnoitre the area of deployment.[25] The gathering of planning data, however, was fragmented and not effectively organised, with the result that UN forces arriving in Cambodia did not have sufficient knowledge about conditions on the ground.

During 1990, the secretary-general sent three separate technical survey teams to Cambodia to examine 'emerging operational issues' relating to the rebuilding of the infrastructure, civil administration and

---

[25] The first fact-finding mission, which also looked into the requirements of UN field operations in the country, was sent by the secretary-general in August 1989.

the repatriation of refugees from Thailand. Another military survey mission was sent in September 1991 to explore the conditions for a stable ceasefire prior to the arrival of the UN Advance Mission in Cambodia (UNAMIC). Another three survey mission – on military arrangements, civil administration, and police and human rights – visited the country between October and December 1991. UNAMIC established its headquarters in Phnom Penh on 9 November 1991 in order to 'maintain the momentum' of the peace process and prevent any 'untoward development' in Cambodia. It was also established with a view to providing more data for mission planning in New York.[26] Once UNAMIC personnel arrived back in New York, the paucity of staff within the DPKO and the preoccupation of planners with the Croatian deployment delayed the process of detailed mission planning.[27] The activities of various survey missions sent to Cambodia before UNTAC's deployment were clearly not coordinated. This prevented the development of an integrated plan. The lack of civil–military integration, in particular, remained a serious problem throughout the entire operation, and was only partly overcome by the creation of Joint Operations Centres throughout the country.[28] Indeed, assessing the operation as a whole, the Force Commander, Lieutenant-General John Sanderson, identified the complete lack of 'any strategic planning within UNTAC' as a major source of the 'many practical problems experienced'.[29]

The most serious planning problem, however, and one which directly influenced the deployment of UNTAC's various components, was the absence of any centralised logistic planning unit within the UN Secretariat where the provision of logistics support was coordinated by the Field Operations Division (in the Department of Administration and Management) which was only obliged to 'consult' with the DPKO.[30] Although the implementation plan noted that the assessment of

---

[26] UNAMIC consisted of a civilian and military liaison staff as well as a military mine awareness unit and support personnel.

[27] Private interviews. See also Jarat Chopra, John Mackinlay and Larry Minear, *Report on the Cambodian Peace Process* (Oslo: Norwegian Institute of International Affairs, February 1993), p. 19. For an account of the weaknesses of UN logistics support and planning generally, see Mats Berdal, *Whither UN Peacekeeping?*, Adelphi Paper 281 (London: Brassey's, for the International Institute for Strategic Studies, October 1993), pp. 32– 5. For an assessment of development since the early 1990s, see William Durch, Victoria Holt, Caroline Earle and Moira Shanahan, *The Brahimi Report and the Future of UN Peace Operations*, The Henry Stimson Center, 2003.

[28] For a more detailed account of the weaknesses in the area of planning at the time of the UNTAC operation, see *UN Peacekeeping: Lessons Learned in Managing Recent Missions* (Washington, DC: General Accounting Office, December 1993), pp. 30–5.

[29] Sanderson, 'UNTAC: Successes and Failures', p. 22.

[30] 'Cambodian Peace Plan "Threatened" by UN Delay', *Daily Telegraph*, 14 January 1992 and private information from UNTAC officials.

resources required for the operation had taken account of 'the varied nature of the topography and vegetation, climatic conditions, the nature of warfare which has been waged . . . the disposition of the forces of the parties and, above all, the degradation or non-existence of infra-structure', this did not amount to a proper logistical estimate. The size of the force, especially its air and engineering component, was simply too small to cope with the range of tasks assigned to it in a country without an effective transport network during the rainy season and with limited refuelling depots and sanitation facilities. Once the specialised logistics elements had been deployed, problems of supply continued because of the existence of different supply doctrines and incompatible equipment among the three countries providing logistics support.

Some of the aforementioned problems might have been overcome by the early deployment of qualified engineers. In fact, the lack of an effective engineering capability was a major problem throughout the operation and illustrates many of the weaknesses in UN planning pro-cedures. For example, no engineering reconnaissance aimed at identi-fying tasks, and local resources took place before UNTAC commenced its deployment. Moreover, apart from the early deployment of the Thai battalion, UNTAC's other engineering units from China and Poland only began to be deployed after the regular infantry units had arrived. At the same time, neither the Chinese nor the Polish contingent was adequately equipped for operations in Cambodia, while the French engineering company was too small (only some 150 men) and the well-equipped engineers provided by Japan were restricted in their deploy-ment to an area south of Phnom Penh. In addition to this, the UN headquarters in New York had not developed appropriate guidelines for the engineering elements. Such guidelines should have been issued to contributing countries before their units began to be deployed.

A further and critical impediment to movement inside the country was the huge number of land mines and sub-munitions in Cambodia. UN's initial de-mining programme as well as subsequent measures taken to remedy the problem, provide perhaps the clearest example of the inade-quacy of pre-deployment planning.[31] The UN's failure to address this problem early on critically undermined the humanitarian relief efforts of the UNHCR, UNDP and ICRC. As one UNHCR representative put it in late 1991: 'the only de-mining going on now is when people tread on them'.[32] In the course of 1992, land mines were planted in Cambodia at a

---

[31] 'UN Blamed for Delay in Clearing Mines', *Guardian*, 22 November 1991.

[32] For an account of the early de-mining efforts in Cambodia, see 'Political Control, Human Rights and the UN Missions in Cambodia', *Asia Watch* (New York: Asia Watch, September 1992), pp. 61–5.

faster rate than they were being removed, and by the time of the elections UNTAC's small Mine Clearance Training Unit (MCTU) had only disposed of some 15,000 mines and 'other pieces of unexploded ordnance'.[33] After the end of UNTAC's operation, it has been estimated that some 8–10 million mines remained.[34]

The UN's failure to anticipate ground conditions and the obvious disadvantages that stemmed from the lack of any systematic reconnaissance capability raises the issue of whether the UN should develop more effective means of gathering intelligence. Anxious to preserve the image of strict neutrality, the UN has traditionally refrained from activities which may be interpreted as involving the collection of military intelligence about the parties to a conflict. In politically fluid and militarily complex situations such as in Cambodia, more advanced technologies and procedures for collecting and assessing intelligence, and the development of a *local* intelligence apparatus, would undoubtedly have enhanced UNTAC's effectiveness. Specifically, once UNTAC began to deploy, it suffered from the lack of a tactical intelligence capability incorporating advanced surveillance and tracking techniques required for the monitoring of movement across borders in dense, malaria-ridden jungles, as well as for the location of arms caches throughout the country. Without such a capability, it was impossible to determine with any degree of accuracy the strength, organisation and operational efficiency of the Khmer Rouge.[35] It also made it difficult for UNTAC to ascertain whether Vietnamese forces, paramilitary or clandestine units, remained hidden within Cambodia as the Khmer Rouge claimed. Equally important, however, such a capability would also have enabled the UN to monitor the performance of its own operation, making sure that the deployment was proceeding smoothly and that the logistics flow was efficiently directed.

This quality of monitoring did not occur. Instead, the lack of accurate planning data, the extremely limited logistical capabilities available to the UN Secretariat and, in particular, the absence of a centralised logistical planning unit within the Secretariat in New York, led to an extremely

---

[33] Craig Etcheson, 'The "Peace" in Cambodia', *Current History*, vol. 91, no. 569 (December 1992), p. 413; and *Fourth Progress Report of the Secretary-General on the United Nations Transitional Authority in Cambodia*, S/25719, 3 May 1993, paras. 52 and 53.

[34] *Cambodia Times* (Phnom Penh), 31 October–7 November 1993, p. 3.

[35] The question of the Khmer Rouge's strength has been a continuing source of controversy and speculation. UNTAC's own military observers rejected the estimates of Western institutes as exaggerated, claiming that the Khmer Rouge strength was no more than 14,000–15,000 troops organised in divisional strengths of about 400. See 'Khmer Rouge Bogey Gets Cut Down to Size', *Business Times*, 16 April 1993.

drawn-out deployment process.[36] Although UNTAC's mandate had been agreed in Paris in October 1991, the UNTAC headquarters in Phnom Penh only became operational on 15 March 1992 when Yasushi Akashi took up his position as head of UNTAC. More serious still were the delays in the deployment of UNTAC's other components. Although priority was given to its military component, it was not until August that all twelve infantry battalions had been deployed. Moreover, military units were also deployed in an inverse order of effectiveness, with infantry troops arriving before logistics and engineering components. By August 1992, only about half of the civilian administrators had arrived and the civilian police component was still some 36 per cent below its planned strength. Initial difficulties in securing sufficient funds for UNTAC, whose operation eventually came to absorb more than two-thirds of the total UN peacekeeping budget, further delayed the deployment of troops. This problem was partly a consequence of the automatic delays built into the UN's complex budgetary allocation procedure. It also reflected, however, reluctance on the part of member states to provide necessary financial support, a problem that was resolved to a limited extent by the pledges made at the International Conference on the Reconstruction of Cambodia held in Tokyo in June 1992.[37]

Command, control and direction from New York

The performance of any UN field operation has always been intimately linked to the effectiveness of its command and control arrangements, both within the theatre of operations and between the headquarters in New York and the field. UN arrangements, however, are subject to a combination of technical and political constraints which invariably reduce the degree to which unified direction can be provided.[38] The size and complexity of UNTAC's mission meant that these constraints had a more detrimental effect on UN operations in Cambodia than on traditional peacekeeping operations. On the technical side, the UNTAC operations revealed just how difficult it is to establish reliable communications within a combined force where contingents arrive with their own equipment stocks, standards and specifications. Communications within Cambodia – that is, the links between the mission headquarters in Phnom Penh and individual battalions in the provinces – were

---

[36] For some of the other sources of delay, see Yasushi Akashi, 'The Challenges Faced by UNTAC', *Japan Review of International Affairs*, vol. 7, no. 3 (Summer 1993), p. 188.

[37] The 31 countries attending pledged a total of US $880 million.

[38] For a discussion of UN command and control problems more generally, see Berdal, *Whither UN Peacekeeping?*, pp. 39–43.

hamstrung not only by the incompatibilities in communications equipment but also by the lack of standardised communications procedures and joint-level planning *before* deployment, which might have eased the problem. The destruction of the local infrastructure meant that the amount of signals traffic which could be carried on the civilian radio network, on which the UN usually relies, was extremely limited.

A further complication arising from the increasingly wide range of countries from which contingents were drawn – more than forty countries provided military and police personnel to UNTAC – was that of language. In Cambodia, several battalions arrived with no knowledge of either French or English, and this in itself gave rise to major communications difficulties. UNTAC also suffered from a general lack of bilingual operators (i.e. proficient in Khmer) which UN's complex recruitment policies were unable to remedy.[39]

As noted earlier, command and control arrangements do not depend on technical factors alone. In Cambodia, the absence of clear and unambiguous chains of command *internal* to UNTAC, as well as proper coordination between the Secretariat in New York and the field, resulted in a loss of operational efficiency. Within UNTAC, a major challenge confronting Akashi and, especially, the force commander, Lieutenant-General Sanderson, from the outset, was how to ensure the loyalty of individual battalion commanders while making them accept the chain of command within the mission. By referring matters to national authorities, or even taking orders from embassies in Phnom Penh, it was often impossible for Akashi to effectively coordinate activities in the field. The Indonesian battalion, for example, was notorious for its tendency to take directions from the Indonesian ambassador in Phnom Penh rather than from the force commander.[40] While the disposition of national authorities to intervene in the day-to-day running of their own contingents is certainly not new, the hostile and dangerous operational environment in Cambodia, as well as the large number of new and inexperienced troop-contributing countries, made that practice more than usually unacceptable.[41]

The relationship between the Secretariat in New York and UNTAC exposed a fundamental problem (which has plagued other contemporary UN field operations) over the lack of clearly defined

---

[39] 'Leichtsinnig, schwerfallig, teuer – Die UN – Operation in Kambodscha: Kein Modell für Afghanistan', *Frankfurter Allgemeine Zeitung*, 3 July 1993.

[40] On one occasion, when the Khmer Rouge held a group of Indonesian soldiers hostage, the ambassador negotiated directly with the captors and after their release requested a helicopter from UNTAC to fly them to safety.

[41] Private interviews.

reporting channels back to the UN headquarters. This failing stemmed in part from the decentralised nature of UN management practices and the lack of horizontal coordination among the four principal departments most directly involved in peacekeeping operations: the DPKO, the Department of Political Affairs, the Department of Humanitarian Affairs, and the Department of Administration and Management (DAM). In particular, as in other peacekeeping operations, the separation of the DPKO and the Field Operations Division (FOD) caused delays and confusion in Cambodia. Even had the reporting channels been properly specified, the general lack of political and military officers in New York, as well as the outdated procurement procedures of the organisation, made it extremely difficult to provide effective guidance and support for an operation on UNTAC's scale. For example, the purchase of medical supplies centrally through the FOD in New York resulted in delays until late September 1992. In the meantime, critical supplies had to be purchased locally in Bangkok. Cumbersome and centralised procurement regulations and decision-making procedures also delayed the introduction of a satisfactory air-control system to support UNTAC air operations for some nine months.

It is worth noting in this context that the efficiency of the UNHCR-led repatriation of refugees owed much to the fact that, by delegating financial and administrative responsibility from New York to the UNHCR in the field, a degree of flexibility in planning and execution was achieved which did not exist for any other of UNTAC's components. As noted above, these were forced to rely on insufficient and poorly coordinated administrative support from the DAM and the DPKO in New York. The experience of UNTAC clearly suggests, therefore, that a greater degree of financial, administrative and operational authority should be delegated to the field in future operations.

Training and quality of UNTAC personnel

The dramatic increase in UN peacekeeping operations in the first half of 1992 meant that the UN could no longer rely only on traditional troop-contributing countries for its operation in Cambodia. Similarly, the composite nature of the UNTAC mission required a high number of civilian personnel and experts recruited directly by the UN or seconded by member states on short-term contracts. In the words of one senior official, the Secretariat could 'not afford to be choosy' when it began to put together a force for Cambodia. The attendant danger was that insufficient attention would be given to the need for familiarising troops with peacekeeping procedures and the specific challenges of operating in Cambodia. Indeed, this turned out to be a major problem as several units failed to maintain even minimum standards of discipline while showing little or no sensitivity to religion or local customs in their area of deployment. In many cases, lack of training and poor disciplinary standards were compounded by the UN payment and allowances system which created very substantial income differentials between civilian and military officials in the field. An additional problem stemmed from the fact that once the cantonment process had collapsed in summer 1992, several infantry battalions were left with little to do. In the eyes of ordinary Cambodians, many UN soldiers appeared to be spending most of their time in bars and brothels or to be driving recklessly in UN vehicles.[42]

Certain contingents did considerable damage to the overall objectives of the operations by undermining the credibility of the UN in the eyes of the local population. The first Bulgarian battalion, and to a lesser extent contingents from Tunisia and Indonesia, are unofficially regarded as having done as much to damage as to advance the cause of UNTAC.[43] The Japanese police contingent was felt by some to be excessively concerned about the domestic political impact of sustaining casualties, especially during the early stage of its deployment. Ideally, UN policy with regard to the hiring of civilian staff should be governed by the relevant Charter provision which holds that 'paramount consideration in the employment of the staff...shall be the necessity of securing the highest standards of efficiency, competence, and integrity'.[44] In practice, however, the stress on merit has become subordinate to that of geographical distribution and, more depressingly, to that of bureaucratic patronage and personal favouritism. This practice, combined with the difficulty of finding sufficient staff to fill specialist functions, explains why the quality of UNTAC staff was so uneven, with the highly competent and dedicated workers working alongside inexperienced and, incompetent personnel. This factor is important to an understanding of the mixed performance of UNTAC's different components. There is little doubt, for example, that a major reason for the impressive record of UNTAC's electoral component, which succeeded in registering more than 90 per cent (4.7 million) of the total number of eligible voters, lay

---

[42] 'UN Cambodian Force Is Malfunctioning', *International Herald Tribune*, 5 October 1992; 'Sex and Inflation End the UN Honeymoon in Cambodia', *The Times*, 26 November 1992. The behaviour of the Bulgarian battalions, the first of which had to be sent back, has been particularly commented upon (interview with UNTAC officials).

[43] 'Leichtsinnig, schwerfallig, teuer' *Frankfurter Allgemeine Zeitung*, 3 July 1993.

[44] Article 101, UN Charter.

in the quality and determination of those working for it (including 460 highly dedicated volunteers). Conversely, the overall performance of the civilian component has been attributed, at least in part, to the lack of proper organisation and motivation and to the poor quality of its staff.

There is a further important dimension to the UN's role in Cambodia which was not properly foreseen: the UNTAC presence was in itself economically and socially destabilising because it fuelled an artificial boom and generated massive inflation in the poverty-stricken country.[45] The dangers of hyperinflation and the 'distorting impact of UNTAC expenditure' on the Cambodian economy more generally should have been anticipated since the civilian per diem 'mission subsistence allowance' (MSA) was as high as US $145 while the average per capita income in the country in 1991 was estimated at only US $150 a year.[46] It has been estimated that the 'total UNTAC budget was of the same order of magnitude as the total Cambodian GDP for the three years 1991–1993' and that this promoted a 'speculative private sector response' more than it encouraged the strengthening of the 'productive and administrative capacity of the economy'.[47] The economic boom in construction also led to an influx of ethnic Vietnamese who were disliked by many Cambodians and therefore inflamed ethnic tensions. The boom and the UNTAC presence also attracted a large number of prostitutes from Thailand, Vietnam and Laos, especially to Phnom Penh. Indeed, several reports indicate that cases of HIV infection, largely unknown in the country before the arrival of UN forces, rose dramatically during the transitional period and that the UN bureaucracy was exceptionally slow in taking preventive action.[48] Such developments generated widespread resentment among the local population, resentment which naturally was exploited by the Khmer Rouge.[49] In February 1993, Prince Sihanouk, in a blunt and forceful attack on the UN performance, said that while the Cambodian people initially had been very willing to support the UN, they now 'detested' and 'hated UNTAC'.[50]

[45] 'With the UN in Town, Phnom Penh Booms – Is This a Good Thing?', *International Herald Tribune*, 23 June 1992.
[46] For a good account of the economic and social consequences of the UNTAC operation, see Edmund Valpy Knox FitzGerald, 'The Economic Dimension of the Peace Process in Cambodia', in Peter Utting (ed.), *Between Hope and Insecurity: The Social Consequences of the Cambodian Peace Process* (Geneva: UNRISD Report, 1994).
[47] *Ibid.*, pp. 78–85.
[48] See 'Die Kambodschaner sterben still', *Frankfurter Allgemeine Zeitung*, 1 June 1993, and 'Child Sex Boom Blamed on UN', *Guardian*, 4 November 1993. See also Judy L. Ledgerwood, 'UN Peacekeeping Mission: The Lessons of Cambodia', *Asia-Pacific Issues* (East–West Center), no. 11 (March 1994), p. 7.
[49] 'Cambodians Fall Out with UN Peacekeepers', *Independent*, 26 January 1993.
[50] 'I Want to Retake Power', *Far Eastern Economic Review*, 4 February 1993, p. 21.

Elections and political aftermath

Some 4.7 million Cambodians were registered for the elections despite the difficulties inherent in that process, but the collapse of the military provisions and the inability of UNTAC's civilian police to maintain law and order meant that a 'neutral political environment' as envisaged did not emerge in the country. Indeed, in the run-up to the elections the security situation deteriorated dramatically throughout the country. Between March and May 1993, incidents of political violence, including attacks on UNTAC representatives, resulted in 200 deaths, 338 injuries and 114 abductions.[51] Many of these fatalities were Vietnamese settlers murdered by Khmer Rouge guerrillas, with the most serious attack taking place on 11 March, when a massacre of thirty-three people in a fishing village sparked off a mass exodus of Vietnamese. At the same time, both Funcinpec and the Buddhist Liberal Democratic Party (an off-shoot of the Khmer People's National Liberation Front) electoral workers were subjected to intensified government violence and obstruction of their campaigning. When, in mid-April, Khieu Sampan left the capital and formally withdrew the Khmer Rouge from the peace process, doubts arose as to whether the elections could be held at all, with foreign diplomats predicting the imminent resumption of full-scale civil war. UNTAC took a calculated risk to proceed, however.

In spite of the upsurge in violence, the elections were held between 23 and 27 May in a relatively peaceful atmosphere. This unanticipated outcome was partly a product of Khmer Rouge inaction, possibly due to the greater prospect of a Funcinpec than a CPP victory, which had been anticipated with apprehension. It also owed much to the UN presence, in particular the role of the electoral component, whose volunteers risked life and limb in the countryside. Moreover, the intoxicating idea of political choice in free elections had been communicated with great effect by Radio UNTAC, a remarkable innovation in peacekeeping practice. It broadcast sixteen hours a day and reached an extensive audience which responded on polling day.[52] Bravely defying threats of violence, an unanticipated 89.56 per cent of the registered voters cast their ballots and on 15 June 1993 the Security Council formally endorsed the election results, declaring the balloting to have been free and fair. The votes cast and the attendant distribution of seats in the assembly gave Funcinpec a near majority, as the following table shows.

---

[51] See 'Statement by the Director of UNTAC Human Rights Component on Political Violence', 23 May 1993. See also 'Pre-Poll Violence Overwhelms UN in Cambodia', *Independent*, 6 April 1993.

[52] Akashi, 'Challenges Faced by UNTAC', p. 195.

Party	Seats in assembly	Proportion of registered voters voting (%)
United National Front for an Independent, Peaceful and Cooperative Cambodia (Funcinpec)	58	45.47
Cambodian People's Party (CPP)	51	38.23
Buddhist Liberal Democratic Party (BLDP)	10	3.81
Molinaka and Nakataorsou Khmere for Freedom	1	1.37[a]

[a] Cambodia Election Results, UN DPI/1389–June 1993.

In late May, the apparent outcome provoked protests from the CPP, which questioned the administration of the elections and called for fresh polls. Before the elections could be officially endorsed by the Security Council, Prince Sihanouk struck a deal with communist veteran hard-liner, Chea Sim, declaring himself head of state in charge of an interim coalition government comprising the CPP and Funcinpec. Although justified by his fear of a military coup, Prince Sihanouk had acted uni-laterally without consulting Akashi, UN officials in New York or his own son, Prince Ranariddh, whose party had just won a plurality in the elections. In face of opposition from both Funcinpec and UNTAC officials, who privately deplored his action as a constitutional if bloodless coup, Prince Sihanouk abandoned the idea some twelve hours later. The abortive initiative indicated the limitations of UNTAC's role. Prince Sihanouk's retreat did not put an end to UNTAC's immediate diffi-culties. For a brief period, the CPP leadership appeared to endorse the formation of 'autonomous zones' in seven eastern provinces following a secessionist attempt led by Prince Norodom Chakrapong, the estranged half-brother of Prince Ranariddh and SOC's deputy prime minister, and General Sin Song, its minister of national security. That gambit was part of a concerted attempt by the CPP to ensure its participation in government, despite losing the elections.

With the collapse of the secessionist move by mid-June, the CPP grudgingly accepted the outcome of the elections and willingly partici-pated in the establishment of a provisional national government of Cambodia with Funcinpec. Prince Ranariddh and Hun Sen jointly assumed the office of co-prime minister which was approved by the new constituent assembly on 1 July. To its credit, the UN had prevailed politically up to a point in refusing to reconsider the election results in spite of threats from the CPP. The post-election interim solution then became a working political compromise encouraged also through Prince Sihanouk's intervention. On 21 September, the constituent assembly approved a new liberal democratic constitution which reinstated the monarchy. Prince Norodom Sihanouk was enthroned as constitutional monarch in Phnom Penh on 24 September 1993, nearly four decades after he had abdicated the throne. This ironic development institutionalised his facility for political intervention which in the last resort worked in the interest of stability, albeit not exactly as UNTAC had intended. The constitutional assembly then transformed itself into a national assembly on 28 September. But it was only at the end of October that a new government was announced with Prince Ranariddh and Hun Sen respectively as first and second prime minister, with the other posts being allocated also on a power-sharing basis. Delay in its announcement occurred primarily because of tensions within the CPP. That party obtained control of the Ministries of Home Affairs, Justice and Defence, while Chea Sim became chairman of the national assembly with a place on the Throne Council, which decides royal succession.

The post-election governing structure comprised a vulnerable political stalemate with the CPP still dominant in the administration, armed forces and police. The Khmer Rouge has been conscious of the tensions and imbalance within the fragile coalition and has sought to exploit them, including the ambitions of King Sihanouk who returned from medical treatment in Beijing in January 1995. It had refused all cooperation with UNTAC but from July 1993 attempted to negotiate a return to public life by offering to provide forces for a new unified army if given 'advisory posts' in the cabinet, which King Sihanouk encouraged in the interest of national reconciliation. Negotiations on the terms for such reconciliation came to nought by mid-1994, after which the government outlawed the Khmer Rouge, which reacted by setting up a competing provisional government. The military resilience of the Khmer Rouge was demonstrated in their successful counter-attacks to government offensives during the 1994 dry season, although a surge of defections took place at the beginning of the following dry season. Thus, within a year of the elections, Cambodia had reverted to civil conflict despite the evident achievements of UN peacekeeping.

When Yasushi Akashi left Cambodia on 26 September 1993 on the completion of his mission as head of UNTAC, he claimed that the UN had succeeded in its objective of 'laying a firm foundation for Cambodian democracy'. Allowing for the inevitable rhetoric which such a valedictory occasion demanded, Akashi had good reason to be pleased with UNTAC's overall performance compared to that of UN peacekeeping in former Yugoslavia and Somalia. That performance, however, revealed a host of shortcomings which should be part of the learning experience of the organisation.

Conclusion

The demise of the Cold War and the apparent achievements of the UN in Afghanistan, Angola, Namibia and Iraq between 1988 and 1991 generated a strong sense of optimism about the future role of the organisation. This optimism reached a symbolic high point at the first ever Security Council summit held in New York in January 1992. It also shaped the approach taken by the principal sponsors of the plan to settle the Cambodian conflict. Underlying the Paris Agreement was the belief that by decoupling Cambodia's civil war from the wider pattern of regional and global confrontation the basis would be provided for a political settlement. The assumption was also made that in order to bring an end to the civil war, the Khmer Rouge had to become a legitimate party to the agreement. The external sponsors involved the UN in a peacekeeping role in Cambodia despite the nature of the internal conflict and the political culture of the country with which they were dealing. They proceeded on the premise that through a comprehensive agreement and democratic rationalism, a lasting settlement could be achieved.

Ironically, a settlement of a kind was attained through UN intervention although the terms of UNTAC's mandate were not upheld. But the responsibility accorded to UNTAC was not underpinned either in authority or capability so as to ensure that all the Cambodian parties kept both to the spirit and letter of the Paris Agreement. Peace enforcement was not, of course, within its purview because the UN had not assumed a trusteeship role with UNTAC as a provisional government. To that extent, the mandate in terms of quasi-administrative responsibility was not matched by the power and resources given to UNTAC. Accordingly, Cambodia should not be regarded as a model for UN intervention. One important lesson of UNTAC's experience, however, is that given the conventions and limitations of peacekeeping, democratic multi-party elections within a short and finite time period are not necessarily a replicable means with which to secure so-called comprehensive political settlements.

This chapter also points to two further lessons from the UN's involvement in Cambodia. First, the UN still lacks the capacity to plan, deploy and administer large-scale multi-component operations. Although more than a decade has passed since the end of UNTAC's mission, this conclusion, depressingly, does not require significant modification. In 2004, a High Level Panel set up to examine the challenges confronting the UN in the field of peace and security described the continuing absence in the UN system of a 'place designed to . . . assist countries in their transition from war to peace', as a 'key institutional gap'.[53] Second, political is still limited and selective among the major powers for the UN to take a more activist, intrusive and long-term role in dealing with internal conflicts, particularly if they are likely to demand enforcement operations and are not seen to involve the vital interests of the major powers themselves. To that extent, the world of the UN at the beginning of the twenty first century would not be unfamiliar to the pioneers of the League of Nations who struggled against corresponding shortcomings shortly after its advent.

More than a decade has passed since UN peacekeepers left Cambodia. It is a length of time that allows for a less tentative verdict on the legacy of the UN's intervention than that which is possible in most of the other cases covered by this volume. Cambodia still falls well short of the standards associated with a mature, liberal democracy. Human rights violations remain widespread, economic progress has been patchy and old habits of settling political scores and doing business are proving hard to eradicate. That said, full-fledged Western-style democracy, with its intricate panoply of checks, balances and guarantees, is hardly a meaningful criterion by which to measure short-term success in this or, indeed, in any comparable case of war-to-peace transition. When viewed against the turbulent and exceptionally bloody backdrop of Cambodia's recent history, the past decade can only be viewed as one of substantial progress towards a more pluralistic and less repressive political system. Civil society groups and NGO's have proliferated; a measure of debate and criticism is tolerated; the country has joined ASEAN; economic growth has been steady if not spectacular; and, crucially, the political system has survived elections and withstood several political crises.

This more balanced and realistic assessment of Cambodia's path towards recovery raises a wider point about post-Cold War UN interventions. In place of a crude and overly simplistic dichotomy between 'success' and 'failure', Cambodia is much more usefully seen as an example of the *possibilities* as well as the *limitations* of the UN's role in transplanting democracy and political stability to countries that are emerging, in what is necessarily a traumatised, weakened and divided condition, from protracted periods of instability, violence and war.

---

[53] 'A More Secure World: Our Shared Responsibility', A/59/565, December 2004, para. 261.

3   Former Yugoslavia

Spyros Economides and Paul Taylor

The experience of the United Nations (UN) in former Yugoslavia up to the end of 1994 was a depressing one, especially as it followed the success of the Gulf War and the prospect of a 'new world order' in 1991. Regional organisations such as the European Union (EU) and NATO were also infected by the miasma of failure. In this chapter the wreckage is examined: what caused the disappointment of the high hopes of a successful intervention? Was the failure as total as some feared? What lessons can be extracted about relations between the regional and the global organisations in protecting the peace?

In the body of the chapter the main currents in the UN's drift to disaster are charted, not in terms of the incidents on the ground, but in the decisions of those who controlled the agenda. In a concluding section some lessons for the future are deduced.

The break-up of the Yugoslav Federation

Following Tito's death, the rigidities of the Cold War international system held Yugoslavia together for a while, but the demise of communism and the ensuing cataclysmic changes in Eastern Europe released the centrifugal pressures which had previously been contained. By the beginning of the 1990s, there was rising tension between the republics of Serbia and Croatia, the two dominant segments of the old state.

Yet it was Slovenia which took the lead in the race for independence, by holding a plebiscite in December 1990, which produced an overwhelming majority in favour of severing links with the Yugoslav Federation. Despite attempts by all parties to renegotiate the constitution of Yugoslavia along looser confederal lines, the political, economic and ethnic fissures between the various republics deepened. On 25 June 1991, Slovenia and Croatia carried out their intentions and declared independence. Rejecting what they considered to be the economically stifling, politically archaic and nationalistically divisive policies of

Belgrade – now dominated by Slobodan Milošević – Slovenia and Croatia seceded, prompting the outbreak of warfare.

The war waged by the Yugoslav National Army against Slovenia lasted a mere ten days, after which the former surprisingly withdrew. But in Croatia the ruptures in Yugoslav society, and the territorial and ethnic divisions bequeathed by Tito to his country, emerged with greater force. The war there was a vicious affair, presaging the descent into inter-ethnic violence which was to be witnessed later in Bosnia-Herzegovina. The fighting arose because the 12 per cent Serbian minority was determined not to relinquish its links with Serbia. But the fighting was not confined to the areas of the Krajina and eastern Slavonia which harboured these minorities. It extended into other parts of Croatia, thus widening and deepening the more profound political and nationalist divisions between Serbia and Croatia. The fighting was between Croatian armed forces and the Yugoslav National Army, but it looked as if the latter was an instrument of Serbian policy. It was this conflict that brought initial international involvement in the Yugoslav crisis.

As a consequence, the outbreak of violence in Bosnia-Herzegovina was sadly predictable. The rights and interests of the three ethnic groups – Muslims, Serbs and Croats – had been guaranteed under Tito's constitutional arrangements, which maintained their equality within a multinational Yugoslav state. As this edifice was now crumbling, the unstable ethnic mix within its frontiers could no longer be held together. The referendum in Bosnia-Herzegovina on 1 March 1992 was boycotted by the Serbian population, but it provided an overwhelming majority in favour of independence. There were ominous signs of what was to follow: Serbs rejected the result of the referendum, indicated their preparedness to escalate the level of protest to defend their interests and raised barricades around Sarajevo. They had decisively rejected an independent Bosnian republic in the knowledge that they would constantly be outvoted by the other two ethnic groups, and that electoral contests would always result in voting along ethnic rather than political lines. The chances of violence were enhanced by an international mechanism: recognition of Bosnia-Herzegovina by the member states of the European Community (EC), precipitated by Germany, which heightened the Serbs' sense of confinement in a framework they were not prepared to tolerate.

This was the situation in which the international community was to become involved: first through the Conference on Security and Cooperation in Europe (CSCE), then the EC/EU and finally through the UN. From the outset the international community faced the difficulty of mediating on the basis of two contradictory principles: the sanctity of the frontiers of states, once recognised, and the right to self-determination and protection of the rights of ethnic minorities. The regional situation in the Balkans made the dilemma worse. A crisis was developing in Kosovo; and the former Yugoslav Republic of Macedonia (FYROM) was also a likely flash point, not least because of the Greek government's refusal to accept its name.

Therefore, by early 1992, the situation in former Yugoslavia was one of increasing chaos and conflicting principles. With hindsight, it was clear that the international community was then also afflicted by uncertainty and a matching irresolution. The 'new world order' of George Bush had quickly faded and the lack of a distinct international order led to a vacuum which various international organisations and states struggled to fill. There were two unfortunate aspects of the intervention: the crisis in Yugoslavia was brutally complex, and the UN and the regional organisations utterly inexperienced and unprepared for dealing with problems of peace and order in the post-Cold War world.

Obstacles to successful intervention in the crisis in former Yugoslavia

When UN-sponsored action in the Gulf in response to the invasion of Kuwait by Saddam Hussein is compared with the intervention in Yugoslavia, three kinds of special difficulties in the latter are highlighted. The first concerns the problems of identifying clearly the territorial dimensions of the problem. The peculiar mix of populations and the uncertainty created by rival claims to territory made it difficult to identify and accept territorial and administrative demarcations; this was the legacy not only of traditional ethnic and territorial problems in the Balkans but also of the Yugoslav federation constructed by Tito which involved a whole series of compromises aimed at making sure that no single constituent republic dominated the state.[1]

It was difficult for any agency contemplating intervention to see a clear point of entry; no frontier could be established behind which the intervening force could safely be assembled, and from where it could move against a clearly located antagonist on the other side. The options of the international community were further complicated by the ethnic

---

[1] See, for example, James Gow, *Yugoslav Endgames: Civil Strife and Inter-State Conflict*, London Defence Studies No. 5 (London: Brassey's, for the Centre for Defence Studies, June 1991); and John Zametica, *The Yugoslav Conflict*, Adelphi Paper 270 (London: Brassey's, for the International Institute for Strategic Studies, May 1992).

diversity within the new entities, even after they had been formally recognised as states. While their borders had previously been generally accepted as internal administrative frontiers without much political significance, when they were transformed into international frontiers they represented a threat to the ethnic minorities living within them, who hence questioned their legality and historical authenticity. Furthermore, any military action that was contemplated ran the risk of incurring unacceptably high levels of collateral damage because of the nature of the conflict which was spread out in small pockets, involving mainly small-arms combat among neighbouring ethnic communities.

A second problem, which emerged very quickly, was that of deciding upon the purpose and style of such an intervention, a problem later developed in the context of the ever-changing mandate of the UN Protection Force (UNPROFOR). In the history of the UN two forms of intervention had emerged: namely, *enforcement* under Chapter VII of the Charter, involving the use of force to pursue an agreed end, such as the exclusion of an invader – as in the Gulf War – and *peacekeeping*, being the interposition of UN forces between the warring parties with the purpose of encouraging them to negotiate a settlement. The latter had no clear basis in the Charter, but was usually thought to derive from Chapter VI which concerned the pacific settlement of disputes. Both procedures could be accompanied by *peacemaking*, the active involvement of the UN in the search for a peaceful settlement, through mediation and the use of good offices.

From the earliest phases of the Yugoslav crisis the intervening agency faced a problem in this context. Should the purpose be humanitarian, intended to alleviate the sufferings of the civilians affected by the dispute, or should it be the assertion of the principle of the sanctity of frontiers? Or should it be a combination of the two? Each of these purposes implied a particular style of intervention, but pursuing the humanitarian goal interfered with the assertion of the principle of the sanctity of frontiers. The former implied negotiation, mediation and peacekeeping, while the latter required enforcement and implied that there should be no compromise or impartiality. It is shown below that the humanitarian concerns made it more difficult to sustain the principle of the sanctity of frontiers (made especially difficult in the light of the question of their validity).

A third set of difficulties may be found in the diplomatic background of the conflict. Throughout the crisis, successive US governments were ambivalent about how to respond, and tended to oscillate between support of enforcement and an anxiety not to be drawn into yet another war. In the early phase the Pentagon was the more cautious, and the

State Department more activist.[2] But the prevalent consensus was that this was something for the Europeans to do: the Americans had made their contribution to the maintenance of international peace and security in the Gulf War.[3] At the outset of the problems in the Balkans in 1991 this was also the view of the Europeans, especially the French and the Germans, who were inclined to see the crisis as an opportunity to demonstrate and test the emerging machinery for foreign policy cooperation in the EC/EU, be it the existing European Political Cooperation (EPC) or the envisaged Common Foreign and Security Policy (CFSP), and the CSCE,[4] and to create a stronger joint conflict resolution and military capacity.

The Russians were, of course, greatly concerned about the crisis and fearful about its implications for the Russian Federation, and for the frontiers of a number of the recently independent states in the Commonwealth of Independent States (CIS), if the principle of the sanctity of frontiers was compromised in Yugoslavia. But circumstances within Russia, and the bankruptcy of the Russian economy, meant that the Russians were unable to adopt an activist line. This became more apparent in spring 1993, especially as the referendum about President Yeltsin's future approached.[5] Indeed, the Russians became more hostile to military action against the Serbs as the crisis developed.[6]

In consequence the permanent members of the UN (the United States, Russia, France, China and the United Kingdom, known as the P5), which had taken a firm lead in the Gulf crisis, were from the beginning not inclined to support firm UN action in the Balkans: their view was that the Europeans should take the lead. This position, which proved to be a serious abdication of responsibility, was reinforced in the early stages by the view of the UN secretary-general, that this was an occasion when Chapter VIII of the Charter, on cooperation between the regional and global organisations, could be tested. In a number of his reports the secretary-general had proposed an extended role for regional organisations in the maintenance of international peace and security,

---

[2] Interview with an official, US mission to the UN, New York, September 1992.

[3] See Paul Taylor and Arthur J. R. Groom, *The United Nations and the Gulf War: Back to the Future*, Discussion Paper No. 38 (London: Royal Institute of International Affairs, February 1992).

[4] See Geoffrey Edwards and Chris Hill, 'European Political Co-operation, 1989–1991', in Ami Barav and Derrick A. Wyatt (eds.), *Yearbook of European Law* 1991 (Oxford: Clarendon Press, 1992), pp. 489–519.

[5] See *The Times*, 23 April 1993.

[6] The reasons behind this gradual shift are highlighted in an ensuing section, pp. 71–2.

and the obvious regional organisations in Europe were the EU and the CSCE.[7]

The purpose of UN intervention: the evolving mandate

One of the greatest difficulties encountered by the UN in its involvement in former Yugoslavia was that the mandate agreed by the Security Council altered as the crisis developed. It was, therefore, impossible to evaluate the success of the UN by enquiring about the *statement of mission* and then measuring the achievement in this light. The mission statement, in the form of the mandate contained in Security Council resolutions, was constantly changing and being modified during the various stages of the crisis. This point is expanded through this chapter, but at this stage it can be briefly developed.

The initial mandate of the UN in former Yugoslavia included Resolution 713, which established a uniform arms embargo on 25 September 1991; it was intended to assist in the preservation of the frontiers of the state of Yugoslavia, unless changes could be agreed by peaceful means and with the consent of all parties. At this stage this was to be done in cooperation with the member states of the EC. This action was taken under Chapter VII of the Charter, and it was explicitly stated that the situation in Yugoslavia represented a threat to international peace and security. It also noted that the action followed from the request of the government of Yugoslavia, acting through its representative in New York.

These conditions were attached to a number of resolutions, including the one establishing the UNPROFOR in Croatia, approved on 21 February 1992 (Resolution 743). The force was created in response to the recommendation of the secretary-general, who in his report of 15 February 1992 judged that, in the context of the ceasefire then in effect, such a force could succeed in consolidating the ceasefire and facilitating the negotiation of an overall settlement (para. 28, S/23592).

As mentioned, in this resolution there was specific reference to the request of the government of Yugoslavia, an indication of the view that the operation was to facilitate the adjustment of the frontiers of an existing state with the agreement of that state. The force was to be established in areas to be determined by UN agents, with a number of administrative responsibilities, and a duty to stop action that could disturb public order. It was to ensure that local police forces reflected

---

[7] In particular see his report, *Agenda for Peace: Preventive Diplomacy, Peacemaking and Peacekeeping. Report of the Secretary-General Pursuant to the Statement Adopted by the Summit Meeting of the Security Council on 31 January 1992* (New York: United Nations, 1992).

the national composition of the populations in the protected areas. The mandate looked, in other words, like that of a traditional peacekeeping force: to be interpositional and impartial, and to provide the framework for negotiations. It nevertheless raised hopes which went beyond traditional peacekeeping in that according to paragraph 5, the force was to 'create the conditions of peace and security required for the negotiation of an overall settlement of the Yugoslav crisis'. In due course this was to be a source of great disappointment to the Croatians, who interpreted the UNPROFOR mandate as being proactively anti-Serbian, but saw UNPROFOR carrying out a more traditional peacekeeping role despite the reference to Chapter VII.

By May 1992, the form of words in the ensuing mandates had changed. For example, Resolution 752 referred to the *former* Socialist Federal Republic of Yugoslavia, and demanded the withdrawal of the Yugoslav National Army from republics other than Serbia and Montenegro and the cessation of operations by Croatian forces in Bosnia-Herzegovina. The UN now dropped the pretence that it was dealing with problems of adjusting the existing frontiers of an established Yugoslav state. In the month following, in Resolution 757, the mandate of UNPROFOR was altered to include a much more active security role with regard to the protection of Sarajevo airport after the withdrawal of the Bosnian Serb forces. It was to be reopened and fortified with a UN special regime (S/24075, para. 5), with the assistance of an extra 1,100 UN troops. The mandate now included the supervision and control of facilities, organisation and security inside the airport; supervision and control of all local civilian personnel; and the dispatch of humanitarian assistance.

In Resolution 770, of 13 August 1992, the mandate of UNPROFOR was further expanded. The force was now asked to deliver humanitarian assistance and was empowered to use 'all measures necessary' to do this: this operation in Bosnia-Herzegovina was to become known as UNPROFOR II. What did this mandate entail in detail? In the words of the UN secretary-general it was to

Support UNHCR's efforts to deliver humanitarian relief *throughout Bosnia and Herzegovina*, and in particular to provide protection, at UNHCR's request, where and when UNHCR considered such protection necessary.

It would remain UNHCR's responsibility, as at present, to determine the priorities and schedules for the delivery of such relief, to organise the relief convoys, to negotiate safe passage along the intended routes, with UNPROFOR's assistance as required, and to coordinate requests from non-governmental organisations and other agencies wishing to join UNPROFOR-protected convoys. UNHCR, after consulting UNPROFOR, would decide which convoys needed protection, and protection would be provided only at UNHCR's request. Other humanitarian agencies seeking UNPROFOR protection for their deliveries of relief supplies would have to address their requests to UNHCR.

(paras 3–4, Report of Secretary-General, S/ 24540, 10 September 1992).

This was the division of labour between UNHCR and UNPROFOR, at least through the end of 1994.

As will be seen later, by late 1993 and 1994 a further question arose with regard to the mandate of UNPROFOR. Was the force authorised to order outside military assistance in pursuit of a further mandate from the Security Council, such as the enforcement of the air exclusion zones created by Operation Deny Flight in late March 1993, or the elimination of weapons which were attacking territory declared by the Security Council to be a 'safe area', as Srebrenica was in mid-April of the same year? UNPROFOR leaders were formally required to address requests for such assistance to the secretary-general's Special Representative in the region who, as the senior local UN official, would decide whether to authorise them in the context of the Security Council mandate. He would consult with the military leaders of the force before doing so.[8]

The escalation of the crisis and the greater involvement of the UN

On 16 October 1992, a leading article in *The Times* contained the following proposals:

- that there should be air strikes against the Serbian warlords and Serbian planes involved in the war in Bosnia-Herzegovina;
- that there should be active defence of convoys if an attempt were made to prevent them from reaching their destinations in pursuit of their mandate;
- that the peacekeeping activities in the area should be positively coordinated under the French commander of UNPROFOR II through NATO; and
- that there should be clear support for the then more moderate prime minister of the remnant of federal Yugoslavia, Milan Panić, against the leader of Serbia, Milošević, who was seen as being responsible for the attempt to create a Greater Serbia at the expense of Croatia, but especially of Bosnia-Herzegovina.

---

[8] The mandate of UNPROFOR was further expanded through Security Council Resolution 795, 11 December 1992, which authorised the initial deployment of 700 troops on a more traditional peacekeeping operation in FYROM, separating Serbia proper from the new republic.

These proposals are indications of trends in the crisis which may be summarised as

- an escalation from minimum peacekeeping to a more activist peacekeeping, tending towards enforcement, culminating in strikes against Serbian heavy weapons;[9]
- the more positive identification of an enemy in the form of the Serbian activists under Milošević and, in Bosnia-Herzegovina, Radovan Karadžić;
- a striking increase in the scale of the presence of the intervening forces in Bosnia – by mid-November 1992 they amounted to 6,500 men – as earlier in Croatia, and the closer involvement of NATO.

This was a process of *creeping escalation*, with a component of more activist peacekeeping, accompanied by an increasingly clear realisation that the regional agencies were incapable of retaining control.

The enhancement of the role of the UN, at the expense of the EC/EU, may be traced through four phases. In the first phase, up until late November 1991, the UN was involved only in that it condemned the violence, and reinforced positions adopted by the EC, as with the approval by the Security Council of an embargo on supplies of arms to all parties in the rapidly disintegrating Federal Republic of Yugoslavia.[10] The EC was more proactive up until November 1991, and was the lead organisation, in the sense that its role combined peacemaking with peacekeeping.[11] This took the form of attempting to mediate a peaceful solution to the break-up of Yugoslavia, the negotiation of ceasefires – which were constantly broken by all parties – and the provision of EC monitors. (The EC had been delegated by the CSCE to take over primary responsibility following the failure of the consensus-seeking CSCE mechanism to make any progress with regard to the fighting in Slovenia and then Croatia.) From the early phase of the conflict the regional organisation sought to attribute primary responsibility for the crisis, first in Croatia, then in Bosnia-Herzegovina, to the Serbs. It directed various pressures against the Serbs, and came to be seen quite quickly by the latter as an enemy, possibly an instrument of Germany, traditionally hostile to Serbia.[12] This was quite starkly reflected in the

---

[9] See *The Times*, 24 April 1993.

[10] According to Resolution 713, 25 September 1991.

[11] This was reflected in the preamble to Resolution 713 (1991), which commended 'the efforts undertaken by the European Community and its member States...to restore peace and dialogue in Yugoslavia'.

[12] See James Gow and James D. D. Smith, *Peace-Making, Peace-Keeping: European Security and the Yugoslav Wars*, London Defence Studies No. 11 (London: Brassey's, for the Centre for Defence Studies, May 1992), p. 36.

role attributed to Germany in the EC's recognition of the secessionist republics of Slovenia and Croatia.

At the start of a second phase, in November 1991, Cyrus Vance was asked to intervene as the secretary-general's personal representative, and the UN played a key peacemaking role in the ending of the first Serbo-Croatian war. This followed the failure of the EC's efforts to end the crisis in Croatia, in part because it was now seen, not as an unbiased mediator, but as an opponent of Serbia. The EC also made mistakes in concluding and administering ceasefires: it did not have the mechanisms or experience of the UN in such matters. Hence the UN became more actively involved with the creation of UNPROFOR and its initial deployment in Croatia.

Nevertheless, in this second phase, the UN role was mainly concerned with *peacekeeping*, it reinforced an effort that was still being directed and conducted primarily by the regional organisation. But the warring sides saw the global organisation as being more impartial in holding the ring. They were also more conciliatory towards the UN position, as espoused by Vance, to ensure that they were not alienating the United States, which was assumed to be backing Cyrus Vance. At the same time, the *peacemaking* function of the EC remained intact; even though the EC had failed in its initial peacebrokering mission, it still retained the authority delegated to it by the CSCE.

In a third phase the UN found itself being pushed into a more proactive role, and was invited to take the lead by Lord Carrington and others, especially after a meeting in London on 17 July 1992.[13] The secretary-general indicated that he accepted the need for a greater UN role in his report of 6 June 1992, though in this phase, as will be shown, there was quarrelling between the regional and global organisations.[14] Greater UN involvement coincided with the more general acceptance of the view that Serbia–Montenegro was the violating state, and the first big step taken was the approval of mandatory sanctions against Serbia–Montenegro at the end of May 1992,[15] followed, on 13 August, by the granting of a mandate to activist states to use 'all measures necessary' against the Serbs if they tried to prevent the provision of humanitarian assistance.[16]

---

[13] This meeting led to the London Agreement of 23 July, described as 'a plan to hand over the baton to the UN with dignity': *Independent*, 3 July 1992.

[14] *Report of the Secretary-General Pursuant to Security Council Resolution 757 (1992)*, S/ 24075, 6 June 1992.

[15] Resolution 757, 30 May 1992, China and Zimbabwe abstaining.

[16] Resolution 770, 13 August 1992, adopted with three abstentions, China, India and Zimbabwe. For text of the resolution, see pp. 185–6 in Appendix B.

In late August 1992 a fourth phase was visible. On his appointment to succeed Peter Carrington as head of the EC's Commission on Yugoslavia on 27 August 1992, David Owen said that any distinction between the role of the two organisations was now defunct. The UN's role as *peacekeeper* was to be merged with the EC's role as *peacemaker*. The two organisations were to set up a joint operation in Geneva to conduct negotiations and research possible forms of settlement on the terms agreed at the London Conference in late August 1992.[17]

After the conference the two organisations worked together in this tandem arrangement and links with the UN were tightened by the direct participation of the permanent members of the Security Council and the secretary-general's representative Vance, and by the role of the British and French governments in New York. The latter became responsible for orchestrating diplomacy among members of the Security Council, particularly the P5, to obtain support for resolutions indicated by the London Conference, and any subsequent proposals.

From peacekeeping to near-enforcement

Several states, including the United Kingdom, declared that their commitment of troops to the crisis would be limited, and that their actions would be confined to the protection of the convoys carrying scarce supplies to those trapped in the conflict areas; they were to protect the UN's humanitarian work in Bosnia. But for a while the possibility of moving beyond the support of convoys to more coercive military action was not positively excluded.

At a cabinet meeting on 18 August 1992 to authorise the use of British troops in Bosnia following the 13 August resolution, and the use of British war planes to create an exclusion zone for Iraqi aircraft in southern Iraq, four stages of commitment in Bosnia were identified.[18] The weakest was preferred as the other three could lead to an escalation of involvement. Nevertheless, it was thought that the British could yet change their minds, and other states, such as the United States and France, occasionally advocated a more muscular approach. But only military assistance for humanitarian missions was explicitly allowed, and only minor further military actions were proposed in the UN, such as the agreement to set up no-fly zones in Bosnia. A decision was also taken

---

[17] *The Times*, 28 August 1992.
[18] See Colin Brown, 'British Troops Will Protect Aid Convoys', *The Independent*, 19 August 1992.

to enforce a naval blockade against Serbia–Montenegro, and to monitor the sanctions.

As the line dividing active peacekeeping and peace enforcement was approached, there were often hints that it might be overstepped, especially from the United States, then hesitation and retreat. A major problem was that there was no agreement on the political objective of enforcement: the optimism, which had followed the recognition of Croatia, was quickly overtaken by evidence of Croatian intentions to share the carve-up of Bosnian territory with Serbia. Although the primary guilt of Serbia was widely acknowledged, the sense that there should be a plague on all their houses was widespread.

The form of words used in the resolution of 13 August 1992, which permitted the use of greater force to protect the humanitarian convoys, was reminiscent of Resolution 678 of November 1990, which had sanctioned the use of force against Saddam Hussein, but, for those who framed it, it had almost the opposite implications. The 1992 resolution included the phrase 'all measures necessary' to protect the convoys, whereas the 1990 resolution mentioned 'all necessary means'. The 1990 resolution was intended to convey the threat of the use of force to evict Saddam from Kuwait, whilst appearing sufficiently ambiguous as to allow those who opposed force to support it. In contrast the 1992 resolution threatened more force than the states were prepared to use, but it was hoped that the Serbs would interpret it in the light of the earlier resolution. But unlike Resolution 678, the threat was not backed with any convincing evidence that it was real.[19]

Until the London Conference of 26–28 August 1992, it was possible to maintain the position that the use of force to impose a settlement in Yugoslavia had not been excluded. But one consequence of that conference was to reinforce the Serbs' doubt that force would be used. The agreement specified the use of sanctions up to and including the complete isolation of the Yugoslav rump state, if that state failed to comply with the agreed terms, but statements by the British and others, and the failure to refer to enforcement, implied that there would be no military coercion. This message was reinforced by the precision with which the non-coercive sanctions were spelled out: they amounted to total isolation for Serbia–Montenegro, but as the sub-text implied, not more than that.[20]

---

[19] It was reported on *The World at One*, BBC Radio 4, on 27 August 1992, that the people of Belgrade had feared that attacks on their city would follow shortly after the approval of the resolution.

[20] *The Times*, 29 August 1992.

By late 1992, it had become apparent that the scale of threat posed by the intervening UN forces had been significantly increased since the creation of UNPROFOR in February. The big step was not Resolution 770 of 13 August 1992, but an earlier resolution. Resolution 761, of 29 June 1992, had pointed the way when it held that the Security Council 'does not exclude other measures to secure aid'. On 11 September, the Security Council confirmed that the new UN force in Bosnia-Herzegovina of up to 8,500 men, UNPROFOR II, could remove those obstructing the convoys by force if necessary. This had been foreseen in the secretary-general's report of 10 September.[21]

By the end of the year, several other indications of the escalation of preparedness to use force were evident. For instance, in early October, UN forces were authorised to use force to resist an attempt to return home by Croatians who had been driven out of UNPROFOR I territory. A senior UN official in charge, Cedric Thornberry, blamed the Croatian government for encouraging this, but stressed that even more trouble would arise if the refugees were allowed back.[22] By mid-November 1992 the British force of 2,400 men had arrived in Bosnia equipped with heavy armoured personnel carriers, Warriors and lighter vehicles, Scimitars. This level of armament was a clear – if to some a symbolic – indication of a determination to be more proactive in protecting troops and removing opposition to the convoys, despite the statement by the British defence minister, Malcolm Rifkind, on 23 November that British forces would keep a low profile. By December, serious incidents involving Serbs and British forces had taken place, and although these had not involved casualties, there was a real danger of this happening. This situation considerably sharpened the dilemma: it could lead either to a sudden increase in commitment, and enforcement, as part of a process of retaliation, or to withdrawal.

In Britain, in late 1992, the former response seemed possible. There had been *creeping escalation* towards a strong version of peacekeeping: if a serious incident took place it was hard in mid-December to predict the outcome. But public opinion and the style of government response in France and Britain suggested they could be provoked into enforcement. Initially this could have involved air strikes against Serbian positions, as recommended in the *Times* leader mentioned earlier.

---

[21] *New York Times*, 11 September 1992. The secretary-general interpreted the rules of engagement as follows: 'self defence is deemed to include situations in which armed persons attempt by force to prevent United Nations troops from carrying out their mandate'. See S/24540.

[22] *The Times*, 2 October 1992.

Plans for peace: the retreat from principle

By January 1993, a plan for peace had been produced by the Vance–
Owen team, which for the first time could be seen as representing a
clearer statement of a political goal. The plan involved not only keeping
the existing frontiers of Bosnia-Herzegovina and a central government
with modest powers, but also dividing the territory into ten cantons
which would have a high degree of autonomy. The difficulty was that it
allowed the Serbs to retain some of the territory they had captured
militarily, and indeed also allowed some of the ethnic cleansing carried
out by the other groups to be kept in place. Despite being the biggest
territorial victors, the Serbs were the main opponents of ratification,
because they would have to relinquish part of the conquered land,
especially the vital land corridor linking the Krajina to Serbia proper
through parts of northern Bosnia.[23] The plan preserved a basic tenet of
international relations – the sanctity of international frontiers – but it
accepted some measure of ethnic cleansing. The new Clinton administration in the United States therefore hesitated to endorse it and the
general failure to agree on implementation of the plan squandered one
of the few real chances of peace.

The approach of the dividing line between active peacekeeping and
enforcement had frightened many in the governments of the leading
Western states involved. But even this 'para-escalation' made the control of the global organisation more necessary to the hesitant states.
Using violence required that the UN be in charge; restraining its use also
had to be pursued through the global organisation. The earlier somewhat unreal oscillations of the EC/EU countries between coercive and
non-coercive measures had gradually given way to a similar oscillation in
the UN, where it was thought the key decisions ought to be taken. The
transfer of the Vance–Owen talks from Geneva to New York in spring
1993 not only facilitated closer teamwork between representatives of the
United States, the P5 and the EC/EU states, but also emphasised the
importance of the UN as the lead organisation.

While the two main mediators continued in their fruitless efforts to
persuade all the three Bosnian groups to agree to the Vance–Owen
peace plan, the UN passed a string of resolutions in early 1993, which
did not positively move to enforcement, but edged in its direction and
kept the pressure on the Bosnian Serbs. Security Council Resolution
807 extended the mandate of UNPROFOR until the end of March
1993 initially, and then until the end of June 1993. More importantly,

---

[23] See *Observer*, 3 January 1993.

this same resolution affirmed that UNPROFOR was acting under Chapter VII of the UN Charter – that is, that it was there to maintain security and that the secretary-general should take all necessary measures for the protection of the force and the provision of heavier weaponry for defensive purposes. Pressure was also maintained by two further resolutions: Resolution 808 which set up an ad hoc war tribunal and requested information about war crimes, and Resolution 816, which finally enforced the no-fly zone over Bosnia. It asked NATO war planes to intercept Bosnian Serb planes in the zones. It had taken over six months for the agreement to acquire these teeth. President Clinton also declared himself prepared in spring 1993 to authorise strikes by US aircraft against Serb positions, for instance, around Sarajevo, a move that the United States argued was sanctioned by Resolution 770. Those with troops on the ground resisted it with some anxiety.

Problems in maintaining the UN's impartiality

Once UNPROFOR was involved, the UN was faced with the difficulty that any proactive role ran the risk of attracting retaliation against the existing UN forces, both in Croatia and Bosnia, thus making it increasingly difficult for the organisation to maintain a reputation for impartiality. The UN secretary-general was at pains to stress this point in his report of 26 May 1992 to the Security Council,[24] which implied a preference for mediation rather than enforcement, though in later reports on 30 May and 6 June, whilst still stressing the risks, he reluctantly accepted the need for a more active role for UNPROFOR,[25] on condition that the parties to the dispute (in Sarajevo) accept and abide by the terms of a ceasefire, and that more personnel and resources be allocated.

But the secretary-general became very irritated (in late July 1992), by what he saw as the EC's unilaterally committing the UN to actions which could increase the chances that UNPROFOR would be seen as partisan. He also noted that Croatia was extremely unhappy about what seemed to be an international validation of the enclaves captured by Serbian forces in Croatia as a result of the positioning of the UNPROFOR forces around those specific enclaves. A rather cynical joke after the initial deployment of UNPROFOR in Croatia was that this force should be called 'UNPROSERB' or 'SERBPROFOR', to

---

[24] Security Council, *Report of the Secretary-General Pursuant to Security Council Resolution 752 (1992)*, S/24000, 26 May 1992.
[25] *Ibid.*

illustrate its true role as seen through Croatian eyes. In late November 1992, the Croatian government threatened not to agree to the renewal of the UNPROFOR mandate in February 1993, a tactic which the Croats have persistently pursued ever since. The secretary-general also expressed great concern at the UN's close involvement with the Balkan crisis at the expense of its involvement in crises elsewhere in the world, particularly in Somalia.[26]

One reason for Croatian complaints was that the UN, through Cyrus Vance, had allowed responsibility for the civilian administration of the UNPROFOR region in Croatia to be placed in Serb hands. The plan called for a reversion of power into the hands of an authority representative of the local populations. Under this specific plan, populations would have been returned to their homes and lands, allowing for representative local government. But as the displaced populations were not returned, because of Serbian intransigence, the Serbs retained control of these areas. There was also clear evidence of serious infringements of human rights by Serbian groups in the area under the authority of the so-called Serbian Republic of Krajina. As the crisis evolved, the UN, like the EC before it, began to attract accusations of partisanship.

At the London Conference in late August 1992, the Bosnian Serbs were allowed a victory, in that discussions about the frontiers of Bosnia with Serbia, and other terms of a possible settlement, were to begin in a week's time (4 September 1992) in Geneva, and there was no guarantee that seized lands would be returned. There was indeed a promise to 'respect the integrity of present frontiers, unless changed by mutual agreement', and the US acting secretary of state, Lawrence Eagleburger, said that the United States would not accept anything other than a return to the status quo ante. But, in the context of the conference, there had been a sell-out: the agreement allowed the Serbs to continue to put pressure on Bosnia in the name of finding general agreement, and to fudge and postpone settlement. A ceasefire was yet to be agreed upon, and although a scheme for placing heavy weapons under UN supervision at eleven centres was accepted by the Serbian leadership in Bosnia, there was no guarantee that all the weapons could be located and disposed of in this way.

By late 1992 the Bosnian Serbs had begun to show a two-fold reaction in their judgement of the UN. The dominant strain, encouraged by Slobodan Milošević in Belgrade, was that they could now play the long game, more confident that they would not be subject to coercive military sanctions, and reassured by the evidence that those who could act were

---

[26] See *International Herald Tribune*, 4 August 1992.

hesitating and that any pressure towards enforcement in the UN was being contained and the UN became vulnerable to the charge that it was continuously chasing after the frontiers of mediation: too often it seemed to be implying mediation on the basis of the most recent gains by the Serbs, a problem which arose in part from its humanitarian role. Agreeing to negotiations about frontiers was a concession to the transgressors, which had been excluded in the Gulf crisis.

On the other hand, the Serbs continued to express doubts about UN intentions and impartiality. There were accusations that the single UN convoy into Gorazde had conveyed arms to the Muslim defenders; this had led to a retreat by the Serbs. The Serbs also complained that some broader, clandestine deal had been struck at the London Conference at their expense and 'this had a shocking effect on Serbian morale'.[27] This also led to a transformation of the image of the UN forces.

The lead states had declined to enforce principles or peace, but despite this the Serbs were beginning to see the UN forces as opponents. Attacks on them seemed to be increasing and on 4 September an Italian military transport aircraft carrying blankets into Sarajevo crashed after having been hit by an anti-aircraft missile. Even though there was strong evidence to suggest that either Croatian or Muslim forces had downed the aircraft, the Bosnian Serbs were to bear the brunt of accusations. Their feeling of persecution by the international community as embodied by the UN mission in Bosnia was heightened.

All this reinforced the latent fears within the governments of the lead states about greater involvement. Unlike in Iraq, as the crisis proceeded they became more, rather than less, tortured by the agonies of choosing between mediation and enforcement. By late April 1993 this dilemma had become unbearable, as the world witnessed the fierce attacks of the Bosnian Serbs on the Muslim town of Srebrenica, and gross violations of human rights.[28] As of December 1994, the agony remained with the Serb aggression against the 'safe area' of Bihać.

But both concern with the humanitarian dimensions of the crisis, and acceptance of the secretary-general's enhanced role, were the result of an ambivalence at the heart of the intentions of the lead states in the UN and the EC/EU: on the one hand, they wanted to defend fundamental principles without reserve or hesitation, and on the other, they were inexorably driven to seek compromise to save costs and lives for themselves. Through spring 1993 the UN was the forum for debate about whether principle should be defended through enforcement, or whether it should play a more limited role. Much of this debate was fuelled by the vacillations in US policy, sometimes suggesting a preparedness to fight to the last Fijian – or European – sometimes implying an active commitment to enforce themselves, and sometimes drawing back from all options. But the United States stopped short of actually providing troops on the ground.

For a number of reasons the precise mix of mechanisms and policy in former Yugoslavia proved to be unstable. Involvement to promote humanitarian assistance spilled over into a more active role, which in turn made it more difficult to protect the organisation's reputation for impartiality, despite the determined efforts of commanders such as General Sir Michael Rose. It also made mediation harder.

Regional and global agencies: forms and fictions

In his report of June 1992 Boutros Boutros-Ghali interpreted the somewhat vague provisions of Chapter VIII of the Charter on relations between regional organisations and the UN:[29] the UN should lead. The secretary-general complained in mid-July 1992 that the EC–UN relationship was the opposite of this. The EC was in some ways directing the UN, but failing to provide the resources for the policies it approved.

This complaint was partly financial. At the London Conference on 26–28 August 1992, the secretary-general, now a joint chairman of the conference, complained that the EC members, which were among the richest states in the world, had been slow to provide enough resources for the tasks that had been agreed. This was a disastrous failing: in summer 1992 the UN was owed US $530 million by member states – mainly the United States.[30] But the EC states showed no sign of being prepared to provide the resources for any more effective role in former Yugoslavia, despite claims that it was primarily their concern.[31] The financial plight of the UN remained serious in 1994. Around US $992.8 million was owed on the peacekeeping fund on 31 December 1993, and US $478 million was owed in unpaid assessments to the regular budget, about 50 per cent of which was owed by the United States.[32] The EU remained unmoved by the need to match concerns with resources.

[29] *Agenda for Peace.*
[30] Paul Taylor, 'The United Nations System Under Stress: Financial Pressures and their Consequences', in Paul Taylor, *International Organization in the Modern World* (London: Pinter, 1993), pp. 159–79.
[31] See Hella Pick in *The Guardian*, 29 October 1993.
[32] See Anthony Mango, 'Finance and Administration', in *A Global Agenda: Issues before the 49th General Assembly of the United Nations* (New York: United Nations, 1994), pp. 304–5.

But it would be misleading to see the EU, or NATO, and the UN as discrete organisations. Two of the permanent members of the Security Council, France and the United Kingdom, were also members of the EU, which took a leading role in the regional organisation's work concerning former Yugoslavia. Three members of the Security Council belonged to NATO. But throughout the development of the EPC and CFSP mechanisms the two EC/EU states had insisted that they had the right to act in their individual capacity with regard to issues that were before the Security Council, and on these questions they declined to be bound by any form of instructions from the EC/EU states.

Agreements between the members of the EC/EU, including the Single European Act of 1985, and the Maastricht Treaty of 1991, confirmed this privileged position for the British and the French. EC/EU member states in the Security Council therefore protected the formal separation of the two organisations in New York and, oddly, declined to appear to act there on behalf of the EC/EU. Within the UN framework they agreed only to inform the other EC/EU members about developments in their weekly meetings in New York. What could have been a useful connection between the regional and the global organisations – overlapping membership of the EC/EU and the Security Council – became a limitation on inter-organisational communication.

In fact, the overlapping memberships and discontinuities meant that distinctions between the regional and universal organisations were unreal, and states in Europe and the UN in practice had no organisational affiliation: in neither case was there any mandate. On the Contact Group it was unclear how far, or in what sense, the five permanent members of the Security Council represented the UN. They had not been authorised to attend in the name of the UN by the Security Council, and did not seem to be acting in the framework of a specific UN mandate, and in any case two of them were also members of the EC/EU. They were there in their individual capacity.

In like vein the meaning of the term *the UN* was also flexible. The UN could mean the Secretariat and the secretary-general, or the collectivity of states working through that organisation. When he spoke of the interests of the UN in former Yugoslavia, Boutros Boutros-Ghali seemed to mean those of the permanent institutions, and his representatives.[33] This interpretation became a convenient device for those states which were becoming anxious to avoid firmer action, as it made it easier to attach blame to the institution rather than to themselves. In this way humanitarian assistance, being a function of the UN more narrowly

[33] *The Times*, 3 September 1992.

defined, became part of a formula by which the cautious elements in member governments sought to abdicate responsibility. In contrast, in the Gulf War the secretary-general was excluded and the image of the UN presented by the governments was of the group of states in alliance with the government of Kuwait.

There were also a number of problems in the relationship between NATO and the UN. NATO had been mandated by Security Council resolutions to enforce the air exclusion zones, and to attack weapons in use against the UN-declared safe areas on the authorisation of the senior UN officer in former Yugoslavia, Yasushi Akashi. Two issues arose. First, it was clear that NATO was the most obvious available mechanism for carrying out these tasks and after it was discovered that the alliance could act out of area, there was no impediment to its doing so under a Security Council mandate. The UN had to authorise such actions, based however on Article 51 in Chapter VII, and not Chapter VIII, of the Charter: the alliance was merely a framework within which a group of states happened to be joined.

Second was the implication of this way of working for the future. There were obvious dangers in accepting the two linked principles of using an organisation like NATO to act, even under licence, outside its own area, and of contracting out the job of maintaining international peace and security to a state or an organisation. Where did the field of NATO action stop? Could it act *anywhere* in the world? In the Middle East, the Far East, or just where the interests of members were directly affected? How was this to be decided? Was it merely a hired gun, or given overlapping membership, simply Security Council power without the Russian or Chinese veto? Was there not the risk that 'contracting out' would reinforce the older *spheres of interest* idea, with local powers asserting their primary responsibility to the exclusion of the global authority? It seemed that the way forward had to be supporting the enhancement of the authority of the UN, and that the option of 'contracting out' discredited the global organisation and licensed local bullies. In the final section of this chapter these points are discussed further.

Alarms and excursions: the main actors in the first half of 1993

In late 1992, the United States seemed to be prepared to mount a massive response to the Serbs, but they were not supported in this by the Europeans, and the proposal evaporated as the Bush election campaign got under way. In fact, it was argued in some circles that the Bush administration's hints at massive intervention were nothing but a ploy in the presidential election campaign, an area in which Bush was emphasising his experience.

The incoming Clinton administration had explicitly placed domestic political and economic options at the top of the agenda and was loathe to announce a major foreign policy decision with regard to the conflict in Bosnia as the government's first important action. Pressure was on Clinton to revive the US economy, to 'put America back to work' and to move away from a primary concern with external affairs. Yet the United States could not simply discard its international role, and there existed some hope within Clinton policy-making ranks that victory for Milan Panić against Milošević in the Serbian presidential election in late 1992 could be the turning point in former Yugoslavia. Moral support was provided for Panić, not least in implying that sanctions against Serbia could be loosened if he won. With the defeat of Panić the Clinton administration was paralysed with indecision: the Vance–Owen peace plan dividing Bosnia into cantons was unacceptable, as it sanctioned ethnic cleansing, the new leadership in Belgrade had a poor track record and in any case foreign affairs was of secondary importance.

By this time the United States had become involved in the Somalian imbroglio – at the behest of the UN. Clinton's attention on US peace-keeping and humanitarian relief missions abroad was dominated by this particular dispute, and for a while the crisis in Bosnia took the back seat. Yet at the heart of the US policy still lay the dilemma of not wanting to extend US commitments in terms of ground troops to Bosnia until a political settlement was reached on the ground; but the flawed premises of the Vance–Owen plan could not be accepted.

Therefore, the United States again pushed for tighter sanctions, but added an air-drop of vital supplies to beleaguered populations. A US envoy was sent to the peace talks in the person of Reginald Bartholomew; and, as mentioned, the Vance–Owen talks were moved to New York, where the participants would be closer to the UN and the US administration. Bartholomew's first action was to travel to Moscow, an indication of US concerns over what they saw as an emerging obstacle to strengthening sanctions against Serbia and enforcing the no-fly zone over Bosnia. This was the increasing alignment of the Russians with the Serbs in Bosnia.

Indeed, as the crisis evolved, the Russians became more prepared to resist increasing the pressures against the Serbs. The Yeltsin government, and the Russian people, were profoundly divided in their loyalties. There was sympathy for the Serbs, but at the same time a great anxiety about allowing a sovereign state to be destroyed without general consent. There was also a hankering after a more independent role among some of Yeltsin's opponents, involving hostility to the west, and certainly opposition to any expansion of NATO to the east as was shown at the December 1994 CSCE meeting, when Yeltsin himself objected to adding eastern European states to NATO. Any demonstration of NATO fire power close to Russian frontiers, as with attacks on Serbian heavy weapons, caused unease. In the Security Council, one factor which discouraged further expansion of the mandate in mid-1993 was the fear that the Russians might prove obdurate. There was a tendency to argue that the general terms of older mandates, like the 'necessary measures' of Resolution 770, could be the legal basis of specific new actions.

Despite deep reservations about the nature of the Vance–Owen plan, by April 1993 the United States was left with no other alternative and showed a willingness to accept it as the best possible bargain that could be struck, if it were to be accepted by all parties. The no-fly zone was pushed through the Security Council on 31 March, and Warren Christopher pressed for the lifting of the arms embargo on Bosnia to allow the Muslims to defend themselves and thus provide, in his words, 'a level playing field'.[34] There was even a hint that the United States would consider using force to ensure compliance, especially through air strikes against Serbian heavy weaponry. Yet the basic premise remained that until a political settlement was found, which the United States then could assist in policing through the employment of a massive NATO-based peacekeeping force, there were no immediate plans for direct US military enforcement measures.[35]

And in Europe, there were, of course, a number of reasons for doubting the others' support if the going got tough. Right at the centre of the problem was the refusal of Germany to provide troops for enforcement purposes in former Yugoslavia, because of the restrictions on activities outside the NATO area then thought to be in the German constitution.[36] The EC/EU therefore lacked several of the conditions of successful collective action.

David Owen also now argued for limited air strikes – a nod towards enforcement. Through the two years of the crisis the Bosnian Serbs had been increasingly, and with mounting vigour, identified as the main transgressors. The UN Security Council had accepted the proposal that

---

[34] *The Independent*, 6 April 1993.   [35] See *The Times*, 11 February 1993.
[36] The German Constitutional Court, in summer 1994, ruled that such action was in fact compatible with the German Constitution.

information about war crimes should be collected, a policy targeted explicitly at the Bosnian Serbs.[37] The earlier uncertainties about who was guilty had been clarified, at least in the minds of Western governments, despite some muddying of the waters as a result of a renewal of fighting between Croats and Muslims in central Bosnia in late April 1993.

Intimations of settlement: from summer 1993 until summer 1994

From summer 1993 into the winter, the warring parties were all embroiled in small-scale fighting to capture or recapture tracts of territory. Despite the repeated extension of the UNPROFOR mandate in Croatia, there were constant rumblings that the Croatian armed forces were preparing for a major military operation to recapture those areas of Croatia in which the Serbian minority lived under the peacekeeping aegis of the UN force. Tripartite fighting in Bosnia, and tension between Serbia and Croatia over the fate of the Serbian enclaves in Croatia, had horrid implications both for the inhabitants of the region and the international community.

Nevertheless, the Serbs, both in Serbia proper and in Bosnia, were becoming more amenable to a solution, albeit for differing reasons. Serbia was increasingly feeling the uncomfortable effects of the comprehensive UN sanctions imposed in March 1992, while the Bosnian Serbs were concerned with consolidating their gains. Similarly, the Croats, both in Croatia and in Bosnia, were contending with problems of their own which leant towards some sort of solution in Bosnia. Croatia's policies on the Serbian enclaves in Croatia, and Croatian President Franjo Tudjman's repeated threats to terminate the UNPROFOR mandate, attracted critical attention; there was even a threat from the international community to impose economic sanctions on Croatia to stop it assisting Croat forces in Bosnia. As with the Bosnian Serbs, the Croats in Bosnia were now more or less content with the ground they had captured and were now primarily interested in defending this territory in the face of increased Muslim military activity. Bosnian Muslims had the least to lose in continuing the fighting, but were still unable to build up a strong enough international coalition to overturn the blanket arms embargo on all former Yugoslav republics, which would provide the so-called level playing field, or to provoke a massive military intervention.

[37] In Security Council Resolution 771, 13 August 1992.

In summer 1993, a further plan for the division of Bosnia was proposed by the Owen–Stoltenberg team (Vance having been replaced by Stoltenberg as the secretary-general's envoy to the peace talks). This plan was a further retreat from the principles on which the international community had originally insisted, a further indication of an increasing anxiety to get out at the minimum acceptable cost.

Peacemaking had initially aimed at keeping a unitary Bosnian republic, thus maintaining the rule that frontiers were not to be changed by force. When this failed, the cantonisation plan was proposed by Vance and Owen, aimed at keeping Bosnia unitary but in a complex puzzle of ethnic divisions, governed by a relatively weak central government. The original intention had been to avoid the division of Bosnia into ethnic provinces, as this would have been seen as a capitulation to armed force and a vindication of the policy of ethnic cleansing. In the new plan this was exactly what was proposed by the EC/EU–UN team. Bosnia was to be divided into three ethnic units, with a loose, and powerless, confederal government in Sarajevo.

A further concession was that after a probationary period of two years, the ethnically based republics would have the right to secede from the confederation with the consent of the other signatories. This would mean that the Republika Srpska (the Serb Republic of Bosnia) and Herzeg-Bosna (the Croatian counterpart) could join their respective parent states of Serbia and Croatia, something which the international community had previously rejected. By winter 1993, therefore, the conclusion could not be avoided that the main states had acted on the principle of regressive mediation, always offering to bargain on the basis of the most recent gains of the aggressor. They had avoided the alternative: enforcement on the basis of principle.

Again there was much discussion between the warring parties and the negotiators about the territorial demarcation of each entity – a problem that had plagued all previous tentative agreements – even when the three groups had in principle agreed to the constitutional side of the arrangement. If the three parties agreed to the plan, the international community was willing to enforce the peace through the deployment of NATO forces under the UN. The Muslim leadership of Izetbegović rejected the plan, however, because of inadequate territorial concessions by the Serbs. Humanitarian missions continued, but the UN contingents were kept under continuing pressure as the peacemaking efforts of the UN and the EU failed.

In the winter of 1993–1994, the fighting on the ground was primarily dominated by hostilities between the Croats and the Bosnian Muslims in central Bosnia, which illustrated the new-found vigour and military organisation of a growing and increasingly better-armed Muslim force. Similarly, on 28 February 1994, international military involvement in the Bosnian crisis took a new twist with the enforcement of the no-fly zone with the use of NATO military aircraft to attack and destroy four Serbian warplanes. This illustrated the increasingly antagonistic stance of the outside world to the Serbian position, but it also put into question the role of the UN operation in the region. This was a clear-cut instance of *creeping escalation* from peacekeeping to peace enforcement by the UN and it naturally reinforced Serb doubts about the acceptability of the global organisation as an impartial peacemaker and peacekeeper, whilst encouraging the Muslims to hope for forceful military intervention on their side. Negatively, it also contributed to the declining reputation of the UN for impartiality.

At the same time, the United States brokered – some would say directed – conciliation between Croatia, the Bosnian Croats and the Bosnian Muslim government, which led to a confederal arrangement between these parties. This reflected in part the rising pressure on the Clinton administration from domestic public opinion and Congress to pursue a strategy which would favour the victims of Serb aggression. The Bosnian Serbs were thus now faced with a united front in negotiations, which was given added strength by the recommendations made by Congress to Clinton to lift the arms embargo against the Bosnian government. By this time, however, the Serbs had taken most of the territory that they wanted in Bosnia, and had no interest in pursuing further large-scale offensive deployments. The conclusion had to be that the anti-Serb coalition was encouraged to continue fighting precisely when the Serbs themselves would have been prepared to negotiate a peace – though on their terms.

Finessing the principles: from summer 1994

Nevertheless, in July 1994, yet another peace plan was announced by the Contact Group comprising the United Kingdom, France, Germany, Russia and the United States – now returned to Geneva from New York. Agreed by the group in July 1994, this plan would have divided Bosnia into mini-ethnic states while keeping the facade of a unitary Bosnian state; it was backed by an explicit threat by the Contact Group that if the Bosnian Serbs did not accept the latest variant of the plan by 20 July 1994 the arms embargo against the Bosnian Muslims would be lifted and further sanctions would be imposed on Serbia itself.

The peace plan demanded that the Bosnian Serbs relinquish some 20 per cent of the territory in Bosnia under their control, and called for the division of Bosnia between the new Croat–Muslim Federation and the Bosnian Serbs on the basis of a 51 per cent to 49 per cent territorial split. The Serbs at this time controlled some 70 per cent of Bosnia. In principle, the plan would apparently keep in place a unitary Bosnian state along loose confederal lines with the two units allowed a great degree of freedom in managing both their domestic and international affairs. The Contact Group proposal accepted that although territorial acquisition through the use of force was unacceptable, some compromise with this principle had to be made.

Pressures against the Serbs were now accumulating. They were facing an international organisation which seemed to be threatening to move from peacekeeping to enforcement with the overt use of the military might of NATO under UN supervision; a united presence from the Croats and Muslims both in the military and diplomatic spheres, which also added extra emphasis to the internationally held view that the Serbs were the villains of the piece; an increase in military activity by the Muslims with the tacit consent of the international community and an increase in the supply of arms entering Bosnia through the Croatian coastline. And Milošević, now president of Serbia–Montenegro, put pressure on the Bosnian Serbs to settle on the terms of the most recent plan, by closing the frontier between Serbia–Montenegro and Bosnian Serbia, thus putting a stranglehold on the latter's supplies. In return Milošević, who was increasingly afraid that the Bosnian Serb leader had larger ambitions to replace him as leader of a Greater Serbia, bargained for the loosening of the international sanctions on Serbia–Montenegro which were producing increasing political and economic strains.

For their part the western Europeans were now quite willing to partition Bosnia, if it meant an end to the fighting. But the United States remained adamant that no partition that was the result of the use of armed force could be condoned. Nevertheless, in the deal the United States went as far as to concede that the constituent units of a confederal Bosnia might secede at a future date. In return the United States extracted from the Europeans the concession that the arms embargo would be lifted if the Bosnian Serbs rejected the plan. The US acceptance of the possibility of partitioning of Bosnia was the biggest shift in US policy since Bush first had to deal with this issue in early 1991.

The first Serb response was neither to accept nor to reject the plan: they demonstrated yet again their skills in diplomatic procrastination. On 20 July 1994, Radovan Karadžić rejected the possibility of a 51–49 per cent territorial split; demanded guarantees for the Serbian corridors joining Serbia proper with the Krajina; demanded access to the Adriatic Sea; and, most importantly, stressed that any acceptance of the plan must include provision for future review of the plan with the right of secession for the two constituent ethnic states. Karadžić also stressed that this was not an outright rejection of the plan but rather part and parcel of an ongoing negotiating process in which the Serbs were asking for certain points of clarification and certain guarantees.

By December 1994, it seemed that all the parties to the dispute and the international mediators had accepted that Bosnia would be divided, sooner or later, in one form or another, formally or informally. But, as with all the plans for the resolution of the conflict since 1992, the maps proved to be the insurmountable obstacle. The continuation of fighting seemed to be the order of the day.

The position in December 1994

In December 1994, it was possible to draw two different sets of conclusions from the crisis about former Yugoslavia. These concerned first the role and contribution of the UN presence in former Yugoslavia, and second the lessons which may be extracted from this experience about the appropriate relationship between the UN and regional organisations in future interventions.

The UN presence in former Yugoslavia

There are some conclusions which must remain a matter of judgement rather than proof. These include the view that humanitarian intervention is a moral obligation, and that as long as it cannot be proved that it costs more lives than it saves, it is incumbent on humanity to do what it can to protect life through all available mechanisms. The argument that intervention in former Yugoslavia has not done this is impossible to prove, and therefore cannot be supported. How can the net balance be calculated of the numbers who have survived because of UN convoys?

The judgement that the UN helped to keep the crisis on the agenda, and that this was itself of benefit, was also impossible to prove. The attention of the international community offered a marginal disincentive to offences against humanity, and some actions that might otherwise have been taken probably were not taken. But this was not just about Bosnia-Herzegovina. UN involvement there was necessary if only to remind other potential malefactors that an international response was always possible, and that the law of the jungle was not the norm.

Lessons about the mistakes of UN intervention may also be deduced by reference to the range of *conceivable* ways of intervening in former Yugoslavia and their implications. First was large-scale intervention to enforce a solution, but this would have required resources, which the states working with the UN were unwilling to provide. In any case such a level of intervention could have been counter-productive in the long term, as it would simply have pushed grievances underground, as if one of the parties had 'won' by force of arms.

Second was a mode of intervention, which committed sufficient resources to make it probable that goals agreed in the Security Council, short of enforcement, would be achieved. This was often not the case: for instance, Resolution 770 promised, as has been seen, more than it was intended to carry out. 'All measures necessary' were never taken to make sure that humanitarian assistance was delivered, and this was probably the first step in the decline of the credibility of the UN. Similarly the decision to introduce safe areas was taken by the Security Council in a kind of resource vacuum: the means necessary to maintain them if attacked were not provided. But such a level of commitment would not have been impossible, and it would have been well short of that necessary for enforcement.

Third was negative intervention: that is, avoiding the commitment of UN forces, though encouraging settlement by diplomatic means, with intervention by the friends of the parties resisted, and peace-keeping forces provided after ceasefires. In this situation, however, there would have been the risk that the Serbs would have been lav-ishly armed by the Russians and the Bosnian Muslims by the Muslim states and the United States. Bosnia would have been destroyed in a proxy war.

Fourth was direct intervention by the large states, say the Russians on the Serb side, at the risk of counter-intervention on the side of the Bosnian Muslims by the West and the Islamic states. This was, of course, the worst-case scenario, and it was precisely because of the horrors it implied that it was an unlikely eventuality. The same rules applied as during the Cold War: each side would avoid too obvious and direct an involvement because of the risk of counter-intervention and escalation to general war.

What conclusions emerge from these possibilities? The best course of action, in that it combined what was practicable with what was the least undesirable, would have been the second option outlined earlier. This course also assumed the impartiality of the UN: it positively committed resources to the pursuit of impartial goals. But there needed to be a sufficient level of force to make it look as if goals agreed by the UN, short of enforcement, would be vigorously pursued. The mistake of the UN was to choose goals without being prepared to do this, and, as is usually the case with hollow threats, they were found out.

Intervention in former Yugoslavia probably had the effect of prolonging the crisis at a lower level of engagement, and discouraged a more rapid conclusion at a higher level. But this was the best that could have been achieved. It avoided the problem of finding massive external forces to impose a settlement which would then have needed policing in the long term at great cost. But it also combined a vigorous pursuit of humanitarian goals, and measures for isolating areas of peace, without compromising with the harsh truth of such conflicts – that the parties to them have to resolve them, even if this means war. The UN was right to intervene, right to fall short of enforcement but go beyond traditional peacekeeping, but wrong in that it failed to match realisable ambitions with affordable means.

The UN could be said to have *managed* the crisis for reasons which add up to the point that intervention was both ineffective in stopping the war *and* required by *both* the main parties to the dispute. The Serbs preferred that the UN stay rather than go, because they retained a preference for a legitimised settlement: hence the tendency for them to continue to push, when given any opportunity, and to make tactical concessions – accepting ceasefires, handing over heavy weapons, etc. – when it looked as if there could be a more powerful response. The UN's departure would also have freed the Islamic countries to arm the Muslims on a much larger scale, probably with the support of the United States. But the threat by the US Congress in late 1994 to allow arms to flow to the Muslims, in defiance of the UN arms embargo, was paradoxically helpful from the point of view of the UN: it encouraged the Serbs to placate the UN in the face of greater dangers. At the same time – and this also tended to prolong the war – the Serbs were constantly encouraged to do what they could to gain territory up to the point at which this was clearly at the risk of UN departure. But the Muslims also wanted the UN to stay because it could be an ally against Serb attack, and a protective umbrella from under which the Serbs could *be* attacked, as in the case of the provocative excursions from the Bihać safe area in November–December 1994.

But the animosity between Milošević and Karadžić, increasingly visible through 1994, was probably also a consequence as much of the structure of the conflict as of personalities. The restraints imposed by the UN presence, without actually preventing Serbian aggression, meant that the Serbs got increasing gains but never enough. Settlement in the framework of Bosnia-Herzegovina, on terms judged acceptable by the Serbs, was always unlikely in the context of UN intervention: the Serbs were always capable of getting enough to encourage them to seek for more, as mediation on the basis of the next gain was always an option.

There was, however, bound to come a point when Bosnian Serb leaders would realise that their ambitions, growing as they were, could never be accommodated in Bosnia-Herzegovina: hence a bid for leadership of a Greater Serbia under Karadžić.

It follows in turn that it was always unlikely that a settlement could be reached without the positive support of the Belgrade government on the side of the UN. This was true under Panić as under Milošević. The former should have been more rewarded for his support of the UN, but in late 1994 so should the latter have been, for instance, by lifting sanctions on Serbia-Montenegro: any settlement in Bosnia-Herzegovina would require the support of Belgrade. Without the whole-hearted support of Milošević, sufficient pressure on Karadžić could not be exerted. But more importantly perhaps, Milošević needed to be brought, and kept, on side, because of what could happen in other parts of the Balkans, especially in Kosovo and in Macedonia (FYROM). The latter crisis could be even more damaging than that in former Yugoslavia, and to contain it the support of Belgrade was essential.

It became apparent, during 1994, that any settlement on former Yugoslavia would be at the expense of the state of Bosnia-Herzegovina. This prospect had ambiguous implications for the UN. From one angle it will be seen as a disastrous betrayal of the key principle on which the UN was founded – respect for the frontiers of nation-states once recognised. But, from another, if this principle had to be suspended, as looked likely in December 1994, it would become clear that it was only the global organisation which has the authority to grant this dispensation and to promulgate its basis.

If there are to be new ways of thinking about the bases of UN's intervention and humanitarian assistance these will have implications for the process whereby states are recognised.[38] The process of recognising the break-away republics in Yugoslavia was, however, controlled by the states of the EC/EU according to tests enunciated by the Badinter Commission attached to the EC Conference on Yugoslavia.[39] This produced a quandary: on the one hand, the UN was the primary forum for the definition of the criteria of statehood, but, on the other hand, their relevance to the circumstances in former Yugoslavia was

---

[38] See Paul Taylor, 'The Role of the United Nations in the Provision of Humanitarian Assistance: New Problems and New Responses', in James T. H. Tang (ed.), *Human Rights and International Relations in the Asia Pacific* (London and New York: Pinter, 1995), p. 141.

[39] See various press releases issued by the Commission of the European Communities on behalf of the Commission for Yugoslavia under reference CEECAN 270066DGO8 and 09, February–March 1992.

determined by the regional organisation. In consequence there was the risk of placing the application of general principles in thrall to local contingency; or even at the mercy of particular state interests within the regional organisation.

In Yugoslavia the recognition process was mishandled by the EC, a lesson which the EU will not easily forget, and was perhaps reflected in its initial reticence to recognise the former Yugoslav republic of Macedonia as an independent state, despite its having seemingly fulfilled all the conditions set out by the Badinter Commission. The major problem was that the EC recognised the regions of former Yugoslavia as successor states before any agreement about frontiers or assuring the rights of minorities, including the Serbs in Bosnia-Herzegovina.

The Badinter Commission had implied recognition before this had happened de jure, by dealing with the central governments in the breakaway territories and accepting the central authorities' statements about the way in which the rights of minorities were to be protected. For instance, evidence of adequate protection for the minority rights of the Serbs was taken merely from assurances contained in a letter from the Bosnian government to say that it had been incorporated in the constitution. There was little direct contact with the minorities, because it might have offended the central regimes. Indeed the Badinter Commission was asked by Lord Carrington to make political judgements, as opposed to strictly legal ones, precisely because the EC states had been subjected to undue pressure in 1991 from the Germans, and asking Badinter to take this on was a useful evasion.

What conclusions follow from these observations? One is that any relaxing of the strict prohibition of intervention in international relations carries with it clear implications for the recognition process. If increasingly there is to be intervention, the global organisation should also have the right to approve states in the first instance, and to de-recognise them if they fall short. If tests to be applied are widened, and applied more explicitly to the rights and welfare of peoples, the global organisation should also have the right to decide upon the justification of a claim to statehood. The reason, as shown by the example of former Yugoslavia, is that it will have to pick up the pieces if that state fails. This is the case for making the recognition of states a global responsibility to be exercised through the UN. Security Council approval would both reflect and enhance its authority. Conversely, it follows that if states cannot accept the transfer to the UN of this traditional prerogative role, then the strict rule of non-intervention cannot be relaxed. A more modest conclusion, however, was that a point has been reached in Yugoslavia, when the global organisation will eventually have to be asked to correct the error of the regional organisation, the EC/EU, which had helped to pre-cipitate it. Only the UN can place the seal of legitimacy upon the resulting new states.

Regional–global organisation relationships

The crisis in former Yugoslavia also provides some lessons on the appropriate relationship between regional and global organisations. The regional organisation should normally act as the agent of the UN, always within a mandate approved in the Security Council, but subject to closer and more direct control as the scale of military intervention moves from that appropriate to traditional peacekeeping towards enforcement. Enforcement should always be managed by the global organisation. Similarly, decisions of a constitutive nature, creating new rules or legitimising new actors, for instance through recognition, should be taken by the UN.

Much has been written about the reform of the global organisation and this is not the place to pursue the matter. But two points may usefully be added: first, if regional organisations are to be a fundamental part of a reformed global security architecture, the arrangements of the Security Council should reflect this; second, the crisis in former Yugoslavia demonstrates the overwhelming importance of relating policies to resources. The Security Council simply should not take decisions without adequate resources. Perhaps there should be a sepa-rate Technical Evaluation Authority to confirm that resources and policy match.

Regional organisations should only act on problems between mem-bers, and not out of their area in crises among non-members. But action by the member states of an out-of-area organisation may be sanctioned by the local regional organisation to act on its behalf in their region. Hence in former Yugoslavia, or other parts of Eurasia, NATO could act if this were requested by the Organisation of Security and Cooperation in Europe (OSCE), which is the responsible inclusive regional organisation. These various forms of supervision are necessary in order to avoid either a return to the spheres-of-influence idea, which creates no-go areas for international authority, or the appearance of the hired gun with overtones of what would look like imperialism.

Such principles mean that, in a number of areas of the world, regional security organisations need to be created where they do not now exist. They should be legitimised by the global authority, and their decisions subject to UN authority, both under the Security Council and the jurisdiction of the International Court of Justice.

Developing the role of regional organisations on the lines of this interpretation of the principles of Chapter VIII can only be carried out in the context of the overall reform of the UN, especially the membership of the Security Council and its relations with the UN General Assembly. The model of the EU is a useful model of links between the regional organisations and the UN, though the French and British insistence on acting on their own account in the Security Council should be abandoned; other regional security organisations should also be represented in the Security Council. The UN and regional organisations should be linked by overlapping memberships, and related through legitimised hierarchies.

The General Framework Agreement for Peace in Bosnia and Herzegovina

In Paris on 14 December 1995, the presidents of the Republic of Bosnia and Herzegovina, the Republic of Croatia, and the Federal Republic of Yugoslavia signed the General Framework Agreement for Peace in Bosnia and Herzegovina, also known as the Dayton Agreement. This agreement, comprising eleven articles, set out the principles for the maintenance of a unitary and sovereign Republic of Bosnia and Herzegovina, consisting of two Entities: Republika Srpska and the Federation of Bosnia and Herzegovina. The latter was to control 51 per cent of the territory of the republic. The agreement also set out a series of constitutional provisions relating to the bicameral legislature of the unitary state, the election of a three-man presidency, the role and responsibilities of central government and the general relationship between the two Entities and the central government.

As a corollary to the seeming willingness of the Balkan parties to seal a peace deal after over three years of fighting in Bosnia, the Dayton Agreement also set out the responsibilities of the organs and institutions of the international community to ensure that the peace would be a lasting one. Included in these provisions were: the definition of the role to be played by the OSCE in the areas of confidence-building, monitoring elections and arms control; the continuing operation of the International War Crimes Tribunal; the creation of a Commission of Human Rights to be monitored by both the OSCE and the Council of Europe; the creation of a UN International Police Task Force; and the nomination of a High Representative to monitor and oversee all civilian aspects of the peace plan. The most important provision relating to the work of the international community in ensuring the success of the peace plan was the direct military involvement of NATO through the Implementation Force, (IFOR). This was a major new development in the international mechanisms involved in attempting to bring peace to this war-torn area: UNPROFOR was to be relieved of its responsibilities in Bosnia and replaced by IFOR, which was to be an implementation and not a peacekeeping force, led by a US general and consisting of some 60,000 NATO troops including a US contingent of some 20,000 troops.

This peace accord had been approached by a long and arduous route. In the public eye it had only been achieved because of the indefatigable work of the US envoy, Richard Holbrooke. In reality, however, events on the ground in Bosnia and its environs throughout 1995 had favoured this outcome. The increasing diplomatic involvement of the United States made a significant difference to the warring parties' perceptions of how much they stood to gain or lose by pursuing conflict, and a series of events in 1995 drew the United States further and further into the Bosnian mire and resulted in the transformation of the UN peace-keeping and humanitarian mission into a peace implementation mission. All the Bosnian parties to the dispute were brought to accept this, although often with great reluctance. Those involved from outside, including President Milošević, the EU and the UN, breathed a sigh of relief.

The move away from a UN-dominated peacekeeping operation began in February 1995, when NATO issued a strong ultimatum to the Bos-nian Serbs, in the wake of the explosion of a mortar shell in Sarajevo market on 5 February which resulted in sixty-eight deaths and left nearly 200 wounded. Even though this was the last of a sequence of NATO-issued threats, which in the past the Bosnian Serbs had scorned, the increasing US diplomatic maneuvering behind the scenes paradoxically lent 'diplomatic muscle' to the existing military potential. This was manifested at the beginning of March by the creation of a Muslim–Croat Federation, heavily brokered, if not forced upon the parties, by the United States, which indicated that the balance of diplomatic and military forces arrayed against the Serbs was growing stronger and more coherent.

The shifting balance of power within the regional context, and the heightened role of NATO, forced the Bosnian Serb leadership into a series of rash retaliatory measures which were to have enormous repercussions. In late May, the Serbs abducted and held hostage dozens of UN peacekeepers and observers from remote positions in an attempt to intimidate NATO into withdrawing its threat to use force against Serb positions if the latters' heavy artillery and other weaponry were not removed from certain key positions, (primarily around Sarajevo). In itself, this move was not considered out of character for the Bosnian Serbs, though it was portrayed in some quarters as a sign of the increasing desperation of the Bosnian Serb forces and leadership in the face of mounting military and diplomatic pressure. Nevertheless, it did trigger a Western response beyond the normal diplomatic negotiations aimed at releasing the hostages, in that Britain and France decided to deploy a newly styled Rapid Reaction Force in Bosnia. This force, consisting of national troops outside UN jurisdiction, was intended to protect the British and French troops operating in Bosnia under the UN flag and mandate. It was a bizarre arrangement, yet one which indicated that the thankless task of the UNPROFOR operation in Bosnia was constantly evolving into an operation in which other regional organisations such as NATO and individual states such as Britain and France were taking the lead. What emerged in the summer of 1995 was a gradual shift of emphasis away from the peacekeeping role of UNPROFOR to a more proactive policy of enforcement, which would later lead to the implementation force agreed at Dayton, Ohio, and signed in Paris.

Two major events in late July and early August 1995 damaged the image of the UN as a viable organisation for dealing with conflicts such as that in Bosnia and the utility and success of peacekeeping operations. These events also dramatically altered the military and territorial scenario on the ground in the Balkans. Their ramifications had two important consequences.

The first involved the collapse of the UN-designated and -protected 'safe areas' of Zepa and Srebrenica to Bosnian Serb attacks and the ensuing mass murders committed by the Bosnian Serbs against the Muslim men of Srebrenica. This discredited the UN and highlighted the impotence of UNPROFOR, as the international community had repeatedly stated that the safe areas would be defended from Serb aggression. It was swiftly followed in early August by the stunning success of the Croatian armed forces in overrunning the Krajina and driving out the local Serbs. This too undermined the authority of the UN, which had commenced its involvement in the wars of the former Yugoslavia by deploying UNPROFOR as a traditional peacekeeping force to keep Croats and Serbs apart in the Krajina while a diplomatic solution was negotiated. Internationally, the UN was discredited and UNPROFOR shown to be an inadequate mechanism through which to attempt to provide an acceptable and lasting peace for Bosnia and other parts of former Yugoslavia.

The second consequence involved the development of the military and territorial situation on the ground, as a result both of Croat successes in the Krajina and the increasingly emboldened attitude of the Bosnian government army in its military operations against the Bosnian Serbs. Throughout August the war in Bosnia flared up with renewed vigour and the Bosnian Serbs were on the receiving end of Croat and Muslim attacks along the whole of their front lines – a precursor to the major offensive to be conducted by the Croats and Muslims, in tandem, in September and October. The Bosnian Serbs were also under political and military pressure from other sources since Milošević steered well clear of providing them with any overt diplomatic support, insisting that they should sue for peace, while NATO with strong US insistence came into the military picture more emphatically.

Towards the end of August, NATO aircraft, and the previously deployed Anglo-French Rapid Reaction Force, pounded Serbian positions around Sarajevo, and targeted and destroyed a range of Serb military, logistics, and command and control installations throughout the Serb-controlled territory. This provided a clear signal of the intent and determination of the international community to pursue a solution to the Bosnian conflict through the use of force if necessary. It also eventually caused enough disruption and dislocation to the Bosnian Serb military machine to allow the Croat and Muslim forces to prosecute their military offensive with great territorial success. Paradoxically, the Bosnian Serb escalation of attacks on UN positions, and the overrunning of the safe areas, helped the UN, as it forced a concentration and relocation of peacekeeping forces to make them less vulnerable to counter-attack in the wake of NATO air strikes.

As the many internationally brokered attempts at negotiating peace had for the most part foundered on the inability of the local warring parties to agree to the demarcation of frontiers on the maps, the NATO bombardment paved the way for a significant redressing in the balance of power on the ground that was fundamental to the final agreement in Dayton. Now on the receiving end of a formidable array of diplomatic and military muscle, the Bosnian Serbs were dragged back to the negotiating table in Geneva in an attempt to thrash out a ceasefire and the basic principles of a peace settlement, including the demarcation of frontiers. This the Bosnian Serbs did with great reluctance, but the mounting pressure placed on them by the United States and Milošević (who could no longer rely on the support of Serbs at large after the disastrous loss of the Krajina and who hence was ready to sign a peace deal to retain his position in power) meant that they had few alternatives.

The final incentive for the Bosnian Serbs was provided by the great territorial gains made by the Croats and Muslims through their renewed, and to date most successful, military campaigns in Bosnia throughout September and early October. While negotiations orchestrated by Holbrooke continued, the Bosnian Serbs were being pushed back in all parts of Bosnia to the extent that even the vital city of Banja Luka came under threat. More importantly, the Bosnian Serb retreat meant that the frontiers in Bosnia were forced back towards the 51–49 per cent Croat–Muslim/Serb split which was the agreed benchmark for any short-term settlement. What had not been achieved since 1992 through international diplomacy and the threat of the use of force was rapidly coming about through the successes of the Croat–Muslim military machine to which the broader international community turned a blind eye under pressure from Washington. A basic set of principles for a peace deal was agreed in Geneva on 9 September, and while war still raged, a ceasefire was set for 12 October, after which intensive negotiations would take place for a final settlement.

The role of the United States in forcing all the parties into signing the General Framework Agreement for Peace in Bosnia and Herzegovina was vital in both military and political terms. The United States lent its weight militarily, through increased participation in NATO operations, and finally indicated its willingness to send troops to the region to police a peace deal. Diplomatically, the United States persuaded Milošević that the time had come for a settlement by making obvious the long-term consequences of war, but also by throwing its weight behind the Croat and Muslim causes by tacitly agreeing to the military campaigns in Krajina and Bosnia; this finally forced the Bosnian Serbs to accept the Dayton accords. What became obvious throughout 1995 was that even though diplomacy could play a leading role in reaching peace, it was the changing military situation on the ground, and the evolving balance of power, which would provide the final catalyst for a settlement. And while the UNPROFOR mission would be disbanded and replaced by the Implementation Force with a different role, the UN's peacekeeping mission had played a significant role in maintaining the Bosnian war on the international agenda. UNPROFOR had neither the necessary military instruments nor political direction to bring peace to Bosnia, but it certainly provided a framework both politically and militarily.

The Dayton Agreement, in many ways, was a reworking of previous plans proposed by the UN and the EU and not a novel departure. By the time of the conference, not only did the participants have the lessons of more than three years of abortive peacekeeping to draw on, there was also a range of Security Council resolutions already in place. These provided the essential context for the final negotiation of the peace. During the course of its involvement, the UN had also pioneered new forms of proactive conflict management, making any retreat to traditional and more passive peacekeeping in the future unlikely. The experience of UNPROFOR was therefore by no means wholly negative. Nonetheless, in many ways the peace settlement indicated that the use of force still pays. While we may have lauded the onset of peace in Bosnia, what we are left with is a country split in two by force of arms – a unitary sovereign state with two *Entities*.

Afterword

Ten years since the first edition of this book and Bosnia still remains on the international agenda and almost in a state of limbo. The façade of unitary sovereign statehood is undermined by the continued difficulties imposed by the division of the country into two entities, and is still underpinned to a great extent but an important international civilian and military presence. Many reforms have been attempted to establish a real unitary state and achieve levels of transparency, the rule of law, democratisation and economic development. But much of this has been limited by the intransigence of local actors – particularly at the entity level – high levels of criminality, serious unemployment and general economic dislocation, and by the persistent declamation that Bosnia is being run by the representatives of external actors and international organisations whose concerns do not tally with those of local actors.

Multiple elections have taken place at all levels of government since December 1995 but it is questionable if a real democracy exists because of the nature of the constitutional arrangements. Attempts at financial and economic reform have fallen foul of a divided state and a truly poor domestic and regional economic environment. Civilian rights and military security have been provided but only because of the continued presence of a large international military and policing operation.[40] In the ten years since the Dayton Accords were concluded, the task of forging a viable, economically sound, multiethnic democracy is nowhere near complete and has relied almost exclusively on a continued international civilian and military presence.

As this book is concerned with the role, effects and implications of UN intervention in a variety of crises since the end of the Cold War, this is not the appropriate place for a detailed discussion of what has passed in the internal affairs of Bosnia since 1995. What is attempted is an overview of the most significant developments and arguments which

---

[40] IFOR was converted into the SFOR (Stabilisation Force), still a NATO military operation. Gradually, this force has been reduced in numbers. In 2005, it was supplanted by an EU military presence EUFOR, even though there is still a US-led rump NATO presence in Bosnia.

have occurred in the last ten years with respect to the UN's role in the internal affairs and international administration of Bosnia.

There are, broadly speaking, three categories which deserve some attention with respect to the UN's role in Bosnia both during the time of the conflict and in the ensuing post-conflict phase.

First, is the growing body of literature by practitioners and academics, which recounts and examines the war in Bosnia and the international diplomatic efforts to achieve peace. What is notable about these accounts and analyses is the extent to which they support if not substantiate many of the conclusions reached in the initial formulation of this case study and especially in relation to the role of the UN and its relationship to the major powers and regional organisations. One could, for example, refer to the experiences of David Owen as co-chair of the Peace Conference on Yugoslavia in his memoir of the international diplomatic effort to achieve peace, *Balkan Odyssey*.[41] Here what is reinforced is not only the near impossibility of delivering solid ceasefires and peace deals when confronted with warring leaders such as Karadžić and Mladić, but also the extreme difficulties inherent in attempting to find consensus for peace between the major Western and other powers who all held their own specific agendas in this particular conflict. Furthermore, and most relevant here, what becomes clear from accounts such as those produced by involved individuals such as Owen is the degree to which the UN – and especially the Security Council – was at the mercy of the interests of the P5, who did not always share the same understanding of the goals that the UN should achieve in the Bosnian conflict or the best way of resolving the conflict. Indeed, much of what these types of accounts centre on is also the growing transatlantic divide and the evolving US position on the Balkans, which in tandem with NATO involvement was crucial to the outcome of international diplomatic efforts. Here one could also refer to another personal memoir of the war in Bosnia – or at least the final stages of achieving a peace deal – that of Richard Holbrooke, who is generally acknowledged as having the prime responsibility for the diplomatic endgame in Bosnia.[42] What is quite clear in this type of account is the force of impact of US political and military might not only on the situation on the ground but also on the US's European allies, the EU and not least the role of the UN.

Indeed the military dimension of the diplomatic endgame has traditionally been seen as the predominance of the US's military muscle, through the vehicle of NATO, as perceived against the relative

---

[41] David Owen, *Balkan Odyssey* (New York: Harcourt Brace and Company, 1995).
[42] Richard Holbrooke, *To End a War* (New York: Modern Library, 1999).

impotence of the UN's military capabilities and the ineffectiveness of its peacekeeping operations. To counter-balance this kind of perception one could point to the diaries of military officers, especially those who commanded UNPROFOR. One of the most robust accounts of the problems faced by UNPROFOR on the ground and in dealing with contradictory messages emanating from UN headquarters in New York is that of General Sir Michael Rose.[43] What emerges from this type of account reinforces the arguments posed earlier in this chapter about the confusing mandates handed down to UNPROFOR, the differences of opinion among the P5 which may have resulted in this, and the resultant, mistaken impression, that the UN and its peacekeeping forces in particular were to blame for the catastrophe which befell Bosnia. Other, more academic, accounts have attempted to apportion blame for the failure to force peace in Bosnia not on the inability of the Western powers and international organisations to do so for lack of a clear understanding or for lack of resources (in the case of the UN and the EU), but on the lack of political will.[44] But they are not without their problems in that they take a more partial view of events in Bosnia, yet still expose the degree of difficulty faced by the UN Secretariat and its military forces on the ground in finding a way through the fighting on the ground and the political and military minefield set by the UN Security Council.

Second, are those analyses to the post-war administration of Bosnia especially in the domains of peacebuilding and democratisation, which among other international organisations the UN had a weighty role to play. Most of this type of discussion is quite critical of these efforts even though some constructively so. The highly ambitious task of state-building and the daunting challenge posed by the desire to construct a multi-ethnic democracy so soon after a vicious war may be an easy target. Nonetheless, many have exposed the inadequacies and hurdles faced by the UN and other international actors in Bosnia since 1995.[45]

The major problem one could point to in this instance is that it is not good enough to pin the blame on the reluctance – if not outright hostility – of certain domestic constituencies to achieving the goals of a democratic, unitary Bosnian state. The constitutional structure bequeathed by the

[43] General Sir Michael Rose, *Fighting for Peace: Bosnia 1994* (London: The Harvill Press, 1998).

[44] James Gow, *Triumph of the Lack of Will: International Diplomacy and the Yugoslav War* (London: Hurst & Company, 1997).

[45] See, for example, Sumantra Bose, *Bosnia After Dayton: Nationalist Partition and International Prevention* (London: Hurst & Company, 2002); and David Chandler, *Bosnia: Faking Democracy after Dayton* (London: Pluto Press, 1999).

Dayton agreements, the conflicting interests of the wide range of 'internationals' involved in the state-building effort have rendered an already confused situation even more confusing. While the UN was at the heart of this effort, especially in the humanitarian domain, and in providing international legitimacy for the whole endeavour, much of the political activity was conducted through other channels (not least the Office of the High Representative). As such, in this case too, while NATO provided the security dimension through SFOR (and latterly the EU through EUFOR), while the OSCE and a multitude of other international organisations and non-governmental organisations were toiling on the ground – often at cross purposes – the UN withstood the brunt of all attacks on the inability to forge ahead with the moulding of the new Bosnia state.

One of the major criticisms levelled at the international presence in Bosnia was the fact that the High Representative, implicitly representing the international community under the aegis of the UN, had powers enabling him to act almost as a viceroy.[46] Indeed for some time, it was the UN which was held responsible for the small degree of 'local own-ership' of efforts at democratisation, capacity building and economic development, when in fact the structures handed down at Dayton were not the product of some kind of UN initiated process. This in time has diminished as the EU has progressively become more important in the administration and reform of Bosnia, but nonetheless the image of UN incompetence and haughtiness still lingers. Where the UN has been most successful though, has been in the humanitarian field, but there has still been much cause for concern – and criticism – about the vast number and transient nature of UN 'internationals' and members of its specialised agencies.

Third, is the attention which has been focused on questions of lessons learned through UN peacekeeping mission in Bosnia and the impor-tance, which has been attached to questions of international criminal justice. One of the major developments which occurred in the ten years after Dayton was the amount of effort devoted to uncovering the actual events surrounding the massacre at Srebrenica and to what extent the UN was responsible for these atrocities. In 1998, the General Assembly requested, from the UN Secretary General, an official report sur-rounding the events at Srebrenica and to the extent to which UNPROFOR contingents could have averted this disaster. This report,

---

[46] One of the most critical accounts of the role and powers of the High Representative (and especially of Paddy Ashdown), which stirred up a big and at times caustic debate is to be found in Gerald Knaus and Felix Martin, 'Travails of the European Raj', *Journal of Democracy*, vol. 14, no. 3 (2003).

issued by the UN secretary general in November 1999,[47] was a frank and almost damning account of the UN's role in Srebrenica. On one level it highlighted the inadequacies of the UN operationally and cast a long, dark shadow on its actions as a 'peacekeeper'. On another level though, it also showed a renewed and transparent effort by the UN to admit to its failures and to learn the lessons of failed operations. The consequences of reports such as that on Srebrenica was to open an agenda of reform not only on the resources and capabilities of the UN in the domain of peacekeeping but also on the general principles of what peacekeeping is and should be in the context of the UN Charter and changing international realities.

As a corollary to this we have also seen the monumental changes that have occurred, in both the promulgation and operation, of international institutions responsible for the indictment and prosecution of individuals suspected of violations of international criminal law, and especially genocide, war crimes and crimes against humanity. The International Criminal Tribunal on Yugoslavia (ICTY) is a UN mandated court and it has brought to trial many of those suspected of such crimes committed during the context of the Bosnia war, not least Slobodan Milošević himself. Similarly, the importance attached to this form of justice as pursued through the UN, has also allowed for the imposition of strict conditionality on a variety of south-eastern European states which do not receive the benefits of EU accession negotiations, or preferential trading agreements if they do not hand over indicted war criminals.[48] In relation to this we have also witnessed the creation of the International Criminal Court which in some ways could only have become a reality because of ICTY and the weight attached to international criminal law through the efforts of the UN.

In conclusion, it is evident that while for the UN, intervention in Bosnia is an ongoing process; the organisation has learned a variety of lessons from this involvement in the last ten years. Many of these have had to do with the whimsical nature of the UN's own constituents – its member states and particularly the P5. Many have had to do with the operational necessities encountered in peacekeeping and humanitarian

---

[47] General Assembly, Report of the Secretary General pursuant to General Assembly Resolution 53/35, A/54/549, 15 November 1999.

[48] This is especially true in the case of Serbia which is constantly under pressure from the European Commission, EU member states and the United States, to hand over Radovan Karadžić and Ratko Mladić to the International Criminal Tribunal of Yugoslavia in the Hague. Croatia is put under similar pressure for the handover of the indicted, Ante Gotovina. In fact, the EU suspended the commencement of accession negotiations with Croatia in March 2005 pending the handing over of Gotovina to the authorities in the Hague.

operations. What is clear from all the above is that the Bosnian experience was a remarkably confused one for the UN, and one that had strong effects on attitudes towards the global international organisation. What is also clear is that despite the confusion encountered during the Bosnian war and in the post-war administration of the country the UN has come away with a degree of success and self-awareness, which has had a positive impact on the principles and practices behind the organisation.

4   Somalia

Ioan Lewis and James Mayall

The involvement of the United Nations (UN) in Somalia was a product of the new international climate created by the end of the Cold War and by the dramatic success of Operation Desert Storm, and its aftermath in 1991. For the UN, the Somali operation, which at its height employed a force of 28,000 at an estimated cost of US $1.5 billion, broke new ground in two ways. Under Resolution 794 of 3 December 1992, the Security Council invoked Chapter VII of the Charter to authorise the establishment of an Unified Task Force (UNITAF), under US command and control, 'in order to establish a secure environment for humanitarian relief operations in Somalia'. This was the first time that an unambiguously internal and humanitarian crisis had been designated as a threat to international peace and security, thus justifying peace-enforcement measures.

Second, with this and subsequent resolutions, the UN dropped the pretence that its involvement in Somalia arose out of an invitation from the government – although the Council continued to refer to 'urgent calls from Somalia . . . to ensure the delivery of humanitarian assistance' – since no government existed with the authority to issue such an invitation. For the first time, statelessness was acknowledged to be a threat to an international society composed of sovereign states.

The UN did not extend its prerogatives in these ways either willingly or as the result of a deliberate and carefully worked out international strategy. Indeed, although the Security Council resolution[1] which established UNOSOM II gave the organisation a wider mandate than UNITAF, from which it took over in May 1993, its political content was sufficiently imprecise to offer many hostages to fortune. If support for UN intervention arose because of the disintegration of all government and the ensuing 'anarchy', the official view remained that 'the people of Somalia bear the ultimate responsibility for national

---

[1] Resolution 814, 26 March 1993.

reconciliation and reconstruction of their own country'.[2] There were periodic suggestions that the UN should establish a formal protectorate for Somalia, or resume the trusteeship responsibilities that it relinquished in 1960. However, no government was prepared to support this view publicly, partly, no doubt, for fear of taking on an open-ended and costly commitment, far removed from their own vital interests, and partly out of respect for Third World sensitivities on the issue of colonialism.

This chapter examines the experience of UN intervention and its local, regional and global implications. As with the other case studies in this volume, more is involved than an assessment of UN peacekeeping in a country where the general commitment to peace barely exists. In Somalia, the issue was whether political reconstruction could be engineered in the absence of a clear-cut political authority, and in a society in which there were a dozen or more major factions, none of which were above manipulating the UN for their own ends.

Somalia as an international problem

Somalia became independent in 1960, when the British Somaliland Protectorate joined with the trusteeship territory administered by Italy to form a single republic. In the aftermath of Second World War, the then British foreign secretary, Ernest Bevin, had advanced a plan that all the Somali territories should be prepared for independence within a single state. This proposal had its origins in Britain's control of the region during the Second World War, but it fell foul of disagreements amongst the four powers (France, the United Kingdom, the United States and the USSR) which had been charged by the newly formed United Nations Organisation (UNO) with devising a solution to the problem of Italy's former colonies.[3]

The international status of the country was thus not a direct issue in the crisis that led to UN intervention. From a historical point of view, however, it must certainly be counted amongst the indirect causes. Somalia has been a problematic member of international society from the beginning. Although the principle of national self-determination was enshrined in the UN Charter as an inalienable human right, it was interpreted in practice as western European decolonisation, ruling out any subsequent territorial revision as a result of irredentist or secessionist claims, except in the unlikely event that these could be peacefully

---

[2] *Ibid.*
[3] See Ioan M. Lewis, *A Modern History of Somalia: Nation and State in the Horn of Africa* (Boulder, CO: Westview Press, 1988), chapter 7.

negotiated between the parties concerned.[4] The Somali nationalists had settled for what they could get, but they remained committed to uniting all Somalis under a single government. This objective was written into the constitution and was symbolised by the national flag, a five-pointed star in which each point represented one of the centres of Somali population. Three remained outside the republic: the Ogaden region of Ethiopia, the north-eastern province of Kenya and Djibouti, at that time still ruled directly by France. Successive Somali governments attempted to secure the 'return' of the lost territories by diplomacy; by supporting both low-level insurgency within the Ogaden and the *shifta*, bandits who operated across the Somali–Kenya border; by directing propaganda and conducting political warfare against the Kenyan and Ethiopian governments; and finally by seeking a military and political alliance with each of the superpowers in turn.

None of these strategies worked. At the founding meeting of the Organisation of African Unity (OAU) in May 1963, Somalia failed to gain any support for its irredentist claims. Indeed, the short border war which broke out in the Ogaden in October 1963 not only failed to modify the status quo but led the OAU to adopt a resolution the following July binding all African governments to respect the frontiers they had inherited at independence.[5] A resumption of the fighting in 1967 was equally unsuccessful, and Kenya and Ethiopia signed a defence pact against their common enemy. Such was the antagonism between Somalia and its neighbours that this pact survived the Ethiopian revolution in 1974.

The military coup by which General Siyad Barre came to power in 1969 temporarily stabilised the regional conflict, although it also involved Somalia more deeply in the Cold War rivalries than previously, and, by giving the regime access to plentiful and relatively sophisticated military supplies, contributed over the longer term to the destruction of the state. General Barre announced Somalia's conversion to Marxism–Leninism and signed a long-term treaty of friendship and cooperation with the Soviet Union. No reliable evidence exists that the Soviet Union, which gained port facilities at Berbera and other military installations, ever encouraged the regime to press its irredentist claims, and indeed for the first few years of his rule, Siyad himself actively discouraged popular provocation of the Ethiopian and Kenyan governments. That he would have been unlikely to succeed for long will become clear when we

[4] See James Mayall, *Nationalism and International Society* (Cambridge: Cambridge University Press, 1990), pp. 50–7.
[5] For text, see Ian Brownlie (ed.), *Basic Documents in African Affairs* (Oxford: Clarendon Press, 1971), pp. 360–1.

consider the nature of Somali society in relation to the current crisis. Here it is sufficient to note that Somali nationalism differs from that in most African countries in that it is in essence a popular (albeit contradictory) rather than merely an elite phenomenon.

Siyad Barre's restraint did not for long outlast the Ethiopian revolution. The fall of Emperor Haile Selassie was followed, after a chaotic interlude, by the establishment of another self-declared Marxist dictatorship under Mengistu Haile Marriam. During this interlude which also saw the gradual withdrawal of US patronage, Ethiopia seemed to be on the point of disintegrating into the state's multiple ethnic components. Given the hostility which the international community had previously demonstrated towards Somalia's irredentist ambitions, it was not surprising that Siyad apparently concluded that the Ethiopian revolution had created an opportunity that was unlikely to recur. For a time, the Soviet authorities tried to consolidate their influence in the Horn of Africa by attempting (in March 1977) to broker a confederation of socialist states to include Ethiopia, Somalia and Yemen. Had it been acceptable, this formula would have reduced the diplomatic costs of shifting their patronage from Mogadishu to Addis Ababa since they had previously supported not only the Somalis but the Eritrean separatists as well. However, when the scheme predictably failed to win regional support, the Soviet government was forced to choose between clients. Equally predictably, it chose Ethiopia.[6]

Meanwhile, Ethiopian–US relations had deteriorated to the point that in April 1977 Mengistu closed US installations in Ethiopia and Eritrea and expelled US personnel. Ethiopia increasingly sought military support from the Soviet Union and, in May, Mengistu visited Moscow and issued a declaration of mutual collaboration against 'imperialist' and 'reactionary' forces which he held responsible for aggravating tension in the Horn. Djibouti's independence from France on 26 June triggered the ensuing Somali–Ethiopian struggle for control of the ethnically Somali Ogaden and the looming seismic shift in superpower allegiances in the region. When the Western Somali Liberation Front (WSLF) rose in revolt in the Ogaden in July, Siyad (whose mother was Ogadeni) first supported it financially and politically and then invaded the territory with his regular forces.

The United States eventually accepted the Somali offer of the vacated Soviet strategic real estate, although not before they had made it clear that they would not support Somali expansionism. By this time the war

---

[6] For a full discussion, see Robert G. Patman, *The Soviet Union in the Horn of Africa* (Cambridge: Cambridge University Press, 1990), pp. 190–254.

was over. Unfortunately, the state of alarm in Washington at what was perceived as a new forward Soviet strategy in Africa was such that there had been influential advocates of the United States in favour of doing whatever was necessary to stop the advance. The national security advisor, Zbigniew Brzezinski, even talked ruefully of the SALT II treaty being buried in the sands of the Ogaden. It is impossible to say whether the Somalis really believed that the United States would come to their assistance. Certainly, the noisy foreign policy debate in Washington allowed them to listen to those they wanted to hear.[7]

In reality, the danger of direct US intervention on the Somali side was remote. The tacit ground rules that had emerged during the first Cold War continued during the second: only one superpower at a time could be directly committed to a regional conflict. In 1977, Moscow was the first to move. Early Somali successes were reversed when the Soviet Union mounted an air-lift of heavy armour and Cuban troops from Aden. The outcome was a crushing military defeat in March 1978. The United States refused to come to Siyad's assistance until Somali forces had been withdrawn from the Ogaden. Thereafter Somalia had American support – after 1979 it was even recruited along with Sudan and Kenya to the favoured group of states that provided facilities for the American Rapid Deployment Force – but it was also effectively forced to abandon the irredentist claims which had formed the corner stone of the state's international policies since 1960. A new constitution, which substituted support for all oppressed peoples for the earlier commitment to liberate Somalis, was an attempt to secure the kind of international recognition and support that the southern African liberation movements enjoyed.[8] But the conceit was so obvious that it impressed no one, and indeed served to illustrate, not for the first or the last time, the depth of Somali misunderstanding of the nature and working of international society.

Somalia is both riven with conflict and politically volatile at the best of times but without the potential safety valve of irredentist enthusiasm, all of these conflicts imploded within the state itself and eventually destroyed it. It was thus that unsuccessful Somali irredentism paved the way for the internal crisis of the 1990s.

---

[7] See James Mayall, 'The Battle for the Horn: Somali Irredentism and International Diplomacy', *The World Today*, vol. 34, no. 9 (September 1978), pp. 336–45.

[8] See James Mayall, 'Self-Determination and the OAU'; and Sally Sealy, 'The Changing Idiom of Self-Determination in the Horn of Africa', in Ioan M. Lewis (ed.), *Nationalism and Self-Determination in the Horn of Africa* (London: Ithaca Press, 1983), pp. 77–92 and 93–109.

The nature of the conflict

The Somali defeat in 1978 had two interlocking consequences. First, it saddled the country with a seemingly permanent refugee population, as over 500,000 people followed the retreating army out of the Ogaden. Second, Siyad was soon faced by an insurrection of northern clans in the former British Protectorate and north-east. The first of these developments helped to create an economy of dependence on humanitarian aid; the second locked the country into the pattern of regional and global rivalries that persisted until the end of the Cold War.

Support for dissidents from neighbouring countries has long been an established feature of the political landscape in the Horn. For example, Eritrean and Tigrean separatists were regularly provided with Somali passports. Mengistu was merely following precedent in seeking to relieve the pressure on his own regime from the Eritrean and Tigrean insurgencies by supporting internal conflict in Somalia. However, the end of the Cold War weakened Siyad's ability to resist. Even as an ally, he had always been regarded with suspicion in Washington, and, under fire from their own human rights activists, the United States now had no compelling reason to support him. In Ethiopia, Mengistu was also having to contemplate survival in a post-Cold War world. In 1988, the two leaders agreed to resume diplomatic relations and to stop helping each other's insurgent movements. The rot had gone too far to be arrested by such tactical diplomatic manoeuvring, although it may have helped Siyad cling on to power for another two years. Indeed, this Ethiopian–Somali agreement spurred on the Somali National Movement (SNM) to a final effort, which, at considerable cost in civilian lives, led eventually to the overthrow of Siyad's forces in the north-west. By August 1990, the three major Somali opposition movements – the SNM, the United Somali Congress (USC) and the Somali Patriotic Movement (SPM) – had joined forces with the aim of ousting Siyad Barre from power, an objective which they finally accomplished on 27 January 1991.

Their loose alliance proved incapable of holding together long enough to bring about the economic and political reconstruction of the country. On the contrary, its falling apart was responsible for a humanitarian disaster of even greater proportions than that over which Siyad had presided, and finally brought about UN intervention. To understand the nature of the Somali conflict and how victory could be turned so quickly and decisively into national disintegration and chaos, it is necessary first to grasp the unique character of Somali political culture.

Somali political culture

The Muslim Somalis (numbering about 5 million) are essentially nomadic herdsmen, roving with their prized camels, sheep and goats (and sometimes cattle) over the plains of the Horn of Africa. Only in the relatively fertile region of the Shebelle and Juba Rivers in southern Somalia, where the Italian colonisers established banana and sugar plantations, is agriculture traditionally practised on any extensive scale. Elsewhere in this semi-desert land, where petrol exploration has proceeded apparently unsuccessfully since the Second World War, Somalis are accustomed to fight for access to pasture and water. Before European colonisation, despite a strong sense of linguistic and cultural identity, they did not constitute a state, but were divided into an elaborate series of clans and sub-clans without a strongly developed dynastic rule. Their uncentralised political organisation belonged to the type classified by political anthropologists as a 'segmentary lineage system' where political identity and loyalty are determined by genealogical closeness and remoteness.[9] A genealogy here was less a historical document than a political charter. The ideological principle was identical to that expressed in the Bedouin Arab maxim: 'Myself against my brother; my brother and I against my cousins; my cousins and I against the world'.

The nineteenth-century English explorer and Arabist, Richard Burton, described the Somalis accurately as a 'fierce and turbulent race of republicans' who lacked both chiefs and experience of a centralised government. If he had been a modern travel writer, he might have added that, with their constantly changing political loyalties – at different levels in the segmentary system – the Somalis lived in what amounted to a state of chronic political schizophrenia, verging on anarchy. Instead, Burton dwelt on what he saw as a redeeming positive characteristic, the pervasive importance of oral poetry in Somali popular culture.[10] He failed, however, to stress sufficiently the crucial role of poetic polemic in war and peace.[11] Burton might also have emphasised the prominence in Somali politics of a form of political contract or treaty, as a means of binding diffuse kinship loyalties at a particular level within and between clans.

---

[9] See Ioan M. Lewis, *A Pastoral Democracy* (New York: Afrikana Press, 1982); and Ioan M. Lewis, *Blood and Bone* (Trenton, NJ: Red Sea Press, 1993), for detailed accounts.

[10] See Bogumil W. Andrzejewski and Ioan M. Lewis, *Somali Poetry* (Oxford: Oxford University Press, 1964); and Bogumil W. Andrzejewski and Sheila Andrzejewski, *Somali Poetry* (Bloomington, IN: Indiana University Press, 1993).

[11] Said S. Samatar, *Oral Poetry and Somali Nationalism* (Cambridge: Cambridge University Press, 1982).

Somalis and the outside world

As a fiercely independent people, with a powerful sense of ethnic exclusiveness and superiority, notwithstanding their myriad internal divisions, the Somalis have lived for centuries outside, or on the edge of, world history and the literate tradition. Characteristically, they have usually impinged on the world outside in contexts of confrontation and conflict. Thus, the earliest extended account of the Somalis in written history is in a sixteenth-century source recording the part they played on the Islamic side in the religious wars of the period between Christian Ethiopia and the surrounding Muslim principalities. It strikes a very modern note in reporting that Somali warriors were particularly famous for their skills in organising ambushes. It also mentions a prominent Somali battle leader belonging to the same clan which in 1969 provided the military dictator of Somalia, Mohammed Siyad Barre.

Muslim 'fundamentalism' is likewise hardly a novel, modern phenomenon in Somali politics. Immediately after the French, British, Italians and Ethiopians had carved up the Somali lands at the close of the nineteenth century,[12] a fiery Somali fundamentalist sheik, who was the most brilliant poet of his age, proclaimed a holy war against the Christian colonisers which dragged on for 20 years. This protracted anti-colonial rebellion, retrospectively considered by Somalis as a protonationalist movement, survived four major British military expeditions and the first use of air strikes in colonial Africa, before it collapsed when Siyad Mohammed, known to the British as the 'mad Mullah', died of influenza in 1920 at a remote village in the Ethiopian Ogaden.

Although it ranged more widely afield, the Dervish War was centred in the north of the Somali region, in the British Somaliland Protectorate and eastern Ethiopia, inhabited by the ethnically Somali Ogaden, the clan of the Dervish leader himself. The Italian colony of Somalia, to the south, was less affected, although the extension of Italian authority was from time to time subject to attacks by Siyad Mohammed's forces. Nevertheless, Somali conscripts were recruited into Mussolini's armies for the long-awaited conquest of Ethiopia. The Italo-Ethiopian War of 1935–1936, which became part of the run-up to the Second World War, was triggered by a minor confrontation between Ethiopian and Italian forces at the oasis of Wal Wal in Ogaden territory in an area disputed by Italy and Ethiopia.

---

[12] See Lewis, *Modern History of Somalia*, pp. 63–91.

The Italian defeat by the Allies in 1942 brought their Somali colony together with those of Ethiopia and Britain under a single British military administration which promoted Somali nationalism, directly and indirectly, particularly through Ernest Bevin's plan proposing that all the Somali people should be administered as a single state and prepared for self-government. When, as we have seen, this pan-Somali plan had to be abandoned, the Somali territories resumed their former colonial statuses, except for the Italian colony of Somalia which became a UN trusteeship, administered by Italy under a ten-year mandate (1950–1960). At the time of independence, ex-Italian Somalia merged with the former British Somaliland Protectorate, which had been hastily prepared for self-government, to form the Somali Republic. The new state was thus based on the principle of self-determination applied to a single ethnic group, parts of which still languished under foreign rule. Unlike the majority of ethnically heterogeneous African states dedicated to 'nation-building', Somalia's predicament was its incomplete statehood, the spur to pan-Somali unification which neighbouring states found so threatening.

The limits of Somali political cohesion

While pursuing these external goals, with little success, the nationalists who dominated the political scene in Somalia strove to maintain the pretension that divisive clan ties had withered away. There was, thus, no serious attempt to address and come to terms with the realities of clan allegiance which had been sharpened rather than diminished by their encapsulation in the exotic structure of a centralised state which provided a new and enlarged arena for clan competition and conflict. These contradictions had even become part of the new political language where politicians spoke of each other's basic allegiance in terms of 'ex-clan', a historical phenomenon which no longer affected them.

After a decade of parliamentary democracy, the seething tensions of antagonistic clans which undermined national cohesion provided the setting for the military coup of October 1969 led by the army commander, Mohammed Siyad Barre. He invoked a crude home-grown version of 'scientific socialism' to consolidate his power, officially outlawing all forms of clannish behaviour.[13] Although the people's inspiration was now supposed to be the curious trinity of 'Comrades Marx, Lenin and Siyad' (the dominant state emblem), Siyad's actual

---

[13] See Lewis, *Blood and Bone*, chapter 7.

power base was a more traditional trinity: his own clan, his mother's clan and the clan of his son-in-law – commander of the secret police. These three clans all belonged at a higher segmentary level to the Darod clan-family which had highjacked the Somali state, and now dominated all the other clans. There was no precedent in Somali history for such clan hegemony.

Siyad's maternal clan allegiance to the Ogaden made him particularly vulnerable to Ogadeni pressure which, as Ethiopia fell apart following the revolution which overthrew Haile Selassie, became increasingly insistent. While his commitment of Somalia's army to help the WSLF guerrillas in their 1977 uprising was initially very popular at home, the crushing defeat which had quickly followed in March 1978 prompted an upsurge of suppressed clan tensions. A critical factor here was the huge refugee influx which flooded Somalia in the wake of the Ethiopian reconquest of the Ogaden. The majority of these Ogadeni refugees (belonging to the Darod clan-family) were grouped in large refugee camps in the north-west regions of the republic, traditionally occupied by the Isaq clansmen who had proved the most recalcitrant subjects of Siyad's dictatorial rule. For centuries, the Isaq and Ogaden had jostled for access to pastureland and water along the Ethiopian border.

In the immediate wake of the Ogaden debacle, it was, however, an abortive coup in April 1978 by predominantly Mijerteyn (Darod) officers which signalled the beginnings of armed insurrection against Siyad's regime. In 1982, the Mijerteyn opposition regrouped with the formation of the Somali Salvation Democratic Front (SSDF),[14] closely followed by the Isaq-based Somali National Movement (SNM).[15] This brought armed insurrection to the north-east and north-west regions, which became increasingly subject to harsh military rule. Both movements organised their guerrilla operations inside Somalia from bases in Ethiopia, with the tacit agreement of Mengistu's government which, despite its dedication to socialism and close ties to the USSR, was after the Ogaden war more rather than less hostile to Somalia than the old regime of Haile Selassie.

Having guardedly replaced the USSR as Somalia's patron, the United States and its Western allies (especially the Italians) added new equipment to what remained of Siyad's Soviet arsenals, with Saudi

---

[14] Daniel Compagnon, 'The Somali Opposition Fronts', *Horn of Africa*, vol. 13, no. 1/2 (1990), pp. 29–54.

[15] Daniel Compagnon, 'Somaliland, un ordre politique en gestation?', *Politique Africaine*, no. 50, June 1993, pp. 9–20; Gérard Prunier, 'A Candid View of the Somali National Movement', *Horn of Africa*, vols. 13/14, nos. 3/4 (1992), pp. 107–20; Lewis, *Blood and Bone*, chapter 8.

Arabia and other Gulf states meeting some of the bills. This was used to counter the insurrections in the north-east and north-west and growing disaffection in other parts of the country, where the dictator's survivalist divide-and-rule tactics relied heavily on the dangerous expedient of bribing and arming friendly clans to attack his enemies. The increasingly desperate fighting in the north eroded the strength of Siyad's forces which became more and more dominated by his own clansmen. In common with the rest of the state, these forces depended critically on supplies of relief food aid for the refugee population – whose size was thus a very controversial issue with UNHCR.[16] The official economy, based primarily on the export of livestock from the war-torn north was collapsing, and was no longer as important as the informal sector based on livestock trading and migrant labour (what Somalis called the 'muscle-drain') in the Gulf states. Banana exports from the riverain plantations in the south had earlier dwindled into insignificance through a mixture of incompetence and corruption. Still paid essentially at the same rates as in the 1960s before the years of hyperinflation, the civil service had virtually ceased to function by the end of the decade.

The descent into chaos

The peace accord signed by the Ethiopian and Somali dictators in April 1988, which obliged each side to stop supporting the other's dissidents, was, ironically, the final precipitant to the full-scale civil war which had already destroyed the Somali state months before the actual overthrow of Siyad in January 1991. The pressure of human rights activists on Western governments, appalled at the ferocious suppression of northern dissidence, led to the virtual cessation of aid by 1990 when the area under Siyad's control hardly extended outside Mogadishu. When the Darod dictator was finally dislodged from the already severely battle scarred capital by USC forces of the Hawiye clans, led by General Aideed, Somalia had already disintegrated into its traditional clan segments. The situation now was exactly as Burton and other nineteenth-century explorers had described it – a land of clan republics where the traveller had to secure protection from each group whose territory he traversed. The only difference was that the volatile relationships between these clan units had been raised to fever pitch by the experience of Darod hegemony, and the bitter fighting with modern weapons which wrought death and suffering on a scale never experienced in the past.

---

[16] Ioan M. Lewis (ed.), *Blueprint for a Socio-Demographic Survey and Re-enumeration of the Refugee Camp Population in the Somali Democratic Republic* (Geneva: UNHCR, 1986).

The scale of the ensuing clan-cleansing in Mogadishu and elsewhere was unprecedented. Siyad's huge arsenals which had largely fallen into the hands of the various clan militia were supplemented by equipment from Mengistu's hastily demobilised army in Ethiopia, where tanks were almost as cheap as second-hand cars, and by continuing imports of arms across the Kenyan border and along the coast.

The trigger to international intervention

Having ousted Siyad, the USC Hawiye leaders, General Aideed (who had links with the Isaqi SNM in the north) and Ali Mahdi (a prominent businessman) could not agree on how to share power. Ali Mahdi, who represented the original Hawiye inhabitants of Mogadishu in contrast to the recent invaders of Aideed's clan, had provocatively already set up an elaborate 'government'. This conflict, which split Mogadishu into two armed camps, polarised along clan lines, quickly engulfing what was left of the city in a protracted blood-bath, killing an estimated 14,000 people and wounding 30,000.[17]

Ferocious fighting outside Mogadishu spread devastation and starvation throughout southern Somalia. The USC Hawiye outlawed or drove out of Mogadishu those Darod clansmen who remained there. The Darod, especially those related to Siyad's clan, regrouped under the leadership of one of his sons-in-law, a general with a particularly brutal record in north-western Somalia (Somaliland). Each side devastated the agricultural region between the rivers which is Somalia's bread basket, killing and terrorising the local cultivators who are less aggressive than the nomadic Somali. As the conflict widened, Aideed allied with Colonel Umar Jess's militia against Morgan who, in turn, joined forces loosely with another of Siyad's former generals, Adan Gabio and his militia. These and the two factions in Mogadishu were the most heavily armed and dangerous militia fighting for control of what was left of southern Somalia. All were based primarily on traditional clan groupings manipulated by a powerful figure and held together by the attractions of the spoils of war. The so-called warlords who led them were all far from illustrious figures from the Siyad regime. Amplifying, on a smaller scale, this relatively organised violence, qat-chewing[18] young gangsters, whose role model was Rambo, spread mayhem, looting and killing in

---

[17] *Somalia Beyond the Warlords*, Africa Watch occasional report, March 1993, p. 5.

[18] Resembling the leaves of the English privet shrub, qat leaves are chewed raw, traditionally on religious or social occasions. Today, they are chewed more widely and frequently by individuals during the day and produce a strong craving for this stimulant which contains benzedrine-type compounds. See Roland Marchal, 'Le *mooryaan* de

Mogadishu.[19] With agricultural and livestock production devastated, famine spread, especially in the arable areas between the rivers. The UN estimated that as many as 300,000 people perished from famine and 700,000 became refugees in Kenya, Ethiopia and to a lesser extent in Yemen, Europe, Scandinavia and North America.

The political and economic magnetism of the capital, Mogadishu, as a spur to conflict is highlighted by the contrasting situation in the north-east and north-west of the country. The north-east is dominated by the Mijerteyn (Darod) clan and, once it was liberated by the clan-based SSDF, remained at peace with a local administration which is a synthesis of the SSDF and the traditional local clan leaders. The only serious threat to order so far has been from militant Islamic fundamentalist groups. In the north-west, which is more heterogeneous in clan composition, the record is even more impressive. While the victorious SNM guerrillas set up a government and distanced themselves from the chronic conflict in the south by declaring unilateral independence in May 1991, clan rivalries within the Isaq federation prevented the 'modern' political leaders from exercising effective authority. Leadership reverted to the clan elders who, employing traditional diplomacy, inaugurated a remarkable series of peace conferences which slowly but surely restored a surprising degree of peace throughout the region – despite the continuing security problems posed by 'freelance' armed gangs. Finally, in June 1993 a new government was formed by a national council of clan elders which elected the former premier of Somalia (1966–1969), Mohamad Haji Ibrahim Egal as president. This reassuring demonstration of the positive side of clanship and the successful potential of genuinely locally based peace initiatives contrasted markedly with the high-profile, extremely expensive and much less successful peacemaking by the UN and other outside bodies in southern Somalia. It indicated also the negative effect of the power-hungry southern warlords and of inequitably distributed foreign aid.[20]

International intervention

In the successive blood-baths into which Mogadishu descended after Siyad's defeat, foreign embassies and most agencies, including the UN,

---

Mogadiscio. Formes de la violence et de son contrôle dans un espèce urbain en guerre', *Cahiers d'Etudes Africaines*, vol. 130, no. 33 (1993), pp. 295–320.

[19] See Lee V. Cassanelli, 'Qat: Changes in the Production and Consumption of a Quasilegal Commodity', in Arjun Appadurai (ed.), *The Social Life of Things* (Cambridge: Cambridge University Press, 1986), pp. 236–60.

[20] See Ahmed Y. Farah and Ioan M. Lewis, *Somalia: The Roots of Reconciliation* (London: Actionaid, 1993).

abandoned southern Somalia to its gruesome fate. In March 1992 a ceasefire between Ali Mahdi and Aideed made possible the resumption of humanitarian relief. However, fighting and looting by various factions seeking to control ports and distribution routes became an important factor in the political economy of the militia and greatly reduced the effectiveness of aid deliveries. Factions levied heavy taxes on cargoes, took direct cuts of 10 to 20 per cent of incoming aid, and charged exorbitantly for providing relief agencies with armed escorts to 'protect' food deliveries which they frequently also looted. Foreign NGOs were thus trapped in a web of protection rackets to an extent that they often failed to appreciate. Clearly, security was a critical issue in what had become Africa's latest famine, widely publicised in the media.[21] The question was how it was to be alleviated in a country where central government had lapsed.

The international community did not immediately conclude that large-scale humanitarian intervention was the appropriate response. On 24 April 1992, the Security Council adopted a resolution (Resolution 751) requesting the UN secretary-general to deploy a group of 50 UN observers to monitor the ceasefire in Mogadishu. This had been negotiated in New York in February under the auspices of the Organisation of African Unity (OAU), the Arab League and the Islamic Conference. Although the resolution also indicated that the Council had agreed, in principle, to establish a UN peacekeeping force once the necessary conditions existed, no one seemed anxious to see Somalia move rapidly up the international agenda. Indeed, so reluctant was the United States to face Congress on the issue that it had to be persuaded by the other members of the Council to allow the observer mission to be paid for out of assessed rather than voluntary contributions over which it had discretionary control. A few days later, the secretary-general appointed an Algerian diplomat, Mohammed Sahnoun, as his special representative in Somalia. Sahnoun energetically set about the task of restoring the UN's credibility in Mogadishu and winning the confidence of faction leaders, donor governments and relief agencies alike. He was less successful in his dealing with the UN itself, a fact which eventually forced his resignation in October after he had repeatedly and publicly criticised the performance of UN agencies in Somalia.[22]

---

[21] See 'Misunderstanding the Somali Crisis', *Anthropology Today*, vol. 9 (1993), pp. 1–3.

[22] Mohammed Sahnoun has written his own account of these events: *Somalia: The Missed Opportunities* (Washington, DC: United States Institute of Peace, 1994). See also Ioan M. Lewis, *Making History in Somalia: Humanitarian Intervention in a Stateless Society*, Discussion Paper 6 (London: The Centre for the Study of Global Governance, LSE, 1993).

The underlying political and security problems remained as intractable as ever. Sahnoun's primary task was to secure effective food distribution to stave off the impending humanitarian disaster – in August he reported that 1.5 million people or one-quarter of the Somali population were at risk – but the UN was not equipped to undertake the required level of armed protection to carry out this task. Following his report, the secretary-general agreed to deploy 500 UN troops to Somalia and under a subsequent resolution, the Security Council authorised an additional 3,500 men to protect food convoys. Implementation did not quickly follow this authorisation. It was not until mid-September that the first contingent of Pakistani troops was flown in on a US aircraft and it was not until the second week of November that they were able to take control of Mogadishu airport.

There is no single explanation for the long delay in organising the international response to the Somali crisis. In part, it was undoubtedly the bureaucratic rigidity of which Ambassador Sahnoun complained so bitterly. In part, it was a consequence of logistical and financial constraints which prevented some countries from responding rapidly, even when they had taken the political decision to do so.[23] But it was also because the situation lay so far beyond the experience of UN peacekeeping that had developed over the previous 40 years – there were simply no precedents for deploying UN forces on a humanitarian rather than a peacekeeping mission when there was no government with which to negotiate and where the practical decision, therefore, was always going to be whether to appease those with the power on the ground or oppose them by force.

By mid-summer it had become clear that, without strong support from the United States, the UN lacked the organisational resources and

---

[23] The nature of the problems involved is illustrated by the Canadian experience. The total lack of modern infrastructure over much of Somalia meant that even a battalion could not be deployed without an off-shore supply ship. The Canadians, who were assigned to the north-east, chartered their own ship which had to be in position by the time they arrived. However, even then they lacked the air transport capability to deploy a battalion quickly, which was obviously desirable if the UN was to take the initiative. Other countries with the capacity were not prepared to meet the cost – by air, US $14 million, compared with US $1 million if they were sent by sea. This meant that the Canadians could not move until the UN Secretariat had chartered two transport ships. This in turn caused further delays as, under the strict procurement rules which the Secretariat operates to avoid charges of profligacy, the UN can only charter vessels after an open international tender. The ships eventually arrived in Montreal on the day that President Bush offered the UN a task force. Once the agreement had been reached with the UN, the Canadians, like the Pakistanis, were shipped to Somalia in US transports, where they were deployed not to the north-east as originally intended, but to an area west of Mogadishu (interview with David Malone, deputy head of the Canadian Mission to the UN, 16 April 1993).

its members the political interest or will to fashion a coherent strategy for Somalia. The trouble was that those elements of the administration which were in favour of intervention and strong US leadership – the Office for Disaster Relief and the Africa Bureau in the State Department – had few cards to play in Washington's game of bureaucratic politics, particularly in an election year. Thus, even after the US president had ordered a food air-lift on 14 August, the White House and the political divisions of the State Department and the Pentagon remained adamantly opposed to any escalation in the US involvement. The election was being fought primarily on domestic issues and the administration was above all concerned to protect the president from a damaging and open-ended foreign entanglement.

There were even persistent rumours of tension between the UN secretary-general and the US administration over the size and composition of UNOSOM I. The United States was well aware that the air-lift was not working but they had estimated that at least 30,000 heavily armed troops would be needed. Neither the numbers of troops available – they were angered by Boutros Boutros-Ghali's plucking the number 3,500 out of a hat at random – nor the mandates were designed to do the job.[24] On the other hand, at this stage they were as reluctant as the other Western governments to see Somalia used as a test case in the reinterpretation (and effective extension) of Chapter VII of the Charter.

By all accounts the change in the American position owed much to George Bush Sr himself. Once he had lost the election, he was, in any case, no longer constrained by domestic considerations. Moreover, as the architect of the 'new world order' he evidently felt it incumbent on him to 'do something'. His speech to the UN General Assembly on 21 September had contained the first indications that the end of the Cold War was changing traditional US attitudes to UN peacekeeping, which had always been considered off-limits by the US military. The speech evidently 'rang bells' in the Department of Defense with the result that when the US president began taking a personal interest in Somalia, they were ready 'to turn on a dime', the Pentagon's opposition to intervention transforming itself into measured support. On 21 November, the Deputies' Committee of the National Security Council reconsidered the

---

[24] This announcement also infuriated Sahnoun, who was not informed in advance and was therefore unable to allay Somali suspicions of UN motives. '[It] was made without informing the UNOSOM delegation in Mogadishu, or the leaders of the neighbouring countries who had previously been informed by me of every intended move. Worse, the announcement was made without consulting the Somali leaders and community elders': Sahnoun, *Somalia*, p. 39.

options on Somalia and on the basis of a recommendation from the chief of staff, Colin Powell, decided in favour of intervention.

Powell's conversion was conditional on the operation being limited in three important respects: its function was to be confined to securing the effective distribution of food to those in need; its geographical scope was to be limited to the most devastated parts of the country in and around Mogadishu, Berbera and Baidoa; and the mission was to be completed preferably before or very soon after the inauguration of the new president in January 1993. Providing that these conditions were met, he favoured intervening with sufficient force and fire-power to overawe any Somali opposition and minimise casualties.

The die was now cast. It remained to secure authorisation from the UN Security Council and to arrange a division of labour with UNOSOM I. While the United States was prepared to act unilaterally, it was understandably anxious to have international support on the ground as well as in the Security Council. The UN turned down the US offer that they should serve in blue berets, that is, as a UN force, as they had done during the Korean War in the early 1950s, since they were not prepared to countenance any weakening in their national chain of command, however nominal. Nonetheless, as one diplomat who witnessed the negotiations remarked, 'The UN gave an almost audible sigh of relief when the Americans made their offer.'

The empowering resolution, Resolution 794 of 3 December 1992, was not only the first to establish an humanitarian operation under Chapter VII of the Charter, and without an explicit invitation from the parties to the conflict, but it also gained the unanimous support of the Council, including China and a number of African members who in the aftermath of Operation Desert Storm had expressed their suspicions that the West might use humanitarian arguments to mask their interference in the domestic affairs of other states. In addition to the Pakistani forces that were already committed to UNOSOM, support for the United States within UNITAF was provided by sizeable contingents from France (Foreign Legion), Italy, Belgium, Saudi Arabia, Egypt and Morocco. More than 20 other contingents of various sizes and specialised functions were either provided or promised (not always the same thing).[25] As in the Gulf in 1990, so in Somalia in 1992: the UN was able to organise

[25] The full list at the beginning of February 1993 consisted of the USA, Canada, France, Belgium, Italy, Australia, Egypt, Pakistan, Norway, Saudi Arabia, Mauritania, Nigeria, Kenya, Argentina, Germany, Sweden, Kuwait, the UAE, Morocco, Turkey, Zimbabwe, Tunisia, Botswana, Algeria, Malaysia, Eire, India, Uganda, Greece, Namibia, Indonesia, Jordan, Zambia, New Zealand and the Republic of Korea. The total deployment was 33,656, of which the United States provided 28,100.

broad international support and so legitimise the operation, but it was left to the United States to impose peace on the warring factions and foster the new interventionist role for which the UN had opted.

Empowered by Resolution 794 to employ 'all necessary means to establish . . . a secure environment for humanitarian relief operations in Somalia', Operation Restore Hope provided force feeding for Somalia, and paved the way for the unique UN peacemaking military administration, UNOSOM II, which followed in May 1993. In line with the Pentagon's original plan, the United States saw its primary objective as being to distribute food and humanitarian supplies securely to the worst affected areas of southern Somalia. They were, understandably, anxious to avoid casualties (especially in the run-up to Christmas) and thus proceeded cautiously and with maximum, even if often ill-conceived, publicity,[26] relying on their sheer numbers and technical superiority to overawe the Somali population.

The operation was directed by an experienced diplomat, Robert Oakley, who had served as ambassador in Mogadishu and knew some of the protagonists personally. He had also the delicate task of coordinating the work of his Unified Task Force (UNITAF) with UNOSOM, which was now led by the Iraqi diplomat, Ismat Kittani, who had replaced Mohammed Sahnoun as Boutros-Ghali's special representative. One of the main tensions arose from UN pressure for UNITAF to enlarge its role to include disarmament, and thus aid the process of negotiation and reconciliation among the main armed groups. The United States for its part was apt to raise the spectre of Vietnam and stress the limited and short-term character of its intervention. Oakley apparently felt that, despite the formidable force at his disposal, the Somali protagonists were not seriously overawed and believed that they could successfully manipulate the United States to their advantage.[27] Events were to prove him right.

Most observers concluded after a few weeks, with a minimum of incidents, that UNITAF had succeeded in opening up the supply routes and getting food through to most of the needy areas in southern Somalia.[28] This entailed establishing military garrisons in key regions to quell oppressive militia, impose peace and control conflict – not always

[26] For assessments, see Ioan M. Lewis, 'Restoring Hope in a Future of Peace', *Cooperazione*, Rome, March 1993; Africa Rights, *Somalia – Operation Restore Hope: A Preliminary Assessment*, Occasional Report, May 1993.

[27] From a personal conversation between Oakley's deputy, John Hirsch, and I. M. Lewis; the Americans were, of course, aware of the irony of their enforcing disarmament on an African people.

[28] Cf. Robert G. Patman, 'The UN Operation in Somalia', in Ramesh Thakur and Carlyle Thayer (eds.), *UN Peacekeeping in the 1990s* (Boulder, CO.: Westview Press, 1995), p. 94.

completely successfully. It also meant trying to re-establish a Somali police force in Mogadishu, where relations between the two local warlords, Ali Mahdi and Aideed, remained tense despite the truce negotiated by Ambassador Oakley prior to the US intervention.

When they realised that it was inevitable, both sides had welcomed the powerful new force and attempted to extract as much advantage as possible from it for themselves. Heavy weapons and military trucks ('technicals') disappeared from the streets; some were hidden locally, others moved to the interior. While many of the citizens of Mogadishu and elsewhere unrealistically saw the Americans as saviours, who would restore normal life and rebuild their country, others felt that the tyranny of the warlords was now sufficiently curtailed to allow them to voice independent views. Outside Mogadishu also, the US military presence enabled local elders, previously terrorised by the rival militia, to regain some of their traditional authority as community leaders.

The policy of re-empowering traditional community leaders, which had been consistently urged on UNOSOM by the Uppsala advisory group[29] had been initiated by Mohammed Sahnoun, but was pursued only in a token fashion by his successor. The UN leadership in Mogadishu was more inclined to concentrate on the high-profile warlords who had gained in legitimacy through their extensive dealings with Ambassador Oakley, despite his efforts to prevent it and despite the fact that their military strength was held in check.

Taking advantage of the precarious lull in the fighting, which had been produced by the huge US military presence, Boutros-Ghali pressed ahead with his own conception of the reconciliation process. Despite a hostile reception when he briefly visited Mogadishu, he succeeded in opening a peace conference of the faction leaders in Addis Ababa in early January 1993. Agreement in principle of a ceasefire was reached, although the terms remained to be settled. Aideed and his allies wanted an immediate ceasefire to consolidate their territorial gains, with reconciliation postponed to a later date. The other groups wanted the militia to return to their traditional clan areas and then proceed immediately to reconciliation. Eventually, formal ceasefire and disarmament agreements were signed, providing for the handing over of heavy weaponry to a 'ceasefire monitoring group' to be completed by March when a further reconciliation conference would be held.

---

[29] Based at the Horn of Africa Centre of the Life and Peace Institute of Uppsala, this small group consists of social scientists with specialist expertise on Somalia drawn from a number of countries. The group has consistently advised UNOSOM to follow a 'bottom-up' regionalist approach with as much decentralisation as possible.

Clearly, the expectation was that UNITAF would now be involved in disarmament in one way or another, and despite the US unease at what it perceived as 'mission creep'. In fact, the uneasy calm which had initially followed US intervention had already begun to break down in the face of renewed outbreaks of fighting in Mogadishu and the southern port of Kismayu. The deteriorating security situation jolted the UNITAF troops into patrolling more aggressively, disarming townsmen who openly carried weapons, and raiding one of the most notorious arms markets in Mogadishu. One of Aideed's encampments was destroyed and a contingent of General Morgan's attacked to prevent it gaining control of Kismayu. Given the vast quantities of weapons in the country and their constant replenishment from Kenya and Ethiopia, such action hardly constituted disarmament, although it was vividly described by Ambassador Oakley as 'bird-plucking' disarmament – feather by feather. There were similar erratic shifts in dealing with the tricky question of the employment by NGOs of privately recruited armed guards; theoretically these freelance security agents were supposed to be unnecessary once UNITAF was established. In practice, arms permits were issued to various categories of guards, as well as to NGO personnel, but the rules kept changing.

Thus, although Somalia was far from fully sanitised, UNITAF and UNOSOM acting together had established an unprecedented level of UN intervention in a previously sovereign state. The terms 'peace-making' and 'peacekeeping' no longer adequately covered the range of activities undertaken. Efforts were being made, especially by UNITAF, to involve the elders – that is, local traditional community leaders – in aid distribution and preparations at the local level for reconstruction. Embryonic police forces were being recruited and in the run-up to the March Addis Ababa meeting of warlords some disarmament took place. Simultaneously, in the United States, preparations were begun for the establishment of UNOSOM II which was due to take over from UNITAF in May 1993.

On the Somali political front, the UN continued to maintain its pressure on the leaders of the movement. The third UN coordination meeting in Addis Ababa in March on humanitarian assistance received donor pledges of US $142 million for relief and rehabilitation. The meeting was attended by a wide range of Somali peace groups who stressed the upsurge of violence in Somalia and the urgent need for improved security. This was highlighted by the brazen incursion of Morgan's forces into Kismayu, which occurred during the Addis Ababa reconciliation conference and under the noses of the UN peacekeepers.

The agreement signed on 27 March by the leading warlords and representatives of sundry clan movements (some of dubious status) evoked local custom in its preamble. 'The serenity and shade of a tree, which according to our Somali tradition is a place of reverence and rapprochement, has been replaced by the conference hall. Yet the promises made here are no less sacred or binding'. It is tempting to conclude from what subsequently occurred that the change of venue was in fact interpreted as having qualified the pledge. Nonetheless, the signatories committed their organisations to 'complete' disarmament and urged that UNITAF/UNOSOM should apply 'strong and effective sanctions against those responsible for a violation of the ceasefire agreement of January 1993'.[30]

In a new departure, which was in line with the UN's understandable but misguided desire to cobble together a Somali government as soon as possible, the agreement also provided for the establishment over two years of a 'transitional system of governance'. This included a Transitional National Council (TNC) with representatives from the 18 regions where Regional and District Councils would be established – a concession to the 'bottom-up' strategy advocated by the Uppsala advisory group and others. The TNC was also to be 'a repository of Somali sovereignty', a particularly unfortunate reference, since the delegation from the self-proclaimed Somaliland Republic in the relatively untroubled north-west had left the Addis Ababa conference before the agreement was signed. It subsequently dissociated itself from these provisions. This insensitive approach to the achievements and aspirations of the people of the north-west was unfortunately characteristic of the UN policy following Sahnoun's departure.

UNOSOM II took over formally from UNITAF/UNOSOM I on 4 May 1993, not as early as Colin Powell had originally hoped, but soon enough to satisfy the new administration whose primary concern was to limit the president's vulnerability in a foreign commitment which he had inherited from his predecessor. But, although they may have hoped to engineer, if not a solution to Somalia's political crisis, at least a situation of sufficient stability to allow them 'to tip toe away', US prestige was now invested in the UN operation whether the United States liked it or not. In these circumstances, both the transition to a UN command, and its organisation and leadership, were of considerable importance to the United States. In the early summer of 1993 the official view was that, having broken new ground with Resolution 794, the United States could not afford to have the Somali operation fail.

---

[30] *Somalia News Update*, Uppsala, vol. 2, no. 12 (30 March 1993), p. 2.

For their part, the UN Secretariat was fully aware that support for UNOSOM would be likely to wither on the vine if it was perceived that the United States was 'dumping' an insoluble problem onto the UN as a way of extricating itself. Boutros-Ghali accurately calculated that if the operation was headed by an American this would guarantee strong US support. It would also be necessary, if as planned a US force was to serve for the first time in their history under a foreign, albeit UN, command.

The arrangement that was reached gave the military command to Lieutenant-General Levik Bir, a Turk who had worked closely with the Americans in NATO, and replaced Ambassador Kittani, the secretary-general's special representative, with Admiral Howe, who had served as security advisor to President Bush. His appointment thus represented continuity between the two administrations. Resolution 814 of 26 March 1993 provided for a multinational force of 20,000 peacekeeping troops, 8,000 logistical support staff and some 3,000 civilian personnel. In addition, the United States undertook to provide a tactical 'quick reaction' force, as required. With the prominence of US logistical support and special forces, this inevitably gave UNOSOM II a strongly American orientation which, when UN forces became embroiled in actual fighting, made it difficult to decide whether the Pentagon or Boutros-Ghali was calling the shots.

The price of intervention, 'new world order'-style

It was not long before the new UN dispensation received a fierce test of its resolve and competence. On 5 June 1993, without any substantial progress towards disarmament, and with new supplies of weapons, forces – presumed to be under Aideed's command – attacked a party of Pakistani blue berets, near Aideed's radio station, killing over 20. Instead of holding an independent legal enquiry and seeking to marginalise Aideed politically, Admiral Howe's forces reacted with injudicious force causing very considerable Somali casualties – not necessarily all supporters of Aideed.[31] The Security Council denounced Aideed, accusing him and the other warlords of committing war crimes. Admiral Howe, behaving as though he were the sheriff of Mogadishu, proclaimed

---

[31] At the request of the UN secretary-general, an independent judicial investigation into the 5 June incident (and further incidents on 12/13 June) was carried out by Professor Tom Farer, a legal specialist at the American University in Washington, who had been an advisor to the Somali police in the 1960s. The report submitted on 12 August convincingly implicates Aideed in masterminding a deliberate and carefully staged ambush which targeted the Pakistani blue berets.

Aideed an outlaw, offering a reward of US $20,000 for his capture. Aideed responded in the same idiom, and both sides were launched on collision course with the UN reacting increasingly aggressively with helicopter gunship strikes and remarkably clumsy and unsuccessful attempts by US special forces to seize Aideed and his henchmen.

Aideed had lured Howe and the unwieldy UN and US war machine into a bitter confrontation in which every raid on southern Mogadishu earned him more support. Indeed, with the aid of simplistic media reporting, he quickly gained an international reputation as an oppressed national hero bravely struggling against overwhelming 'imperialist' forces. He had also managed to distort UN operations into concentrating far too much of their efforts on attempting to deal with him.[32] The inevitable denouement occurred at the beginning of October when his forces succeeded in shooting down a number of helicopters, capturing an American airman and inflicting serious casualties on US personnel. US/ UN forces could not win in the back streets of Mogadishu without inflicting and sustaining unacceptable levels of casualties. Thus, Aideed succeeded in cocking a snook at the mighty United States. The American public, horrified by grisly television pictures from Mogadishu and haunted by memories of Vietnam, clamoured for withdrawal.

The joint US/UN plan for a smooth transition had gone well, but the aftermath confirmed the worst fears of the operation's critics. What had gone wrong? Inevitably, it was the United States that bore the brunt of the criticisms. And no doubt the complexities of the dual command structure had much to do with it. Nonetheless, much of the responsibility lies with the UN organisation itself, although it is difficult to know whether the rapid deterioration of the situation should be laid at the door of the secretary-general and his representatives, who mounted the vendetta against General Aideed, or rather should be understood as an unintended outcome which flowed with tragic necessity from the Security Council's reaction to the events of 5 June.

Understandably, the Americans themselves were drawn to the first of these explanations, and administration spokesmen were openly critical of Howe's policies and actions. No doubt he could have interpreted his mandate with more caution and subtlety – in particular the UN seemed insensitive to the fact that their attempts to capture Aideed would inevitably be interpreted as an attack on his clan group with the deliberate intention of favouring their rivals. But Howe had acted under Resolution 837 which had been passed *unanimously* on 6 June. This resolution called on UNOSOM 'to arrest and detain for trial and

---

[32] See Ioan M. Lewis, 'Ambush in Somalia', *The Guardian*, 7 October 1993.

punishment the Somalis responsible for the slaying of a . . . Pakistani unit of the UN peacekeeping force'. The resolution also condemned the USC and SNA broadcasts inciting attacks against the UN and recalled a statement by their president – Aideed – promising to take action against anyone found guilty of violent attacks on UN personnel. What lay behind this strong and explicit resolution was, of course, the need to shore up the authority of the UN in general and to reassure the Pakistan government in particular.[33]

That such a reassurance would be needed became abundantly clear on 7 October when public outcry forced President Clinton to announce that all US forces would leave Somalia by 31 March 1994 and to state publicly that they were all under US command.[34] Withdrawing with honour, the United States evidently believed, would require short-run military reinforcements and a change in political direction. To meet the first requirement, President Clinton announced that he was sending an additional 1,700 army troops and 104 army vehicles plus an aircraft carrier and two amphibious groups of Marines, offshore; while to secure the second, he reappointed Ambassador Oakley to go out to Somalia once more, ostensibly to lend US support to new Ethiopian and Eritrean efforts to broker a political settlement, in reality to secure the release of the prisoners taken by Aideed's forces. Probably hurt by US media coverage depicting his forces as barbarians, and delighted with this new attention, Aideed welcomed Oakley's return and released the prisoners on terms which were not made public but evidently involved the holding of a further enquiry into the notorious incident of 5 June. Aideed was also brought back into the unfolding political discussions. How this might affect Resolution 837 of 6 June remained unclear. There was, in any event, serious doubt about whether UNOSOM would be able to continue in the absence of active involvement of any of the major industrial countries with the capacity to provide the logistical support on which the operation depended. By the end of the year the Belgians,

---

[33] Cf. Ken Menkhaus, 'Getting Out v. Getting Through: US and UN Policies in Somalia', *Middle East Policy*, vol. 3, no. 1 (1994), p. 157.

[34] The issue of the command of US forces within UNOSOM II had been a sensitive one from the start. In a report submitted to Congress on 13 October 1993 the command structure was described as follows: 'all US military personnel are under US command. In addition, all US combat forces are under US operational control. The logistic units that support the overall UN military presence are assigned to the UN commander for operational control through the UNOSOM deputy commander, Major-General Thomas Montgomery, US Army. That means that for purposes explicitly agreed in writing between the United States and the United Nations, the UN commander may provide them direction in their logistic mission of supporting UN units. These units do not have any combat role': Official text, United States Information Service, London, 15 October 1993.

French and Italians had all announced that they too would withdraw all their forces in early 1994.

The projected US withdrawal in March 1994 was not entirely out of gear with the existing UN timetable for organising District and Regional Councils with a view to establishing the Transitional National Council envisaged in the Addis Ababa agreements. Criticism of Howe's obsessive, but not impressively successful, pursuit of Aideed encouraged more attention being given to this process of setting up local Councils. In the absence of any informed, independent assessment, however, it was difficult to decide how well this was proceeding and whether there was a realistic prospect of establishing a genuinely representative National Council which was not dominated by the power-hungry warlords.

The announcement of the United States and other withdrawals inevitably had a further destabilising effect in Somalia, and led on 24 October to a brief clash in Mogadishu between Ali Mahdi's and Aideed's supporters. There was obvious anxiety that Aideed (who still seemed to possess plenty of weapons) would attempt to seize power when the Americans left, and Ali Mahdi publicly threatened to 'rearm' his own followers. To demonstrate the UNs' continuing commitment to Somalia, Boutros-Ghali, against US advice, made a brief visit to Somalia on 22 October and opened a flurry of negotiations with OAU and Arab League leaders, with the Ethiopian president, Meles Zenawi, playing a prominent role. Although Aideed was now back in the unwieldy negotiations, they proceeded at a snail's pace, taxing the patience of all the major negotiators – especially the Americans, who naturally wanted to leave behind at least an impression of achievement.

By the end of March 1994, following hectic meetings in Addis Ababa, Cairo and Nairobi, involving the original Addis Ababa signatories and other Somali dignitaries arbitrarily assembled by the UN, an agreement was finally signed by Aideed and Ali Mahdi ostensibly on behalf of their allies as well as themselves. The 60 participants whose hotel bills were reported to run to US $150,000 per day were apparently informed that UNOSOM was not prepared to incur further expenses and the junkets would have to end on a positive note. The resulting agreement issued the usual ritual declarations forswearing violence and urging the implementation of general disarmament as a precondition for reconstruction. It also set a date three weeks later for the signatories to establish rules and procedures for voting and participation in a national reconciliation conference, which was scheduled for 15 May 1994 when an interim government was to be formed. These rather vague and certainly extremely optimistic developments were foreshadowed by Resolution 897 which revised UNOSOM's mandate from peace-enforcement to peacekeeping and envisaged a reduced military establishment of 22,000 at best and drawn exclusively from the Third World after the impending departure of the United States, French, Belgian and Italian contingents. Admiral Howe and the head of UNOSOM's political section had already left Mogadishu, leaving the acting special envoy in charge. The latter had already been promoted to a senior position in the UN hierarchy in New York which he was due to take up at the end of May, on the assumption that his assiduous negotiations with the warlords would by then have led to the actual formation of a Somali government, or something that might be represented as one. The UN had by now reverted to its earlier tactic of dealing primarily with the military leaders and their henchmen, and had given up its never-convincing efforts to 'empower' local leaders, which it had neither the resources nor the local knowledge to do effectively.

No real progress was made towards disarmament or the division of power in an interim Somali administration. The leading protagonists were unwilling to make any substantial concessions and, with mounting uncertainty about the future after the US withdrawal, busily rearmed their militias.

All these negative trends continued to gather momentum throughout the remainder of 1994. Inter-clan violence and attacks on UN personnel increased as the reduced UN force withdrew its garrisons from the hinterland to concentrate in Mogadishu and prepare for the final UN withdrawal from Somalia by the end of March 1995. The new UN special representative and his colleagues redoubled their efforts to cajole the Somali 'faction-leaders' to form a government, any government would do, to enable the residual international forces to pull out in as orderly a fashion as possible, leaving some equipment behind and taking such heavy equipment as they could with them. Money for 'expenses' was lavished on these 'leaders', adding to the substantial benefits they had already derived from careless UN largesse and such memorable unofficial hand-outs as the 'theft' of almost US $4 million in dollar bills stored overnight in a UNOSOM filing cabinet.[35]

Following a litany of ever-less-credible reports from UNOSOM via the UN secretary-general to the Security Council, whose members were losing patience at the deteriorating situation in Somalia and the faction leaders' manifest inability to reach any workable agreement, the UN finally announced in September 1994 that the Somali operation would be wound down as soon as possible.[36] One current of opinion in the

[35] Patman, 'UN Operation in Somalia', p. 100.
[36] *Report by the Secretary-General Concerning the Situation in Somalia,* S/1994/1968, 17 September 1994, paras. 17–21. In Resolution 953 of 31 October 1994, the Security Council called for withdrawal by 31 March 1995.

mounting chaos of Mogadishu believed, apparently, that the United States would return again to rescue Somalia. In fact, the final UN evacuation was carried out under the protection of US Marines and with the aid of a small multinational flotilla in which even the United Kingdom, reluctant to the last, played a minor role. Since so much also went wrong with the UN's operation in Somalia, it is worth recording that the secure and orderly withdrawal for which the Security Council had called in Resolution 953 was accomplished in time and without serious mishap.

Assessment

While Ambassador Sahnoun, who initiated UNOSOM I, and Oakley, who led Operation Restore Hope, were both relatively well informed about Somali politics, the same cannot be said for their successors, nor does UNOSOM seem to have been well served by various ad hoc advisors. The UN headquarters were located in southern Mogadishu, dominated by Aideed's Habar Gaddir clansmen who, in the main, had invaded Mogadishu during and after the guerrilla operations which overthrew the Darod dictator, Mohammed Siyad Barre, in 1991. Without adequate consideration of the consequences, large numbers of Somali ancillary staff were recruited from this clan which helped to finance Aideed's operations while at the same time supplying him with vital intelligence. Very few adequately representative Somali advisors were recruited, and UN officials generally could hardly have been more inadequately briefed about Somali society and culture. The huge gap between traditional Somali methods of dealing with foreigners and US high-tech put most of the UN staff at a great disadvantage in their local dealings. This is perhaps most graphically illustrated by US helicopters dropping leaflets on a population with a primarily oral tradition whose sensitivity to radio broadcasting is famous in Africa.

While both Sahnoun and Oakley negotiated directly with the various Somali figures and had some awareness of the partisan interests involved, their successors relied on indirect contacts through various deputies and aids, a style of diplomacy calculated to sow suspicion in the minds of their interlocutors. The demanding Somali situation, in which each group vigorously sought to influence UN activity to its own advantage, required skilful, shrewd diplomacy of a high order, making the job of UN special envoy exceedingly difficult and taxing. The distance between the fortified UN bureaucracy in Mogadishu and the local population was further magnified by the failure of the UN to employ a range of Somali professionals spanning the different clans, and this was greatly intensified as

Admiral Howe became increasingly embattled in the feud with Aideed. In addition, with the cumbersome UN bureaucracy and the multi-national military force, logistically linked to Washington rather than New York, with an ineffective command structure and national components like the Italians with their own agenda, the possibilities for mis-understanding and confusion were enormous. Put at its simplest, this vast, unwieldy UN organisation was ill adapted to the Somali environ-ment and poorly equipped to encourage the grass-roots political initia-tives that were developing so notably in the north.[37]

This was, perhaps, to some extent an unfortunate unintended effect of the over-concentration of resources in Mogadishu (despite Sahnoun's earlier plans for decentralisation) which, of course, stimulated conflict between rival Somali groups. Indeed, three weeks after the US depar-ture, Aideed's forces seized the area adjoining Mogadishu airport, routing the previous inhabitants, and were clearly poised at some future opportunity to assume control of the airport itself. While Aideed, who had benefited so much from the shifts of US policy towards him, remained outside Somalia, posturing like a head of state in Nairobi, Addis Ababa and other African capitals, his forces steadily extended his conquests at home. Outside and to the south of Mogadishu, they had captured the port of Merca, heavily defeating the local militias, and menacing the more important and repeatedly contested port of Kismayu. UN forces continued to control Mogadishu airport itself and to provide aid convoy protection while prudently turning a blind eye to the engagements which were becoming more and more frequent between rival Somali factions. Thus, the political situation, despite the much-publicised formal peace agreements, remained extremely fluid and unstable and, with the new pattern of UN action or inaction, came to resemble Bosnia ever more closely. These were not circumstances which suggested that the UN-brokered negotiations could have any positive outcome. Indeed, any viable future government that could be realistically envisaged would almost certainly have to be minimalist with a much higher degree of regional decentralisation than the UN officials contemplated.

Here, as we have repeatedly seen, there is a recurrent problem in the UN's dealings in Somalia, namely their reliance on the warlords and other so-called Somali 'leaders'. These figures have been consistently endowed with a degree of power and authority which they would like to, but do not actually, have, as has been demonstrated time and again by their failure to deliver on their various promises. This approach simply

---

[37] See Farah and Lewis, *Roots of Reconciliation*.

fails to grasp the shifting and situationally focused character of political groupings and leadership in this profoundly uncentralised but not literally anarchic society. The Somali political economy was, moreover, grossly overheated by the protracted clan wars in which modern weapons had produced casualties on an unprecedented scale. This is not a setting conducive to the 'quick-fix' solutions purveyed by the UN and other international organisations.

The most that might be said for this inordinately expensive, poorly led and coordinated, and incredibly cumbersome UN operation is that with all its glaring inadequacies, it offered something for everyone.[38] In the short run, the inter-riverine agro-pastoralists who had earlier been driven to starvation by the ravages of Aideed's and Morgan's marauding forces, had been rescued and protected. Aideed's henchmen who had invaded and seized control of part of Mogadishu when Siyad Barre was overthrown, quickly developed a monopoly in supplying local services and housing at exorbitant cost to UNOSOM. The blue berets themselves earned for their governments almost US $1,000 per month per soldier, as well as generous allowances for work which was extremely dangerous. Supplying troops was thus a profitable business, especially for Third World countries short of hard currency. Foreign contractors providing international transport and other services also did very well out of UNOSOM. At the same time despite the exigencies of life in Somalia, UN careerism flourished and even quite junior officials, few if any adequately trained or briefed, made quite significant financial gains. In stark contrast to the money lavished on the construction of the UN headquarters compound, with its modern services, shops, bowling alleys and other US home comforts, no serious humanitarian development of benefit to the Somali public has been accomplished, despite an inordinate outpouring of rhetoric. Of the US $1.6 billion allocated for UNOSOM's military operations in the period up to the end of 1993, it was estimated that only 4 per cent would work its way into the Somali economy, mostly into the hands of the warlords and other operators whose financial activities, subsidised by UNOSOM, had distorted, perhaps irrevocably, the Somali economy.[39] It would require quite remarkable ignorance to consider all this a UN success.

---

[38] If humanitarian assistance and UN assessments are included with expenditures by the Department of Defense, the cost to the US government alone of all Somali operations amounted to nearly US $2.3 billion between April 1992 and July 1994. See John G. Sommer, *Hope Restored? Humanitarian Aid in Somalia 1990–1994* (Washington, DC: Refugee Policy Group, Center for Policy Analysis and Research on Refugee Issues, November 1994).

[39] These figures are quoted from Rick Atkinson, 'For UN Force in Mogadishu, the Comforts of Home', *International Herald Tribune*, 25 March 1994, p. 1.

Afterword

Ten years have elapsed since the publication of this account of the international intervention in Somalia. Unfortunately, perhaps, it set the tone for many of the subsequent so-called humanitarian interventions of the 1990s. Subsequent research has added to our knowledge of particular aspects of the operation, but has not challenged the fundamental analysis. The failure was political not humanitarian. Lives were saved and there has been no return to the anarchy-induced famine that preceded Operation Restore Hope. But the south of the country – the target area for both UNITAF and UNOSOM – still lacks an effective central government whose authority is acknowledged by the rival contenders for power. Relative peace and stability has come to the two northern provinces of the former Somali Republic, the self-styled but still unrecognised Republic of Somaliland and Puntland in the north-east. An EU-sponsored project that attempted to provide options for decentralised reconstruction indirectly provided some of the ideas on which the constitution of Puntland was based,[40] but in both cases stabilisation was driven by local rather than international initiatives. Indeed, such order as has been achieved in Somalia seems to have been positively correlated with international neglect.

Is this a necessary consequence of all humanitarian intervention? If so, then it will be seen to be misconceived across the board, and not just in Somalia. No such general conclusion, however, can be safely drawn from the Somali experience. Every case is different and must be treated as such. On the other hand, the Somali experience does point to the central importance of paying close attention to the local political culture in any operation. In Somalia, the state had not only failed, it was an exotic import in the first place. It had also struck very shallow roots. The legitimacy of the intervention, therefore, had to be established at the local, not at the state, level. Some contingents did achieve this. The Australian UNITAF contingent in Baidoa, for example, won local support by providing security for the humanitarian relief sector, by disarming the criminal gangs and the SLA and by creating an indigenous police force and judicial system.[41] It seems doubtful that all contingents could have been similarly effective, thus establishing more

---

[40] Professor Brendan O'Leary who was one of the constitutional experts employed on this project, which was directed by the authors of this chapter, subsequently advised the provincial authorities on an appropriate constitution for Puntland.

[41] Michael Mersiades, 'Peacekeeping and Legitimacy: Lessons from Cambodia and Somalia,' *International Peacekeeping*, vol. 12, no. 2, (Summer 2005), p. 217.

widespread support for the UN and creating the prospects of long-term peace. At any rate, it did not happen.

As Clarke and Herbst correctly pointed out, it would have required, at the very least, the disarming of all the war lords and not just Aideed.[42] This was a mission that went well beyond what the United States had been prepared to entertain when it embarked on the intervention. The United States is also right to suggest that the distinction between the two operations can be exaggerated. The introduction of 30,000 troops into a civil conflict will inevitably expose the artificiality of the distinction between an intervention designed to reverse a humanitarian catastrophe, and an enforcement action to put an end to the conflict and rebuild the society. The United States was never prepared to accept the political implications of its intervention, and while some in UNOSOM may have wanted to engage in nation building, they lacked the resources, local knowledge and indeed the will, to carry it through.

It may be the case that by starving the operation of civilian staff, the United States deprived itself of the means of local economic planning. But had it accepted that the scale of the intervention implied a commitment to nation building, that there was no humanitarian 'quick-fix' available, it would have had to accept that the logic of humanitarian intervention is imperial. In other words, the United States would have had to be prepared to stay as long as it took, and to expend whatever resources might be necessary, to transform Somali society. To be fair to the United States, no modern government has been prepared to interpret humanitarian intervention in this way. As Michael Mann has suggested it is difficult to generate a coherent imperial ideology in an era of nation-states.[43] This is a general problem. It means that for any humanitarian intervention to stand a chance of success there must be a modern national state, that may be broken but which in principle can be rebuilt with outside help. In Somalia there was an ancient and powerful national culture but no recoverable state in this sense.

[42] Warren Clarke and Jeffry Herbst, 'Somalia and the Future of Humanitarian Intervention', *Foreign Affairs*, vol. 75, no. 2, (1996), p 80.

[43] George Lawson, 'A Conversation with Michael Mann', *Millenium, Journal of International Studies*, vol. 34, no. 2, (2005), pp. 487–508.

5   Rwanda

Bruce D. Jones

Scholarly studies and policy debates about peacekeeping in Rwanda have largely focused on the question of whether or not it was possible, in the immediate aftermath of the outbreak of genocide in April 1994, to rapidly reinforce the small peacekeeping presence on the ground and thereby halt the ongoing mass killing that killed over 750,000 people in three months. Against a series of arguments that this was a feasible policy option, most forcefully made by the serving Force Commander Romeo Dallaire, and also by the Carnegie Corporation project on Preventing Deadly Violence's Scott Feil, scholars such as Alan Kuperman have made strong arguments to the contrary.[1] This debate has shaped the lessons learned, and unlearned, from Rwanda.

While this debate remains unresolved, this chapter argues that the real failures in peacekeeping in Rwanda occurred far earlier than this juncture. The real failures occurred in 1993 in designing a 'neutral international force' – which became the United Nations (UN) Assistance Mission in Rwanda (UNAMIR) – to help implement the Arusha Accords. These failures were in part the result of poor communication and coordination; in part the result of political dynamics between the UN Security Council and the UN Secretariat; in part of the conception in the UN Security Council that Rwanda was a mission of tertiary importance. These factors led to the deployment of a mission that was poorly matched to the real challenges that awaited it. They were compounded by Secretary-General Boutros Boutros-Ghali's lack of leadership and his unwillingness to take risks, notwithstanding intelligence gained that suggested threats to the mission; by the limited conception

---

[1] Alan Kuperman, 'Rwanda is Retrospect', Foreign Affairs vol. 79, no.1 (January/February 2000), pp. 94–118; Scott Feil, *Preventing Genocide: How the Early Use of Force might have Succeeded in Rwanda* (Washington DC: Carnegie Commission on Preventing Deadly Conflict, 1998), pp. 28.

of contingency planning that pervades the UN Secretariat; and by political decisions taken by key member states, especially the United States and Belgium.

These failures hugely increased the difficulty of mounting an effective response in April 1994. When the mission encountered a robust challenge from the *génocidaires* forces in April 1994, the missions' response options were limited, as were the UN's. Rwanda was not a case – as Sierra Leone and Liberia later proved to be – where a handful of Western soldiers would have been able to alter the military balance. A more comparable case is East Timor, where a swift response of several thousand effective soldiers deployed by a capable military power, along with concerted international pressure, including from the United States, did alter the dynamics on the ground. Neither of these responses was present in Rwanda, and the mission collapsed, as did the peace process, giving way to mass genocide. A subsequent peacekeeping mission, UNAMIR II, deployed only in the beginning of August, after the genocide had been halted and the war won, contributed nothing to conflict management. UNAMIR did facilitate the delivery of humanitarian assistance to parts of Rwanda's traumatised population, though it encountered coordination problems and other management challenges. This model of peacekeeping as humanitarian stopgap has not been repeated since.

The failings of Rwanda and the policy implications of those failings have been well documented, the lessons identified. More important, they have also been learned – at least in part. This chapter traces these arguments in three sections. First, it sets out the backdrop in terms of a brief history of the civil war in Rwanda, of the peace process to try to end it, and of a growing genocidal movement that was in part a response to the success of that peace process. Second, it provides an analytical account of why UNAMIR was inadequate to the task of implementing the Arusha Accords and responding to the resumption of (far more virulent) violence in 1994. To do so, it lays out the process by which UNAMIR was negotiated, conceived, planned and implemented – in that order. In this section, it also touches briefly on UNAMIR II. Finally, the chapter concludes by tracing the lessons learned, and some that remain to be learned, for later peace operations.

It argues that some of the presumed lessons of Rwanda, about the need for decisive response to crisis, have been influential in shaping peacekeeping policies and decisions in the period since. And it argues, faced with the same situation today, the UN would try to respond differently. But it also argues that continuing limits on UN peacekeeping capacity means that a different response today might well fail.

Background to the mission: war, negotiations and response

From the mid-1960s to 1990, Rwanda was governed (comparatively well by regional standards) by an oligarchic party, the Mouvement Rwandaise National pour le Development (MRND), under the lead of President Juvenal Habyarimana. As a political party, the MRND represented and was predominantly composed of northern clans of Hutus, Rwanda's dominant ethnic group. Both southern Hutus and the minority Tutsi and Twa were progressively excluded from positions of authority or economic opportunity, and from the ranks of the military.[2] Rising inequalities were exacerbated in the late 1980s by a combination of collapsing global prices for coffee, Rwanda's principal export, and the resulting IMF-imposed structural adjustment policies – which respectively cut state revenues and the state's employment roll.[3]

Civil war in Rwanda began on 1 October 1990 when a rebel movement, the Rwandese Patriotic Front (RPF), crossed from southern Uganda into Rwanda. Largely comprised of Rwandan Tutsis, who had been well trained by fighting alongside Ugandan President Museveni's National Revolutionary Army in the 1970s, the RPF fought well and won a series of rapid victories against government forces, the Forces Armées Rwandaise (FAR). Within days the RPF had captured the important northern town of Gibaro and were moving fast south towards the capital Kigali.[4] On 5 October, France intervened, sending 150 paratroopers from bases in nearby Central African Republic to bolster Habyarimana's regime.[5] France's troops backstopped the FAR in Kigali, securing the airport and other major sites. Zaire also sent roughly 1,000 troops to Rwanda.[6] Backed by the French and Zairian troops, the FAR re-engaged the RPF in the north and quickly succeeded in pushing the RPF back into Uganda.

However, shortly thereafter and under a new leadership, the RPF re-entered Rwanda and established bases in the east and north-west of the country. From vantage points in the high mountain country of

---

[2] For a rich history of Rwanda's governance during this period, see in particular Catherine Newbury, *The Cohesion of Oppression: Clientship and Ethnicity in Rwanda, 1860–1960* (New York: Columbia University Press, 1988).

[3] Peter Uvin, *Aiding Violence: The Development Enterprise in Rwanda* (West Hartford CT: Kumarian Press, 1998).

[4] Interview with Reuters Correspondent Aidan Hartley, Nairobi, June 1996.

[5] France's troops were deployed under a French–Rwandan Military Cooperation pact signed in 1975.

[6] Zaire's troops were also deployed under a cooperative agreement, this one sub-regional: the Communite Economique de Pays des Grands Lacs.

the Virungas in the north-east, they staged raids and attacks on FAR positions, weakening the FAR and destabilizing Rwanda, especially economically.[7] A low-intensity war continued until mid-1992.[8] Then, following a failed FAR offensive in November 1991, the RPF launched more ambitious attacks, holding territory for the first time and creating a *de facto* RPF-held zone extending along almost the entire Uganda–Rwanda border, creating a serious economic and financial impact on the Rwandan state and also displacing more than 500,000 persons.[9]

Throughout this period, the Organisation of African Unity (OAU), Belgium, France and the United States undertook a variety of diplomatic efforts to bring the warring parties into negotiations. This led to a series of desultory negotiation sessions between the FAR and RPF in 1991, some of which produced ceasefires and declarations on various topics, but little true change in the situation. As fighting intensified in early 1992, France and the United States, with additional support from the Vatican and Belgium, undertook coordinated pressure on the RPF and FAR, pressuring them to agree to start peace talks. In June 1992, both parties agreed to participate in comprehensive political negotiations. The talks were to be facilitated by Tanzania and held in Arusha.

The Government of Rwanda had been further pressured, principally by France and the United States, during this period to begin to democratise and by spring of 1991 had re-constituted itself as a multi-party government. It was this multi-party government that represented Rwanda at the Arusha talks when they began in July 1992. Talks advanced rapidly and by 7–18 September 1992, agreements on power-sharing, unification and political cooperation were initialed, though not signed, by the RPF and the FAR negotiators. The two sides returned to their headquarters for consultation with their respective parties.

These consultations were particularly difficult for the FAR's negotiator, Foreign Minister Ngulinzira, who had joined the multi-party

---

[7] In June 1996, the RPF took the author up to their old bases in the Virungas. A steep hike up a bamboo entangled face – perfect ambush territory – led to a series of hard-to-find plateaus, where the RPF encamped. It was evident how difficult it would be for any army to find, let alone dislodge, the RPF from these positions.

[8] For a detailed account of the war during this period, see Gerard Prunier, *Rwanda Crisis: History of a Genocide* (New York: Columbia University Press, 1997). Also see Bruce D. Jones, *Peacemaking in Rwanda: The Dynamics of Failure* (Boulder, CO: Lynne Reinner, 2001).

[9] Towards the end of the war, this number would rise to 900,000. John Borton, Emery Brusset, Alistair Hallam (core team) et al., *Humanitarian Aid and Effects: International Response to Conflict and Genocide: Lessons from the Rwanda Experience – Study III* (London and Brussels: Steering Committee of the Joint Evaluation of Emergency Assistance to Rwanda, 1996).

government in 1991, and was not a member of Habyarimana's MRND, nor of his inner circle. It emerged that Ngulinzira had acted in Arusha without Habyarimana's full support. Negotiations in Kigali, between Habyarimana and the opposition parties, produced an agreement on instructions for Ngulinzira, who returned to Arusha for a further round of talks on 6 October. By 12 October, the FAR and RPF had reached an agreement on the issues of the nature of presidential power under a Broad-Based Transitional Government (BBTG), and on the establishment of a Transitional National Assembly (TNA).[10] However, agreement could not be reached on the fundamental issues of the distribution of seats in the TNA and the allocation of cabinet posts, leaving the question of political control unresolved. A penultimate round of talks in Arusha commenced on 25 November 1992. The agenda focused on the difficult topic of the precise composition of the transitional institutions whose frameworks had been agreed. The talks reached no conclusion, and the parties broke away from the talks.[11]

On 8 February, the RPF launched a major offensive from their positions in the north-east of Rwanda. What had previously been a war of small skirmishes and guerrilla tactics evolved into a full-scale confrontation. Within days of launching the attack, the RPF had fought to within 23 kilometres of Kigali.[12] The offensive provoked further French intervention: two waves of paratroopers, totalling 600 new troops, were sent to Kigali to shore up the FAR's defences.[13] In the face of the added strength provided by France, and under intense diplomatic pressure to hold off from outright military victory, the RPF halted their offensive and both parties returned to the negotiations.

A final round of negotiations in June–July 1993 dealt primarily with the questions of the composition of a neutral military force to oversee implementation, the integration of the armed forces into a single national army, and the composition of the BBTG. The most difficult negotiation in this phase concerned the critical issue of integrating the two armies into one national army, and the percentage split of army command positions. An eventual agreement was brokered wherein the

---

[10] Filip Reyntjens, *L'Afrique des Grands Lacs: Rwanda et Burundi, 1990–1994* (Paris: Khartala, 1994). Reynjtens provides an excellent analysis of this Protocol, on which I have drawn.

[11] It should be noted that although the Arusha talks formally adjourned between these periods, discussions and negotiations continued in Kigali, Kampala, Addis Ababa and Dar-es-Salaam throughout these intervals, both under the aegis of the JPMC and in informal meetings at various embassies and high commissions in the region.

[12] *Africa Research Bulletin*, 1–28 February 1993, p. 10902.

[13] Lt. Cameron, NGO Liaison Officer, Rwandese Patriotic Front, personal interview, Washington, DC, December 1995.

command level was to be split 50–50 between the RPF and FAR, and the infantry was to be drawn at a rate of 60 per cent from government forces and 40 per cent from RPF forces. At senior levels, the RPF would be given the head of the *gendarmerie* and the government was to keep the head of the armed forces. Both armies would be integrated into a 13,000 strong army supplemented by a 6,000 strong *gendarmerie*. The announcement of this agreement on 24 June seemed to presage an imminent signing of a comprehensive peace package.

This putative agreement was taken back to Kigali on 24 June by the government's negotiating team, where it was rejected by Habyarimana.[14] A major sticking point, which emerged, was the question of what actually constituted a 'command level' position. When the issue was returned to Arusha, the RPF not only stood their ground, they raised the stakes in anger over the government's reneging on the agreement, and called for a 60–40 per cent split weighted in their favour. After heavy intercession by the Tanzanian, French and US teams, the two sides agreed again on the original deal, with the clarification that 'command level' extended all the way to field command positions. This represented a significant victory for the RPF in terms of their capacity to control the merged security forces, and underscored the strength of their negotiation position, bolstered by their recent military victories.

Planning for Genocide

It could be argued that these talks constituted a classic case of empty words short of real negotiation. While the talks were in progress, an extremist movement of northern Hutu elites was building its capacity to constrain the negotiations and their implementation. As Alison des Forges in particular has documented, a network of senior clan-family members holding senior positions in government, the army, and the business sector – known as the *akazu*, or little house – cohered into a quasi-party called the Committee for the Defense of the Republic (CDR). The *akazu* launched a political struggle to undermine Arusha. They offered large bribes, loan forgiveness, and promises of future benefit in state positions to many within the government and opposition parties – people who had signed onto the Arusha process – in an attempt to turn them against the Arusha deal.[15]

---

[14] Interview, Lt. Col. Anthony Marley, US Department of State.

[15] For a comprehensive account of the planning for the genocide, see Alison des Forges, *Leave None to Tell the Story: Genocide in Rwanda* (New York: Human Rights Watch, 1999).

Furthermore, the *akazu* were building a malign second option. While in public the struggle was over control of the peace process, in the shadows a force was being constructed by the *akazu* to destroy the peace in its entirety through violent means. A plan for genocide had been formed and was being hatched. The centrepiece of the plan was the creation of a militia movement in late 1993. The *impuzamugambe* and *interahamwe* militias were formed under the direct control of the CDR which was in effect the political party through which the *akazu* organised itself and financed illegally through the ruling political party, many of whose members were also in the CDR. Small arms and light weapons, as well as machetes, were imported from sources in Europe in violation of a UN ban, and distributed to 'citizens' – code for the militia groups. The militias trained in Kigali for their 'citizens' defence role. The *akazu* also organised logistics: orders went out from the central ministries to government offices throughout the country, instructing local administrators to have trucks and jeeps and other equipment on standby for 'purposes of national defence'.[16] An *akazu*-financed radio state, *Radio et Television Libre Milles Colines* (RMLMC) played hate-filled propaganda that warned Hutus that the RPF's return to Rwanda presaged a return to pre-independence days when the Tutsi, with Belgian support, had ruled over the Hutu majority – and warned of the potential for violence at the hands the 'foreign invaders' and 'cockroaches'. The *akazu* was gearing up for a major escalation.

By early 1994, the *akazu* put into motion a programme of assassination and disruption. The elements of this plan were outlined in the confessions of a senior figure in the regime that had gone along with the CDR but was having doubts. As revealed in a now infamous 11 January cable, this individual revealed to the UN that the extremists' plan had several elements.[17] First, assassination of key opposition leaders, and other steps to disrupt the establishment of a power-sharing government – this included staged mass demonstrations in front of the Parliament to disrupt efforts to install new members. Second, an attack on the UN peacekeeping mission, which by this time had been deployed in Rwanda (see the next section on peacekeeping in the face of mounting threat), to force its withdrawal. And finally, critically, a plan to kill *en masse* the RPF's presumed political base – the Tutsi population of Rwanda.

---

[16] A copy of such a letter was shown to the author by an official of the Rwandan Embassy in Washington, DC, 18 December 1995.

[17] Howard Adelman and Astri Suhrke with Bruce Jones, *Early Warning and Conflict Management in Rwanda: Report of Study II of the Joint Evaluation of Emergency Assistance in Rwanda* (Copenhagen: DANIDA, 1996).

In early April, pro-Arusha forces tried to regain the initiative. A meeting was convened in Dar-es-Salaam, which was designed to have regional political actors pressurise President Habyarimana to put the Arusha peace deal in place. On 5 April, Habyarimana agreed to a series of concrete measures designed to accelerate the timetable for peace. On 6 April, however, the aircraft carrying President Habyarimana, a handful of senior aides as well as the president of Burundi back from Dar-er-Salaam was shot down and all its passengers were killed.

Kigali had fallen to a coup. The upper hand was quickly gained by Colonel Bagasora, *Chef de Cabinet* at the Ministry of Defence, and a central architect of the CDR's programme (known in Arusha circles as 'the Colonel of Death'). Within hours of the shooting down of President Habyarimana's aircraft, an 'interim government' had been formed under Colonel Bagasora. Rallying together the forces of opposition to peace, Bagasora led a two-pronged strike: a return to war with the RPF and the launch of a mass genocide. In the first days of the killings, this 'interim government' organised the execution of the Tutsi population of Kigali, and wiped out the ranks of moderate politicians and civil society leaders, most of them Hutu. Over the next three months, the *génocidiares*, as they have become known, systematically slaughtered Tutsi populations across the country. The RPF renewed the civil war. By the time they had won it, on 17 July 1994, an estimated 900,000 Rwandans had been slaughtered.[18]

Peacekeeping in the face of mounting threat

That the *génocidiares* were able to implement their plan in the face of a UN peacekeeping presence already deployed in Rwanda is evidence enough of the failure of UNAMIR and of the overall UN response. But this failure was multi-faceted. A brief history of the negotiation of the formation and deployment of UNAMIR reveals several large gaps in the mission, which were skilfully exploited by the *akazu* to undermine the UN's capacity for response.

Negotiating, planning and financing UNAMIR

The UN's involvement in Rwanda began in March 1993, following the offensive in February 1993 launched by the RPF. International pressure on the warring parties, together with French reinforcements of the FAR, pushed the parties back to the negotiating table. This was accomplished

---

[18] See des Forges, *Leave None to Tell the Story*.

in part through a UN mission, in which staff members of the Departments of Political Affairs (DPA) and Peacekeeping Operations (DPKO) travelled to Rwanda to assess the prospects of UN assistance to the negotiations. The beginning of the UN involvement represented an important shift in responsibility for the peace process, which to date had rested largely in the hands of the OAU.

Earlier discussions in the Arusha negotiations had reviewed the question of the provision of a neutral international force (NIF) to secure the implementation of the BBTG, which would govern Rwanda until national elections could be held, 22 months later. The agreement specified that the NIF should be deployed within 37 days of the signing of the agreement, and should provide security and protection to the members of the BBTG. It would also take over the task of monitoring a demilitarised zone around Kigali, which up to that point had been carried out by an OAU mission, the Neutral Military Observer Group (NMOG).

Discussions about the force started with a proposal that the OAU should provide the neutral force, building on their experience in managing NMOG. This proposal met resistance from two quarters. First, the Government of Rwanda had reservations about an OAU force, seeing the OAU as pre-disposed to the RPF position (in part because the OAU was at the time led by a Tanzanian, Salim A Salim; the Government of Rwanda perceived a gradual shift in the Tanzanian position at Arusha, towards the RPF, and feared that this would prejudice an OAU force). Second, a number of international observers at Arusha, on the basis of the poor performance of NMOG, argued that the OAU was not capable of mounting an effective security force.

The discussions around the NIF thus turned to proposals to have the UN provide the force. In fact, the Rwandan government, with backing from the French, had been lobbying for a UN force from the outset of the negotiations. The RPF initially resisted the UN proposal, fearing that France's position on the Security Council would allow it to control the UN force in a way, which would be contrary to the RPF's security concerns. In the end, however, the RPF had to give way when their preferred option of an OAU force fell through. An agreement was reached that the UN should provide the NIF in the form of a Chapter VI peacekeeping operation.

Ironically, given the UN Secretariat's resistance to an OAU force, when discussions moved from Rwanda to the Security Council, the idea of a UN peacekeeping mission for Rwanda ran into serious resistance. The time, it should be recalled, was mid-1993, a period when the US hostility to UN peacekeeping had reached a peak, soured by the cost and seeming ineffectiveness of the UN's operations in Bosnia, and scarred by the US experience in Somalia.[19] At the Security Council, both the UN and Russia initially objected to yet another peacekeeping operation, this time for a small country with a small civil war that barely registered on the radar screen. Of the actors involved in Security Council deliberations, only France had any significant interests in Rwanda. As J. Matthew Vaccaro establishes, the political will to engage seriously in Rwanda was absent among those actors with sufficient capacity to do so.[20] However, France eventually brokered a compromise wherein the UN and Russia would support UNAMIR if France agreed to support missions in Haiti and Georgia for which the UN and Russia were lobbying respectively. The UN Assistance Mission in Rwanda was voted into effect on 5 October 1993 through UN Security Council Resolution 872.

The political reluctance, which attended the birth of UNAMIR, shaped its destiny. At key moments, the lack of political support within New York would place serious limitations on UNAMIR's ability to interpret its mandate broadly, communicate effectively with its political masters, respond to events and information on the ground, or in other ways help to shape the implementation phase in Rwanda.

Planning

On 15 August 1993, as negotiations over UNAMIR were getting under way, the UN secretary-general, Boutros Boutros-Ghali, decided to send a reconnaissance mission to Rwanda led by Brigadier-General Romeo Dallaire – at the time, the Force Commander of a small UN monitoring mission deployed along the Rwanda–Uganda border earlier in 1993 (UN Observer Mission Uganda–Rwanda – UNOMUR). In meetings in Kigali, Rwandan officials stressed the urgency of the mission and the fact that the neutral force had been asked, by the Arusha Peace Accords (which the UN had signed) to guarantee security throughout the country.[21] They also stressed that the deployment of the mission was

---

[19] For an account of US views about UN peacekeeping operations, in particular with respect to Rwanda, see Michael Barnett, 'The Politics of Indifference: The Professionalisation of Peacekeeping and the Toleration of Genocide', unpublished paper, December 1995. Also see Michael Barnett, *Eyewitness to a Genocide: The United Nations and Rwanda* (Ithaca, NY: Cornell University Press, 2002).

[20] Matthew J. Vaccaro, 'The Politics of Genocide: Peacekeeping and Disaster Relief in Rwanda', in William J. Durch (ed.), *UN Peacekeeping, American Politics, and the Uncivil Wars of the 1990s*, first edition (New York: St. Martin's Press), p. 374.

[21] UN Department of Political Affairs, *Report of the Reconnaissance Mission* (New York: United Nations, March 1993), 21 March, pp. 4–6.

central to the whole peace process, especially to the establishment of the BBTG. RPF officials warned that late deployment of the NIF would give an opportunity to hardline opponents of the peace deal, who would use the delay to portray the Arusha Accords as mere pieces of paper.

Dallaire reported back that there were some serious risks to a peacekeeping operation in Rwanda and on the basis of this assessment argued, in an initial, informal report, that an optimal mission would comprise 8,000 troops; 4,500 to 5,000 men was seen as the minimum responsible level.[22] Nevertheless, the general conclusion from the reconnaissance mission was that UNAMIR was achievable despite the risks. Some diplomats in the region, who were consulted by Brigadier-General Dallaire, recall his optimism: 'We can do this thing', Dallaire reported to the Canadian mission in Dar-es-Salaam.[23]

In New York, it quickly became apparent that there was limited support for a large mission: advance messages from the US delegation in particular made this clear.[24] The UN DPKO eventually recommended a mission designed mindful of 'what the traffic would bear' – that is, bearing political considerations in mind.[25] The 'risky but achievable' assessment reached by DPKO's reconnaissance mission was toned down for Security Council consumption. Indeed, by the time proposals were being floated to the Permanent Five (P5), Rwanda was increasingly being depicted as a 'winnable' mission, a potential flagship success story that could restore credibility to the tarnished image of UN peacekeeping. This was perhaps a necessary misrepresentation; the Security Council was not likely to authorise a risky mission, given the trauma of the UN's operations in Somalia and Bosnia. However, the perception that Rwanda was going to be an easy success meant that the mission was only approved with a minimum of political backing.

UNAMIR's mandate was given under Chapter VI of the Charter. It would be a traditional peacekeeping operation based on the consent of the local parties. Specifically, it was mandated to perform the following tasks:

- to contribute to the security of the city of Kigali, *inter alia*, within a weapons-secure area established by the parties in and around the city;

---

[22] Interviews with DPKO officials, New York, May 1996.
[23] US Embassy and Canadian High Commission, confidential author interviews, Dar-es-Salaam, December 1993.
[24] DPKO interviews.
[25] As documented in Adelman and Suhrke with Jones, *Early Warning and Conflict*.

- to monitor the observance of the cease-fire agreement, which called for the establishment of cantonment and assembly zones and the demarcation of the new demilitarised zones and other demilitarisation procedures;
- to monitor the security situation during the final period of the transitional Government's mandate, leading up to the elections;
- to assist with mine clearance, primarily through training programmes;
- to investigate, at the request of the parties, or on its own initiative, instances of alleged non-compliance with the provisions of the Protocol of Agreement on the Integration of the Armed Forces of the Two Parties, and to pursue any such instances with the parties responsible and report thereon as appropriate to the Secretary-General;
- to monitor the process of repatriation of Rwandan refugees and resettlement of displaced persons to verify that it was carried out in a safe and orderly manner;
- to assist in the co-ordination of humanitarian assistance activities in conjunction with relief operations; and
- to investigate and report on incidents regarding the activities of the *gendarmerie* and police.[26]

The mandate given to UNAMIR by the Security Council conformed to the tasks foreseen for it in the Arusha Accords, with one major exception. Missing from the Security Council resolution was any reference to the *primary* task ascribed to the NIF by Arusha: namely, ensuring overall security in the country.[27]

The Rules of Engagement established by UNAMIR reflected this trestricted mandate. The Force Commander's Directive establishing the Rules stated that 'the use of weapons is normally authorised for self-defence only. The use of force for deterrence or retaliation is forbidden'.[28] This reflected a philosophy that 'the whole *raison d'être* of peacekeeping is that peace should be achieved without the use of military force'.[29]

Deploying, financing & equipping UNAMIR

UNAMIR was to be deployed in four phases. In Phase I, starting immediately after authorisation, 1,428 troops were to be sent to Rwanda

---

[26] Security Council resolution establishing UNAMIR for a six-month period and approving the integration of UNOMUR into UNAMIR. Security Council Resolution 872, 5 October 1993.

[27] See UN, *The United Nations and Rwanda, 1993–1996*, DPI/1768 (New York: Department of Public Information UN), p. 23.

[28] General Romeo Dallaire, *Force Directive No. 01: Rules of Engagement*, UNAMIR, October, 1993, p. 1.

[29] *Ibid.*

to establish a presence in the DMZ, and await the departure of French forces from Kigali – a condition of deployment of the NIF established by the Arusha negotiations. Phase I was estimated to have a duration of 90 days. Phase II was to commence after the establishment of the transitional government and would focus on preparations for the disarmament and demobilisation of the armed forces. During this phase, UNAMIR would also provide security in Kigali and in a weapons-free zone surrounding the city. Troop strength would rise during this period to 2,217 troops. These reinforcements would, during Phase III, oversee the demobilisation, disengagement and integration processes. The force would gradually be thinned out during Phase IV but would maintain a security presence during the transition to elections.

Starting on 1 November 1993, the first contingent of troops in UNAMIR deployed in five sectors: in the DMZ; in Kigali; in RPF-held territory near the frontline with the Rwandan army; in government territory; and along the Uganda–Rwanda border (incorporating the eighty-one observers of UNOMUR). In Kigali, UNAMIR was deployed in several small detachments, rather than as a concentrated force. In his compelling autobiography, former Force Commander Romeo Dallaire ruefully comments on this decision. He stresses that his preference was to concentrate his forces, to enhance their deterrent capacity, but that the rules governing the deployment of the Belgian contingent prohibited him from doing so – a striking example of the way in which contingents' national doctrine and regulations complicates the business of UN peacekeeping.[30]

UNAMIR slowly built up its presence. By 27 December 1993, UNAMIR had 1,260 troops on the ground drawn from Belgian, Bangledeshi, Tunisian, Ghanaian and Canadian contingents.[31] Despite the fact that the transitional government had not been established, the UN secretary-general's December report recommended that a further battalion be sent early to Rwanda, and on 6 January 1994 further troops for UNAMIR were approved by the Security Council, bringing UNAMIR's total strength to 2,548.

UNAMIR's deployment was constrained by the extraordinarily tortuous budget procedure that in that period accompanied the establishment of UN missions.[32] The initial budget for UNAMIR went to the UN Fifth Committee on 3 January 1994; the Advisory Committee on Activities and Budgetary Questions (ACABQ) began

[30] Romeo Dallaire, *Shake Hands with the Devil: The Failure of Humanity in Rwanda* (New York: Avalon Publishing Group, 2004).

[31] UN, *The United Nations and Rwanda*, p. 28.

[32] Confidential author interviews: Diplomatic mission, Permanent Member of the Security Council, Official in charge of UN budgetary issues, New York, June 1995.

consideration of the budget on 17 March. ACABQ issued its recommendations to the Fifth Committee on 30 March, which were endorsed on 4 April.[33] On 18 April, requests were issued to contributors for $61 million, the first instalments of which were received on 26 August. In short, UNAMIR's budget was approved two days before the start of the genocide, and the first instalment of funds was received one month after the genocide ended. At the time, UNAMIR was described as 'financially and logistically very weak'.[34]

Further, UNAMIR was never equipped with two assets, which might have proved critically useful; an intelligence capacity, and defensive equipment, such as armoured personnel carriers (APCs).[35] No member state contributed a unit equipped with such vehicles, so DPKO scavenged spare equipment from the UN operation in Mozambique, and contacted commercial contractors. Several APCs arrived from Mozambique but were largely non-functional. Just before the outbreak of genocide, UNAMIR was often in the position of having to tow one non-functioning APC behind a second – presenting a disastrously accurate symbol of weakness to the *génocidiares*. Whatever intelligence capacity UNAMIR did have was provided informally by the Belgian contingent (the First Paratroop Battalion). Commenting on these two issues, a staff officer of Brigadier-General Dallaire's would later argue that the experience of Rwanda established that 'the UN must drop its aversion to intelligence operations', and that, 'the continued deployment of contingents without the requisite equipment ... placed a large, immobile and largely ineffective force in the middle of an increasingly hostile environment'.[36]

Mounting threat, non-response, withdrawal

On the ground UNAMIR was challenged from the very outset. The Force Commander and an advance party of 21 troops arrived in Kigali between 21 and 27 October 1993, several weeks after the date agreed at Arusha. On the day the Force Commander arrived, the Tutsi-dominated army of Burundi assassinated the newly elected President Melchior Ndadaye, a Hutu – an act that sparked widespread killing resulting in the deaths of a reported 150,000 Burundians.[37] The

---

[33] UN General Assembly, A/RES/48/248, 5 April 1994.
[34] UNAMIR/IC/08, 14 December 1993.
[35] For details about the process by which UNAMIR was supplied and equipped, see Adelman and Suhrke with Jones, *Early Warning and Conflict*.
[36] Confidential, unofficial document given to Astri Suhrke and Howard Adelman by a senior officer in UNAMIR, New York (June 1995).
[37] A subsequent study by the US Agency for International Development suggested that the number killed was between 35,000 and 50,000, and that the killings were evenly

assassination and killings were rich material for the extremists in Rwanda, who used the events to lend credence to their claims that the Tutsis of the RPF were returning to Rwanda to re-establish their historic dominance over the Hutu. The contrast could not have been starker between the violence in Burundi and the late, partial arrival of the NIF whose ostensible task, at least in Rwandan eyes and in the language of Arusha, was to 'secure' the implementation phase. UNAMIR's role as guarantor of the peace agreement was already in jeopardy.

Despite having its resources stretched by the general deterioration in security in Kigali, UNAMIR managed to maintain order in the capital, and even to restore it following a series of assassinations in February 1994. But the damage was done and a sense of chaos and impending catastrophe had already pervaded the Rwandan political system. UNAMIR's minimal ability to contain a rapidly disintegrating situation in Rwanda was quickly being eroded.

The weakness of UNAMIR was matched by the weakness of other international efforts to control the situation: in both the military and diplomatic realms, international responses to the deteriorating situation were anaemic. From the late Arusha period onwards, it had been clear that there was substantial opposition to the Arusha process, and especially to the final deal. Moreover, the groups that opposed the deal, and especially the CDR, were free in their use of totalistic rhetoric and even apocalyptic references to signal their opposition. The risk to Arusha was widely noted by diplomats in the region.[38] But little was done to counter the risk.

Non-response Warnings and signals emanating from Rwanda were falling on ears in New York that if not deaf were clearly attuned to different sounds. Signals were read, and processed, but not highlighted or brought to the attention of the Security Council. When they were,

balanced between Hutus killed by the army and Tutsis killed by Hutu groups (US Agency for International Development, confidential author interview, Washington, December 1995). Nevertheless, the important point in terms of the dynamics of politics in Rwanda was the far larger, more one-sided figure that was widely reported through the region. The author was in Tanzania shortly after the Burundi killings, and repeatedly heard the 150,000 figure. This point was also made by Gérard Prunier at a US Committee for Refugees-sponsored meeting of the Joint Evaluation team in Washington, DC, 18 December 1995 (author notes).

[38] For example, on 29 November 1993, Canadian diplomats sent the following message to Ottawa: 'Country is tense as political actors manoeuvre to keep or gain advantage among three shifting corners of power: President and his MNRD party, RPF, and opposition parties (several of whose members are cabinet ministers). Within each corner, there are divisions and intrigue which contribute to general sense of unease over likelihood that Arusha Accords can be fully implemented and peace maintained'. Canadian High Commission, Dar-es-Salaam, Cable, 29 November 1993.

they were cleaned in a routine manner.[39] In this process, and given the background of a presumption of an easy mission, the rapid deterioration of the situation in Rwanda was missed in the Security Council. This was so despite the fact that national intelligence units were also beginning to consider the possibility of a serious threat to Arusha. Notably, the CIA conducted a desk study of options, one of which suggested a worst-case scenario of 500,000 dead. This report was never shared beyond the CIA.[40]

Throughout this period, moreover, UNAMIR was being managed in a way, which minimised its capacity to respond to challenge. As the Force Commander reported a worsening situation, and sought approval to interpret his mandate widely in order to respond, he was consistently denied. The critical juncture for this came in response to the 11 January cable that Dallaire sent to headquarters. The Force Commander requested approval to conduct a search for weapons caches revealed by a high-level government informant. DPKO's response was that the matter should be raised with the parties, and that no weapons searches should be undertaken. They noted that the mandate referred to a weapons-free zone established 'by the parties'.

The unwillingness of New York to take an expansive view of the mandate was in substantial part a consequence of the weak political support for UNAMIR. The timing was not auspicious: the Security Council was still reeling from the news of the disastrous results from a similar 'hunt-and-destroy' mission in Mogadishu that ended with a disastrous UN death toll. A clear 'Mogadishu line' had been set, and it was not to be crossed. As Michael Barnett shows in his account of the period, the Mission in New York was under clear instructions to dissuade the UN from an ambitious response.[41] This coupled with the basic lack of support for UNAMIR, limited the mission's capacity to investigate the growing signals of opposition to the implementation of Arusha. The combination of political indifference and poor intelligence

---

[39] One diplomat (from a Permanent Five country) who dealt with the Security Council during this period alleged that cables from UNAMIR were 'cleaned' before being shared with the Council. While a certain degree of cleaning of language and presentation is normal practice, it is not normal that UN Secretariat officials would alter the central meaning of cables from the field before sharing them with the Council. However, this allegation has not been substantiated. Confidential author interview, New York, June 1995.

[40] US Department of State, Confidential author interview, Washington DC, December 1995. This was confirmed in separate interviews by Astri Suhrke and Howard Adelman at the US Central Intelligence Agency. See Bruce Jones, 'The Arusha Peace Process', Background paper for Study II of the Joint Evaluation (London, 1995) editors' comments in the footnotes.

[41] Barnett, *Eyewitness to a Genocide*.

meant that the direction of the political war, and signals of impending violence, went unheeded if not unheard in New York.[42] As the signals grew louder, and civil violence in Kigali and throughout the country increased with each step towards implementation of Arusha, New York failed to respond. No proactive measures to block Arusha's opponents were taken; no contingency planning occurred. Thus, UNAMIR was denied the tools, which might have helped generate better options when the violence of the political war overtook the peace process in the military war.

Withdrawal When genocide was launched, the UN was in no position to respond. Indeed, UNAMIR was among the early, successful targets of the *génocidaires*. The targeting of UNAMIR had actually been revealed to the UN in the 11 January cable; the plan included killing ten Belgian peacekeepers to provoke the withdrawal of the UN force.

The plan worked. The peacekeepers were waylaid by a FAR company, creating a standoff. The peacekeepers radioed-in for instructions and were ordered to lay down their weapons. The order was given by the head of the Belgian contingent, Colonel Luc Marchal who relayed the situation to General Dallaire. Dallaire did not respond to the situation directly but continued with a meeting with a 'Crisis Committee' of the ruling MRND and CDR officials that had declared itself the acting 'interim government'. The peacekeepers were then placed in a small shed. A lengthy interval ensued, the only explanation for which is that the FAR were waiting for UNAMIR's response. When no response was forthcoming, the peacekeepers were attacked and killed. Their bodies were then brutalised: limbs were severed, bodies were hacked at with machetes, and the soldiers' genitalia were hacked off and stuffed in their mouths.[43]

A senior Rwandan official familiar with the planning of the genocide talked about the inspiration for the attack as having come from watching the UN's experience in Somalia: 'We watch CNN too, you know'.[44] The extremists believed that the Western nations supplying the core of

---

[42] Bruce Jones and Astri Suhrke, 'Preventive Diplomacy in Rwanda: Failure to Act, or Failure of Actions Taken?', in Bruce Jentleson (ed.), *Opportunities Taken, Opportunities Lost: Preventive Diplomacy in the Post-Cold War* (New York: Carnegie Commission on Preventing Deadly Conflict, 1999).

[43] For a highly detailed account of the first three days of the genocide, see Filip Reyntjens, *Rwanda. Trois jours qui ont fait basculer l'histoire* (Bruxelles et Paris: Institut Africain-L'Harmattan, Cahiers Africains, 1996). For details on the brutalisation of the ten Belgian peacekeepers, see in particular George Koch, 'The Cross', *Saturday Night*, vol. 1 (September 1996), pp. 64–84.

[44] Confidential author interview, Kigali, June 1996.

the force would not be able to stomach even a handful of casualties. The attack was a test and UNAMIR failed. Within five days, Belgium announced the imminent withdrawal of its UNAMIR contingent.[45] Ten days later, the UN decided to draw down its force to symbolic levels.[46]

The decision to draw down UNAMIR followed heated debate in the corridors of the Security Council. Notable in this debate was the effort of Nigeria, then holding an elected seat at the Security Council, to generate a substantive response. Options for reinforcement, the status quo, and evacuation of the force were provided by the Secretariat.[47] On 14 April, Nigeria offered to provide the necessary troops, if the United States and others would provide both the strategic lift and would loan Nigeria the necessary armour, especially APCs; but even with this offer, the Security Council was unable to generate an active response.

Notwithstanding the cynicism of decision-making at the Security Council, the withdrawal of the Belgian contingent had already crippled the mission. In what stands as the most cynical decision of the episode, Belgium's Defence Minister Willy Claes actively sought to persuade other troop-contributing nations to join Belgium in withdrawing their troops from UNAMIR – apparently to minimise the embarrassment to Belgium of withdrawing.[48]

Furthermore, UN Secretary-General Boutros Boutros-Ghali failed to provide leadership within the Secretariat or at the Council at this critical juncture.[49] It is true that the responsible parts of the UN Secretariat were enormously overworked during this period, and as Vaccaro points out, two weeks earlier, US troops had withdrawn from Somalia, leaving the UN in the lurch.[50] It is nevertheless the case that the lack of a vigorous response by the UN Secretariat undermined its moral credibility and therefore its ability to prompt action from the Council. Moreover, the Secretariat's own sense of responsibility lagged from the

---

[45] Letter from the Belgian Permanent Representative to the UN to the UN secretary-general (New York, 13 April 1994.)

[46] The decision to draw down, established by UNSCR 912, was never fully implemented. Only 270 officials were supposed to remain in Rwanda; in fact, over 450 stayed. Adelman and Suhrke with Jones, *Early Warning and Conflict*, Chapter 5.

[47] Adelman and Suhrke with Jones, *Early Warning and Conflict*, Chapter 5.

[48] Official of the Belgian Permanent Mission to the UN, Confidential author interview, New York, June 1995.

[49] Barnett, 'The Politics of Indifference'.

[50] The attack on the UN's peacekeepers in Rwanda occurred in April 1994; just days earlier, on 25 March 1994, the US forces assigned to Operation Continue Hope completed their withdrawal from Mogadishu. Simultaneously, the UN (and NATO) were coping with attacks on the 'safe areas' in Goradze; air strikes against Serb forces were launched on 10 and 11 April. In short, the Department of Peacekeeping Operations was coping simultaneously with two major crises before the situation in Rwanda deteriorated dramatically.

outset. One senior peacekeeping official later admitted that it was only after the outbreak of the genocide that he learned of the Genocide Convention and of the UN's legal capacity and moral obligation to respond.[51]

The net result was that on 20 April, the bulk of UNAMIR's troops withdrew from Kigali airport. On boarding the planes which flew them out, Belgian peacekeepers cut up their blue berets in disgust at being forced to abandon a mission that had already claimed ten Belgian soldiers' lives. Apart from a few hundred officers left behind, who did manage to protect a few thousand civilians in Kigali, the UN effectively left Rwanda's genocide planners a clear field to put their killing machine in motion.

UNAMIR II

Only once the genocide in Rwanda had reached its peak, in mid-May, did the Security Council take some active decisions.[52] On 29 April, according to statistics from the Office of the UN High Commissioner for Refugees (UNHCR), just over 250,000 Rwandans crossed into neighbouring Tanzania. This massive outflow of refugees focused attention on the scale of what was occurring inside Rwanda. At the same juncture, the UN issued an estimate that over 200,000 people had been killed inside Rwanda. These facts managed to jolt the Security Council back into 'action': on 6 May the Council reopened the debate on Rwanda, and asked the Secretariat for plans. This eventuated, by 17 May, in Resolution 918 under which the Council sought to reinforce UNAMIR (hereafter known as UNAMIR II) to a total strength of 5,500, at a budgeted cost of $115 million for six months. However, requests to troop-contributing nations produced no readily available troops. Indeed, no new troops were deployed to UNAMIR II until the middle of August, by which point the genocide and the civil war were well over. Thus, on the ground, UNAMIR II played not a peacekeeping/security role, but primarily a humanitarian role.

From the start of the refugee crisis, UNAMIR II undertook a series of operational humanitarian activities in collaboration with UN humanitarian agencies and non-governmental organisations, especially after the deployment to the force in August 1994 of British, Canadian, Australian and other contingents that included medical, logistics and

---

[51] Confidential author interview, UN, New York, June 1995.
[52] See in particular, Adelman and Suhrke with Jones, *Early Warning and Conflict*, Chapters 5 and 6; Vaccaro, 'The Politics of Genocide', in Durch (ed.) *UN Peacekeeping*; and Prunier, *The Rwanda Crisis*.

communication units. Among the activities undertaken by the various contingents were rebuilding hospitals and deploying field ambulances, restoration of telephone systems to aid communication, as well as undertaking security functions such as the management of security and logistics at the airport that were crucial to the delivery of humanitarian supplies. Military airlift was during some periods the major source of supplies to the humanitarian operation. Some contingents also became directly involved in distributing relief supplies.[53]

At later stages of the humanitarian crisis, once the RPF had established a functioning government in Kigali and the situation in Rwanda itself had stabilised somewhat, UNAMIR II also become involved in operations designed to resettle internally displaced persons (IDPs), including a major such undertaking known as *Opération Retour* – during which UNAMIR II contingents' trucks were used to transport IDPs.[54]

The issue of IDPs however was also one, which showed the oddity of a peacekeeping force deployed primarily to humanitarian taskings. This was revealed in particular when the Rwandan government agreed – under considerable pressure – to resettle several large camps of IDPs in the Kibeho area, where IDPs had complained of acute insecurity. UNAMIR II agreed to play a substantial role in the resettlement operation. Before it could occur, however, large-scale killings occurred in the camps, with perhaps 2,000 IDPs killed during what became known as the Kibeho massacre. The contrast between UNAMIR II's transport and humanitarian role on the one hand, and its lack of a security or protection role on the other, was thrown into sharp relief.

Progressively, UNAMIR II's mandate was broadened – to encompass good offices, national reconciliation, monitoring with military and police observers, training of a national police force, contributing to the security in Rwanda of personnel and premises of UN agencies, and of the International Tribunal for Rwanda, and to assist in the establishment and training of a new, integrated, national police force. However, relations between UNAMIR II and the government of Rwanda were bad from the outset, and never improved. The roles assigned to UNAMIR II by the Security Council were far removed from its actual role on the ground. Tensions between the UN force and the Rwandan government mounted after the Kibeho incident, and in March 1996 the Rwandan government withdrew its support from the mission, and UNAMIR was disbanded.

---

[53] Borton et al., *Study III Humanitarian Aid*, pp. 40–59.
[54] *Ibid.*, p. 57.

Learning from failure: evolution of peacekeeping policy and practice[55]

This UN's actions and inactions in Rwanda stand as one of its greatest failures. It is therefore unsurprising that perceived lessons of Rwanda have significantly shaped UN policy and peacekeeping response in the period since.

Lessons learning, policy evolution

The UN's experience in Rwanda sparked a substantial body of analysis and lessons learning, commensurate with the scale of the failure, some of it commissioned by the UN itself, some by major state actors at the UN.

External analysis

The first major effort to learn lessons from Rwanda was an exercise undertaken jointly by the Danish, Norwegian, Swedish, US and UK governments. This group of governments commissioned four separate analyses, of the background, conflict management efforts, humanitarian efforts and early post-conflict efforts that accompanied the Rwanda crisis. A multi-year, multi-author effort, the Joint Evaluation produced in 1996 a five-volume study that set out a series of conclusions and lessons about what had gone wrong in Rwanda. The scale of the study – involving 51 official institutions, and dozens of research institutes – arguably contributed to a substantial degree of dissemination of these conclusions and lessons.

The report reached a broad range of conclusions about humanitarian assistance, strategic coordination, early warning, conflict management and other issues. In terms of issues with specific salience for peacekeeping, the study reached five key conclusions:

- that the mission as deployed was insufficient in scale to deal with the potential challenges from opponents known to exist;

---

[55] This section of the chapter is written from the perspective of the UN Secretariat, where the author was a staff member from 1997 until 2002, dealing *inter alia* with such issues as early warning, mutli-dimensional peacekeeping (including in Sierra Leone), and specifically with UN missions in Kosovo, East Timor and the Middle East. The argument made below is thus developed in substantial part from material taken from this period, some of which can be cited, some not. This chapter is not the place to engage the methodological issues of internal versus external knowledge, of counterfactual analysis and of tracing causality in complex social organisations: but these issues are present in any effort to trace the impact of lessons learning on decision-making.

- that poor budgeting and procurement procedures further hobbled the effectiveness of the force as deployed;
- that inadequate planning for the contingency of opposition removed options from the UN at the moment of attack;
- that the secretary-general was at fault in terms of lack of leadership, for failing to try to generate an adequate response from the Security Council, when the genocide first got underway;
- and that irrespective of these points, the Security Council failed in its basic responsibilities, at a critical time to undertake a response to the outbreak of genocidal violence.

Simultaneously, several individual governments commissioned separate studies of what had gone wrong.[56] The Canadian government published an independent examination of the failures of Rwanda that reinforced the conclusions of the Joint Evaluation. Many academic institutions and think-tanks also commissioned studies, notably the Carnegie Commission on Preventing Deadly Conflict, which resulted both in an analysis of peacekeeping options by Scott Feil and of the failure of early warning efforts (by this author, together with Astri Suhrke.)[57]

Within the humanitarian community, lessons learned from Rwanda – the scale of the post-genocide disaster of which had overwhelmed the humanitarian community – immediately became a major source of policy and practice reform. In particular, the traumas and dilemmas associated with providing humanitarian relief in the refugee camps in eastern Zaire, to which much of the FAR had fled in the face of RPF advances, became a central theme in the humanitarian community's effort to struggle with the political impacts of humanitarian relief provision. Several post-operation analyses recognised that the humanitarian response in eastern Zaire had inadvertently helped the fleeing genocide movement to reconstitute itself in the camps. Reliance on local leaders within the camp to help organise the distribution of relief supplies, in particular, allowed those leaders to reassert their authority over the camp population; intimidate them into not returning from Rwanda; and effectively hold the refugee population hostage to their political objectives. On the other hand, of course, withdrawing aid support to that population would have condemned tens of thousands

---

[56] Of particular note, Paul La Rose-Edwards, *The Rwandan Crisis of April 1994: The Lessons Learned*, Report for Regional Security and Peacekeeping Division (IDC) International Security, Arms Control, and CSCE Affairs Bureau, Department of Foreign Affairs and International Trade, Ottawa, November 1994.

[57] Feil, *Preventing Genocide*.

to die. To this day, the Zaire camps haunt the humanitarian community, which continues to struggle with the dilemmas they highlighted.[58]

Within the peacekeeping community at the UN, the impact of lessons learned from Rwanda apparently took longer to develop.

Internal analysis

Within the UN, during the continuing tenure of Boutros Boutros-Ghali, the first effort at lessons learned (by DPKO's Lessons Learned Unit) was so desultory as to constitute a whitewash. The Unit's Rwanda report avoided any direct criticisms of internal decisions or decision-makers, avoided any direct political criticism of member states, and was in general abstracted in its tone from the real horrors of Rwanda. This was not out of keeping with general practice at the time, in which internal UN evaluation – to the extent that it occurred – tended to be defensive and uncritical.

The beginnings of real 'lessons learnt' by the UN from its intervention in Rwanda can be traced to Kofi Annan's election as secretary-general in 1997. Soon after taking office, Annan commissioned independent studies of two of the UN's' great failures of the 1990s, UNAMIR, and UNPROFOR's role in the safe areas in Bosnia. These documents, when published, were unusually frank, not just by UN standards: they specified responsibility for failures, and named names (Annan's among them). Among the key conclusions that the documents drew, apart from those already drawn by the Joint Evaluation, were that the principal failing of the Secretariat had been in providing to the Security Council a too-rosy analysis of the likely requirements of the Rwanda mission. The failure to provide to the Security Council an accurate picture of the likely needs of the mission was identified as a critical (and recurrent) failure of the Secretariat.[59]

This conclusion was picked up by a further report then commissioned by the secretary-general in an effort to redress some of the weaknesses identified by the Rwanda and Bosnia reports. The secretary-general's Report on Strengthening Peace Operations (commonly known, after its

---

[58] For a recent discussion, see Stephen J. Stedman and Fred Tanner, *Refugee Manipulation: War, Politics, and the Abuse of Human Suffering* (Washington, DC: The Brookings Institution, 2003).

[59] UN, Report of the Independent Inquiry into the Actions of the UN during the 1994 Genocide in Rwanda, 15 December 1999, www.un.org/News/ossg/rwanda_report.htm.

chairman, as the Brahimi Report[60]) not only reinforced the prior conclusion that this was a central weakness of UN peace operations and of the Secretariat, but actively recommended that the Secretariat, in effect, 'speak truth to power' – that the Secretariat should provide the Security Council with clear, realistic assessments of new missions, and even refuse to undertake missions if inadequately resourced. Though the Brahimi Report made many other recommendations, this is widely taken to be its core political contribution to the evolution of doctrine at the UN.

Evolved practice

There is, thus, a relatively clear line of continuity between lessons identified from the failure of Rwanda, and the evolution of peacekeeping policy, at least in terms of the Secretariat. But what about practice?

It is arguable that the experience of Rwanda has altered peacekeeping practice, in four important ways: by changing the bureaucratic culture related to the management of early warning information; by generating some limited improvements in the financing of and planning for peacekeeping missions; by influencing the Secretariat's political leadership in terms of its willingness to stand firm in the face of crises; and – most tenuously – in terms of the willingness of member states to authorise more adequate responses for peacekeeping, including in Africa. It also seems evident that there remains within the Secretariat – or at least in the dynamics between the Secretariat and the Security Council – an unwillingness to engage in contingency planning for negative scenarios within existing missions.

Early warning

Since 1997 there has been a robust development of early warning capacities, practices and procedures at the UN. Experience suggests that UN staff members' awareness of the fact that early warning signals for the Rwandan genocide were missed inside the Secretariat has led to a phenomenon wherein desk officers and staff aides are pre-occupied with 'not being the person sitting on the next Rwanda cable'. Warnings from field cables or field colleagues about potential upsurges in violence are quickly passed upwards for decision-making, rather than cleaned, buried or ignored, for fear of contributing to another catastrophe of Rwanda's proportions. More formally, the UN has in recent years put in

---

[60] UN General Assembly, *Report of the Panel on United Nations Peace Operations*, A/55/305, 21 August 2000.

place a series of early warning and analyses functions, including the Early Warning Unit of the Office for the Coordination of Humanitarian Affairs (OCHA), the 'Framework team', and others. These capacities, and others within specific agencies, now routinely review country information coming from UN field presences, commission external analysis, and in other ways seek to identify warning sides of potential risk of conflict, and to identify preventative strategies.

Financing and planning

Rwanda, along with several other missions that experienced the same set of logistical and financial constraints, spurred on efforts by the Security Council, the Special Committee on Peacekeeping Operations, the ACABQ and DPKO to improve the mechanisms for financing new operations. Notably, the secretary-general was given the authority to allocate up to $50 million for advance spending on newly authorised missions, prior to budget authorisation. This, and a series of other technical improvements to the UN's logistics and finance capacity – well documented in two studies that have examined the implementation of agreed reforms[61] – have significantly improved the capacity of the UN to mount operations within a limited time period. The financial obstacles to mission start-up have been minimised, if not entirely removed. At this technical level, there is evidence of progress in peacekeeping reform – though, as of early 2004, some of the limits of this progress were being revealed as the UN struggled to deploy stocks for a sequence of upcoming missions. Here, however, it is impossible to isolate the impact of lessons from Rwanda, versus those of the several other missions of the early 1990s that experienced the same set of technical obstacles.

The Brahimi Report and the subsequent implementation process also generated improvements to other aspects of planning for missions. For example, a greater number of desk staff has been allocated to DPKO, meaning that a single mission is now routinely managed by two (or at least one and a half) desk officers, rather than the two-mission-per-desk-officer ratio that held during the pre-Brahimi era. In addition, there have been improvements to mission planning capacities inside DPKO, in areas such as logistics and preparation for police deployments.

Less progress has been made on contingency planning or scenario planning at the onset of operations. UN planning still tends towards the variety of identification of a likely scenario, and planning for that scenario

---

[61] William J. Durch, Victoria K. Holt, Caroline E. Earle and Moira K. Shanahan, *The Brahimi Report and the Future of Peace Operations*, Stimson Center, December 2003.

within estimated resource limits. By contrast, most national defence ministries or armed services undertake scenario planning in a very different sense, looking at a range of possible outcomes or developments and planning for what would be required to deal with the *worst* of them. The UN's predilection for more limited planning is a function both of Secretariat culture and, importantly, the political constraints placed on mission planning by member states. An important example came during the UN's experience in East Timor, where the UN was assisting the Indonesian authorities and the East Timorese mounted a referendum on the future relationship between Djakarta and Dili. During the course of planning for the referendum, warnings were received that violence might result from a pro-independence vote. Initially the UN peacekeepers were to be deployed in the event of a pro-independence vote in the referendum. Now the question was posed as to whether a peacekeeping force should be deployed as a preventative measure prior to the referendum. This suggestion was rejected, not by the Secretariat, but by a key member state involved in the negotiating process. The result was that when, indeed, a vote for independence was swiftly followed by violence, the UN was caught without any peacekeeping or security presence on the island and a potential disaster on its hands. East Timor is not the only case where no contingency planning occurred: the culture within the Secretariat is still resistant to planning for various contingencies either in existing or upcoming missions.[62]

Responding to crisis

When faced with crisis, there is clear evidence that the Secretariat has learned to act in a different way than it did during Rwanda. In 1998, the UN peacekeeping mission in Sierra Leone (UNAMSIL) came under attack from the Revolutionary United Front, rather than rapidly withdrawing the mission as it had done in Rwanda, the organisation responded differently. The secretary-general immediately went to the Security Council and demanded action. He dispatched his under-secretary-general for Peacekeeping Operations, Bernard Miyet to Freetown, to signal that the UN was not intending to leave.[63] The UK government responded to the secretary-general's urgings for action by deploying a contingent of Royal Marines to Freetown, which bolstered

---

[62] Author notes, Office for the Coordination of Humanitarian Affairs, Department of Peacekeeping Operations, and Department of Political Affairs/United Nations Special Coordination, 1998–2002.

[63] Author notes, Office for the Coordination of Humanitarian Affairs, 1999.

UNAMSIL and helped re-train a national army, leading in quick order to a sustained though fragile peace.

Similarly, despite the arguable mishandling of early warnings and contingency planning in East Timor, when violence did occur, again the secretary-general went immediately to the Security Council to make the case for an enhanced response.[64] The initial result was a Security Council mission to Dili, which, along with a number of private efforts to lobby President Clinton for the United States to take a more active role in preventing a broader tragedy, eventually led to the rapid deployment of an Australian-led multi-national force (INTERFET), and a withdrawal of the Indonesian army from Dili. Also similar, when a mission came under attack in the Democratic Republic of the Congo, a French-led (though European Union flagged) operation, Operation Artemis, was quickly deployed to bolster the UN's force – which was small and thinly spread over a huge territory.

These experiences have very recently given rise to a secretary-general proposal for the establishment of 'strategic reserves' for UN peace-keeping, designed in part to fill this gap. The proposal is for a set of high-readiness brigades, probably maintained, in part, on UN peace-keeping financing, for rapid deployment to field operations. Foreseen by the Brahimi Report, the establishment of a capacity of this kind would give the UN itself the operational tools to respond at short notice to an escalating situation, using 'over-the-horizon' forces with real punch. At the World Summit in 2005, governments cautiously endorsed further deliberation of the proposal.[65]

Speaking truth to power

There is limited evidence that the lessons from Rwanda, as translated in policy and particular by the Brahimi Report, have finally begun to have an impact on the way in which the Secretariat interacts with the Security Council in calling for new missions. Here, the salient example is Liberia. Faced with lukewarm support for a new mission in Liberia, the Secretariat – both the secretary-general's Special Representative Jacques Paul Klein and DPKO – spoke forcefully both in private to the Security Council and even in public, calling for a sizeable mission to handle the Liberia situation and stating its unwillingness to mount a mission with less than adequate mandates or resources. The Security Council responded by authorising 15,000 troops for Sierra Leone, as requested,

---

[64] Author notes, Department of Peacekeeping Operations, 1999.
[65] A/Res/60/1.

albeit with a slightly weaker mandate than asked for, and 1,500 military observers, several hundred more than the Secretariat has requested.

Of course, there are still several missions where the UN's troop presence is grossly inadequate by comparison with the scale of challenge – the starkest being the Democratic Republic of Congo (DRC), where the UN's 6,000 observers are deployed across an enormous country providing the only third-party military presence in a country that has lost an estimated 3.4 million people to war. Nevertheless, in the most recent UN peacekeeping decisions, the trend has been improving.

Continued obstacles to effective peacekeeping

All this being said, several of the broader implications of the Rwanda crisis remain unaddressed, or under-addressed. At the operational level, the most important among these is the argument – not new to Rwanda but reinforced by it – that to have an effective peacekeeping capacity, the UN must have a stand-by, rapid-deployment capacity to deter new Rwandas. Much negotiation and policy effort in the late 1990s has gone into this issue. By 2002, the UN did have a Stand-By High Readiness Brigade (SHIRBRIG), comprising stand-by components from several Western countries. SHIRBRIG – which primarily constitutes a rapidly deployable mission headquarters capacity, but can be accompanied by troops – was deployed in the Ethiopian–Eritrean context, and later in Liberia. This is without doubt a significant improvement for the UN, giving it a capacity to stand-up a mission within 30 to 90 days. It is not, of course, an actual rapid deployment peacekeeping capacity able to check sudden upsurges in violence, of the style of Interfet.

Most recently, a joint proposal by the United Kingdom and France to create a stand-by force of roughly 1,500 troops points to some further improvement, even on this difficult issue. Efforts to increase this stand-by force with contributions from other European countries may well succeed. If so, and if the strategic reserves proposal noted above is acted upon, we may begin to be at a point where capacity meets the need.

At a broader political level, the more fundamental point is that Rwanda highlighted the fact – simply – that the enormous differences in power and import of different states, and different peoples, meant that the international community effectively stood by while a mass crime against humanity took place. The cynical claim, often repeated in peacekeeping circles in the 1990s, that 1,000 African lives equated to one hundred South Asian lives equated to ten European lives equated to one American life, proved tragically too optimistic. A total of 800,000

Rwandan lives were not worth the insurance risk of providing APCs to Nigerian troops.

Conclusion

In assessing the impact of Rwanda on peacekeeping policy and practice, the key question remains: if faced today with the situation it was faced with on 6 April 1994, would the UN act differently, and with a different result? In all likelihood, the answer to the first question is yes; but to the second question, perhaps no.

For the first, the evidence both of policy changes and more importantly of actions – in respect of Sierra Leone, East Timor and Liberia, at least – suggest that faced with an imminent crisis, the UN Secretariat and the secretary-general would react by facing the Security Council with a realistic appraisal of the situation, and a demand for action. By recent experience, and being optimistic, one could surmise that the Council would respond, authorising a mission. But lacking a rapid-deployment capacity, the UN would be reliant on a combination of neighbours' troops, small European stand-by forces, and US strategic lift capacity to mount the operation. A realistic estimate of the amount of time it would take – under good circumstances – to generate the necessary level of troops in Rwanda would be perhaps 30 days – the target deployment rate for the United Kingdom and French rapid-response troops just mentioned. By May 6, in Rwanda, 30 days into the genocide, roughly 500,000 people were dead. Would a month-late response be better than the three-month late response of 1994? Unquestionably. But it also demonstrates the continued gap between potential need, and UN capacity, in peacekeeping.

David M. Malone and Sebastian von Einsiedel

Introduction

In 2004, Haiti's fortunes executed a full circle. Shortly after leading the celebrations marking Haiti's bicentennial anniversary of its independence in February 2004, Jean-Bertrand Aristide, three-time president of Haiti, was swept from power by violent rebellion. Aristide's departure and the preceding turmoil, the culmination of a political and economic crisis that had festered for years, provoked a US and French military intervention, shortly thereafter replaced by a United Nations (UN) peacekeeping force to restore order and create the conditions for long term stability and democracy.

These unhappy developments are all the more striking for following on intense international involvement in Haiti's affairs throughout the 1990s. In particular, the UN engaged in a broad range of activities in support of democracy in Haiti, including election monitoring in 1990, UN Security Council (UNSC)-mandated sanctions in 1993–1994, a naval blockade in 1993–1994, UNSC-authorised use of force in 1994 against the military regime that had removed Aristide from power three years earlier and a major peacekeeping operation (PKO) in the years 1994–1996, subsequently reduced to a small international force aimed at building a domestic police force.

The case offers the first, and to date only, instance of the UNSC authorising the use of force to effect the restoration of democracy within a member state. Unlike in a number of other situations, democratic processes were not seen as a means of national reconciliation, nor were elections seen as a mechanism to anchor fragile peace agreements. Rather democratic rule was asserted as the goal in and of itself.

The Haiti file reveals themes present in many other of the UN's efforts to address internal crises following the end of the Cold War: promotion and monitoring of human rights; concern over the humanitarian plight of a civilian population affected by political turmoil; a desire to bring to justice those responsible for gross human rights violations; and an effort at peace building through national economic development.

The case sheds light on how leadership is exercised, coalitions are built and burden sharing is negotiated within the Council. It also highlights how the UN can work in partnership with a regional organisation, in this instance the Organisation of American States (OAS). It provides indications of the extent to which the UN in general and Security Council members in particular, improvised action in response to events on the ground they did not control. Most importantly, this case presents an instance in which UN operations were broadly successful, but in which the patient failed to recover and eventually collapsed fully in 2004 requiring massive renewed international intervention. While it provides sobering lessons on the UN's readiness for overseeing long-term peace building, the main responsibility for failure, in our view, lies with Haitian political actors.

Haiti's crisis of democracy

When Haiti in February 1990 sought assistance from the OAS and the UN for elections, the challenges to genuine democracy in Haiti were immense. Ever since gaining independence from French colonial rule in 1804, Haiti has been unable to establish a stable political system. The tradition of 'one-man rule' flourished through a system of institutional corruption. The US occupation, which lasted from 1915 until 1934, failed to produce a more responsive governing system. The notoriously brutal Duvalier dynasty, ruling Haiti from 1957 until 1986, was only the culmination of almost two centuries of misrule.[1]

Yet, the elections in December 1990, monitored by the UN and the OAS, unfolded well, bringing to power a young Roman Catholic priest and partisan of liberation theology, Jean-Bertrand Aristide.[2] Aristide's government made serious efforts to address the country's formidable challenges, with uneven skill and results. However, faced with numerous obstacles, Aristide's exercise of power became increasingly personalised and authoritarian. On 29 September 1991, Raoul Cédras,

---

[1] Many distinguished Haitian scholars have surveyed Haiti's history. These include Patrick Bellegard-Smith and Michel-Rolph Trouillot in a number of riveting books. For a comprehensive overview, see Robert Debs Heinl Jr and Nancy Gordon Heinl, *Written in Blood: The Story of the Haitian People 1492–1971* (Boston, MA: Houghton Mifflin, 1978).

[2] *Electoral Assistance to Haiti: Note by the Secretary-General*, A/45/870/Add.1, 22 February 1991.

the commander of Haiti's armed forces, fearing mass revenge violence against the protagonists of the former regime, overthrew his government.

Aftermath of the coup in Haiti

From his exile in Venezuela, Aristide successfully mobilised the international community, notably through the OAS and the UN. The OAS Council, which had only recently proclaimed its Santiago Declaration to foster democracy, immediately rejected the coup, calling for the 'diplomatic isolation' of the military regime.[3] The UN secretary-general and the president of the UNSC soon followed suit, the latter calling for 'the immediate reversal of the situation'.[4]

The OAS on 8 October adopted a resolution urging member states to impose a trade embargo on Haiti.[5] The OAS embargo, subsequently endorsed by the UN General Assembly,[6] began to produce some effects by the end of October 1991, but 'exemptions' covering supplies for US-owned local industries severely undermined the effectiveness of the sanctions. Meanwhile, large numbers of Haitians took to the seas, threatening to engulf Florida with boat-going refugees.

In order to sustain momentum at the UN, a grouping of Canada, France, the United States, and Venezuela was constituted in mid-1992 as the Group of Friends of the secretary-general on Haiti. Prodded by the General Assembly, UN Secretary-General Boutros Boutros-Ghali by late 1992 adopted a more proactive approach. On 11 December he appointed Dante Caputo, a former president of the UN General Assembly and former foreign minister of Argentina, as his special envoy for Haiti.[7] Caputo, with strong support from the Friends, laid the groundwork for a joint deployment in February of the following year of UN and OAS staff, known as the International Civilian Mission in Haiti (MICIVIH), to monitor human rights in Haiti. MICIVIH was to

---

[3] For the declaration's enabling a resolution, see Organisation of American States, Resolution 1080: Representative Democracy, AG/Res. 1080 (XXI-0/91), 5 June 1991.
[4] Statement by the UN secretary-general, SG/SM4627 HI/4, 1 October 1990.
[5] OAS Resolution MRE/Res. 2/91, 8 October 1991.
[6] General Assembly Resolution 46/7, 11 October 1991.
[7] On 13 January 1993, Caputo was named Special Envoy for Haiti of the OAS as well as of the UN, an innovation in cooperation between the UN and regional organisations, and a demonstration that in spite of 'turf' wars, they could cooperate with each other in the right circumstances. This joint appointment was echoed by that of Mohammed Sahnoun as Special Representative of both the UN and the OAU for the (African) Great Lakes area in January 1997.

prove perhaps the most successful multilateral effort in Haiti of the 1990s.

Security Council involvement and the Governors Island Agreement (GIA)

By May 1993, consensus emerged among the Friends that UN mandatory sanctions were required to nudge Cédras. However, anticipating objections on humanitarian and legal grounds, they did not seek to universalise the broad OAS sanctions but focused on weapons and oil, the latter seen as the de facto regime's Achilles's heel. Countries that in other circumstances would have opposed the imposition of sanctions in support of democracy, such as China, acquiesced due to strong lobbying from Latin American and Caribbean countries. On 16 June 1993, the Security Council unanimously adopted Resolution 841, instituting mandatory sanctions on weapons, oil and petroleum products against Haiti.[8]

Cédras now agreed to negotiate.[9] Caputo convened a meeting involving both Aristide and Cédras on 27 June 1993, at Governor's Island. Banging heads, Caputo managed to extract from both leaders an agreement, which foresaw successively a new civilian government, the suspension of sanctions, the deployment of UN peacekeepers, an amnesty, retirement of Cédras, and the return of Aristide. Aristide only signed it reluctantly, believing that it provided insufficient guarantees for his return to Haiti.[10] Its most serious flaw, however, lay in a critical path for implementation that was too long and a deployment of the UN PKO too late in the process.

The Governor's Island Agreement's application proved uneven, but plans proceeded for the peacekeeping force, the UN Mission in Haiti (UNMIH), with one hundred Canadian and one hundred French police at its core. Washington agreed to provide troops for a small peacekeeping force also including Canadians and some others. With the ratification of a new prime minister selected by Aristide, the UNSC in Resolution 861 of 27 August suspended the sanctions against Haiti. However, upon the arrival of the USS *Harlan County* in Port-au-Prince

---

[8] In an OAS Council meeting on 22 June, Baena Soares suggested that the UN resolution created a 'serious mutation' in the international treatment of the Haiti crisis but even those OAS members opposed to the UN measures were not prepared to fight for Baena Soares' turf.

[9] 'Document 68', in United Nations, *Haiti* (1993), p. 308. Sanctions were imposed on 23 June, maintaining pressure on the de factos.

[10] Interview with Jean-Bertrand Aristide, Port-au-Prince, 21 May 1996.

harbour on 11 October, carrying the bulk of the United States and Canadian UN peacekeepers, thugs in the pay of the de facto regime prevented the landing of the troops, screaming, 'We are going to turn this into another Somalia!'[11]

This incident challenged US resolve at a time when Washington was in shock over eighteen US Army Rangers killed eight days earlier in Mogadishu. On 12 October, without US consultation of the UN, the *Harlan County* received orders to depart from Haitian waters. From this astonishing failure of US nerve, at least one lesson was learned: when the UN in 1994 prepared for UNMIH redeployment, roughly ten times more military personnel were planned than in 1993.

The UNSC re-imposed sanctions on 13 October in Resolution 873. A few days later, the Clinton administration, eager to cover its embarrassment, prodded the Council to adopt Resolution 875, imposing a naval blockade on Haiti. China's reservations were allayed by the resolution's assertion that 'unique and exceptional circumstances' required the measures.[12] The naval blockade, on its surface a very strong measure, in fact signalled desperation following the collapse of the Governor's Island Agreement. The blockade could not be effective, due to Haiti's extensive land border with the Dominican Republic (which did not enforce the sanctions). However, the humanitarian and economic costs of the embargo were to prove lastingly crippling for Haiti with the poor hardest-hit.

Towards the use of force and Aristide's return

Aristide, hitherto publicly opposed to military intervention to restore him to power, in early January 1994 signalled support for a surgical intervention to overthrow the de facto regime.[13] The United States, however, was not yet willing to adopt this course and exerted pressure on Aristide to yield more to his opponents, creating splits among the Friends. Aristide began to play the 'immigration card', implicitly threatening further floods of boat-going Haitian refugees, in an effort to create pressure on the United States.

Aristide's backers included Democratic members of the Congress, Hollywood royalty and much of the quality media in the United States. The Congressional Black Caucus began agitating energetically for a more sympathetic US policy. Randall Robinson, chairman of Tran

---

[11] Howard French, *New York Times*, 12 October 1993.

[12] S/PV 3293, 16 October 1993.

[13] This suggestion was rejected as 'not helpful' by the State Department. See article by Gwen Ifill, *New York Times*, 6 January 1994.

Africa, an organisation addressing foreign policy issues of interest to US blacks, launched a hunger strike on 12 April 1994, calling the administration's policy of forced repatriation of Haitian refugees 'cruel and . . . profoundly racist'.[14]

The Clinton administration gave in to the pressure. On 21 April it affirmed its support for Aristide, expressing commitment to secure the Dominican Republic–Haiti border against sanctions violations. On 8 May, after the White House announced that the United States would no longer automatically send boat-going Haitian refugees back to Haiti, Robinson ended his hunger strike. In his showdown with the administration, Aristide had won.

A new, stronger sanctions regime came into effect on 21 May 1994.[15] The Dominican Republic was pressured to accept a multination embargo-monitoring mission.[16] The United States imposed additional financial and travel sanctions against Haiti.[17] The endgame was nigh.

The Friends agreed that UNMIH's mandate could not, as in 1993, simply consist of training and engineering projects but had to envisage self-defence and security for senior Haitian officials and key installations. Although the United States had wanted a UN force, if only because the UN flag would be useful in attracting participation by a number of countries, Boutros-Ghali, believing that the UN had neither the resources nor the capacity to enforce Aristide's return, preferred a US-led multinational force (MNF). The UN's involvement in Rwanda, where its small force was overwhelmed by local violence only a month earlier, and its recent setbacks in Somalia, contributed to his caution.[18] In the end, the Friends agreed on a non-UN MNF under Chapter VII, followed, once a 'secure and stable environment' had been established, by a Chapter VI UN Peacekeeping Operation.

---

[14] Dispatch by Alan Elsner, *Reuters*, 12 April 1994.

[15] In its resolution MRE/Res. 6/94 of 9 June 1994, the OAS also called on member states to 'suspend financial transactions with Haiti'.

[16] The United States pulled together a Multinational Observer Group (MOG) of 88 members, the bulk American, with 15 Canadians and a contingent of Argentineans joining them. The MOG operated only from 30 August until the lifting of sanctions, 15 October 1994.

[17] President of the United States, *Prohibiting Certain Transactions with Respect to Haiti*, Executive Order 12920, 10 June 1994, www.archives.gov/federal_register/executive_orders/pdf/12920.pdf; US Department of Transportation, Order 94–6–28 of 17 June 1994. On 30 July, the last Air France flight departed from Port-au-Prince, virtually isolating the country by air; President of the United States, *Blocking Property of Certain Haitian Nationals*, Executive Order 12922, 22 June 1994, www.archives.gov/federal_register/executive_orders/pdf/12922.pdf.

[18] See *Yearbook of the United Nations* 1994, vol. 48, (The Hague: Martinus Nijhoff, 1995), pp. 281–317.

The UNSC adopted Resolution 940 on 31 July 1994, authorising the MNF. The adoption of Resolution 940 was groundbreaking in several respects. It marked the first time that the United States had sought UN authority for the use of force within its own hemisphere. The resolution was also unprecedented in authorising force to remove one regime and install another within a member state. By 15 September 1994, the Pentagon had recruited nineteen countries with a total of 2,000 troops to join a 20,000 strong US force within the MNF, including Argentina, Australia, Belgium, Bolivia, Israel, Jordan, the Netherlands, many Caribbean and Central American countries and the United Kingdom. However, Canada, Venezuela and France did not join in.

On 16 September in a political coup de théatre, former president, Jimmy Carter, led a US mission to Haiti in a final attempt to secure the departure of the Haitian military leadership. When word arrived on 18 September that US military aircraft were preparing to take off for Haiti, Cédras agreed to leave.[19] The MNF thereupon deployed smoothly, accompanied by the small UN team charged with monitoring it.[20] On 16 October the UNSC lifted sanctions and the blockade, the day after Aristide's return to Haiti.[21]

Peacekeeping

Following Aristide's return, the UN faced a number of new challenges in Haiti. The most pressing problem was that of institution building, in order to achieve a sustainable democracy, including support for credible elections to a bewildering range of national offices. Concerns existed over Aristide's likely course, with international players able to exert less leverage over him than they had previously: would he revert to a populist, possibly xenophobic, leadership or would he remain true to his rhetoric of national reconciliation? Both the MNF, now essentially occupying Haiti, and the UN, soon to take over from it, faced an uncertain relationship with Aristide, Parliament and the Haitian Armed Forces.

[19] Colin Powell, *My American Journey* (New York: Random House, 1995), p. 600; and Robert A. Pastor, 'The Clinton Administration and the Americas: The Postwar Rhythm and Blues', *Journal of Interamerican Studies and World Affairs* vol. 38, no. 4 (Winter 1996), p. 106.

[20] See Annex to *Letter from the Permanent Representative of the United States of America to the President of the Security Council*, S/1994/1148, 10 October 1994; see also UN Secretary-General, *Reports on the Question Concerning Haiti*, S/1994/1143, 28 September 1994, and S/1994/1180, 18 October 1994.

[21] Security Council Resolution 948, 15 October 1994.

Fears of violence in Haiti following Aristide's return initially proved unfounded. He worked to promote calm, going out of his way to consult members of the economic elite, who might have preferred a return to the old order, but could no longer count on the armed forces to secure this end.

In January 1995 the US MNF force commander certified a 'secure and stable environment'[22] and the hand-over from the MNF to UNMIH comprising 6,000 troops and almost 800 civilian police officers, took place in March.[23] UNMIH's mission originally outlined in Resolution 867 (1993) and revised in Resolution 940 (1994), was to provide security, stabilise the country, create a new police force and professionalise the Haitian armed forces.

The latter were eventually eliminated altogether by Aristide – against US wishes. Disbanding the army in the absence of serious efforts on disarmament and reintegration would later constitute a serious burden for peace building, providing an incentive for discontented soldiers to regroup as militias. (Indeed, the militias that plunged Haiti once again into chaos in early 2004 were largely comprised of well-armed former members of the Haitian army.)

One of the early challenges the UN faced in its peacekeeping mission was not linked to the adverse environment in Haiti but to the renewal of UNMIH's mandate. The problem arose from the fact that the Haitian government had indulged in public diplomacy with Taiwan. Aristide had sought and received $20 million at the time of the breakdown in cooperation with the International Monetary Fund (IMF) and the International Bank for Reconstruction and Development (IBRD) over his resistance to privatisation of several loss-making national enterprises. Also, Taiwan's vice-president was the most senior guest at the inauguration of René Préval, who succeeded Aristide in February 1996.

That same month the enraged Chinese government privately hinted that it was disinclined to support an extension of a smaller UNMIH. The Taiwan sub-text was clear to all. At the instigation of its Latin American and Caribbean members, the Non-Aligned Movement, with which the Chinese had traditionally asserted solidarity, expressed support for UNMIH extension. This pressure yielded some fruit but China ultimately consented only to 1,200 military and 300 police for a period of four months. The Secretariat and the Friends considered that

---

[22] Security Council Resolution 975, 30 January 1995.

[23] Annex II of the *Letter by Representatives of Countries Participating in the Multinational Force to the President of the Security Council*, S/1995/55, 19 January 1995; UN Secretary-General, *Reports on the Question Concerning Haiti*, S/1995/46, 17 January 1995, and S/1995/305, 13 April 1995.

UNMIH could not discharge its mandate with only 1,200 soldiers. Canada, which had, in principle, agreed to take over military command of the mission, refused to contemplate this without the personnel it believed necessary. It looked for a time as if the Friends would force China into a veto, a situation nobody wanted. At the last moment, on 28 February, Canada offered to dispatch 700 soldiers on its own account, to work alongside those 1,200 the Council could mandate with Chinese concurrence. Russia's position, meanwhile, had been to reduce UNMIH costs, through voluntary financing and other means. It was also seeking to exchange its support for UNMIH extension for authorisation of a UN PKO in Tajikistan. After this flare-up, the Friends remained under pressure from China and also Russia to downsize UNMIH and shut it down as soon as possible, in spite of a deteriorating security, economic and social situation there.

Peace building: from restored to fledgling democracy

The first peaceful transfer of power through what international observers agreed were free and fair elections in February 1996, constituted a significant step towards bringing democracy to Haiti, even though it was obvious to most observers that Préval, Aristide's handpicked successor, was largely dependent on him for his political legitimacy. The UNMIH operation itself, which ended in June 1996 was also seen as a success, which, in the highly positive final report of the US contingent in UNMIH was attributed to two main factors: (a) there was a clear mandate from the Security Council, facilitating effective planning and resource allocation; and (b) there was plenty of time to pull the force together (from 31 July 1994 to 31 March 1995) creating the conditions essential for a smooth transition between the multinational intervention force and the follow-on UN peacekeeping force.[24]

While UNMIH was a success on its own terms, the UN's broader peace-building efforts failed. Establishing a new police force that respected human rights and that was immune to politicisation proved a difficult and slow process. Disaffection among former army personnel and the continued existence of paramilitary networks kept the security situation fragile. And the archaic state of the judicial system and poor economic prospects were aggravated by a years-long political impasse that followed the legislative elections of April 1997.

[24] US Army Peacekeeping Institute, *Success in Peacekeeping: United Nations Mission in Haiti: The Military Perspective* (Carlisle Barracks, PA: US Army Peacekeeping Institute, 1996), p. 19.

The mandate of UNMIH's three follow-up missions (the UN Support Mission in Haiti (UNSMIH) from June 1996 to July 1997; the UN Transition Mission in Haiti (UNTMIH) from July 1997 to November 1997; and the UN Civilian Police Mission in Haiti (MIPONUH) from November 1997 to March 2000) became increasingly narrow. The central task, carried out by 300 international civilian police (CIVPOL), remained to assist the government of Haiti to establish and train an effective national police force. However, the successive UN missions were also encouraged to coordinate the activities by the UN system to promote institution building, national reconciliation and economic rehabilitation in Haiti.[25] At the same time the military peacekeeping dimension gradually receded and after the last UN military personnel was withdrawn upon the completion of UNTMIH's mandate in November 1997 the UN's presence on the ground was purely civilian.

To carry out the peace-building tasks the subsequent SRSGs were placed at the centre of an array of other international actors involved in Haiti, including MICIVIH, a number of UN specialised agencies and the International Financial Institutions. This structure was very much in line with the reform efforts initiated by the Secretary-General Annan in 1997 to integrate country-level work plans and bring UN operations in each nation 'under one flag'.[26] Giving the SRSG political backing and providing a link to the Security Council, the Group of Friends continued to be deeply involved, meeting with the SRSG on a weekly basis.[27]

The UN's task on the ground was made increasingly complicated by a succession of long constitutional crises that started when Haitian Prime Minister Rosny Smarth resigned in June 1997 in protest at the outcome of senatorial elections in April.[28] The dispute led to an open confrontation between the legislature and the executive and caused a huge rift between two once-aligned factions of former Aristide followers. Following Smarth's resignation, the Haitian parliament refused to approve Préval's appointments for replacement and the country was left without a prime minister for almost two years. The institutional crisis escalated further when a disagreement arose between the executive and the legislature over the length of the parliamentarians' terms and the date of new elections.

---

[25] This task was only spelled out once, in Resolution 1063, 28 June 1996, which declared the Council would support the role of the SRSG in this coordination effort.

[26] UN Secretary-General, *Renewing the United Nations: A Program for Reform*, A/51/950, 14 July 1997.

[27] Personal interview with Julian Harston, 5 February 2003.

[28] UN Secretary-General, *Report on the United Nations Civilian Police Mission in Haiti*, S/1998/144, 20 February 1998.

Throughout 1998, international efforts to induce the Haitians to find a solution to the impasse failed. A series of meetings between Haitian political leaders and civil society representatives held under the auspices of the International Peace Academy, an independent research organisation in New York, were as fruitless as were the démarches sent in June to President Préval by leading EU countries and the Group of Friends to convey the concern of the international community.[29] The Security Council, in March 1998 focused on process (free and fair elections) refusing to take sides in the bitter political polemics.[30]

Failure to resolve the crisis through negotiations led President Préval in January 1999 to declare the lawmakers' and most of the country's mayors' terms expired and to rule by decree. This move made him one of only nine elected officials in the whole of Haiti.[31] The achievements of 'Operation Restore Democracy' seemed to be lying in shambles.

The political crisis dealt a further blow to the country's already dismal economy.[32] In 1995, Haitian per capita Gross Domestic Product (GDP), at \$242.1, was by far the lowest in the Western Hemisphere.[33] Haiti ranked only 159 out of 174 in the 1998 UNDP's global Human Development Index.[34] The World Bank and others estimated that the sanctions regime might have cost the country up to 30 per cent of its GDP.[35] Investment failed to materialise given the uncertain political and security situation. What modest signs of life the economy showed in 1995 and in 1996 were due entirely to massive infusions of foreign assistance, but donors rapidly grew disenchanted with Aristide's political and economic management priorities.[36] The paralysis of the political process that caught Haiti in the following years further undermined international economic development efforts. Between 1995 and 1998 foreign aid payments dropped by about 35 per cent,[37] ostensibly due to limited absorptive capacity and non-approval of available loans by the

---

[29] UN Secretary-General, *Report on the United Nations Civilian Police Mission in Haiti*, S/1998/796, 24 August 1998.

[30] UN Secretary-General, *Report on the United Nations Civilian Police Mission in Haiti*, S/1998/434, 28 May 1998.

[31] Catherine Orenstein, 'The Roads Built in Haiti Only Go So Far', *The Washington Post*, 30 January 2000.

[32] The World Bank Group, *Haiti: The Challenges of Poverty Reduction* (Washington DC: World Bank Group, August, 1998).

[33] IBRD Haiti Assistance Strategy Document 15945-HA, 13 August 1996.

[34] *Ibid.*

[35] Richard Garfield, *The Impact of Economic Sanctions on Health and Well-being*, Relief and Rehabilitation Network Paper, no. 31 (London: Overseas Development Institute, November 1999).

[36] *Eleventh Report of the Multinational Force in Haiti*, S/1995/149, 21 February 1995.

[37] Economic and Social Council, *Report of the Ad-hoc Advisory Group on Haiti*, E/1999/103, 2 July 1999.

Haitian parliament but donor fatigue played a significant role.[38] By mid-1998, at least US $340 million in aid was held up by foreign exasperation at the lack of a trustworthy government.[39] A 1998 World Bank Report pointed to 'political instability, woefully poor governance, and corruption'[40] – in spite of the considerable international efforts. More recently, however, there have been hints that international development actors are sensitive to the appearance and reality that withholding loans in some respects played into Aristide's position that the international community was out to harm Haitians. Donor conditionality was lost on Aristide, who had portrayed meeting international conditions as moral corruption claiming that 'poverty is how we guarantee our freedom today.'[41]

The security situation also deteriorated as the political crisis proceeded. While in early 1998 the UN secretary-general could still report that 'most instances of lawlessness do not appear to have a political motivation',[42] the numerous murders and attempted murders of human rights activists, and high profile political figures or their relatives in 1999 made it clear that political violence was on the rise. Significantly, the UN trained Haitian National Police (HNP) initially performed surprisingly well in spite of the rising tensions and the police's political neutrality was remarkable in the Haitian context.[43] A 1998 USIS poll showed that 70 per cent of Haitians had confidence in the HNP as an institution.[44] However, against the backdrop of rising political tension in 1999 and 2000 there was increasing criticism of the police's violent performance during anti-government demonstrations and passivity in the face of often-brutal demonstrations by Aristide's supporters.[45] In addition, by November 1999, of the original 5,300 strong force, around 1,000 had been dismissed for corruption, drug offences and human rights abuses.[46]

---

[38] 'Help Wanted: One Government,' *The Economist*, 25 July 1998.

[39] *Ibid.*

[40] The World Bank Group, *Haiti*.

[41] Carol Williams, 'Road to Democracy in Haiti Hits an Impasse', *Los Angeles Times*, 26 June 2003.

[42] S/1998/144.

[43] UN Secretary-General, *Report on the United Nations Civilian Police Mission in Haiti*, S/1999/181, 19 February 1999.

[44] UN Secretary-General, *Report on the United Nations Civilian Police Mission in Haiti*, S/1998/1064, 11 November 1998.

[45] UN Secretary-General, *Reports on the United Nations Civilian Police Mission in Haiti to the Security Council and the General Assembly*, S/1999/908, 24 August 1999, and A/55/154, 17 July 2000.

[46] David Gonzalez, 'Civilian Police Force Brings New Problems to Haiti', *The New York Times*, 26 November 1999.

The UN's task of creating a police force from scratch took place in a particularly adverse environment. The HNP suffered from severe lack of resources.[47] The mushrooming drug trade, which according to one estimate increased fourfold in 1997–1998,[48] offered a potent incentive for corrupt behaviour. Deportation of 300 or so Haitian criminals annually from the United States did not help.[49] Finally, police reform was only insufficiently complemented by efforts to reform the penal and judicial system. The fact that in 1999, 88 per cent of the prison population was in pre-trial detention underscored the justice system's weakness.[50]

An exit strategy?

Throughout 1999, nervousness increased over the scheduled end of the UN's peacekeeping presence. General elections in Haiti were scheduled for the end of the year and the UN secretary-general and others feared that withdrawing MIPONUH during the election period might undermine security at a particular sensitive moment.[51] However, China had never overcome its reservations towards the mission and some Council members expected that the Chinese would veto any renewal.[52] Russia was also lukewarm at best and both countries had abstained when MIPONUH got extended the last time for a full-year term in November 1998.[53] However, had the United States thrown its weight behind an extension of MIPONUH, this might have been agreed.[54] But in the United States support for any involvement in Haiti was also gradually waning and Washington was increasingly frustrated with 'Mr. Préval's passivity and Mr. Aristide's duplicity'.[55] In

---

[47] UN Secretary-General, *Report on the United Nations Civilian Police Mission in Haiti*, S/1998/1064, 11 November 1998.

[48] 'Help Wanted: One Government', *The Economist*; S/1999/908; Serge Kovalski, 'Haitian Police Tinged by Thin Blue Line', *The Washington Post*, 23 October 1999. According to other estimates, the volume of cocaine into the US from Haiti rose from around 5 per cent of the annual US import in the early 1990s to 13 per cent in 1999, then fell back to 8 per cent in 2000 where it remained through 2003, see US Department of State, *International Narcotics Strategy Reports*, 2003, 1 March 2004.

[49] Serge Kovalski, 'Haitian Police'.

[50] Jamal Benomar, 'Rule of Law Technical Assistance in Haiti: Lessons Learned', World Bank Conference, St. Petersburg, 8–12 July 2002.

[51] UN Secretary-General, *Report of the Secretary-General on the United Nations Civilian Police Mission in Haiti*, S/1999/579, 18 May 1999.

[52] Barbara Crossette, 'UN Diplomats Search for Ways to Avoid Violence in Haiti,' *New York Times*, 27 August 1999.

[53] United Nations Daily Highlights, 25 November 1998, www.hri.org/news/world/undh/1998/98–11–25.undh.html.

[54] Confidential interviews.

[55] Larry Rohter, 'Political Feuds Rack Haiti: So Much for Its High Hopes,' *The New York Times*, 18 October 1998.

mid-1999, the Pentagon decided that the United States pull out the remaining 500 soldiers, who were performing nation-building tasks outside the UN mission, saying that it had been unable to create stability in Haiti.[56] In January 2000, almost all US soldiers left the country and thus ended an almost six-year military presence in Haiti.[57] Republicans in Congress used every opportunity to undermine the Clinton administration's efforts to support Haiti, for instance sitting on funding for MICIVIH, which was slated to start its phase out.[58] Moreover, Haitians themselves were unhappy with any continued foreign military presence on their soil, which reinforced the view of those Council members who began to see the situation in Haiti as more a matter of development than a question of international peace and security.[59]

In the face of these difficulties, the Group of Friends tried to move the issue to the General Assembly to ensure a continued UN presence in Haiti at a precarious time. On 17 December, the General Assembly mandated a drastically reduced follow-up mission, the Civilian Support Mission in Haiti (MICAH), which was to consolidate MIPONUH's meagre achievements.[60] With the withdrawal of MIPONUH in March 2000, a decade of Security Council involvement in Haiti came to an end – at least temporarily. The Friends, with strong support from the Italian president of the UN Economic and Social Council (ECOSOC), sought to place this UN organ in charge of overseeing the UN's continued peace-building efforts in Haiti, but the results were disappointing. Meeting only once a year and not being imbued with the power of mandating and ending a mission, ECOSOC was even less well positioned than the Council to manage a peace-building mission.[61]

In May 2000, general elections finally took place, after the polling date had been rescheduled four times. Although the vote itself was surprisingly peaceful it only resulted in further dissension over what was widely considered a flawed method of calculating the election results, and the electoral mission of the OAS quit in protest.

---

[56] Douglas Farah, 'General Calls for Pullout from Haiti; Region's Commander Says Instability Threatens Safety of US Troops on Island,' The Washington Post, 13 March 1999.

[57] David Gonzalez, 'Haiti's Paralysis Spreads as US Troops Pack Up', New York Times, 10 November 1999.

[58] Jennifer Bauduy, 'US Forces UN to reduce Haiti Human Rights mission,' Reuters, 16 June 1999.

[59] Interview with Michel Duval, former Deputy Permanent Representative of Canada to the United Nations, New York, 10 March 2003.

[60] General Assembly Resolution 54/193, A/RES/54/193, 18 February 2000.

[61] Interview with Michel Duval, 10 March 2003.

Just as Aristide was elected as president for a second time, Kofi Annan recommended the termination of MICAH when its mandate would expire in February 2001. He contended that the climate of instability made it inadvisable to extend the mission, but funding constraints certainly played a role.[62] Indeed, by March 2000 no voluntary contributions had been received for the MICAH trust fund and the mission had therefore begun its mandate on 16 March without any of the substantive staff necessary for the implementation of its mandate.[63] The pull-out came at a time when the 'human rights situation in Haiti was more worrying than at any time since the 1994 return to democracy'.[64] The UN then turned back the lead international role in addressing Haiti's political problems to the OAS.[65]

While the UN's withdrawal was premature relative to the scale of the challenge, particularly in retrospect, it is important to remember that the organisation's engagement in Haiti became increasingly unproductive. The case highlights the difficulty of interaction between UN and local actors. The secretary-general has self-critically pointed out, that the UN has 'failed to develop necessary and productive partnerships with the Haitian society at all levels'.[66] However, short of international trusteeship, UN peace-building efforts often stand or fall with the commitment and quality of local leaders. The UN's efforts were severely undermined by Aristide who turned out to be an increasingly unhelpful and unreliable partner, and by other Haitian political actors. Haiti's opposition also displayed a woefully uncompromising attitude, highlighting again Haiti's 'winner takes all' political culture. In that, Haiti stands in contrast to peace-building endeavours as East Timor, where the UN encountered credible and committed counterparts in leaders such as Xanana Gusmao.

Renewed crisis and intervention

Between 2000 and 2004, the political stalemate hardened, the economic situation remained dire, and the security and human rights situation

[62] Amnesty International, 'Haiti,' in *Amnesty International Annual Report* 2001.
[63] *UN Secretary-General, Report on the International Civilian Support Mission in Haiti*, A/55/154, 17 July 2000.
[64] Amnesty International, 'Haiti'.
[65] The OAS Secretariat, notably its much admired Assistant Secretary-General Luigi Einaudi, had devoted considerable time and attention to Haiti, regularly deploying missions to Port-au-Prince in an effort to produce common ground between President Aristide and his opponents in the *Convergence Démocratique*. Haiti was one of the most active topics at the extraordinary Summit of the Americas in January 2004, during which President Aristide undertook to schedule parliamentary elections.
[66] UN Secretary-General, *Report on Haiti*, S/2004/300, 16 April 2004.

continued to deteriorate. By late 2003, the OAS pressed for and Aristide agreed to the stationing of 600 international police in Haiti to stabilise the situation but the initiative was aborted after it became clear that donor countries had no intention of footing the bill.[67] By January 2004, President Aristide was reduced to governing by decree, with the term of the lower house of parliament expiring. Public protests and casualties mounted. Aristide's much feared militia supporters, the *Chimères*, elicited nightmare memories of the *Tontons Macoutes* under the Duvalier dictatorship.[68] Aristide latched onto a populist distraction, an attempt to extract from France compensation for the reparations that had been imposed on Haiti by Paris in the nineteenth century as indemnity for the dispossessed French colonists post-independence, but this quixotic venture did little to address Haiti's severe political crisis, and reinforced Aristide's diplomatic isolation.[69] Neither the president nor the opposition leadership appeared disposed to compromise with each other in the national interest, a familiar state of play in Haiti.

In early 2004, following the celebrations commemorating the bicentennial anniversary of Haiti's independence, anti-Aristide protests grew and became more violent. Armed conflict broke out in the city of Gonaïves and quickly spread to other cities. Local militia groups took control of provincial capitals and closed in on Port-au-Prince. Without an army, and with declining public support, the government was unable to resist the advance of well-armed groups. The HNP almost completely collapsed.

Amidst the turmoil, the OAS Council called upon the UN Security Council to 'take all the necessary and appropriate urgent measures to address the deteriorating situation in Haiti'[70] and CARICOM submitted a formal request to send troops to 'end the spiral of violence'.[71] However, there was no appetite in the Council to put the deeply compromised Aristide regime on life support. Last minute mediation offers and diplomatic initiatives spearheaded by CARICOM and supported by the OAS, the United States, France, Canada and the Bahamas were rejected by the opposition, which didn't see much to be gained from

---

[67] International Crisis Group, 'A New Chance for Haiti?', in *ICG Latin America/Caribbean Report*, no. 10, (Brussels: ICG, 18 November 2004), p. 14.

[68] 'Des heurts entre partisans du président Aristide et opposents ont perturbé le bicentenaire d'Haiti: Le président sud-africain, Thabo Mbeki, était le seul chefs d'état présent aux cérémonies...', Agence France Presse text in *Le Monde*, 3 January 2004.

[69] Jose de Cordoba, 'Haiti Seeks its Fortune in a Nineteenth Century Pact with the French: Impoverished Country Demands Restitution for Gunboat Diplomacy', *Wall Street Journal Europe*, 2–4 January 2004.

[70] OAS Permanent Council Resolution 862, CP/Res. 862 (1401/04), 26 February 2004.

[71] International Crisis Group, 'A New Chance for Haiti?', p. 16.

negotiating with the crumbling Aristide government.[72] Soon it became clear that Aristide's forces could not stem the tide. Overcoming their disagreements over the 2003 Iraq crisis, and disregarding the fact that Aristide was democratically elected, the United States and France joined forces to exert pressure on Aristide to step down. Ten years after the United States brought Aristide back to power through the threat of military force, it was Washington that played an important role in removing him. Haiti had gone full circle.

On 29 February 2004, Aristide departed from Haiti for exile on a US aircraft, later claiming that he was 'kidnapped' by US forces, a far-fetched allegation that the US government denied. That same day, in an instance of *déja-vu*, the UNSC in Resolution 1529 authorised the deployment of a 3,000 strong multinational interim force (MIF) composed of US, French, Canadian and Chilean troops, which, three months later was replaced by a UN peacekeeping mission, the UN Stabilisation Mission in Haiti (MINUSTAH). Depressingly, French and US activism in removing Aristide from power was not matched by a willingness to stay heavily involved to pick up the pieces. Instead, both Paris and Washington, whose forces were already stretched thin by their respective involvements in Iraq and Côte d'Ivoire, insisted on scaling back militarily at the time of the handover from the MIF to its UN successor force. By the end of June 2004, the US and French forces had left Haiti.[73] On a happier note, Latin American countries, Brazil in the lead, came forward with significant offers of peacekeepers, for the first time in a UN operation in the Western Hemisphere. A distinguished Chilean, Juan Gabriel Valdés, was appointed Special Representative of the UN secretary-general and mandated to coordinate international efforts to support a transition back to electoral democracy.

As in the early 1990s a Friends Group emerged in March 2005, composed of the main players on the ground: the United States, France, Brazil, Chile and Canada. Given that all but Canada also had a seat in the Security Council, this group served as the Council's drafting committee on Haiti, holding the pen on the original texts of resolutions and presidential statements. Unlike in the 1990s, however, this group operated mostly on the expert level and did not emerge as a high-level coherent actor with the aim of steering international action *vis-à-vis* Haiti.

---

[72] S/2004/300.
[73] UN Secretary-General, *Report on Haiti*, S/2004/698, 30 August 2004.

Rebuilding a failed state

The UN was saddled with challenges far more daunting than in 1995. With widespread poverty and hunger, record unemployment rates, spiking crime and gang violence, and among the world's highest corruption levels, many Haitians have lost hope for a better future after ten years of failed peace-building efforts. Already adverse humanitarian circumstances were aggravated when a series of tropical storms hit Haiti later that year, burying entire cities in mud killing thousands. Moreover, the 1994 intervention brought back to power a democratically elected leader who at the time enjoyed widespread support among Haiti's population. By contrast, his successor in 2004, Gérard Latortue,[74] an international technocrat installed to govern the country until elections were held in 2006, never enjoyed such legitimacy and lacked the political support to carry out much needed political and economic reforms. Caribbean leaders, furious over the course of events in Haiti seen by them and many others as undermining democratic order in their region, demanded a UN-led investigation into the events leading to Aristide's ouster (an initiative that was successfully blocked by the United States and France) and never granted recognition to the transitional government in Port-au-Prince. Not surprisingly, Haitian support for the international presence seems much weaker than it was in the 1990s.

Moreover, the UN mission is haunted by Aristide's flawed dismantling of the Haitian army in 1995, which weakened state authority and filled the slums with disgruntled and well-armed former soldiers. This was compounded by the failure of intervening forces systematically to disarm state security forces and militias, first after reinstating President Aristide in 1994 and later, after his removal in 2004.[75] Haiti's fledgling police force, whose strength shrank from 5,000 prior to the crisis to merely 2,500 during the violent uprising, are sometimes outnumbered and generally outgunned by the well-armed militias and gangs (estimated to be around 25,000 strong) that continue to take advantage of the security vacuum prevalent in Haiti today.[76] Belatedly, the Haitian government, with the UN help, has

---

[74] While, technically, Aristide's successor is President Boniface Alexandre, it is in interim Prime Minister Latortue that political power now resides with the president only carrying out ceremonial functions.

[75] Eirin Mobbekk, 'Enforcement of Democracy in Haiti', Paper for the Political Studies Association; UK Fiftieth Annual Conference, 10–13 April 2000, London; Rachel Stohl, 'Haiti's Big Threat: Small Arms,' *Christian Science Monitor*, 23 March 2004, www.csmonitor.com/2004/0323/p09s02-coop.html.

[76] S/2004/300 and S/2004/698.

started to address these problems, initiating efforts in October 2004 to reintegrate former officers of the Haitian army.[77]

Against this unpromising background, it is clear to all that there are no quick fixes and no plausible early exit scenario.[78]

Indeed, the UN secretary-general in early 2004 asserted that to induce sustainable stability and economic growth in Haiti a much more interventionist and longer-term engagement was required than proved possible during the 1990s. The secretary-general's special advisor for Haiti at the time, John Reginald Dumas, called for a twenty-year peacekeeping presence in Haiti, which he deemed necessary to (re-) establish the rule of law.[79]

The Security Council in Resolution 1542 of 30 April 2004, equipped MINUSTAH with a chapter VII mandate, authorised force levels of 1,622 Civilian Police and over 6,700 troops (still not fully deployed by December 2004)[80] and tasked it, *inter alia*, to carry out police reform, to assist in comprehensive disarmament, demobilisation and reintegration measures, and to promote the political transition process. Yet, the Security Council continues to rely on distressingly short (and thus unrealistic) mandates, placing mandate renewals at the mercy of notoriously fickle Council politics. This hardly inspires confidence in the Council's long-term commitment. Further, as the experience of previous missions has shown, short mandates prevent missions from recruiting highly qualified experts, since most such experts were unwilling to take on short-term assignment.[81]

In particular re-establishing an effective police force seems a daunting task that will take time and considerable resources. The UN Secretariat estimates that such a force would need to be at least 10,000 strong to maintain order;[82] independent experts put the figure twice as high.[83] Yet, as of early January 2005, MINUSTAH has been only involved in the training of around 1,000 officers.

---

[77] UN Secretary-General, *Report on the UN Stabilization Mission in Haiti*, UN Doc., S/2004/908, 18 November 2004.

[78] S/2004/300; David Cloud, 'Haiti to Delay Vote Until Next Year,' *Wall Street Journal*, 6 April 2004.

[79] Bill Varner and Glenn Hall, 'UN Peacekeepers Should Stay in Haiti for 20 Years, Envoy Says', *Bloomberg*, 30 March 2004.

[80] By early November 2004, six months into the mission, the strength of both troops and civilian police stood barely at two-thirds of the number authorised by the Security Council. See S/2004/908.

[81] Lama Khouri-Padova, *Haiti: Lessons Learned*, UN Department of Peacekeeping Operations, Best Practices Unit Discussion Paper, March 2004, http://pbpu.unlb.org/pbpu/library/Haiti per cent20lessons per cent20learned per cent2030 per cent20March per cent202004 per cent20final.pdf.

[82] S/2004/300.

[83] Tim Weiner and Lydia Polgreen, 'Facing New Crisis, Haiti again Relies on US Military to Keep Order,' *The New York Times*, 7 March 2004.

In one hopeful sign, many Latin American countries have offered troops for MINUSTAH with Brazil, for the first time and perhaps in a bid to strengthen its claim to a permanent seat on the Security Council, taking the lead and providing the mission's largest contingent. By contrast, in July 1994, Brazil was far more cautious on the Council and had abstained when the Council adopted Resolution 940 to use force to reinstall Aristide, arguing that Brazil's constitution and political traditions precluded support for military intervention. In another 'first', China, signalling a willingness to play a somewhat bigger role in UN peacekeeping and putting aside earlier hostility towards UN presence in Haiti, contributed a contingent of specially trained riot police to the UN's mission. Finally, a donors' conference in July 2004 yielded pledges of $1.3 billion, although most of these promises have yet to be cashed in.[84]

However, repeated outbursts of unrest and violence from September 2004 onwards seriously called into question the UN's and the transitional government's ability to induce stability in Haiti.[85] Independent observers on the ground warned of armed gangs developing 'into either coherent insurgencies as in Colombia or formidable war-lord-led groups along the Somali model'.[86] MINUSTAH responded by carrying out a series of robust raids against militia leaders residing in the capital's slums. This reflected a generally welcome new willingness of UN forces to violently confront spoilers not only in Haiti but also in the Democratic Republic of the Congo, in Cote d' Ivoire and Sierra Leone.

Looking from afar, it is also hard to discern a political strategy that promises to bridge the paralysing divides in Haitian politics and society. Having been repeatedly postponed, parliamentary and presidential elections finally took place in early February 2006. These cannot serve as an exit strategy. Rather, they need to be viewed as merely a first step in a long process of helping to establish legitimate, sustainable government. Unfortunately, in the recent past, elections in Haiti have mainly served to polarise political life and disputed election results have repeatedly triggered political crises.

As in the 1990s, international efforts in 2004 and 2005 failed to address the lack of consensus between the country's different sectors on fundamental social and economic goals and on the means for achieving

---

[84] Alex Halperin, 'Haiti Wins Donors' Help with Reconstruction Plans', *Financial Times*, 21 July 2004. See also 'Operation Deep Pockets', *The Economist*, 18 December 2004, pp. 93–94.

[85] International Crisis Group, 'A New Chance for Haiti?', p. 7.

[86] Ibid., p. 23.

them.[87] To the distress of the Group of Friends, Aristide remains the most potent political force within Haiti, and the re-ascendence to the presidency of his former close associate René Préval might spell a potential further challenge to international assistance.

Conclusions

What explains Security Council involvement, disengagement and renewed intervention in Haiti? In the early 1990s, the Security Council's involvement in Haiti was strongly driven by the domestic interest of the United States to contain refugee flows to Florida. US dominance of the issue within the Council has been moderated by the Group of Friends and, occasionally, by interested Latin American countries such as Brazil. But once Washington loses interest, as it did in the late 1990s when its hostility to Aristide increased, there is little these other countries could do to sustain peacekeeping or credible peace building in Haiti. The willingness of China in 1996 to disrupt its normally close relations with the non-aligned movement, and to inconvenience the UN, over Haitian ties to Taiwan also demonstrates the importance of national interests as the prime motivator for Council members.

The Security Council ended its involvement in Haiti in 2000 because the United States had grown progressively frustrated with Haiti's leadership and decided to cut its (short term) losses. The Council passed the baton on to the UN General Assembly and ECOSOC, whose follow-up mission was atrophied by the lack of voluntary financial contributions. In 2001 the UN abandoned the country altogether without a strategy for the future, leaving the OAS once again in the lead. However, in spite of creditable efforts by the OAS secretariat, it was unable seriously to influence events on the ground, which continued quietly to deteriorate.[88] The new engagement of the OAS in the promotion of democracy, further to the Santiago Declaration, was severely tested by Haiti's serial convulsions, and the OAS, though shrinking from association with the use of force, has often performed well. Its joint sponsorship with the UN of MICIVIH played a valuable role at the worst point of the crisis and beyond in defence of human rights.

---

[87] Chetan Kumar, 'Sustainable Peace as Sustainable Democracy: The Experience of Haiti', *Politik und Gesellschaft Online*, April 1999, www.fcs.de/ipg/ipg4_99/artkumar.htm.

[88] See Lotta Hagman, 'Lessons Learned: Peacebuilding in Haiti,' in *International Peace Academy Conference Report*, 23–24 January 2002 (New York: IPA); See also Peter Dailey, 'Haiti: The Fall of the House of Aristide', *New York Review of Books*, vol. 50, no. 4 (13 March 2003), pp. 41–47; and his 'Haiti's Betrayal', *New York Review of Books*, vol. 50, no. 5 (27 March 2003), pp. 43–46.

When the Council re-engaged in 2004, the United States was again the main driver. However, US activism was motivated less by the prospect of thousands of boat people reaching the shores of the United States than the desire to prevent large-scale armed clashes and to halt the process of state failure that risked turning Haiti into a major hub of the international cocaine trade. France, resenting Aristide's populist attempt to extract reimbursement of nineteenth century (admittedly odious) debt payments from its former colonial master and in its own spheres of influence every bit as interventionist as the United States is on a global level, actively reinforced US policy.

What other conclusions arise from the Council's experience with Haiti over the past fifteen years?

First, the UN's growing ambivalence towards mandatory economic sanctions was reinforced by the Haiti experience in 1993 and thereafter. The Haiti sanctions policy exacted a significant humanitarian toll and produced lasting economic costs that the UN and other multilateral actors were later unable to counteract. Adding insult to injury, the sanctions significantly enriched the de facto regime. Unfortunately, such is the aversion to the use of force that the Security Council is more inclined towards imposition of sanctions, even draconian ones, than towards credible threats of military force. Yet against a relatively weak adversary, the threat of force would have stood a much better chance of bringing the de facto regime to heel after the coup.

Second, the tendency of the Council in addressing conflict to aim for a cease-fire followed by neutral mediation of differences may not be the appropriate course in every instance. Both Aristide and Cédras undermined the Governor's Island Agreement, which they signed under great international pressure. Had the agreement been fully implemented, a showdown between the military and Aristide, with unpredictable results, would probably only have been postponed.

Third, the UN's financial constraints in Haiti eventually became crippling. MICIVIH's modest funding requirements became problematic as early as 1996 and the mission terminated for lack of funding in 2000. UNMIH's follow-on missions were not supported by reliable funding arrangements and were saddled with impractically short mandates. 'The fact that these had to be renegotiated every few months...hampered UNMIH's ability to gain the initiative or to maintain momentum' *vis-à-vis* the Haitian parties.[89] The Secretariat

---

[89] Mission of the Netherlands to the United Nations, 'No Exit without Strategy', background paper for an open debate in the Security Council, New York, October 2000.

commented on 'leaving the peacekeeping operation as an insufficient single prong in what was intended to be a multi-pronged strategy,' seriously short-changing peace-building objectives.[90]

Fourth, and most importantly, the Haiti case suggests that the UN remains woefully unprepared, through its intergovernmental decision-making and funding approaches, as well as in its institutional culture, to lead effectively on medium and long-term peace-building efforts. An even more sweeping criticism of the UN's peace-building activities is that they failed to address the lack of consensus between the country's different sectors on fundamental social and economic goals and on the means for achieving them.[91] It is tempting to blame the international actors for the sorry outcome. But the Haiti case demonstrates that local actors matter critically in the success of UN mediation and peace-building activities. The international community supported to the hilt Jean-Bertrand Aristide's restoration to power in circumstances still unique to international relations. The UN could certainly have done better in many respects, but this is one case in which the UN was able to summon not only the political will but also very significant resources necessary to help the Haitians help themselves. It is also a case in which the international community was fairly well coordinated both politically and in terms of technical and developmental assistance.[92] The UN was poorly repaid. Adhering to established patterns of Haitian political life, Aristide and his opponents reverted to 'winner-take-all' strategies precluding compromise or any serious commitment to national interests. In these circumstances, the conditionalities donor governments and institutions attempted to use as leverage for better policies failed miserably. International interveners have not developed alternative strategies. The Haitian political community has squandered not only considerable international goodwill but also the huge resources poured into its stabilisation in the years 1994–1997. Myopic, self-serving Haitian leadership has plunged the country back into a crisis both familiar and desperately sad.

It is unclear whether the newly elected government of René Préval can, with UN and OAS support, achieve the degree of political consensus on democratic process necessary for Haiti to move towards stability. It is also hard to predict how international actors will react to

---

[90] UN Secretary-General, *No Exit without Strategy: Security Council Decision-Making and the Closure or Transition of United Nations Peacekeeping Operations*, S/2001/394, 20 April 2001.

[91] Chetan Kumar, *'Sustainable Peace as Sustainable Democracy: The Experience of Haiti,' Politik und Gesellschaft Online*, (April 1999), www.fes.de/ipg/ipg4_99/artkumar.htm.

[92] Hagman, *Lessons Learned*, p. 5.

further upheavals in Haiti. Haitians of all stripes, resident in country or in Haiti's impressive diaspora, must assume responsibility for their country's future rather than hoping that the UN can solve the problem for them. Their engagement is a sine qua non condition of future multilateral success in Haiti. This factor is now crystal clear to all international interveners and to many Haitians. What remains is to witness a shift in the domestic politics of Haiti from posturing to political entrepreneurship in the public interest. May we see this soon!

7   East Timor

Simon Chesterman

On 20 May 2002, UN Secretary-General Kofi Annan, joined East Timorese President Xanana Gusmão and the heads of state from over a dozen countries to lower the United Nations (UN) flag and raise the Timorese one. Four months later, Timor-Leste became the 191st member state of the UN.

East Timor presents two contradictory stories in the history of UN peace operations. On the one hand, it is an outstanding success. In two and a half years, a territory that had been reduced to ashes after the 1999 referendum on independence held peaceful elections and celebrated independence. On the other hand, however, East Timor can be seen as a series of missed opportunities and wastage. Of the UN Transitional Administration's annual budget of over $500 million, only around one-tenth actually reached the East Timorese. At one point, $27 million was spent annually on bottled water for the international staff – approximately half the budget of the embryonic Timorese government, and money that might have paid for water purification plants to serve both international staff and locals well beyond the life of the mission. More could have been done, or done earlier to reconstruct public facilities. This did not happen in part because of budgetary restrictions on UN peacekeeping operations that, to the Timorese, were not simply absurd but insulting. Such problems were compounded by coordination failures, the displacement of local initiatives by bilateral donor activities and the lack of any significant private sector investment. When East Timor (now Timor-Leste) became independent, it did so with the dubious distinction of becoming the poorest country in Asia.[1] Unemployment remains high, literacy remains low and the foundations for a stable and democratic society are untested.

The powers exercised by the UN in this transition to independence were extraordinary. Though the UN had assumed quasi-governmental

---

[1] 'Getting Ready for Statehood', *Economist*, 13 April 2002. This chapter draws upon passages in Simon Chesterman, *You, the People: The United Nations, Transitional Administration, and State-Building* (Oxford: Oxford University Press, 2004).

authority on a number of previous occasions, from limited responsibilities in Cambodia (1992–1993), to temporary administrative control
of Eastern Slavonia in Croatia (1996–1998) and effective control of
Kosovo (1999–), this was the first time that the UN found itself
effectively in control of a country. In addition to civilian and military
responsibilities, UN officials effectively negotiated treaties on behalf of
the Timorese. Such an exercise of power was controversial and may be
exceptional. The Brahimi Report on UN Peace Operations, issued less
than a year after the establishment of the UN Transitional Administration in East Timor (UNTAET), observed that there was 'evident
ambivalence' among member states and within the UN Secretariat
concerning such operations. Nevertheless, the report went on, the
circumstances that demand transitional administration are likely to
recur:

Thus, the Secretariat faces an unpleasant dilemma: to assume that transitional
administration is a transitory responsibility, not prepare for additional missions
and do badly if it is once again flung into the breach, or to prepare well and be
asked to undertake them more often because it is well prepared. Certainly, if the
Secretariat anticipates future transitional administrations as the rule rather than
the exception, then a dedicated and distinct responsibility centre for those tasks
must be created somewhere within the United Nations system. In the interim,
[the Department of Peacekeeping Operations] has to continue to support this
function.[2]

This was not the subject of any recommendation and was not addressed
in the secretary-general's response to the report.[3]

   This chapter outlines the background to UN involvement in East
Timor before examining the five key challenges that confronted the
transitional administration during its twenty-nine-month period of
governing East Timor: ensuring peace and security, governing the territory on a day-to-day basis, laying the foundations for the rule of law,
beginning the process of development, and overseeing a constitutional
process that would provide an exit strategy.

Background to the UN operation

The origins of the complex role played by the UN in East Timor lie in
Indonesia's 1975 invasion of the former Portuguese colony. Since the

---

[2] *Report of the Panel on United Nations Peace Operations* (Brahimi Report), A/55/305–S/
2000/809, 21 August 2000, www.un.org/peace/reports/peace_operations, para. 78.
[3] *Report of the Secretary-General on the Implementation of the Report of the Panel on United
Nations Peace Operations*, A/55/502, 20 October 2000.

purported annexation of East Timor by Indonesia was never explicitly recognised by the vast majority of governments (Australia's recognition in 1978 was a notable exception), it is questionable as to what legitimate interest Indonesia had in the territory's transition to independence.[4] In practice, however, East Timor's independence only became possible following the replacement of Indonesian President Suharto by B. J. Habibie, who offered to hold a plebiscite on the territory's future. An agreement dated 5 May 1999, between Indonesia and Portugal (as the administering power of a non-self-governing territory), provided for a 'popular consultation' to be held on East Timor's future on 8 August of the same year.[5]

The date of the consultation fell squarely in the middle of Indonesia's first presidential elections in 44 years. Crucially, the agreement left security arrangements in the hands of Indonesia's military – the very forces that had actively suppressed the East Timorese population for 24 years. On 11 June 1999, the Security Council established the UN Mission in East Timor (UNAMET) to organise and conduct the consultation.[6] A month later, with the consultation postponed until the end of August, the secretary-general reported to the Council that 'the situation in East Timor will be rather delicate as the Territory prepares for the implementation of the result of the popular consultation, whichever it may be'.[7] Despite threats and intimidation, 98 per cent of registered East Timorese voted in the referendum, with 78.5 per cent choosing independence.[8]

It is still difficult to understand the violence that consumed the island in the weeks following the vote. What is confusing is that unrest before the popular consultation was both sporadic and, it seemed, controllable. When pressure was placed on the Indonesian Armed Forces (TNI), the

---

[4] See Antonio Cassese, *Self-Determination of Peoples: A Legal Reappraisal*, Hersch Lauterpacht Memorial Lectures (Cambridge: Cambridge University Press, 1995), pp. 223–30.

[5] *Agreement on the Question of East Timor, Indonesia–Portugal*, S/1999/513, done at New York, 5 May 1999, Annex I; *Agreement Regarding the Modalities for the Popular Consultation of the East Timorese Through a Direct Ballot, Indonesia–Portugal Secretary-General of the United Nations*, done at New York, 5 May 1999, S/1999/513, Annex II; *East Timor Popular Consultation (Security Provisions), Indonesia–Portugal Secretary-General of the United Nations*, S/1999/513, done at New York, 5 May 1999, Annex III.

[6] Security Council Resolution 1246, 11 June 1999.

[7] *Question of East Timor: Report of the Secretary-General*, S/1999/862, 9 August 1999, para. 5.

[8] The East Timorese were asked to vote on the following question: 'do you accept the proposed special autonomy for East Timor within the unitary state of the Republic of Indonesia? Or, Do you reject the proposed special autonomy for East Timor, leading to East Timor's separation from Indonesia?' See generally Ian Martin, *Self-Determination in East Timor: The United Nations, the Ballot, and International Intervention*, International Peace Academy Occasional Paper Series (Boulder CO: Lynne Rienner, 2001).

limited instances of intimidation stopped. Moreover, there was little trouble on the day of the vote itself. If the intention had been to prevent East Timor's independence, this could have been achieved easily by killing a few UN volunteers, or burning down some of the buildings used by expatriates.

With the benefit of hindsight, two key factors were at work. The first was that most of the Indonesian cabinet, relying on remarkably bad intelligence, genuinely believed that in a free vote the Timorese would choose to remain within Indonesia (or, perhaps, that the result would be close enough to dispute). Officials at the UN and in concerned governments anticipated precisely the opposite result, but were constrained from planning openly for independence by the delicate political balance that had made a vote possible in the first place. This set the stage for a very swift transition, with little planning for either the logistics of independence or management of the inevitable political crisis it would cause within Indonesia. The second factor was the erroneous assumption on the part of most international actors that the Indonesian government and military could be assumed to work in concert. Quite apart from the dubious reliance placed on Indonesia's occupying forces to maintain 'peace and security' during the vote, there appears to have been great reluctance within the TNI to leave the battleground – sometimes described as Indonesia's Vietnam – as anything other than scorched earth. Many of the Timorese, by contrast, appear to have known precisely what was going to happen. Across the island there were reports of entire towns packing their belongings and leaving in anticipation of the violence to come. One UN observer in Maliana reported a day before the vote that his entire town had disappeared, only to find people streaming back from the hillsides from 4 a.m. to queue up, vote and depart once more.[9]

Much of the violence took place under the direction of the Indonesian military, if not the government itself.[10] At the time there was great reluctance within the international community to intervene, despite the

---

[9] See generally Paul Hainsworth and Stephen McCloskey (eds.), *The East Timor Question: The Struggle for Independence from Indonesia* (London: I.B. Tauris, 2000); Damien Kingsbury (ed.), *Guns and Ballot Boxes: East Timor's Vote for Independence* (Clayton, Australia: Monash Asia Institute, 2000); and United Nations, *The United Nations and East Timor: Self-Determination Through Popular Consultation* (New York: UN Department of Public Information, 2000).

[10] The Security Council mission to Dili and Jakarta included analysis by UNAMET that the violence was 'nothing less than a systematic implementation of a "scorched earth" policy in East Timor, under the direction of the Indonesian military': *Report of the Security Council Mission to Jakarta and Dili, 8 to 12 September 1999*, S/1999/976, 14 September 1999, Annex, para. 1.

apparent double standard given the international response to the situation in Kosovo only months earlier. There was no legal basis for requiring Indonesia's consent to such an operation, but as a practical matter, it was clear that no form of enforcement action would have been possible without it. A fortuitously timed meeting of the Asia Pacific Economic Cooperation Forum (APEC) in Auckland, New Zealand, enabled political and economic pressure to be brought to bear on Indonesia, and Resolution 1264 (1999) welcomed a 12 September statement by the Indonesian president that expressed the readiness of Indonesia to accept an international force under the auspices of the UN.[11] Australia – driven by domestic political pressure, concern about a refugee crisis and some measure of contrition for its previous policies on East Timor – offered to lead a multinational force under unified command and on 15 September the Security Council, acting under Chapter VII, authorised the International Force in East Timor (INTERFET) to 'take all necessary measures' in achieving three tasks: 'to restore peace and security in East Timor, to protect and support UNAMET in carrying out its tasks and, within force capabilities, to facilitate humanitarian assistance operations'.[12]

INTERFET arrived in Dili on 20 September 1999; by the end of the month, force headquarters were operational in the capital's burnt-out public library and 4,000 troops had been deployed. Over a period of six weeks, INTERFET extended its presence to every district, following an 'oil spot' strategy of expanding operations from secured locations. The strategy was criticised for being overly cautious, but force commander Major General Peter Cosgrove justified his caution on the basis of risks to his troops as well as to regional confidence in the operation. At its peak, INTERFET comprised 11,000 troops from 22 countries, of which around 5,000 were Australian. In its five-month deployment there were no battle fatalities and only two non-battle-related deaths.[13]

On 25 October, the Security Council passed Resolution 1272 (1999), establishing UNTAET. The resolution, also adopted under Chapter VII, mandated UNTAET to provide security and maintain law and order throughout the territory of East Timor; to establish an effective administration; to assist in the development of civil and social services; to ensure the coordination and delivery of humanitarian assistance, rehabilitation of humanitarian assistance, rehabilitation and

---

[11] Security Council Resolution 1264, 15 September 1999, preamble. See Martin, *Self-Determination*, pp. 106–7.
[12] Security Council Resolution 1264 (1999), para. 3.
[13] Michael G. Smith, *Peacekeeping in East Timor*, International Peace Academy Occasional Paper Series (Boulder, CO: Lynne Rienner, 2003), pp. 45–8.

development assistance; to support capacity-building for self-government; and to assist in the establishment of conditions for sustainable development. UNTAET was established with a governance and public administration component, a civilian police component of up to 1,640 civilian police, and a UN peacekeeping force of up to 8,950 troops and 200 military observers. Humanitarian assistance and rehabilitation components were incorporated within the structures of the transitional administration. Sergio Vieira de Mello, fresh from setting up the UN Interim Administration Mission in Kosovo (UNMIK), commenced duties as Special Representative of the UN secretary-general and transitional administrator in Dili on 17 November. To finance the transitional activities of the transitional administration, a donors' meeting on East Timor, convened in Tokyo in December 1999, pledged more than $520 million in assistance.

Peace and security

In the wake of the post-referendum violence in East Timor in September 1999, INTERFET had to decide how to respond to denunciations of alleged former militia. Such matters formally remained in the hands of the Indonesian police and judiciary, though this was on paper only. It was clear that this would soon become the responsibility of UNTAET and an East Timorese judiciary, but these had yet to be established on the ground. INTERFET's Security Council mandate was silent on its responsibility or authority to carry out arrests. The Council resolution did, however, stress the responsibility of individuals committing violations of international humanitarian law and demand that they be brought to justice.[14] INTERFET ultimately decided that its broad mandate to restore peace and security could encompass arrests of individuals accused of committing serious offences – failure to do so might encourage Timorese people to take the law into their own hands.[15] INTERFET's commander therefore issued a Detainee Ordinance, creating various categories of prisoners. INTERFET troops were authorised to detain persons suspected of committing a serious offence prior to 20 September, and were required to deliver them to the Force Detention Centre in Dili within 24 hours. If a detainee was held for more than 96 hours, he or she was provided the grounds

[14] Security Council Resolution 1264 (1999), para. 1.
[15] See, for example, *First Periodic Report on the Operations of the Multinational Force in East Timor*, S/1999/1025, 4 October 1999, Annex, para. 23; and Michael Ware, 'Murder Charge Bolsters INTERFET Get-Tough Policy', *The Australian* (Sydney), 17 December 1999.

for being held, together with material considered by the commander of INTERFET as the basis for continuing detention. Defending officers were available to assist the detainee to show why he or she should not be so held, and a number of detainees were released because of insufficiency of evidence. The INTERFET Detention Centre handed over 25 detainees to UNTAET Civilian Police and the East Timorese judiciary on 14 January 2000.[16]

A persistent, if slightly unfair, criticism of UNTAET is that it relied too greatly on the experiences of the immediately preceding operation in Kosovo. The Department of Peacekeeping Operations assumed control over UNTAET following an internal turf battle with the Department of Political Affairs, which had overseen the 5 May agreement and had been the lead agency throughout the UNAMET referendum. Much as the International Criminal Tribunal for Rwanda was substantially modelled on the Hague Tribunal for the Former Yugoslavia, UNTAET drew directly upon the institutional and personal knowledge of UNMIK. The planning staff was, it seems, told to 're-jig' the Kosovo plan for East Timor; Vieira de Mello himself came from a position as head of UNMIK, bringing many core personnel with UNMIK backgrounds.[17]

The criticism is unfair because when the UN entered East Timor it was reasonable to assume that it was entering an area of potential conflict. Kosovo represented the most relevant experience in pacifying territory that had come under UN control, where a deeply polarised society faced the continued threat of violence. In Kosovo, the failure to contain and demobilise the Kosovo Liberation Army (KLA) had caused problems that continued to plague the mission. Building upon previous experiences in the former Yugoslavia, the result was that centralised control and neutrality dominated the mandate and initial activities of UNTAET personnel.

The problem, rather, was that the mandate and mindset, once established, was slow to change with the reality on the ground. It was quickly established that the violence in East Timor had been caused by militia, supported and organised by the Indonesian military. When INTERFET arrived, many of the militia had left East Timor. By 26 January 2000, the UN secretary-general was able to report that internal

---

[16] *Report of the Secretary-General on the United Nations Transitional Administration in East Timor*, S/2000/53, 26 January 2000, para. 45.

[17] Joel C. Beauvais, 'Benevolent Despotism: A Critique of UN State-Building in East Timor', *New York University Journal of International Law and Politics*, vol. 33, no. 4 (2001), pp. 1101–79. See also Jarat Chopra, '*The UN's Kingdom of East Timor*', *Survival*, vol. 42, no. 3 (2000), pp. 27–40; and [Australian] Department of Foreign Affairs and Trade, *East Timor in Transition 1998–2000: An Australian Policy Challenge* (Canberra: Brown and Wilton, 2000).

security had greatly improved: 'For most people, there is now no threat of violence and they can circulate freely.'[18] UNTAET was, therefore, established first and foremost as a peacekeeping operation. But with the evacuation of most of the militia and the arrival of over 8,000 troops, the demands of security were supplanted by demands for political and economic development in preparation for independence. Both were hindered by the initial choices made in New York in 1999. A further difference worth noting is that the UN played a more muted role in Kosovo thanks to the burden assumed by European institutional actors. The absence of such actors in East Timor both increased the demands on UNTAET and reduced the opportunity for engagement by interested states with senior UN staff over differing interpretations of the situation on the ground.

Consultation and accountability

In contrast to the missions in Bosnia and Kosovo, East Timor had a uniquely clear political endpoint. The outcome of independence was never really questioned after the UN Transitional Administration was established, but the timing and the manner in which power was to be exercised in the meantime soon became controversial.

The widespread assumption that East Timor in late 1999 was a political and economic vacuum was perhaps half true. Even before the vote to separate from Indonesia, East Timor was one of the poorest parts of the archipelago; in the violence that followed, the formal economy simply ceased to function. Unemployment during the period of Transitional Administration remained at around 80 per cent, with much economic activity being parasitic on the temporary market for expatriate food and entertainment. The political situation was far more complex.

Many of the expatriates working for UNTAET and the 70-odd international non-governmental organisations (NGOs) tended to treat the Timorese political system as a *tabula rasa*. This attitude led to the first significant civic education initiative proposed by the UN being rejected by the Timorese. A letter from Timorese NGOs to UNTAET's Director of Political Affairs, Peter Galbraith, complained of inadequate consultation in the development of the project, and the fact that the vast majority of the $8 million budget was earmarked for the salaries of international staff. This greatly underestimated the interest and capacity of Timorese actors to play an active role in civic education. Following

---

[18] S/2000/53, para. 2.

changes of personnel and the formation of a steering committee with substantial local representation, Timorese civil society agreed to resume participation in the process in January 2001.

Many of these problems were referable to a contradiction within Security Council Resolution 1272 (1999). It established UNTAET in order to give the East Timorese eventual control over their country, stressing the need for UNTAET to 'consult and cooperate closely with the East Timorese people'. At the same time, however, UNTAET followed the Kosovo model of concentrating all political power in UNTAET and the Special Representative,[19] while endowing the administration with all the institutional and bureaucratic baggage that the UN carries. The failure to elaborate on the meaning of 'consult and cooperate closely' gave UNTAET considerable latitude in its interpretation of the mandate. The initial approach was to establish a non-elected council, comprising representatives of UNTAET and local political factions. Created in December 1999, the 15-member National Consultative Council (NCC) was a purely advisory body, though it reviewed (and endorsed) all UNTAET regulations.[20] Nevertheless, as the situation in East Timor became more stable, there were calls for wider and more direct participation in political life.

On 5 April 2000, Vieira de Mello announced the appointment of Timorese deputy district administrators to operate under the 13 international district administrators. New district advisory councils would also be established. These were to have 'broad participation of representatives of political parties, the Church, women and youth groups.' In particular, Vieira de Mello noted, 'We wish to establish advisory councils in the districts that are representative of the East Timorese civil society more than was possible in the NCC.' In addition, he announced that proceedings of the NCC, which had been criticised by some as overly secretive, would be opened to representatives of NGOs and of Falintil, the Timorese guerrilla force that had long resisted Indonesian rule.[21]

The criticisms of UNTAET in Dili were echoed and amplified in the districts, where district administrators complained of their exclusion from policy decisions. In a letter to Deputy Special Representative and head of UN administration Jean-Christian Cady, they warned that the appointment of deputy district administrators might worsen the problem if it was not accompanied by meaningful reform in the

---

[19] Security Council Resolution 1272, 25 October 1999, paras. 1, 8.
[20] UNTAET Regulation 1999/2, 2 December 1999. See S/2000/53, para. 4.
[21] Sergio Vieira de Mello, *Press Briefing* (Dili, East Timor, 5 April 2000).

decision-making process: 'These high-level posts might satisfy the international community's demand for involvement but will not increase our authority at a local level if the process is not handled correctly. Unless it is part of a broader integration strategy it is likely to be perceived as tokenism.'[22] Weeks earlier, the head of district administration, Jarat Chopra, had resigned in a very public disagreement with senior UNTAET staff.[23]

As Vieira de Mello later acknowledged at the National Congress of the National Council of Timorese Resistance (CNRT), an umbrella organisation of groups that opposed Indonesia's occupation, more radical reform was needed:

UNTAET consulted on major policy issues, but in the end it retained all the responsibility for the design and execution of policy. What is more, the NCC came under increasing scrutiny for not being representative enough of East Timorese society, and not transparent enough in its deliberations. Faced as we were with our own difficulties in the establishment of this mission, we did not, we could not involve the Timorese at large as much as they were entitled to.[24]

In May 2000, the Special Representative presented two options to Timorese leaders. The first model was a 'technocratic model', by which the administration would be fully staffed with East Timorese, so a fully national civil service would be in place at independence. The second was a 'political model', whereby East Timorese people would also share responsibility for government in coalition with UNTAET and hold several portfolios in the interim government. He explained that the latter option was a mixed blessing, as those East Timorese would also share UNTAET's role as a 'punching bag'.[25]

The latter model was chosen, and a National Council (NC) was established by a regulation passed on 14 July 2000. Importantly, Vieira de Mello did not chair the NC and its members were exclusively East Timorese (though all appointed by the Special Representative). Its 33 (later 36) members comprised representatives of CNRT and other parties, together with representatives from the Church, women's and youth organisations, NGOs, professional and labour organisations,

---

[22] Mark Dodd, 'UN Peace Mission at War with Itself', *Sydney Morning Herald*, 13 May 2000.

[23] Mark Dodd, 'UN Staff Battle over Independence Policy', *Sydney Morning Herald*, 13 March 2000.

[24] Sergio Vieira de Mello, *Address of Sergio Vieira de Mello to the National Congress of CNRT* (Dili, East Timor: 21 August 2000)

[25] *Security Council Briefed by Sergio Vieira de Mello, Special Representative for East Timor*, SC/6882, 27 June 2000.

the farming and business community and Timor's thirteen districts.[26] On the same day, a 'Cabinet of the Transitional Government in East Timor' was established.[27] Of the eight posts initially created, four were assigned to East Timorese (Internal Administration, Infrastructure, Economic Affairs and Social Affairs) and four to international staff (Police and Emergency Services, Political Affairs, Justice and Finance). In October 2000, the NC was expanded to 36 members and José Ramos-Horta was sworn in as Cabinet member for Foreign Affairs.[28]

Soon after establishing the National Council, UNTAET announced at a daily press briefing that the East Timorese Transitional Administration (ETTA) had replaced the Governance and Public Administration pillar, and that ETTA should now be referred to as a 'government'.[29] The idea, as senior UNTAET officials later explained, was that UNTAET should eventually be regarded as a UN assistance mission to ETTA. This was sometimes described as a 'co-government' approach, in contrast to the earlier 'two-track' approach.[30] Such an arrangement could only ever be theoretical, as the Special Representative retained ultimate power, but it represented a decisive shift in thinking less than one year into the mission.

With the benefit of hindsight, UNTAET officials later described the early attempts at consultation as 'confused at best', and as leading to justified criticism on the part of the East Timorese. Capacity building and preparation for government were originally seen as requiring a 'bottom-up' creation of an East Timorese civil service, with minor consultation at senior levels. The inadequacy of that consultation, combined with the failure to achieve significant headway in 'Timorising' the civil service, led to pressure to reform UNTAET's structure. Unlike the NCC, which was generally presented with draft regulations for approval, the National Council had power to initiate, modify and recommend draft regulations; to amend regulations; and to call Cabinet members before it to answer questions regarding their respective functions.[31]

---

[26] UNTAET Regulation 2000/24, *On the Establishment of a National Council*, 14 July 2000, para. 3.2.

[27] UNTAET Regulation 2000/23, *On the Establishment of the Cabinet of the Transitional Government in East Timor*, 14 July 2000.

[28] *Report of the Secretary-General on the United Nations Transitional Administration in East Timor (for the period 27 July 2000 to 16 January 2001)*, S/2001/42, 16 January 2001, para. 9.

[29] UNTAET Daily Briefing, 8 August 2000.

[30] See generally Beauvais, 'Benevolent Despotism'.

[31] UNTAET Regulation 2000/24, 14 July 2000, para. 2.1.

Nevertheless, these powers did not reflect the reality of governance in East Timor – at least, not to the satisfaction of the Timorese. Xanana Gusmão, a guerrilla leader imprisoned in Indonesia for over six years who became the charismatic political leader of the Timorese and later president, expressed the collective frustration in October 2000, arguing that the Timorese experience of the UN presence was limited to watching hundreds of white four-wheel-drive vehicles driving around Dili and receiving a succession of regulations passed by the UN administration.[32] The Timorese Cabinet members shared these sentiments; in December 2000 they threatened to resign. In a letter to Vieira de Mello, the Timorese Cabinet members (excluding José Ramos-Horta, who was out of East Timor at the time) complained of being 'used as a justification for the delays and the confusion in a process which is outside our control. The East Timorese Cabinet members are caricatures of ministers in a government of a banana republic. They have no power, no duties, no resources to function adequately'.[33]

The threat of resignation was used frequently as a political tool in East Timor. The Cabinet members' threat came soon after Gusmão himself threatened to resign from his position as speaker of the NC. Earlier that year, in the August 2000 CNRT Congress, both Gusmão and Ramos-Horta resigned, twice, only to be reinstated. Gusmão resigned once again from the NC in March 2001. In the absence of real political power, resignation – essentially an attempt to challenge UNTAET's legitimacy by undermining its claims to be consulting effectively – was the most effective means of expressing frustration and trying to bring about change.

In East Timor, talk of 'Timorisation' was sometimes conflated with the idea of genuine ownership. As a result, significant effort was put into appointing local staff without focusing on the training that would enable them to do their jobs. The lack of skilled local workers was initially addressed by importing international staff (of varying quality and interest) who, it was assumed, would not only be able to fulfil civilian functions in the transitional administration but to train Timorese staff to do the same. Doing a job and training another person to do it are, however, quite distinct skills. The result, as UNTAET officials later acknowledged, was that Timorese staff spent less time receiving on-the-job training than standing around watching.

Such considerations are quite separate from administrative barriers to the transfer of power peculiar to the UN. East Timor's experiment with

---

[32] Mark Dodd, 'Give Us a Say, Urges Gusmao', *The Age* (Melbourne), 10 October 2000.
[33] Mark Dodd, 'Give Us a Free Hand or We Quit, Leaders Say', *Sydney Morning Herald*, 5 December 2000.

the ETTA structure, for example, ran into bureaucratic stonewalling when it was suggested that international staff should work directly under Timorese managers. There was great unwillingness on the part of international staff to submit to such oversight, which might have entailed Timorese officials completing field evaluation reports for mission staff, with consequences for subsequent mission placements and promotions. This reflected the reality that the UN was not operating under the control of the nascent Timorese institutions, but also raised squarely the question of to whom these international staff are accountable for their performance in the governance of such territories.

Justice and reconciliation

In East Timor, the UN faced the task of building a judicial system literally from the ground up. As the UN prepared to establish a transitional administration, the secretary-general observed that 'local institutions, including the court system, have for all practical purposes ceased to function, with . . . judges, prosecutors, and other members of the legal profession having left the territory'.[34] This apocalyptic view of the situation was borne out by early estimates that the number of lawyers remaining in the territory was fewer than ten.[35] A Transitional Judicial Service Commission was established, comprising three East Timorese and two international experts,[36] but the absence of a communications network meant that the search for qualified lawyers had to be conducted through leaflet drops by INTERFET planes.

Although there was an initial assumption that East Timor required quick law and order measures to maintain peace and security (learning, in part, from the experiences of Kosovo), it soon became clear that the main focus should be on developing institutions that would be sustainable. Balancing the need to respect international human rights standards against the need for sustainability – and the reluctance of Indonesia to cooperate with any form of international tribunal[37] – led to

---

[34] *Report of the Secretary-General on the Situation in East Timor*, S/1999/1024, 4 October 1999, para. 33.

[35] See Hansjoerg Strohmeyer, 'Building a New Judiciary for East Timor: Challenges of a Fledgling Nation', *Criminal Law Forum*, vol. 11, no. 3 (2000), p 263. The World Bank estimated that over 70 per cent of all administrative buildings were partially or completely destroyed, and almost all office equipment and consumable materials were totally destroyed: World Bank, *Report of the Joint Assessment Mission to East Timor*, 8 December 1999, www.worldbank.org, para. 15.

[36] UNTAET Regulation 1999/3, 3 December 1999, para. 2.

[37] Such a tribunal had been called for by, among others, the International Commission of Inquiry on East Timor: *Report of the International Commission of Inquiry on East Timor to the Secretary-General*, A/54/726-S/2000/59, 31 January 2000, Annex, para. 152.

the establishment of special panels for serious crimes. Plagued by various concerns irrelevant to the situation of the Timorese (such as internal UN management difficulties), this panel enjoyed less legitimacy than the Timorese-driven Commission for Reception, Truth and Reconciliation – an innovative variation on the South African Truth and Reconciliation Commission that linked the need for reconciliation to the need for reconstruction. The Commission was empowered to establish non-prosecutorial 'Community Reconciliation Processes' (usually some form of community service) that barred future prosecution for criminal acts not amounting to serious crimes.[38] Meanwhile, frustration with the pursuit of serious offenders and the questionable efforts by Indonesia to prosecute its own nationals led to renewed Timorese calls for a full international criminal tribunal to be convened.

As in Kosovo, the decision to rely on inexperienced local jurists came from a mix of politics and pragmatism. Politically, the appointment of the first Timorese legal officers was of enormous symbolic importance. At the same time, the emergency detentions under INTERFET required the early appointment of judges who understood the local civil law system and who would not require the same amount of translation services demanded by international judges. In addition, appointment of international judges would necessarily be an unsustainable temporary measure that would cause further dislocation when funds began to diminish.

UNTAET was more aggressive in Timorising the management of judicial systems than the institutions working in political and civil affairs. The trade-off, of course, was in formal qualifications and practical experience. Some of the appointees had worked in law firms and legal aid organisations in Indonesia; others as paralegals with Timorese human rights organisations and resistance groups.[39] None had ever served as a judge or prosecutor. Timorisation thus referred more to the identity of a particular official, rather than the establishment of support structures to ensure that individuals could fulfil their responsibilities. UNTAET developed a three-tier training approach, comprising a one-week 'quick impact' course prior to appointment, ongoing training and a mentoring scheme. Limited resources and difficulties in recruiting experienced mentors with a background in civil law posed serious

---

[38] UNTAET Regulation 2001/10, 13 July 2001. See Frederick Rawski, 'Truth-Seeking and Local Histories in East Timor', *Asia-Pacific Journal on Human Rights and the Law*, vol. 3, no.1 (2002), pp. 77–96.

[39] Hansjoerg Strohmeyer, 'Collapse and Reconstruction of a Judicial System: The United Nations Missions in Kosovo and East Timor', *American Journal of International Law*, vol. 95, no. 1 (2001), p. 54.

obstacles to the training programme, however, which UNTAET officials later acknowledged was grossly insufficient.

Even more so than Kosovo, the destruction wrought in East Timor presented substantial practical difficulties in the administration of justice. The first judges to be sworn in worked out of chambers and courtrooms that were still blackened by smoke. The judges lacked not merely furniture and computers, but virtually any legal texts. Some books were retrieved from the destroyed buildings, but most had to be sought in the form of donations from private law firms and law schools in Indonesia and Australia.[40]

A non-obvious priority in the first months of the operation was to construct correctional facilities. Virtually all detention facilities had been destroyed prior to the arrival of INTERFET, limiting the capacity to detain alleged criminals. This problem was inherited by UNTAET, with the result that UN civilian police were forced to release alleged criminals in order to detain returning militia implicated in the commission of grave violations of international humanitarian law during the post-referendum violence. One of the barriers to dealing with the shortage of space was the reluctance of donors to fund, either directly or indirectly, the building of prisons.[41]

Many of the gaps in the legal system, in particular the provision of legal assistance, were filled by enterprising NGOs, such as the civil rights organisation Yayasan HAK.[42] Such initiatives deserve the support of international actors, particularly where bureaucratic or political obstacles delay UN initiatives in the same area. Nevertheless, by November 2000, the Security Council Mission to East Timor found that 'the judicial sector remains seriously under-resourced. Consequently, the current system cannot process those suspects already in detention, some of whom have been held for almost a year.'[43] These delays, combined with the lack of access to qualified defence lawyers, were blamed when over half the Timorese prison population escaped in August 2002.[44]

In Kosovo, the judicial system existed parallel to the ongoing jurisdiction of the International Criminal Tribunal for the Former Yugoslavia. In East Timor, no such international tribunal existed.

---

[40] Strohmeyer, 'Building a New Judiciary', pp. 268–9.
[41] Human Rights Watch, *Unfinished Business: Justice for East Timor*, (Press Backgrounder) August 2000, 23 October 1988, www.hrw.org/backgrounder/asia/timor/etimor-back0829. htm.
[42] Yayasan HAK (Foundation for Law, Human Rights and Justice) was established in 1997 by a group of young East Timorese intellectuals and NGO activists. See 23 October 1988, www.yayasanhak.minihub.org.
[43] *Report of the Security Council Mission to East Timor and Indonesia*, S/2000/1105, 20 November 2000, para. 8.
[44] See Jill Jolliffe, 'Jail Breakout over Delays', *The Age* (Melbourne), 17 August 2002.

Prosecution of those accused of the most serious crimes was therefore handled as part of the East Timorese domestic process. In March 2000, UNTAET passed a regulation establishing the exclusive jurisdiction of the Dili District Court and the Court of Appeal in Dili in relation to serious crimes. These were defined as including genocide, crimes against humanity, war crimes and torture, as well as murder and sexual offences committed between 1 January 1999 and 25 October 1999. The cases were to be heard by mixed panels of both international and East Timorese judges and prosecuted by a new Serious Crimes Unit. The first hearings took place in January 2001.[45]

In addition to the constraints on resources, management problems contributed to the extremely slow functioning of the serious crimes panels. By early 2001 there were over 700 unprocessed cases in the serious crimes category alone and detention facilities were filled to capacity with pre-trial detainees, with the result that some alleged perpetrators had to be released.[46] These problems continued through 2001 with a number of resignations from the Serious Crimes Unit. Dissatisfaction with the progress in serious crimes was one factor that encouraged the East Timorese to look for alternative accountability mechanisms for the abuses of September 1999. More importantly, however, the inadequacy of Indonesia's efforts to deal with alleged perpetrators in its territory led many to believe that an international tribunal was the only way in which high-level perpetrators would ever face justice.[47] This might have been based on unrealistic expectations of what such a tribunal could achieve; in any case, such a proposal appeared unlikely to draw much support from governments.

The aggressive policies in promoting Timorese leadership in the law and order area were laudable, but the slow pace of the legal system that was created undermined faith in the rule of law as such. A major test of this system will be on the question of land title. For essentially political reasons, UNTAET deferred consideration of the land title issue until after independence – and therefore beyond its mandate. This enormously complex problem includes claims arising from Indonesian and Portuguese colonial rule, and perhaps claims under customary norms pre-dating Portuguese colonisation.[48] How East Timor deals with this

---

[45] UNTAET Regulation 2000/11, 6 March 2000, para. 10; UNTAET Regulation 2000/15, 6 June 2000; *Report of the Secretary-General on the United Nations Transitional Administration in East Timor (for the period 27 January to 26 July 2000)*, S/2000/738, 26 July 2000, para. 42.

[46] Beauvais, 'Benevolent Despotism', p. 1155.

[47] Ian Martin, 'No Justice in Jakarta', *Washington Post*, 27 August 2002.

[48] See Dennis Schulz, 'East Timor's Land Rights Mess', *The Age* (Melbourne), 23 December 2000.

issue, and the incentives for corruption that go with it, will undoubtedly challenge this newest of countries' political and legal systems. Although the outcome is clearly up to the Timorese themselves, how the new regime responds to that challenge will be a measure of the success of the rule of law policies put in place by UNTAET.

Relief and reconstruction

> We are not interested in a legacy of cars and laws, nor are we interested in a legacy of development plans for the future designed by [people] other than East Timorese. We are not interested in inheriting an economic rationale, which leaves out the social and political complexity of East Timorese reality. Nor do we wish to inherit the heavy decision-making and project implementation mechanisms in which the role of the East Timorese is to give their consent as observers rather than the active players we should start to be.
>
> Xanana Gusmão[49]

The political economy of humanitarian and development assistance in conflict territories is the subject of an entire literature in its own right.[50] Assistance is notoriously supply- rather than demand-driven, with the result that it is more influenced by donor politics than those of the recipient communities. At the same time, a large foreign presence in a territory like East Timor typically has perverse economic effects – in particular, the destabilising effect of a bubble economy for providing services to expatriates and the distortions it causes in the labour market.

In post-conflict situations administered by the UN, a further layer of complication is the bureaucratic framework within which funds supporting a transitional administration must be spent. Funding for such operations typically comes from two sources: assessed and voluntary contributions. Assessed contributions for peacekeeping operations are calculated on the basis of gross national product (GNP) and range from 0.001 per cent of the budget to 25 per cent. The 2003–2004 budget for peacekeeping was $2.2 billion.[51] Voluntary contributions from member

---

[49] Xanana Gusmão, quoted in Dodd, 'Give Us a Say, Urges Gusmao', *The Age* (Melbourne), 10 October 2000.

[50] See Mats R. Berdal and David M. Malone (eds.), *Greed and Grievance: Economic Agendas in Civil Wars, A Project of the International Peace Academy* (Boulder, CO: Lynne Rienner, 2000); Paul Collier, *Breaking the Conflict Trap: Civil War and Development Policy, A World Bank Policy Research Report* (New York: Oxford University Press, 2003); and Karen Ballentine and Jake Sherman, *The Political Economy of Armed Conflict: Beyond Greed and Grievance* (Boulder, CO: Lynne Rienner, 2003).

[51] Press Release, UN Doc GA/AB/3570, 4 June 2003. Assessed contributions for peacekeeping vary slightly from those to the regular budget of the UN, taking into account the 'special status' of the permanent members of the Security Council.

states support specialised agencies and subsidiary organisations of the UN family, including UNDP, the UN High Commissioner for Refugees (UNHCR) and so on.

In East Timor, despite the repeated assertions that this was a unique operation, the mission was subject to the same budgetary procedures as other peacekeeping operations – thus meaning a strict division between funds that could be used to support the peacekeeping mission and funds that could be used for humanitarian and development assistance. This might be reasonable in a country where the UN operation sits parallel to an existing government, but when the UN *was* the government it led to absurdity. Speaking in June 2000, Vieira de Mello noted Timorese frustration with the slow pace of reconstruction. In part this was due to the slow rate of disbursement into the World Bank Trust Fund, but on a more basic level he acknowledged that criticism was certain to continue while UN engineers were prohibited from fixing buildings used by Timorese officials.[52]

These problems were exacerbated by the distortions that a sudden influx of wealthy foreigners caused to the Timorese economy. Every significant UN mission creates a parasitic and unsustainable economy to serve the needs of the transient internationals. As in cities from Freetown to Kabul, for example, the rental market in Dili exploded in early 2000, accompanied by dubious evictions of existing tenants to make way for more lucrative foreign occupants. This can be a benefit to the economy if, as sometimes happened in East Timor, families move into a back room and rent out the rest of the house, using some of the income to renovate their property. When disputes arise over the microeconomic impact of a UN presence, they tend to focus on the question of salaries. East Timor experienced typical problems, with those Timorese bearing qualifications being tempted by the higher salaries offered for work as a driver or a security guard than were available to electricians or businessmen. Ultimately, such problems solve themselves. As the international presence peaks and begins to decline, the job and property balloon bursts.

Elections and exit strategies

As indicated earlier, there was no question that East Timor would become independent after its brief period of UN virtual 'trusteeship'.[53]

---

[52] Press Release, UN Doc. SC/6882, 27 June 2000. See also Smith, *Peacekeeping*, pp. 136–7. In practice, these funding distinctions are often blurred – de-mining, for example, is sometimes funded through assessed contributions when it coincides with a peacekeeping operation.

[53] Richard Caplan, *A New Trusteeship? The International Administration of War-Torn Territories*, Adelphi Paper 341 (Oxford: Oxford University Press, 2002).

Though there had been diverging views about the time within which this should take place – with some Timorese initially calling for an extended international presence of a decade or more – the patience and the pockets of donors, combined with the strengthening Timorese commitment to governing themselves, imposed an implicit time limit on UNTAET of a few years. A viable exit strategy, however, required a legitimate and sustainable government that could assume power.

In this context, East Timor exhibited an atypical form of political life. As the territory prepared for its first elections in August 2001, many ordinary Timorese expressed doubts about the need for political parties. This stemmed from the view that divisions between the Revolutionary Front of Independent East Timor (Fretilin) and Timorese Democratic Union (UDT) parties in 1974–1975 had been exploited by Indonesia and facilitated its invasion and subsequent annexation.[54] Significantly, Xanana Gusmão, who later became East Timor's first president, was not formally associated with any political party. He was president of CNRT but repeatedly stated that this was not a political party and that it would not run in the elections. (It was eventually dissolved in June 2001.) CNRT's status was important because it was the vehicle through which UNTAET haltingly attempted to carry out its mandate to consult with the Timorese population. Soon after UNTAET's deployment, CNRT was regarded as representing the Timorese people, giving enormous political sway to its leadership – arguably at the expense of other sections of the population. The questionably representative nature of CNRT was reflected in its August 2000 decision to adopt Portuguese as the official language of East Timor, a language understood by fewer than 10 per cent of the population and by virtually no one under thirty.[55] This was compounded when Fretilin broke from CNRT in the same month, leading to a proliferation of smaller parties.

The most concrete political legacy that UNTAET left East Timor was its constitution. UNTAET officials stated repeatedly that they had no intention of involving themselves directly in the drafting process. UNTAET did, however, organise the vote for the Constituent Assembly and remained committed to a 'perfect election'. These positions reflected competing and potentially inconsistent obligations. On the one hand, the UN was committed to disseminating the values enshrined in the UN Charter and other treaties: the promotion of self-determination,

---

[54] See, for example, National Democratic Institute and the Faculty of Social and Political Science of the University of East Timor, *Carrying the People's Aspirations: A Report on Focus Group Discussions in East Timor* (Dili, East Timor: NDI, February 2002), p. 9.

[55] Outcomes of the CNRT National Congress, 21–30 August 2000 (English Version), Commission III, Recommendation B(4)(c), adopted by the National Congress 362–0–3.

democracy, freedom of association and the rule of law. On the other, the choice of the political system to be adopted had to lie with the Timorese themselves. In discussions on a draft regulation on political parties, for example, UNTAET resisted a push to exclude parties that had opposed Timor's independence.

A related problem was the possibility that East Timor would become a one-party state. Fretilin was always certain to win an overwhelming majority of the vote in the August 2001 elections – some estimates were as high as 90 per cent – and there were fears that it would then impose whatever constitution and legislative programme it wanted. Senior UNTAET staff confessed that they regarded such an outcome as undesirable, but were reserved as to what they should (or could) do to avoid it. As a start, they encouraged the Timorese to adopt a mixed voting system with proportional representation in the hope that smaller parties would be represented in the process. (Fretilin eventually won 55 of the 88 seats.)

Procedural difficulties also arose. The elected Constituent Assembly was tasked with drafting and adopting a constitution, which it did on 22 March 2002. The Assembly then transformed itself into the first legislature prior to presidential elections, held in April. But two of the most contentious questions for a constitution are (i) how the legislature is elected and (ii) what powers it holds *vis-à-vis* the other organs of government. The process followed in East Timor presumed the existence of a consensus on at least the voting method before the assembly could be elected, and mandated that legislature-in-waiting to define the scope of its own powers.[56]

At the same time, some UNTAET staff warned of 'worrying authoritarian tendencies' within the Timorese leadership. Locally organised civic education programmes were sometimes likened to propaganda campaigns. 'I have grave doubts that anything democratic will come out of this,' observed one senior international official. 'Look at Cambodia: everyone regards it as a success but it was an utter disaster – look who we put in power!' The *Jakarta Post* ran a story along these lines bearing a title of fulsome irony for an Indonesian paper: 'The New Timor: A Xanana Republic?'[57] Gusmão railed against such criticisms in his 2001 New Year's speech, deriding those who 'spout forth points of view ... in a remote-control-style'. He went on to draw what he saw as

---

[56] The new legislative assembly, not surprisingly, endorsed the method by which the legislature was elected and gave itself broad powers.

[57] Damien Kingsbury, 'The New Timor: A Xanana Republic?' *Jakarta Post*, 16 December 2000.

broader lessons from East Timor's engagement with international actors:

> We are witnessing another phenomenon in East Timor; that of an obsessive acculturation to standards that hundreds of international experts try to convey to the East Timorese, who are hungry for values: democracy (many of those who teach us never practised it in their own countries because they became UN staff members); human rights (many of those who remind us of them forget the situation in their own countries); gender (many of the women who attend the workshops know that in their countries this issue is no example for others); NGOs (numerous NGOs live off the aid 'business' to poor countries); youth (all those who remind us of this issue know that in their countries most of the youth are unemployed).
>
> It might sound as though I am speaking against these noble values of democratic participation. I do not mind if it happens in the democratic minds of people. What seems to be absurd is that we absorb standards just to pretend we look like a democratic society and please our masters of independence. What concerns me is the non-critical absorption of [universal] standards given the current stage of the historic process we are building.[58]

This bore interesting similarities to the 'Asian values' arguments of the 1990s, when south-east Asian leaders (and some Western commentators) defended authoritarian political systems on the basis of their alleged effectiveness in promoting economic success. Few UN staff felt comfortable even discussing the idea that good governance might not always be coterminous with multiparty democracy. For its part, of course, UNTAET could hardly lay claim to democratic legitimacy. Vieira de Mello held absolute power in East Timor at the pleasure of the UN Security Council, a body whose permanent members continued to reflect the balance of power at the end of the Second World War. Neither he nor his staff were accountable in any direct way to the Timorese population.

Criticism of the Timorese leadership's style was not limited to expatriates, however. Aderito de Jesus Soares, of the Timorese Jurists Association, spoke of the need to change the 'culture of command' in Timorese political life that developed within a clandestine resistance.[59] Other Timorese NGOs were also critical of the closed nature of Timorese political processes. The greatest point of leverage for international actors will be Timor's continued reliance on development assistance over the coming years, so it is highly unlikely that independent East Timor will be overtly draconian. There is, however, a real

---

[58] Gusmão, *New Year's Message*, 31 December 2000.
[59] Aderito de Jesus Soares, interview with the author, Dili, East Timor, 15 January 2001.

danger that Timorese civil society will become regarded as simply a channel for aid rather than as a legitimate part of political life.[60]

The territory's small size and the concentration of political actors in Dili meant that municipal or regional elections were never seriously contemplated, though Jarat Chopra has argued forcefully that the failure to decentralise Timorese political authority missed an opportunity to introduce genuine democracy rather than a simulacra that disguised a one-party state.[61]

Unlike the first elections in post-apartheid South Africa, where people celebrated in the long queues to vote, East Timor's first elections on 30 August 2001 were so calm as to be almost boring. This was unfortunate for the journalists who had journeyed to East Timor – a few left even before the election – but it was the best possible news for the Timorese people. They queued up peacefully to cast their ballots and then went home. Such boredom is a thing worth fighting for. Fretilin, the dominant party of national liberation, won a clear majority – 55 of 88 seats – but fell short of the two-thirds majority it needed to be able to impose a constitution unilaterally. Presidential elections followed, and on 14 April 2002 Gusmão was elected with an overwhelming majority of the vote, though his powers were limited by the constitution adopted the previous March. East Timor was declared independent on 20 May 2002 and UNTAET was replaced by the UN Mission of Support in East Timor (UNMISET), which remained with a scaled-down peacekeeping presence until a projected departure in June 2004.

East Timor's elections were formal successes, enjoying large turnouts and swift certification as 'free and fair' by, among other organisations, the Carter Centre and the European Union. But the translation of institutions into local terms sometimes effaced elements of their meaning. 'Democracy', for example, was translated into Tetum as *biti boot* (big mat), referring to the woven grass mats on which elders sat when they discussed communal problems.[62] Like 'good governance', this is close to, but not identical with democracy.

The actual voting in the 30 August 2001 elections went off with only a few minor hitches, contested by 16 political parties and five independent candidates. There was a clear commitment to a peaceful vote, helped by Gusmão's statement a week earlier that he would run for president only if not a drop of blood was spilt. Turnout was high and

---

[60] Cf Jarat Chopra, 'Building State Failure in East Timor', *Development and Change*, vol. 33, no. 5 (2002), pp. 979–1000.

[61] See *Ibid.*

[62] Tanja Hohe, 'Totem Polls: Indigenous Concepts and "Free and Fair" Elections in East Timor', *International Peacekeeping*, vol. 9, no. 4 (2002), p. 78.

calm. Voter education seemed to have been broadly successful, and most people seemed to understand the voting process. In particular, there was evidence of strategic voting. This was clearest in Aileu district, where the new Timorese Social Democratic Association (ASDT) was a popular party. In each district, voters could vote for a national and a district candidate; the national ballot was chosen by proportional representation, the district candidate by simple plurality. In Aileu, however, ASDT did not field a district candidate. The result was that in the national ballot from Aileu ASDT won 52 per cent of vote. In the district vote, Fretilin won, but 40 per cent of the votes were spoiled (compared with 4–5 per cent of votes spoiled in other districts).

People appeared to know, then, how to vote, but not necessarily why. Civic education left a great deal to be desired: by January 2001 the UN had not run a single programme of significance. Confusion about the vote was not simply a matter of education, however. A country of around 800,000 people was electing an 88 member constituent assembly, with the dual functions of coming up with a constitution and serving as a provisional legislature. These two functions are not necessarily compatible. Most obviously, while one might want a strong government to implement policy and push through legislation, a dominant party may be the last thing one wants when drafting a constitution.

A senior Timorese official acknowledged that the population voted for party symbols in the constituent assembly. There was, naturally, strong support for the Fretilin flag, which many associated with the independence struggle. Others equated support for Fretilin with a kind of neutrality, not wishing to hear about other parties because they felt it was up to educated people to deal with politics.[63] Once constituent assembly representatives were chosen, however, it became apparent that many people did not know the individuals for whom they had voted – in particular, they did not realise that they were electing a subgroup of the diaspora (the 'Mozambique clique') to executive power.

Conclusion

East Timor's independence on 20 May 2002 concluded the most expansive assertion of sovereignty by the UN in its history – in addition to administering East Timor, passing laws and overseeing the judiciary, UNTAET had negotiated treaties for the territory. Even so, as indicated earlier, East Timor celebrated independence as the poorest country in the region. It faced a period of great economic instability at least until

---

[63] See *Ibid.*, p. 74.

tax revenues from oil taken from the Timor Gap begin to accrue – estimated at up to $3 billion over 17 years beginning in around 2006. There was also evidence of political instability. On 4 December 2002, riots in Dili left two dead and Prime Minister Marí Alkatiri's house burned to the ground. A month later, 20 to 30 men armed with automatic weapons attacked villages in the Ermera district, killing five. With UNMISET's consent, the Timorese Defence Force (Falintil-FDTL) was given temporary responsibility for the defence of the area, where they detained ninety people.[64]

The disturbances led to discussion about the possibility of delaying the drawdown of UN peacekeepers, though there was little enthusiasm for this on the part of the states contributing troops. Instead of an extension of the projected mandate, the speed of the drawdown was paused for 2003, keeping troop strength at just under 4,000. This would then be followed by an accelerated withdrawal in 2004 handing over defence responsibility to Falintil-FDTL on 20 May 2004.[65] In the absence of a riot control capacity within the Timor Leste Police Service (TLPS), it is expected that Falintil-FDTL will continue to be active in internal as well as external security. Some UNMISET officials worry that East Timor may now follow a path not dissimilar to Indonesia, where the military operates largely independent of civilian political control while on occasion playing a capricious role itself in government.

Through embracing formal processes that led to Fretilin's domination of the political landscape while endorsing the charismatic legitimacy of Gusmão, UNTAET sowed the seeds of a possible confrontation between Fretilin, which consolidated power in the institutions of government, and a president who commands the affection of the population and the loyalty of the military. It is not clear that this will force a choice between one-party rule and violent political confrontation,[66] but it is far from ideal as an exit strategy. After investing so much in East Timor, the UN and its member states have a considerable interest in remaining engaged to ensure that this was not an investment in a failed state.

The UN may never again be called upon to repeat an operation comparable to East Timor, where it exercised sovereign powers on a temporary basis. Even so, it is certain that the circumstances that demand such interventions will recur. Lessons derived from past experiences of transitional administration will be applicable whenever the UN or other international actors engage in complex peace operations

---

[61] *Special Report of the Secretary-General on the UN Mission of Support in East Timor*, S/2003/243, 3 March 2003, paras. 6–8.
[65] *Ibid.*, paras. 24–9.   [66] Cf. Hohe, 'Totem Polls', p. 85.

that include a policing function, civilian administration, development of the rule of law, establishment of a national economy, the staging of elections or all of the above. Learning from such lessons has not, however, been one of the strengths of the UN. A senior Secretariat official describes this as an unwritten rule that 'no wheel shall go un-reinvented'.[67]

The later operations in Afghanistan and Iraq present corrections to the trend of greater UN interventionism in post-conflict reconstruction that led to its expansive role in East Timor. The 'light footprint' in Afghanistan and the exclusion of the UN from much of Iraq suggested a recognition of the limited capacity available for post-conflict reconstruction: feasible in a small territory like East Timor or Kosovo, but unrealistic on the scale of Afghanistan or Iraq. The tendency to view these problems as technical, however, at times occluded the more basic contradictions between means and ends, and the question of whether it is possible to establish the conditions for legitimate and sustainable national government through a period of benevolent autocracy.

---

[67] Alvaro de Soto, interview with the author, New York, 12 August 2003. Alvaro de Soto is Special Representative of the secretary-general for Western Sahara at the rank of under-secretary-general.

8   Kosovo

Spyros Economides

Introduction

The inherent paradox in the United Nation's (UN) interventionary role in Kosovo is that it did not occur until after a ceasefire had been reached on the ground. In fact, as this chapter examines, one of the two major questions relating to the UN's role in the Kosovo war was that the UN Security Council (UNSC) in particular, was bypassed by the major Western powers that employed NATO as the vehicle for their intervention. As a result, this undermined the authority of the UNSC as the legitimating body for international interventions both in terms of the maintenance of international peace and security and on the basis of humanitarian concerns giving rise to the 'doctrine of humanitarian intervention'. As NATO dispensed with the normal practice of seeking a UNSC resolution to mandate its action, both the legality and moral underpinning of the operation were heavily questioned.

A second major issue raised for the UN by the Kosovo crisis relates to the evolution of the UN's functions as the lead organisation in the international administration of war-torn territories. Through the UN Interim Administration Mission in Kosovo (UNMIK), the UN assumed responsibility for the civilian administration of post-War Kosovo. In practice, UNMIK has been governing a de facto protectorate, kept in relative peace by the maintenance of a weighty, NATO-led military and security presence, the Kosovo Force (KFOR). In this case too, the UN has been accused of lacking in success, an unwarranted criticism in the light of the ill-defined parameters and prospects for a permanent settlement in Kosovo and the fragile inter-communal situation on the ground.

This chapter traces the origins and evolution of the Kosovo crisis, examines the UN's role – or indeed the lack of a role – in the subsequent NATO intervention, addresses the implications this has for international interventionary practice in general, and analyses the UN's performance in the administration of post-conflict Kosovo. While the UN's Kosovo experience, as with that in Bosnia, has been repeatedly cast in a negative light, it is argued here that the UN is criticised for actions beyond its control. As such, intervention in Kosovo sheds much light not only on the activities of the UN, its various organs and agencies, but more importantly on the role and utility of the UN in the calculations of powerful state actors and especially the Western powers.

History

Myth and reality are interwoven features of Kosovo's role in the demise of Yugoslavia. And, these myths and realities are inextricably linked to the emergence of a Serbian national consciousness – and nationalism – as they are to the rise and fall of Slobodan Milošević who is widely held responsible for the tragedy that befell Yugoslavia during the 1990s.

The element of myth and symbolism arises from the supreme standing of Kosovo in the history of the Serbian nation and the Serbian Orthodox Church. A leap of imagination would allow us to trace the origins of the contemporary crisis in Kosovo to 1389, however unusual it may be to root Europe's last twentieth-century conflict in the fourteenth century. But such is the centrality of the Kosovo myth to the Serbian nation and Serbia nationalism to the Kosovo war, that such as historical detour cannot be ignored.[1]

The year 1389 is fixed in Serbia's history as the year in which a Serbian national consciousness emerged and a national identity was forged. In this year Serbian forces suffered a major military defeat at the hands of the expanding Ottoman Empire at the Battle of Kosovo. While defeat may seem an unlikely source for nascent national identity, the symbolism of the resistance offered to the invading (Muslim) Ottomans by the (Christian) Serbs embedded the idea of a heroic Orthodox Serbian nation standing alone against the invader. That this defeat, and the resultant mythology and symbolism which defined emerging Serbian nationhood, occurred in Kosovo cemented the historical importance of Kosovo to the centre of Serbian national history.[2] In the case of Serbia/ Kosovo the effect is doubly-important in that Kosovo is also the seat of

---

[1] See generally Tim Judah, *The Serbs: History, Myth and the Destruction of Yugoslavia* (New Haven, CT: Yale University Press, 1997), Chapters 2 and 3; David Bruce Macdonald, *Balkan Holocausts? Serbian and Croatian Victim-Centred Propaganda and the War in Yugoslavia* (Manchester: Manchester University Press, 2002), pp. 69–78; Noel Malcolm, *Kosovo: A Short History* (London: Macmillan, 1998), Chapter 4; and Miranda Vickers, *Between Serb and Albanian: A History of Kosovo* (London: Hurst & Company, 1998), pp. 12–16.

[2] Macdonald, *Balkan Holocausts?*, p. 63.

Serbian Orthodoxy – such a vital part of national culture that even in 2004 it was referred to as 'Serbia's Jerusalem'.[3]

How and why are events in 1389 relevant to crisis and war in 1999? Simply put, the centrality of Kosovo to the mythology of Serbian nationhood was manipulated by Milošević in furthering his own political ambitions. One argument would suggest that the employment of nationalist sentiment by Milošević was the key instrument by which to achieve the broader end of a Greater Serbia: 'a Serbian project . . . to establish the new borders of a set of territories linked to Serbia that would be "for" the Serbs – and which would mostly be ethnically pure'.[4] Another argument suggests that the manipulation of Serbian nationalism by Milošević was primarily about holding onto power; while it was almost impossible to retain public support through other economic and political platforms and policies, nationalism and national victimisation still motivated people to support Milošević.[5] And this sense of national victimisation was felt more strongly nowhere else but in relation to the standing of Serbs in Kosovo and the link between Kosovo and Serbian nationalism.

It is indicative that in 1987, a few years before the outbreak of full-scale violence in former Yugoslavia, Milošević cemented his hold on power in Serbia by invoking the Kosovo myth. Milošević lit the fuse of Serbian nationalism by pledging to defend the rights of Serbs living in Kosovo and by implication of all Serbs outside Serbia in neighbouring republics.[6] The key to unlocking the importance of the centrality of Kosovo to Serbian nationalism is that by the late twentieth century Kosovo was not Serbian. By the late 1980s, the Serb population in Kosovo amounted to some 10 per cent of the population, the vast majority of the Kosovar population being ethnic Albanian.[7] In coming

---

[3] Wim van Meurs, *Kosovo's Fifth Anniversary – On the Road to Nowhere?* (Munich: Centre for Applied Policy Working Paper, 2004), available at www.cap.lmu.de/download/2004/2004_Kosovo.pdf. In fact, to Serbs the province is known as Kosovo and Metohija, the latter denoting church estates and that the land encompassed 'is the cradle of the Serbian Orthodox People and their Church . . . the very heart of Serbian spiritual and national identity', see, www.kosovo.com, the official website of the Serbian Orthodox Diocese in the area.

[4] James Gow, *The Serbian Project and its Adversaries: A Strategy of War Crimes* (London: Hurst & Company, 2003), p. 2.

[5] For example, Independent International Commission on Kosovo, *Kosovo Report: Conflict; International Response; Lessons Learned* (Oxford: Oxford University Press, 2000), pp. 53–5; and Tim Judah, *Kosovo: War and Revenge* (New Haven, CT: Yale University Press, 2000), pp. 150–3.

[6] For a fuller account of this event see, Laura Silber and Allan Little, *The Death of Yugoslavia* (London: Penguin/BBC Books, 1996), pp. 37–8.

[7] The last census whose figures were generally accepted as valid was conducted in 1981, and showed that Serbs amounted to some 13 per cent and Albanians some 77 per cent of

to the defence of the Serbs in Kosovo, Milošević was equating the events of 1389 to those of 1989 (and later 1999); in his estimation he was defending a Serbia under threat from a foreign force, this time not the Ottoman invader but an ever growing Albanian population with a massive demographic preponderance in the Serbian province of Kosovo.

At the heart of the Kosovo conundrum lay the fact that indeed Kosovo was an integral part of Serbia and sovereign Yugoslavia, as a province and not a constituent republic; yet another piece of fabric in the tapestry sewn together by Tito in the formation of the Yugoslav state. It was never given the status of a republic both because of its significance to Serbian history and the rapidly inverting sizes of Serbian and Albanian populations. The safeguarding of Serbian rights in Kosovo was achieved initially through the federal status of Yugoslavia which provided equal constitutional guarantees for all national groups and subsequently through Kosovo's status as a province of Serbia and not Yugoslavia (while Serbs may have been a minority within Kosovo, the latter's provincial status within Serbia meant that in fact the Kosovar Albanian were a majority within Kosovo but a minority within Serbia).[8]

In effect, Kosovo was legally and territorially part of Serbia – and hence 'Serbian' – while the vast majority of its inhabitants were ethnically Albanian. Furthermore, this majority was progressively being marginalised, and repressed within Kosovo, and increasingly making demands in defence of their rights.

Resistance

There had always been an opposition tendency among Kosovo's Albanian population, resisting the effects of Serbia's authority. This increasingly grew in size and impact following Tito's death, and really emerged as a considerable force during the late 1980s as a result of Milošević's policies. The main Kosovar Albanian demands did not initially centre on independence – even though that was always an issue high up on the Albanian agenda. What the Albanians argued for was greater autonomy and equality within the political and economic system of Kosovo where ethnic criteria for selection would be abandoned. In addition, the freedom and opportunity to use their own language – and indeed teach it in school – and acknowledge their own history were

the population. The 1991 census is not accepted as valid and figures for that year are generally estimated by non-Yugoslav sources.

[8] For some details of the importance of the Yugoslav construct and its constitutions on the national question see James Gow, 'Deconstructing Yugoslavia', *Survival*, vol. 33, no. 3 (1991), pp. 291–311.

central to the Albanian 'opposition'.[9] Sporadic outbursts of violence directed at Serbian authorities within Kosovo – and occasionally at Serb civilians – were the extreme manifestations of discontent. But this discontent had yet to evolve into general unrest. But there were two main streams to the Albanian 'opposition' movement. The first revolved around the leadership of Ibrahim Rugova and took the form of passive resistance to the increasingly radicalised and extreme positions adopted by Belgrade on Kosovo. By the early 1990s, Kosovo's Albanians were second-class citizens.

Rugova countered this repression by advocating and practicing a policy of passive resistance, and his moderate leadership held sway through the period of uncertainty preceding Yugoslavia's violent disintegration. Hope remained that, as various Yugoslav constituent republics moved towards independence, Kosovo would be carried along in their wake and a peaceful transition to some form of autonomy would be achieved. This was also reflected in Rugova's secondary policy of creating the basis for a shadow administration of the province, following a secret referendum in 1991, and an array of 'para-institutions' to safeguard the rights and well-being on the Kosovar Albanians. But both policies foundered on the political reality that Kosovo was still part of Serbia within Yugoslavia. While passive resistance – and the creation of a parallel, phantom state – still mustered support among a majority of the Kosovar Albanians, cracks were beginning to appear in their united front.[10]

That cracks appeared was no great surprise. By early 1992, Yugoslavia was being ripped apart in a bloody struggle. Despite the bloodshed, Kosovar Albanians were beginning to cast envious glances at the success of Slovenia and Croatia in pursuing their independence and in their ability to gain international support for their cause. As a result a second form of opposition appeared in Kosovo, directly challenging the policies adopted by Rugova and his Democratic Alliance of Kosovo. This was the Kosovo Liberation Army (KLA), largely funded by a more radical Albanian diaspora and committed to a more aggressive and violent challenge to Serbian authority in the province. The KLA intended to provoke with the gun what Rugova was accused of failing to deliver through passive resistance. The KLA advocated an open struggle to deliver independence and within a decade its name would reverberate internationally. The Serbian police and military presence in Kosovo soon became the targets of the KLA, which was also not reticent to target Serbian civilians. But the radicalisation of the Kosovar Albanian

[9] Vickers, *Between Serb and Albanian*, pp. 246–8.   [10] Judah, *Kosovo*, Chapter 3.

population took longer for the KLA to achieve than it expected. There was no enunciation of a clear political agenda and certainly Kosovo did not register on the international diplomatic agenda which, at least in Western European and Transatlantic terms, was dominated – if not consumed – by the Bosnian conflict.[11]

The year 1995 was a turning point in the ability of the KLA to radicalise the Kosovar Albanian resistance to Serb rule and the raising of political stakes through the use of the gun. The catalyst proved to be the end of hostilities in Bosnia and the conclusion of the Dayton Accords. Through KLA prompting, the Dayton Accords were presented as a betrayal of the Kosovar Albanians by the international community. Some had seen Dayton as an opportunity to include Kosovo on the negotiating agenda at a time of weakness for Milošević in which significant concessions could have been gained. But there was no such interest internationally. The KLA exploited this by arguing in favour of increased use of force and proselytising among the Albanian community that passive resistance had yielded limited results, the outside world was not at all engaged in the plight of Kosovo's Albanians and since the independence of Slovenia, Croatia and – to a lesser extent – Bosnia were only achieved through violence, this should be emulated in Kosovo as well. While there could be a great human cost to this strategy, it was underpinned by the assumption that as the international community was now fully engaged in the Balkans, and that engagement had only come about as the result of war in Croatia and Bosnia, violence would be the only way to encourage attention on the Kosovo question.[12]

Events in neighbouring Albania added to the momentum of radicalisation among the Kosovar Albanians. The collapse of several large pyramid schemes in early 1997, resulted both in public economic dislocation and great political unrest, bordering on civil war, with the state held responsible for the crisis. The repercussions on Kosovo were immense. The close communal and political links between Albanians had immediate knock-on effects and a de facto anarchy in Albania was exploited by the KLA especially through the pilfering of arms from denuded Albanian authorities, which were then transported into Kosovo.[13] Effectively, the KLA's political agenda and its ability to pursue it were gradually coming together.

Progressively, and into 1998, Rugova's policy of passive resistance was being superseded by the KLA's more radical agenda. As the KLA

---

[11] Independent International Commission on Kosovo, *Kosovo Report*, pp. 51–3.
[12] *Ibid.*, pp. 62–4.
[13] Paulin Kola, *The Search for Greater Albania* (London: Hurst & Company, 2003), pp. 330–1.

stepped up its attacks on Serbian targets, Serb reprisals became harsher. This was both a case of self-defence and a reflection of the increasingly difficult position of the Milošević regime which was in need of a cause to reinvigorate its supporters among the Serbian population. Dayton may have signalled the end of a war but it also signified, in some circles, Milošević's betrayal of the Serbian cause; he may have been lauded as a peacemaker but his commitment to Serbia was in question. In the face of a growing public opposition – and in light of his unwillingness to promulgate serious political and economic reforms – Milošević re-energised a nationalist agenda. Reprisals against increasingly widespread KLA actions became harsher and were caught in the public spotlight in Kosovo and beyond. The regime in Belgrade argued that it was taking action in the interests of former Yugoslavia in what essentially was an internal matter of jurisdiction in a sovereign state. Milošević, by now president of Yugoslavia, steadfastly defended these actions in the face of mounting international pressure along these lines, accusing the KLA of terrorist actions and generally impugning the legality if its cause and methods.

By spring 1998, the United States and the United Kingdom, started paying greater attention to the possibility of a new Balkan crisis. Consequently, the 'international community' encouraged dialogue between the moderate Albanian leadership and the Yugoslav authorities in the hope of brokering an agreement which, while falling short of independence, would quell support for the KLA by granting greater autonomy to Kosovo (while simultaneously affirming Yugoslav sovereign rights and compelling Milošević to cease actions against the KLA).

It was through UNSC Resolution 1160, on 31 March 1998, that the Security Council attempted to intervene in the unfolding crisis by promoting a peaceful settlement. UNSC 1160 welcomed the efforts of both the six member Contact Group and the OSCE to bring a peaceful resolution to the situation in Kosovo. It clearly condemned 'the use of excessive force' by Serbian police, 'as well as acts of terrorism by the Kosovo Liberation Army', in an attempt to differentiate the latter from the moderate leadership of Rugova which it was hoped could be persuaded to negotiate with Serbia.[14] But while promoting the use of peaceful means by all parties to the dispute in pursuing a settlement, the resolution also confirmed the UN's commitment to the sovereignty and territorial integrity of the Federal Republic of Yugoslavia.[15]

This seemingly even-handed approach which condemned both Serbia and the KLA for the use of force in the pursuit of their respective goals,

---

[14] Security Council Resolution 1160, 31 March 1998, para. 3.   [15] *Ibid.*, para. 7.

while placing the burden of blame on Serbia also reaffirmed the commitment of the great powers to the respect of the sovereign and territorial rights of Federal Yugoslavia. This was an indication not only of the existing uncertainty as to whether the situation in Kosovo warranted intervention along humanitarian grounds – and to what extent the sovereignty of Yugoslavia should be doubted as a result of gross violations of human rights – but also because of a developing political dispute between the Permanent Five (P5) as to the consequences of any humanitarian intervention. While the United Kingdom and the United States were becoming increasingly prepared to consider military action against Yugoslavia, the Russian Federation and others, continued to promote Yugoslavia's sovereign rights both as a point of principle in relation to the maintenance of one of the most fundamental rules of international order, and also due to internal and geopolitical consideration on Russia's part.[16]

The Western powers, nevertheless, were faced by serious dilemmas of their own making. First, the brewing Balkan crisis was not initially considered humanitarian in nature. The prevailing, perennial Western strategy of containment in the Balkans placed events in Kosovo within the context of the broader south-eastern European landscape, and especially the safeguarding of the fragile peace in Bosnia. Hard fought gains made at Dayton would not be sacrificed for the situation in Kosovo, even if the possibility of escalation and spillover were real. Therefore what topped the Western agenda was not the protection of the rights of Kosovo's Albanian population but rather the stability of the region as a whole.[17] And, this stability included a heavy dose of realism especially with respect to the regional role of Serbia. Second, Western policy was temporarily stalled by the observation made by a high-ranking US envoy to the region, that in fact the KLA was a terrorist organisation.[18] If so, then the Yugoslav authorities had every right to pursue a heavy-handed policy against an illegal organisation threatening the integrity and sovereignty of a recognised state. This characterisation of the KLA as a terrorist organisation reinforced Milošević's belief not only in the legality of his actions but also that the international community neither had the basis nor stomach for the fight. But in attempting to retain his grip on power, he was stirring up a hornet's nest

---

[16] See the ensuing discussion of the Russian Federation's UNSC resolution which was rejected on 26 March 1999 for more detail.

[17] For more details of this argument see, Spyros Economides, 'Balkan Security: What Security? Whose Security?', *Journal of Southeast European and Black Sea Studies*, vol. 3, no. 3 (2003), pp. 105–29.

[18] Judah, *Kosovo*, p. 138.

of international disapproval which would quickly turn more demanding if not aggressive towards him.

Dialogue between Rugova and Belgrade proved futile and by late summer 1998, Serb forces were openly operating in large numbers against the KLA, conducting large sweeps in the countryside and rural villages suspected of harbouring 'terrorists'. There was now a growing international concern at the situation in Kosovo with the fear both of a threat to regional stability and a strong challenge to the authority of a Western-led 'international community'. The response was to threaten the reimposition of economic sanctions on Yugoslavia and not to preclude the possibility of military intervention at a later date.

It was at this juncture that the UN made its first forceful diplomatic intervention into the Kosovo crisis. Prompted by the United States and the United Kingdom – and a very recalcitrant Russia – the UNSC passed Resolution 1199 on 23 September 1998, calling for an immediate ceasefire and threatening the possible use of force against the FRY if it did not cease its offensive operations and proceed to a withdrawal of its forces. Behind the UNSC resolution lay an array of diplomatic initiatives and threats orchestrated by Richard Holbrooke, the architect of the Dayton Accords, and now US special presidential envoy to Yugoslavia. Inherent in his initial communications with Milošević was the potential threat of NATO action which lay behind UNSC 1199, already aired in June 1998.[19] It was indicated to Milošević that non-compliance could bring the full force of NATO to bear on Serbia. Under pressure from all international fronts, Milošević reluctantly complied.

The agreement struck consisted of three main elements. First, Milošević agreed to the withdrawal of 4,000 Serb special police troops which had been transferred into Kosovo during 1998. Second, it was also agreed that a 2,000 strong OSCE observer contingent, the Kosovo Verification Mission (KVM), would be deployed in Kosovo to monitor the above withdrawal.[20] Third, Milošević was forced to accept further negotiation with the Kosovo Albanian leadership to find a long-term solution.[21]

---

[19] William G. O'Neill, *Kosovo: An Unfinished Peace* (Boulder, CO: Lynne Rienner, 2002), p. 24.

[20] *Agreement on the Kosovo Verification Mission of the Organization for Security and Cooperation in Europe*, S/1998/978, 20 October 1998; *Kosovo Verification Mission Agreement between the North Atlantic Treaty Organization and the Federal Republic of Yugoslavia*, S/1998/991, 23 October 1998.

[21] Independent International Commission on Kosovo, *Kosovo Report*, p. 76.

While the Serbian withdrawal began on 27 October, and the KVM arrived to carry out its monitoring duties, there was no 'outbreak of peace'. On the one hand, the KLA saw no sense in an agreement predicated on further negotiation between Serb authorities and Rugova which could only go as far as limited autonomy for Kosovo. In addition, the fact that the UN (and NATO) had entered the fray and confronted Milošević was understood by the KLA as showing implicit support for Kosovo's independence. It concluded that the only way to achieve a quick and favourable solution – with this implicit Western backing – was to step up its 'military' operations.[22] On the other hand, Milošević still refused to take seriously the threat of international military intervention.[23] Holding the mistaken assumption that the United States – among others – would refuse to support the KLA, having already branded it a terrorist organisation, Milošević's forces met fire with fire.

In the winter of 1998–1999, the international community's role *vis-à-vis* Kosovo changed dramatically from that of mediator and interlocutor to both sides, to that of open opponent to the policies of Milošević (but not necessarily open supporter of the KLA). The first catalytic event in this transformation was the Račak massacre.[24] On 15 January 1999, the bodies of 45 Kosovo Albanians were discovered near the village of Račak. Called to the site, William Walker, the head of the KVM, immediately attributed the deaths to the actions of Serb forces. That Walker was requested to leave Kosovo by the Serb authorities, who would portray the massacre as an event stage managed by the KLA to attract external support, simply heightened tension. But the key was that the discovery of these bodies sparked off a vicious circle of hostilities between the KLA and the remaining Serb forces. In the face of such implacable hostility and disregard for the efforts to move the peace dialogue forward under UNSC Resolution 1199, the international community attempted to assert its authority by issuing an ultimatum.

This ultimatum stipulated that both sides should cease hostile actions and enter into intense negotiations to be held at Rambouillet under the aegis of the six nations Contact Group.[25] It was clear that there were still deep misgivings about the UN's perceived failure in Bosnia, and as the Contact Group had been instrumental in driving forward the Dayton Process, it was under this authority that the Serbs and Kosovar Albanians would be pressurised into reaching a solution. The talks at Rambouillet, which convened on 6 February, were scheduled to last one

---

[22] *Ibid.*, pp. 78–80.

[23] For more detail see, Gow, *The Serbian Project and its Adversaries*, pp. 204–5.   [24] *Ibid.*

[25] *Statement by the Contact Group Issued in London*, S/1999/96, 29 January 1999.

week. For the Kosovar Albanians this was an opportunity to press their case for independence under the watchful eye and with the support of an increasingly engaged, 'Western'-led international community. For Milošević, it was an opportunity not only to stall but also conduct a damage limitation exercise in which some – insignificant – concessions could be made while hammering home the point of sovereignty and domestic jurisdiction over internal affairs.

For various international actors, the opportunities offered by Rambouillet were less clear mainly because there was no agreement – let alone consensus – as to the causes and consequences of violence in Kosovo. Within the Contact Group, the United Kingdom and the United States were the most vociferous supporters of Kosovar Albanian rights. With the Bosnian experience and the plight of the Bosnian Muslims clearly in mind – and within the framework of promoting an ethical dimension to foreign policy-making (especially in the case of the Blair government in the United Kingdom) – there was a strong case for the defence of basic human rights through direct intervention against the Milošević regime. But the lack of clear support for the KLA, French and Russian reticence for military action against Milošević, and issues of regional stability and former Yugoslavia's state sovereignty, limited the Contact Group's scope of action at this point. While human rights were being violated, the realities of international and regional politics precluded early interventionary action.

Rambouillet

The negotiations at Rambouillet failed for a number of reasons. First, there was no common agenda or consensus for action among those who convened the talks. Second, the Serbs and Kosovar Albanians came to the table with very little intention of reaching a commonly agreed or viable settlement. This was reflected in the composition of their delegations. The Kosovar Albanians were a fragmented delegation, including Rugova, Hashim Thaçi and Veton Surroi, representing rival groups and agenda within Kosovo. As the lowest common denominator they could only agree, under immense pressure from their respective domestic constituencies, to push for an early referendum on the question of Kosovo's independence. This was a position that Thaçi and the KLA could sustain. The more moderate Kosovar Albanian elements believed that such a maximalist position would endanger Western goodwill and support (when the Contact Group was recommending a more limited compromise solution). On the other side of the table, they were faced by a united but impotent and inflexible FRY delegation that had no authority or agenda with which to negotiate. The scheduled first week of talks quickly spilled over into a second, and this scenario continued with constant extensions of the negotiating deadlines. Paradoxically it was the Kosovar Albanian delegation, which, until the last possible moment, refused to agree to the convoluted compromise solution, proposed by the Contact Group. Its inability to work to a common agenda or provide a common front – as they each jockeyed for popular support within Kosovo – meant that individuals within the delegation were increasingly susceptible to pressure from the Contact Group. In this context the FRY delegation retreated into its shell and wished the onus of refusal to negotiate to be heaped onto the Albanian delegation. By late February, under intolerable Western pressure, the Kosovar Albanian delegation agreed to sign up to the plan on offer.[26]

The weight of responsibility now lay on Milošević. For much of the latter stages of the talks, the FRY delegation agreed to many of the political elements of the Contact Group's proposals, believing that the Albanian delegation's inability to reach a consensus would render them meaningless. Once international pressure told on the Albanian delegation, Milošević was left with no alternative but refusal to sign. On one level he attacked the method by which the final position had been drawn up – in secret consultation with the Albanian delegation – indicating that the Western powers had caved in to Albanian demands so as to be able to call the talks which they had initiated a success. On another more substantial level, the FRY delegation argued that they could not sign an agreement that was so imbalanced that it violated the basic rights of a sovereign state. The main objections centred on provisions for a three-year 'cooling-off period', during which the Kosovar Albanians would be granted growing degrees of autonomy and self-government, leading to a referendum on independence.[27] On 18 March the Albanian delegation signed, the FRY delegation refused to do so.[28]

In the following nine days, Holbrooke orchestrated a concerted international effort to persuade Milošević that it was in the best interests of Serbia to sign up to the deal. Holbrooke made it clear to him, in no uncertain terms, that failure to agree would result in NATO

---

[26] For discussions of the build up to Rambouillet talks and the talks themselves, see Richard Caplan, 'International Diplomacy and the Crisis in Kosovo', *International Affairs*, vol. 74, no. 4 (1998), pp. 745–61; and Marc Weller, 'The Rambouillet Conference on Kosovo', *International Affairs*, vol. 75, no. 2 (1999), pp. 211–51. See also Alex J. Bellamy, *Kosovo and International Society* (Basingstoke: Palgrave, 2002), pp. 120–53.

[27] Including 'military intervention' in the form of a NATO-led implementation force.

[28] For the full text of the Rambouillet Accords, see *Rambouillet Accords: Interim Agreement for Peace and Self-Government in Kosovo*, S/1999/648, 7 June 1999.

bombardment of FRY on an unimaginable scale.[29] But for Milošević, signing up, would be viewed not only as backing-down on the isolated issue of Kosovo, but the dismantling of his nationalist construct on which his political power now relied.[30] Impervious to diplomatic pressure, and unable to imagine international intervention against Serbia, Milošević made the likely inevitable, by permitting the stepping up of the campaign against the Kosovar Albanians. Serbian troops and paramilitaries drove thousands of Kosovar Albanians from their homes, villages and towns. The growth of FRY military activity and refusal to sign up to Rambouillet left little room for manoeuvre for the international community. It had become not only a question of defending Albanian lives in Kosovo; a NATO-led international diplomatic effort could not be seen to be crumbling and ineffective in the face of FRY intransigence. The only remaining options were to concede failure, both at Rambouillet and all the preceding 'peace efforts', and face international humiliation and perhaps fragmentary tension within the Western alliance, or military intervention.

Taking the moral high ground, and espousing a doctrine of humanitarian intervention, NATO launched its aerial bombardment on the night of 24 March 1999. That the intervention took the form of a massive aerial bombardment represented the dual view that an attack on such a scale would force Milošević into concessions and also minimise NATO casualties. Its limited effectiveness was evident in that it lasted for 78 days. Target selection, involving a tortuous process at SHAPE, which required various levels of clearance, was initially limited to Serb forces and military installations within Kosovo.[31]

By the end of March it appeared that this policy was not having the desired effect. Indeed instead of damaging Serbian military capacity to act against the Albanian population, the campaign was pursued even more intensively. It has been argued that as a result of NATO's aerial bombardment, Milošević accelerated the policy of forcible expulsion of Kosovar Albanian's with the aim of purging Kosovo of all its Albanian population and rendering the minority question redundant.[32] Television images of hundreds of thousands of Albanian refugees streaming across the borders into neighbouring Albania and Macedonia was a telling

---

[29] Wesley K. Clark, *Waging Modern War: Bosnia, Kosovo and the Future of Combat* (New York: Public Affairs, 2001), pp. 180–2.

[30] For Milošević it was not only about Kosovo's potential independence and the loss of domestic prestige that would entail but about the stationing of foreign (NATO) troops on Yugoslav soil.

[31] Clark, *Waging Modern War*, p. 183.

[32] Independent International Commission on Kosovo, *Kosovo Report*, pp. 89–92; Gow, *The Serbian Project and its Adversaries*, pp. 206–9.

confirmation of this policy and of the ineffectiveness of the NATO air campaign. As a result, NATO extended its attack to encompass targets within FRY as well. Belgrade and other urban centres were targeted, as were major river crossings on the Danube, the remnants of the FRY's industrial capacity, oil refineries, electricity plants, as well as the obvious military and logistics targets across the country. This too had a short-term marginal effect as it did not hamper the operations of the Serb forces in Kosovo; the displacement of the Kosovar Albanians continued at a heightened pace.

The aerial campaign caused immense damage to the military capacity and civilian infrastructure of the FRY and its economic, psychological and political damage on the Milošević regime was extensive but not enough so as to put an end to the situation in Kosovo. The decision by NATO to pursue this form of military campaign hinged on two vital considerations. The first stemmed directly from previous NATO experience in the Balkans, and the misperception that aerial bombardment had driven the Serbs to the negotiating table at Dayton. The second emerged from the conviction that this 'new kind of war' would minimise 'allied' and especially US casualties, which was a vital concern in the context of the US experience in Somalia.[33]

These two considerations were instrumental not only in how the intervention was conducted, but also in its outcome. Bosnia's war was not terminated as a direct result of aerial bombardment; humanitarian intervention by aerial bombardment was ineffectual and in certain instances deemed not humanitarian. These were two important controversies arising out of the conduct of the war. The major controversy arose not out of how the war was conducted but why war and on whose authority?

The UN and NATO

The UN's role in the military intervention in Kosovo was minimal. Yet the intervention took place on humanitarian grounds and in the interest of maintaining international peace and security, by a regional organisation invoking the defence of humanitarian law on behalf of an international community based on a previous, but indecisive, resolution by the UNSC. The two key UNSC resolutions on which the intervention was based were UNSC 1199 (September 1998) and UNSC 1205

---

[33] Clark, *Waging Modern War*, p. 183. Minimising US casualties was the prime consideration in planning and executing the air campaign.

(October 1998), and particularly the former which provide the focus for the legality – or not – of NATO's actions in Kosovo.

The crucial dispute arising from NATO's intervention in Kosovo is between the morality and legality of the operation. This is also where the role of the UNSC as the main legitimating authority for this type of humanitarian intervention is of paramount importance. Did the UNSC authorise and hence legitimise the intervention in Kosovo? Or was this form of 'proper authority' lacking? If it was lacking then the operation was illegitimate and illegal. But first let us deal with the moral dimension of the question.

There is no doubt that the general framework for international humanitarian law (as distinct from international human rights law) allows for but does not provide for intervention on humanitarian grounds. It may be that the use of force for humanitarian purposes became increasingly accepted after the interventions in Somalia and Bosnia. But that does not preclude the fact that there is no international legal instrument providing for humanitarian intervention by military means.[34] In short, there was in the late 1990s a growing consensus based on fundamental moral considerations, and precedents set in at least two instances, that it was *morally* right to act – using force – to prevent or bring to an end humanitarian catastrophes. But these moral considerations, and notions of what was right, were brought into tension with what was legitimate and legal.

In this context a strong case can be built, on moral grounds, for forceful intervention in Kosovo to terminate a growing humanitarian 'catastrophe'; the killing and/or expulsion of the Albanian population of Kosovo by the authorities and actors of the FRY. This had been recognised not only by those NATO member states which ultimately condoned and/or participated in the military operation but also by the UNSC itself.

The international protection of human rights, especially in the case of the gross violation of human rights on a large scale, was becoming an increasingly important issue of concern for the Western world post-1989. Bosnia and Rwanda, for example, had brought focus to the debates on preventing large-scale abuses of human rights as well as for creating the justification and mechanisms for intervention when and where it was deemed to be necessary (and possible). As a result, strong arguments were put forward suggesting that, in the context of the UNSC, the use – or threat of use – of the veto by any member(s) of the

---

[34] Adam Roberts, 'NATO's "Humanitarian War" over Kosovo', *Survival*, vol. 41, no. 3 (1999), p. 108.

P5, in the case of a human rights issue was not only anachronistic, the product of a bygone age of power politics, but also plain wrong. This was not only an issue of institutional design and voting rights in the UNSC but one of moral imperative in relation to humanitarian intervention and the international protection of human rights. As one author put it, 'some support this position on the grounds that morality should trump legality in the exceptional cases where governments commit massive violations of human rights within their borders'.[35]

Moral indignation was compounded by the fact that the refugee crisis resulting from 'ethnic cleansing' in Kosovo was having an immediate regional impact in south-eastern Europe and beyond. All these considerations were reflected in UNSC Resolution 1199 which not only noted the concern with the fighting in Kosovo, 'and in particular the excessive and indiscriminate use of force by Serbian security forces and the Yugoslav Army',[36] but also condemned 'all acts of violence by any party, as well as terrorism in pursuit of political goals by any group or individual', clearly pointing a finger at the KLA.[37] The levels of refugees, and an affirmation of their right to return to their homes, figured highly in the resolution. Of great importance in the context of the moral argument were the references to the 'humanitarian situation in Kosovo', its 'rapid deterioration', 'the impending human catastrophe' and 'the need to prevent this from happening'.[38] The resolution emphasised deep concern about 'reports of increasing violations of human rights and of international humanitarian law' and also that the situation 'constituted a threat to peace and security in the region'.[39]

The resolution was clear in its condemnation of Serbian actions, highlighted the humanitarian dimension to the crisis, and proposed a series of criteria by which Serbia could meet UN demands. Basically, the resolution laid out a relatively solid moral case for intervention in Kosovo with the notable departure of also implicitly criticising the KLA and its method of operation through the use of the term 'terrorism'. The major problem arising from the resolution for 'pro-interventionists' was that there was no reference to 'the use of all necessary means', the acknowledged short-hand terminology authorising the use of armed force, even though it went on to say that the UN would 'consider further action'.[40]

---

[35] Nicholas J. Wheeler, 'Humanitarian Intervention after Kosovo: Emergent Norm, Moral Duty or the Coming Anarchy?', *International Affairs*, vol. 77, no. 1 (2001), p. 114.

[36] Security Council Resolution 1199, 23 September 1998, preamble.

[37] *Ibid.*   [38] *Ibid.*   [39] *Ibid.*

[40] Security Council Resolution 1199 (1998), para. 16.

This could be portrayed as a semantic argument. But the precedent of UNSC resolutions in using this language to telegraph intent and authorise, and legitimise, the use of force is widely accepted. While this is an important issue, the reality was that the UN neither officially authorised nor legitimised – let alone participated in – Operation Allied Force. As such, the moral case for intervention was a strong one but the legal case, and that of the UN's legitimising authority, remained open.

The first issue arising out of the legal dimension of this argument was that of FRY's sovereign statehood and the possible violation of that status through Operation Allied Force. Intervention may have been 'necessary on moral and political grounds',[41] but it may not have met the criteria of non-intervention into the internal affairs of a sovereign state. The FRY's right to domestic jurisdiction, as enshrined in the UN Charter, was violated albeit for a 'just cause'. But this violation, whatever the moral considerations, provided a big shock to the foundations of the international system of states. By enforcing the predominance of humanitarian issues over the principle of state sovereignty, NATO's intervention impinged on a most basic organising principle in international relations. But many, including eminent international lawyers, would argue that this is unproblematic.[42]

This was also brought to the fore in the UN Security Council by the draft resolution tabled by the Russian Federation – and co-sponsored by Belarus and India – on 26 March 1999 immediately after the beginning of the NATO bombardment.[43] This draft, which was resoundingly defeated in a vote, called for the cessation of the NATO operation, judging it as a violation of the UN Charter on a number of counts and most importantly as a violation of Article 2 (4). While the obvious reason for the this draft was the Russian concern with the protection of Yugoslavia's sovereignty and territorial integrity, numerous other factors were behind it. Most of them were specific to domestic Russian politics and Russia's geopolitical concerns and it's general relationship with the western world. Yeltsin's political position was rather precarious in the

---

[41] Catherine Guicherd, 'International Law and the War in Kosovo', *Survival*, vol. 41, no. 2 (1999), p. 19.
[42] For example, Christopher Greenwood argued both in evidence to the House of Commons Select Committee on Foreign Affairs and in the media that state rights do not always take precedence over human rights especially where there was a threat to international peace and security as a result of massive human rights violations. See the *House of Commons Select Committee on Foreign Affairs, Fourth Report, 1999*, para. 130, www.publications.parliament.uk/pa/cm199900/cmselect/cmfaff/28/2813.htm; and Christopher Greenwood, 'Yes, but is the war legal', *The Observer*, 28 March 1999.
[43] UN Security Council Draft Resolution, S/1999/328, 26 March 1999.

face of a serious domestic opposition in the run-up to elections and the bolstering of his nationalist credentials – a sure way of gaining electoral support – was partly achievable by supporting Slav Serbia. But Russia's grievances also stretched to the extending influence of NATO in to central and eastern Europe both in the context of the expansion of NATO's membership but also the physical expansion of NATO's military involvement in south-eastern Europe.

Russia's concerns about NATO humanitarian intervention in Kosovo, and the challenge this posed to sovereignty and territorial integrity as the mainstay of international order, was also an important consideration shared by a number of other (non-Western states) such as India and the People's Republic of China. They argued that the evolving doctrine of humanitarian intervention, was a Western way of establishing new norms and rules of international behaviour, which would undermine the existing bases of international order based on the sovereign, territorial state, which would then be used against them and especially against 'weaker states' which had no way of defending against Western power.

This set of arguments did not prove convincing in the context of the Russian draft resolution which was resoundingly rejected. The UNSC was mindful of the issue of sovereignty but a majority of its members argued that in such times of humanitarian crisis action had to be taken, and while the UNSC has the primary responsibility for the maintenance of international peace and security, this responsibility is not exclusive and when it cannot act because of institutional restrictions then other avenues must be pursued which are equally legitimate both legally and morally.

The centrality of state sovereignty to this debate continued and will continue to do so. One key development arising from this debate was the establishment of the International Commission on Intervention and State Sovereignty. The Commission and its ensuing report,[44] using the Kosovo war as the starting point, concentrates specifically on the right of humanitarian intervention. At the heart of this report is indeed this conundrum of the relationship between sovereign state rights and the evolving right to intervene in times of humanitarian catastrophe, as well as the legal and moral debates which were pitted against each other in the context of Kodso.

What is most revealing about the centrality of the state sovereignty issue to Operation Allied Force is that the agreement signalling the end

---

[44] The International Commission on Intervention and State Sovereignty, *The Responsibility to Protect* (Ottawa, ON: International Development Research Centre, 2001).

of hostilities and relating to Kosovo's status, NATO and thus the international community, had to explicitly acknowledge the maintenance of FRY's sovereign rights in Kosovo. While NATO went to war in violation of those sovereign rights, it laid down that right as a basic condition for the future resolution of the Kosovo issue.

But the moral or 'just war' tradition for the intervention in Kosovo also raises a further set of legal issues. In the just war tradition, proper authority is a pre-requisite of military action. In the case of Kosovo the primary sources of proper authority; self-defence; an invitation to intervene; or the authority of the UN as the universal international organisation are not met, at least not overtly or transparently.[45] But this is more than a legal issue.

Let us assume that the moral concerns for intervention in Kosovo were real, but secondary, to a host of political considerations and political expediency on behalf of the interventionary powers (and especially the United States and the United Kingdom).[46] Even if Operation Allied Force was a manifestation of realpolitik and based on the defence of NATO's integrity or of regional peace and security, UNSC authority was not sought. It has been argued that Operation Allied Force was 'implementing UNSC resolutions without Security Council authorisation'.[47] But that does not necessarily make it right. It could point to political tension within the UNSC, where there lurked a real possibility of a Russian or Chinese veto, which would have scuppered all chances of the operation going ahead, but these may have been overcome. Nor is it adequate – even though it seems powerful – to suggest that NATO was acting on behalf of the international community, as it represented an international community based on the values of liberty and freedom enshrined in the democratic practices of the alliance's member states acting en bloc.

There existed within NATO a wide range of positions, and differing policy preferences with regard to the situation in Kosovo, which indicated that in fact the NATO operation did not take place with the

---

[45] Kosovo was not a recognised sovereign state, thus not subject to the jurisdiction of international law allowing it to invoke self-defence not did the Kosovar Albanians or the KLA have the sovereign rights, according to international law to request outside intervention. While NATO intervention was justifiable under the relevant Charter provisions allowing for the actions of regional organisations, it has been shown that the authority of the UN, which is needed in these cases, was not as clear as some would like to make out.

[46] Economides, 'Balkan Security', pp. 105–27. Even though others would argue that moral and normative issues actually became the interests of states such as the United Kingdom. See for example, Nicholas J. Wheeler, *Saving Strangers: Humanitarian Intervention in International Society* (Oxford: Oxford University Press, 2000), pp. 267–8.

[47] Roberts, 'NATO's "Humanitarian War" over Kosovo', p. 102.

unanimous acclamation of NATO allies, let alone the international community, more broadly speaking.

While the legitimacy of Operation Allied Force may have been compromised by the lack of proper authority, and its moral under-pinning questioned by others, the means used to conduct the intervention also lay open to criticism; conduct during warfare also led to disputes. Irrespective of the moral implications of the decision to intervene, it was argued that the method of intervention and the conduct in war rendered the intervention susceptible to doubt if not altogether wrong. The operation was conducted from the air, over a sustained period of time, targeting military as well as military-related targets, in Kosovo and beyond. As a result of the wide range of targets and the type of campaign it was, there was much collateral damage. And as mentioned before, US insistence on conducting such an air campaign hinged on the need to minimise US casualties. One notable international lawyer, Ian Brownlie, questioned not only the legitimacy of the operation but also its morality as a result of the type of operation conducted: 'a blitz with high explosives, which was intended in part to put pressure on the population and which lasted 78 days, has nothing in common with humanitarian intervention'.[48]

This argument suggests that as humanitarian intervention is rooted in morality, and seeks to safeguard the rights of people based on a moral concern for their 'well-being', then any such intervention also has to be conducted according to accepted principles of conduct in war. In essence, the criticism is levelled not only at the methods used in the intervention but also at the operation as a whole. If indeed, the lives of NATO soldiers – and in this case primarily US soldiers – were considered more valuable than those of the Kosovar Albanians being killed or chased from their homes, and hence determined the nature of the campaign, then the operation as a whole could not be justified.

The same question has been raised by Adam Roberts, albeit in a slightly different manner. His focus is not conduct in war but rather the practical effects of the intervention: 'The fact that the campaign failed in the intended manner to avert a humanitarian disaster in the short-term, even though it did eventually stop it, makes it a questionable model of humanitarian intervention'.[49] As humanitarian intervention is predicated on moral concerns, then the morality of the entire operation is cast into doubt both by the methods employed and the short-term

---

[48] *House of Commons Select Committee on Foreign Affairs, Fourth Report, 1999, Appendix 2,* para. 102, www.parliament.the-stationery-office.co.uk/pa/cm19990/cmselect/cmfaff/28/28a.

[49] Roberts, 'NATO's "Humanitarian War" over Kosovo', p. 120.

outcomes (especially since, as was argued previously, the short-term outcomes were a direct result of the methods used).

As we can see, the debates concerning the morality, legality and political expediency of NATO intervention in Kosovo are extensive. In the context of this book, what is most relevant is that the UN was sidestepped by the intervening states for a number of reasons. In name, NATO may have acted on behalf of the common morality of the international community and, as has been argued, in accordance with the spirit of the UN Charter and specific UNSC resolutions. In practice, its actions did not receive direct UN authorisation. While a moral cause was undoubtedly served in the longer term, the causes of the intervention and the conduct in war cast a shadow over Operation Allied Force.

The biggest paradox is that in a volume dedicated to UN interventionism in the post-Cold War, the Kosovo episode (at least in its period of war) is one in which the UN was marginalised. The UN is significant, in this case, not because of its actions, or the actions of its agencies of forces operating under its aegis, but because of the inability or unwillingness of key members to utilise its Charter provisions to make an intervention legally and morally airtight. We are still left with the afterthought that intervention in Kosovo did have a humanitarian motivation but was primarily the result of other more political questions. That NATO proceeded with Operation Allied Force on the premises of both a pending humanitarian catastrophe and a threat to international peace and security does not mitigate the unwillingness to ensure UN legitimation.

The fallout of Kosovo on the UN, and on the UNSC in particular, should not be underestimated. It solidified the emerging view that the United States found the UNSC a redundant forum for multilateralism. Undoubtedly, the Bosnian experience and the multiple and unachievable mandates handed down by the UNSC in that conflict had a telling effect on US attitudes. The objections of the PRC and especially Russia also left their mark on US and UK policy-makers. But, the reluctance to employ the tried and tested (and legitimate) avenue of the UNSC to authorise 'the use of all necessary means' also signalled the beginning of growing US unilateralism, the novel use of NATO as the vehicle for international intervention, and the return to a special 'special relationship' between the United States and the United Kingdom.

There is a paradox within the paradox of the UN's role in the Kosovo crisis. While in the run-up to the war the principles and institutions of the UN were marginalised, and the whole organisation was deemed irrelevant in security terms, with the cessation of hostilities, these principles and institutions were pushed to the fore in dealing with the

Kosovo question. I will stand on only two here, the issue of sovereignty and the role of the UN. These are the two most prominent factors relevant to the argument.

Moral concerns and concerns with the protection of human rights seemingly took precedence over sovereign state rights in 1999, and NATO unleashed a military intervention to avert a humanitarian catastrophe. With the signing of the Kumanovo Technical Agreement in June 1999, which put an end to NATO's military campaign, the sovereign rights of the FRY – which, arguably, had been trampled upon – were reinvoked and reinstated. Pending a final status for Kosovo, Serbian sovereign rights were to be respected in principle and were embodied in the agreement concluding the hostilities and which set out the framework for the governance of Kosovo.[50] Immediate independence for Kosovo was impossible, even though that is what the KLA had fought for and what the Kosovar Albanians aspired to. Indeed, independence will be the most likely long-term outcome for Kosovo and it was widely perceived by Kosovo's Albanian community that the NATO had intervened with this result in mind.

Until the cessation of hostilities and the signing of the Kumanovo Agreement, the UN had a non-role in the Kosovo crisis. The UN's indirect authority had been utilised by the intervening states but direct legitimation had not been sought or given. The prevailing argument that 'needs must' and that the immediacy of the moral and humanitarian crisis in Kosovo made imperative an immediate intervention without the formal or legal backing of a UNSC resolution, promoted the idea of the predominance of human over state rights. And yet, at the end of the conflict, the intervening powers sought both to re-establish Yugoslav sovereign rights and the legitimacy of UN sponsorship.

The P5 returned to the Security Council at the end of the conflict to seek this legitimacy. UNSC Resolution 1244 sought to restore the authority of the UN, and most importantly that of the UNSC and its 'primary responsibility for the maintenance of international peace and security', and in a sense thus justifying Operation Allied Force in UN terms ex post facto. Acting under Chapter VII of the Charter, the UN would provide the auspices under which both civilian administration

---

[50] The Kumanovo Agreement concentrated on the military dimension to the end of hostilities, the withdrawal of Serb forces from Kosovo and the establishment of an international security force (KFOR) to maintain peace and stability in Kosovo. This was the *Military Technical Agreement between the International Security Force (KFOR) and the Governments of the Federal Republic of Yugoslavia and the Republic of Serbia*, www.nato.int/kosovo/docu/a990609a.htm. This went in tandem with Security Council Resolution 1244 (1999), which established the political, legal and civilian administration framework for the governance of Kosovo and its future.

and a military security force would bring peace and stability to Kosovo, 'pending a final settlement'.[51] UNSC Resolution 1244 reaffirmed the commitment of all member states to the sovereignty and territorial integrity of FRY, while also calling for substantial autonomy and 'meaningful self-administration for Kosovo'.[52] These contradictory processes have clouded the debate on Kosovo's final status ever since.

UNSC Resolution 1244 also confirmed and authorised the call made in the Kumanovo Technical Agreement for an international military presence in Kosovo. This would be in the form of the KFOR, acting under UN auspices, but essentially a NATO force allowing for some non-NATO contingents. KFOR, initially numbering over 40,000 men, would guarantee international peace and security under a Chapter VII mandate and also maintain a secure environment for all citizens of Kosovo. KFOR would be responsible for monitoring and enforcing the agreed Serbian military withdrawal, protect against future threats from FRY, and safeguard against 'all terrorist acts by any party',[53] and including the demilitarisation of the KLA.[54] The enablement of refugee return was another role for KFOR as was the protection of the international civilian presence.[55] KFOR operated under a UN mandate but was in reality an independent force commanded and controlled by NATO.

The international civilian presence would be an 'interim administration for Kosovo', 'to provide transitional administration' under which the people of Kosovo could enjoy substantial autonomy within FRY and 'establishing and overseeing the development of provisional democratic self-governing institutions'.[56] The organisation, which was to administer this process, was termed UNMIK. It was to work closely with other international organisations and agencies to ensure economic stability and development, and political reform, to meet the criteria of UNSC Resolution 1244.

UNMIK's activities were hamstrung from the outset. The contradictions implicit in its mandate rather than operational constraints made its task almost unfeasable.[57] Operationally, it was robust, especially at the levels of executive powers and the ability to intervene in all aspects of the province's political and socio-economic life.[58] To facilitate in the

---

[51] Security Council Resolution 1244 (1999), para. 11(a).   [52] *Ibid.*, preamble.
[53] *Ibid.*   [54] *Ibid.*, paras. 9(b) and 15.   [55] *Ibid.*, para. 9.   [56] *Ibid.*, para. 10.
[57] Richard Caplan, *A New Trusteeship? The International Administration of War-Torn Territories*, Adelphi Paper 341 (Oxford: Oxford University Press, 2002), pp. 17–8. See also Alexandros Yannis, *Kosovo Under International Administration: An Unfinished Conflict* (Athens: Hellenic Foundation for European and Foreign Policy, 2001), pp. 27–31.
[58] For the clearest exposition of the structure of UNMIK and its 'pillars' see, Caplan, *A New Trusteeship?*, pp. 22–5.

twin tasks of economic reconstruction and development, and political transition, UNMIK was also required to guide institutional and capacity building, as well as providing for the day-to-day administration of the province in tandem with local groups and institutions. For protection, UNMIK turned to KFOR. For finances, UNMIK relied on substantial contributions from the European Union (and various special agencies set up for Kosovo) as well as the pledges of special donor conferences that earmarked funds for the province.

Therefore, functions were expansive but quite clearly delineated, international support existed both in political, economic and military terms, authority was exerted through all encompassing powers, and legitimacy was guaranteed through a UN mandate. But there was no clear idea what the final status of Kosovo would be, and as such it remained impossible to plan for the length of stay or the ultimate nature of the transition. In terms of the economy this vagueness about the final resolution of Kosovo's status was less problematic; economic reconstruction and development would occur irrespective of the future of the province. While it would remain unclear what the final beneficiary of economic reform would be, that is an independent state of Kosovo, a province of Serbia or an entity somewhere in between. It was perfectly clear that the people of Kosovo would be the beneficiaries irrespective of the status of the province. Politically, though, reform could only achieve broad acceptance if the end status was clear and agreeable, and if both the issue of the rights of the people of Kosovo (of all ethnic backgrounds) and the state of FRY/Serbia could be addressed to the satisfaction of all parties. This was impossible in light of the open-ended process of political transition.

Politically, thus, UNMIK was limited from the outset, and the politics of the international presence in Kosovo dominated all other activities. Unless Kosovo's final status was made transparent and acceptable to all, the work of UNMIK would always be met with suspicion if not obstruction from all sides. And, final status was not readily attainable because of the nature of the agreements reached in June 1999 and in UNSC Resolution 1244. The latter recognised and guaranteed FRY's sovereignty and included Kosovo within that sovereign territory. Simultaneously, it promoted 'substantial autonomy and meaningful self-administration for Kosovo'.[59]

The guarantee of sovereignty served the interests of the FRY, the Serb minority in Kosovo, as well as broader organisational principles in international affairs dealing with the use of armed force to change

[59] Security Council Resolution 1244 (1999), preamble.

borders, secession, domestic jurisdiction, defence against terrorism, and the fact that international intervention had occurred to maintain international peace and security, maintain the integrity of NATO and avert a humanitarian catastrophe – and not to support the independence of Kosovo. The promotion of autonomy and self-administration served the interests of the Albanian majority, relieving it of Serbian domination and oppression, and indicating a desire to ensure the well-being of this population through a degree of autonomy if not self-determination.

The Serbs saw the return of their sovereign rights as hypocritical yet indicative of the justice of their rights and condemnation of the 'terrorist' activities of the KLA. The Albanian community saw the latter as an explicit commitment to future independence. But in the interim period neither side would be happy with a political arrangement which did not grant them fully and immediately what they saw as their right; their support for UNMIK was therefore reluctant and at times non-existent. As far as FRY was concerned its sovereign rights and the rights of the Serb community in Kosovo were not being met according to the expectations laid out in UNSC Resolution 1244. As far as the Kosovar Albanians were concerned, UNMIK was just not moving the transition movement on towards the perceived goal of independence fast enough. Elections were regularly postponed and even when they were staged, one side or the other – or both immediately challenged their legitimacy. Violence, though controlled by KFOR and not widespread, was a constant low-level reminder of the intractability of the Kosovo problem and of the horrors which could revisit the inhabitants of the province. When the situation did boil over into open violence, as it did in March 2004 when 19 people lost their lives, 900 were injured and over 700 homes, 30 Orthodox Churches and monasteries and 10 public buildings were destroyed and over 4,500 Serbs were 'displaced',[60] the true nature of the problem confronting the international community reared its head.

Technical solutions and a technocratic approach were all well and good, but there seemed to be no agreed progress on the underlying ethnic divisions and sovereign status of the province. Consequently, as uncertainty reigned and there was no progress towards an agreed end status, not only was there a political stalemate, but also a general reticence by foreign funders and investors to participate in a constitutionally unclear potentially unstable territory.

At heart, the main sticking point is the conflict between the Serbian demand for the maintenance of their sovereign rights and the Albanian

---

[60] International Crisis Group, 'Collapse in Kosovo', *ICG Europe Report No. 155* (Brussels: ICG, 22 April 2004), p. 1.

demand for self-determination and independence. Nevertheless, to actually reach negotiations on this fundamental conflict, the international community set up a road map, which caused further uncertainty and divisions, the so-called standards before status policy. It was in a speech to the Security Council, in April 2002, that the secretary-general's Special Representative to Kosovo, Michael Steiner, first set the foundations for this policy. It was a policy, which set 'benchmarks' for behaviour, and the protection of rights and institutions, as well as, economic development, which he proposed, was, 'an exit strategy (from Kosovo), which is in reality an entry strategy into the European integration process'.[61] Swiftly following this speech the term 'standards before status' became the *lingua franca* of the international community's attitude towards the Kosovo impasse and a strategy, which was formalised in the Kosovo Standards Implementation Plan, produced in March 2004.[62] But, while concentrating on the vital issue of standards of life and behaviour as the key for the solution of Kosovo's ills, this strategy sidestepped the fundamental political and legal issue of the status of the province.

In essence the issue is of rule: who would be administering and protecting these standards? Would it be an independent Kosovo in which the Serb minority would feel insecure (especially after the events of March 2004), or a Serbian Kosovo which would be a throwback to the pre-1999 situation, totally unacceptable to the Albanians and to vast parts of the international community as a whole? Without a clear vision of what the final status of the province would be and who would govern, standards were of secondary importance, or at least of equal importance only if monitored and enforced by the 'internationals', whether civilian or military.

The sovereignty issue in itself is not intractable for the international community; it can easily assume support for the Albanian position and push for independence. Arguably in Kosovo this would make sense, as could a partition or cantonisation of the province between the two ethnic groups. But in terms of international politics it would have to be done slowly and over a longer period of time to avoid accusations of the total flouting of international law and open support for a group which as late as 1999 had been branded a terrorist organisation. What is intractable is the bind of the 'standards before status policy' in which it is very difficult to agree upon or enforce standards, which in their own

---

[61] See 'Kosovo: More needs to be done on security, economic development, Annan reports', 5 October 2006, www.unmikonline.org/archives/news04_02full.htm.

[62] *Kosovo Standards Implementation Plan*, 31 March 2004, www.unmikonline.org/pub/misc/ksip-eng.pdf.

right are very popular, when it is unclear to whom those standards will apply, who will enforce them in the future, and on which territory.

While the UN is still in charge of the civilian administration in Kosovo – with the continued military support of the international security force, some of its powers have been devolved to an elected government while more importantly the international effort to reach a solution has been taken up by the revitalised Contact Group. While the latter operates under the aegis of the UNSC – and will have to ensure that any plans it proposes are cleared with the UN who will have to authorise any final settlement – it is clear that the running will be made by the P5 and especially the United States and the United Kingdom (with the consent of the European Union). What is becoming evident is that the standards before status policy will have to be modified if the Contact Group is to fulfil its ambition to reach a final settlement by 2007. And there are indications that this will happen especially following the publications of two significant, independent reports, which propose a variety of possibilities for the future of Kosovo.

The first of these argues forcefully for a timeline for the settlement of the Kosovo issue suggesting that this should happen swiftly, and that it should be on the basis of 'standards and status'.[63] It goes on to suggest a variety of different possibilities for the outcome of the discussions of status and concludes that the only viable settlement will be based on Kosovo's independence, 'albeit a somewhat conditioned independence'.[64] This would be the only way in which the consent of Serbia would be forthcoming and which would satisfy the demands of the Albanian community in Kosovo, as well as giving the international community a degree of leverage if not control of the situation and eradicating the possibilities of regional instability resulting not only from conflict within Kosovo but that arising from any moves towards the unification with the Albanian community in neighbouring FYROM and Albania proper.

The second, equally influential, report is just as urgent in tone as that of the International Crisis group: 'Time is running out in Kosovo. The international community has clearly failed in its attempts to bring security and development to the province ... [W]e do not believe that Kosovo's independence will solve all the territorial problems, but we are concerned that postponing the status talks will lead to a further deterioration in the situation in the province'.[65] This report also suggests a

---

[63] International Crisis Group, 'Kosovo: Towards Final Status', *ICG Europe Report No. 161* (Brussels: ICG, 24 January 2005), p. 2–3.

[64] International Crisis Group, 'Kosovo: Towards Final Status', pp. 25–7.

[65] International Commission on the Balkans, 'The Balkans in Europe's Future' (April 2005), pp. 19–20, 20 November 2006, www.balkan-commission.org.

settlement short of full independence by way of an independent but not sovereign Kosovo, which will then undergo a period of 'guided sovereignty' and ultimately be subsumed within the European Union.[66]

But it is generally acknowledged that any settlement is contingent on one fundamental obstacle, the lack of direct discussion between Belgrade and Pristina. The Serbian authorities are unwilling not only to contemplate an independent Kosovo but more importantly, involvement in discussions culminating in this form of settlement for which they will be held responsible by their domestic constituency. Similarly, the Albanian leadership in Pristina is holding out for full independence and does not see the need to deal away what it perceives as a strong hand. The intractability of this problem is yet an added burden to the UN quite apart from the travails of the day-to-day administration of Kosovo.

Conclusion

The origins of the conflict in Kosovo are lengthy and convoluted. They are mired in the potent symbolism and imagery of a national awakening which was linked with a complicated contemporary Balkan political scene in the context of Yugoslavia's disintegration. The manipulation of Kosovo's status increasingly became the cornerstone of Sobodan Milošević's political edifice. Kosovo's Albanians had a major role in this tragic act. They became the targets of a policy initially aimed at their repression and subsequently at their displacement (if not death). They were an indirect target in that their persecution served the ulterior motive of maintaining Milošević's grip on power. But Kosovo's Albanians were not passive actors. Their major role was acted out through the violent activity of the KLA in its drive to secure Kosovo's independence. It was the escalation of conflict in Kosovo in the wake of Yugoslavia's other bloody wars of disintegration, which drew in the outside world and resulted in international intervention.

The UN's role in the Kosovo conflict and subsequent intervention was on one level minimal and on another level extensive. As the acknowledged authoriser and legitimating agent of international humanitarian intervention it played a minimal role, and not by its own design. Those states, and particularly the United States and the United Kingdom, who wished to prosecute war against Serbia, sidestepped the UN (especially the UNSC). It was not deemed necessary to acquire the

---

[66] International Commission on the Balkans, 'The Balkans in Europe's Future', pp. 20–3.

legal or moral backing of a UNSC resolution in carrying out the intervention in Kosovo; NATO would act as the agent transmitting and enforcing the moral, humanitarian concerns of the international community. The legal, moral and political fall-out of the marginalisation of the UNSC has subsequently been repeated elsewhere and especially in the case of Iraq. Nevertheless, the issue of legality and moral authority of Operation Allied Force still remains open to debate. Some would have it that the moral justification for this operation remains beyond doubt even if it does not carry the imprimatur of the UNSC. In preventing a humanitarian catastrophe, and maintaining its commitment to international humanitarian law and the defence of human rights, the Western alliance led an intervention on behalf of the broader international community. Grave doubts still remain as to the effectiveness of the operation, over the methods used and the collateral damage caused, and over the political outcome.

A ceasefire was imposed and stability restored to Kosovo, but the operation did not resolve Kosovo's ethnic and political problems; this remained an open-ended process. International intervention on humanitarian grounds was interpreted by one side as clear support for the independence of Kosovo. The Kumanovo agreement, and especially the subsequent UNSC resolution mapping out the future political framework for negotiation, was interpreted by the other side as an acceptance of Yugoslavia's sovereign rights in Kosovo. And while this uncertainty and conflict of interpretation remained on the table, the UN was called in to govern Kosovo almost as a protectorate pending a final agreement on status. Marginalised in terms of the intervention, the UN was now required to 'pick-up' the post-conflict 'pieces'. So long as a negotiated political solution remained unreachable – or a solution is not externally imposed – the UN shouldered the responsibility for the social, economic and political administration of a territory of unresolved status. Standards may have been set in terms of governance and human rights but they cannot be imposed or are not readily accepted, when there is no agreement on the final status – on whom these rights will be applicable to and who will guarantee them.

9   Sierra Leone

Adekeye Adebajo and David Keen

Introduction

Since the early 1990s, West Africa has been an innovative laboratory for United Nations (UN) peacekeeping. In 1993, the UN deployed military observers in Liberia, alongside a regional organisation – the Economic Community of West African States (ECOWAS) Ceasefire Monitoring Group (ECOMOG) – for the first time in its history. The UN also sent military observers to Sierra Leone (UNOMSIL) in 1998 and took over ECOMOG's peacekeeping responsibilities in the country by 2000.[1] ECOWAS peacekeepers were 're-hatted' as Blue Helmets in Liberia and Côte d'Ivoire in 2003 and 2004 respectively. After providing a brief background of the domestic, regional and external dimensions of Sierra Leone's conflict, this chapter examines the evolution, performance and politics of the UN mission in Sierra Leone (UNAMSIL), as well as peacekeeping cooperation between the UN and ECOWAS.

The chapter argues that the UN (particularly the most powerful members of the fifteen member Security Council) was shamefully negligent in African countries like Sierra Leone for most of the 1990s

---

[1] For a background, see Ibrahim Abdullah and Patrick Muana, 'The Revolutionary United Front of Sierra Leone: A Revolt of the Lumpenproletariat', in Christopher Clapham (ed.), *African Guerrillas* (Oxford, Kampala and Bloomington IN: James Currey, Fountain Publishers and Indiana University Press, 1998), pp. 127–94; Adekeye Adebajo, *Building Peace in West Africa: Liberia, Sierra Leone and Guinea-Bissau* (Boulder, CO and London: Lynne Rienner, 2002); Adekeye Adebajo and Ismail Rashid (eds.), *West Africa's Security Challenges: Building Peace in a Troubled Region* (Boulder CO and London: Lynne Rienner, 2004); Ibrahim Abdullah and Yusuf Bangura 'Youth Culture and Political Violence: The Sierra Leone Civil War', *African Development*, special issue, vol. 22, nos. 2 and 3, (1997); John Hirsch, *Sierra Leone: Diamonds and the Struggle for Democracy* (Boulder CO: Lynne Rienner, 2001); Mark Malan, Phenyo Rakate and Angela McIntyre, *Peacekeeping in Sierra Leone: UNAMSIL Hits the Home Straight* (Pretoria: Institute for Security Studies, 2002); William Reno, *Warlord Politics and African States* (Boulder CO and London: Lynne Rienner Publishers, 1998); and Paul Richards, *Fighting for the Rainforest: War, Youth and Resources in Sierra Leone* (Oxford and New Hampshire: James Currey and Heinemann, 1996).

following debacles in Somalia (1993) and Rwanda (1994).[2] Although
there was criticism of rebel atrocities, much of the international community and UN agencies failed to condemn the gross human rights
abuses committed by government troops during Sierra Leone's civil war
or to support disarmament efforts effectively. Indeed, Sierra Leone
hardly appeared on international radar screens at all until the late 1990s.
In the context of a major security vacuum and lack of strong UN
interest, ECOWAS took up the burden of peacekeeping – with mixed
results. Sierra Leone's civil society actors – particularly women and
religious groups – also contributed to peace efforts. However, it was only
after May 2000 – with the UN's logistically ill-equipped peacekeeping
force facing the humiliation of having 500 peacekeepers captured by
rebels – that the world body began to develop a viable strategy in Sierra
Leone. In the end, the results were impressive – if highly improvised –
demonstrating what can be achieved by a coordinated effort to push for
peace and a willingness to fund it.

The 'malign' neglect of Sierra Leone's civil war, 1991–1997[3]

The civil war in Sierra Leone began in March 1991 when about 300
rebels moved into the diamond-rich areas of the south and east, backed
by Liberian warlord Charles Taylor (who was elected president of
Liberia in 1997). Though claiming to be fighting corruption, the rebels
quickly alienated the great majority of Sierra Leoneans through their
attacks on civilians. Those fighters of the Revolutionary United Front
(RUF) opposing such atrocities, often the more educated members,
were eliminated by the RUF leadership. Significantly, this seems to have
reflected, in large part, the hostility of rebel leader, Foday Sankoh, and
his supporters towards an educated strata that were seen as complicit in

---

[2] See Adekeye Adebajo, 'From Congo to Congo: United Nations Peacekeeping in Africa
after the Cold War,' in Ian Taylor and Paul Williams (eds.), *Africa in International
Politics: External Involvement on the Continent* (London: Routledge, 2004), pp. 195–212;
Oliver Furley and Roy May (eds.), *Peacekeeping in Africa* (Aldershot and Vermont:
Ashgate, 1998); Ibrahim Gambari, 'The United Nations', in Mwesiga Baregu and
Christopher Landsberg (eds.), *From Cape to Congo: Southern Africa's Evolving Security
Challenges* (Boulder, CO: and London: Lynne Rienner, 2003), pp. 255–74; Marrack
Goulding, 'The United Nations and Conflict in Africa since the Cold War', *African
Affairs*, vol. 98, no. 391 (April 1999), pp. 155–66; Norrie McQueen, *United Nations
Peacekeeping in Africa since* 1960 (Harlow: Pearson Education Limited, 2002); and
Agostinho Zacarias, *The United Nations and International Peacekeeping* (London: I.B.
Tauris and Co., 1996).

[3] The next two sections borrow from Adekeye Adebajo and David Keen, 'Banquet for
Warlords', *The World Today*, vol. 56 no. 7 (July 2000), pp. 8–10.

a corrupt one-party regime under Siaka Stevens' All People's Congress (APC) had allowed the country's valuable mineral resources to drain away, while Sierra Leone languished at the bottom of global development league tables.

Despite its growing unpopularity, the small group of rebels could not be defeated. The key to this paradox was the role of the government army. Underpaid, under-trained and frequently under-aged, its ill-disciplined and ill-equipped recruits were sent into resource-rich areas to do battle with an elusive and often invisible enemy. Like the under-paid policemen and soldiers who had been sent out to suppress the smuggling of Sierra Leonean diamonds and other commodities in the 1960s and again in the late 1980s, many of these soldiers soon became drawn into the activities of an annual $250 million diamond trade that they were ostensibly seeking to suppress. Encouraged by international pressures for privatisation and austerity, the Sierra Leonean state had privatised most of its sources of revenues.[4] The salaries of state officials had been run down. And education and health were hugely neglected. The state, now a 'shadow' of its former self,[5] was generating massive resentment, but its treasury was being deprived even of the resources to suppress this resentment with a disciplined counter-insurgency.

Increasingly drawn from the same social strata as the RUF, the young men of the Sierra Leonean Army (SLA) saw in the war an opportunity to wield power and make money. After disillusioned soldiers from the war-front seized power, under the youthful leadership of Captain Valentine Strasser in April 1992, there was virtually no check on military abuses. Given the drastic collapse in educational opportunities in the 1970s and 1980s and the shrinking employment prospects, the opportunities offered by war were often far more attractive than those offered by peace. Many government soldiers realised that they could profit from robbing civilians and depopulating resource-rich areas. Many seemed to want to keep the war going, rather than to win it. And many were drawn into complicity with the RUF, sometimes participating in rebel attacks, coordinating their movements with those of the rebels, and even selling arms to their ostensible enemy.[6]

It was this growing collusion between government soldiers and rebels – the *sobel* phenomenon – that spurred the rapid expansion of the civil

---

[4] David Keen, 'Liberalisation and Conflict', *International Political Science Review*, vol. 26, no. 1 (2005), pp. 73–89.

[5] On the 'shadow state', see, notably, William Reno, *Corruption and State Politics in Sierra Leone* (Cambridge: Cambridge University Press, 1995).

[6] These dynamics are explained more fully in David Keen's *Conflict and Collusion in Sierra Leone* (Oxford: James Currey/Palgrave Macmillan/International Peace Academy, 2005).

defence forces based on traditional hunting societies or *Kamajors*, as civilians bravely stood up to the twin threat of soldiers and rebels. Together with *Executive Outcomes*, the South African-based mercenary outfit, the *Kamajors* managed to weaken the RUF and rogue government soldiers sufficiently to allow elections to take place in February 1996. Sierra Leone's courageous civil society actors, particularly the women's movement, were instrumental in pressuring the military to conduct these elections.[7] Yet the rebels and soldiers-turned-rebels (or *sobels*) were not finished. Their shared interest in warfare, in avoiding prosecution, and in resisting the continued rise of the *Kamajors* helped to explain the bizarre military coup in May 1997, when soldiers of the Armed Forces Revolutionary Council (AFRC) entered into government and were joined with suspicious speed by the RUF rebels that they had ostensibly been fighting for the previous six years. This formalised the unholy alliance between armed groups at the expense of those without arms – an alliance that helps explain why many youths have been tempted to locate themselves in the armed rather than the unarmed camp.

Given the key role of government soldiers in the violence, the single biggest contribution that the UN and other international actors could have made as the war developed in the early and mid-1990s would have been to prevent the collapse of Sierra Leone's counterinsurgency by addressing the issue of soldiers' poor conditions; by publicly criticising the abuses of soldiers; and by linking aid and loans more closely to ending corruption and military rule as well as improving the government's abysmal human rights record. Donor governments were less than enthusiastic about the 1992–1996 military government of the National Provisional Ruling Council (NPRC), something that impeded any systematic attempt to improve conditions in the military. The scarcity of Western embassies and intelligence in Sierra Leone and the shortage of media (especially TV) coverage also fed the climate of neglect and ignorance. Nor was there much interaction between Western officials and researchers.[8] In the event, donor governments and UN agencies were remarkably silent about abuses by government forces. ECOWAS itself was split into pro- and anti-NPRC camps.

Meanwhile, the willingness of the NPRC to implement structural adjustment measures (and particularly its success in bringing down inflation in the early 1990s), encouraged donors and international financial organisations (principally the World Bank and the International

[7] See Yasmin Jusu-Sheriff, 'Civil Society', in Adebajo and Rashid (eds.), *West Africa's Security Challenges*, pp. 272–5.

[8] We thank John Hirsch, former US Ambassador to Sierra Leone, for drawing our attention to the point on researchers and the media.

Monetary Fund) to look favourably on NPRC requests for aid, loans and debt rescheduling. Paradoxically, the NPRC's very success in reducing inflation owed something to the 'self-funding' (and abusive) nature of the counter-insurgency. While the British government seemed reluctant to criticise the NPRC, the French government was reluctant to criticise either Liberia's Charles Taylor or his allies in Burkina Faso and Côte d'Ivoire. The United States, more focused on Liberia, regarded Sierra Leone as the United Kingdom's 'sphere of influence' and its peacekeeping debacle in Somalia in 1993 had adversely affected its support for similar missions in Africa.

With the lack of common purpose among its most powerful members and its own bureaucratic inertia, the UN was doing little to address the human rights crisis in Sierra Leone in the early to mid-1990s. According to the World Food Programme's (WFP) 1996 evaluation of assistance to the region (which also included Liberia as well as refugee populations in Guinea and Côte d'Ivoire): 'while the UN has spent over half a billion dollars on its humanitarian response, its diplomatic efforts have been characterised by a lack of understanding and commitment, and have, thus far, had very little impact on conflict resolution'.[9] A particular problem was the role of the UN Development Programme (UNDP). As a development agency, UNDP was used to working through governments and adopted this approach in Sierra Leone. The RUF was difficult to track down, but UNDP showed little interest in any overtures that might alienate the government in Freetown.[10] In general, UN agencies contributed very little worthwhile analysis of the conflict. One symptom of the international attention deficit was the significant 'diplomatic' role played by International Alert, a London-based non-governmental organisation (NGO) whose representative, Akyaaba Addai-Sebo, established contact with Sankoh in 1995 and played a negative 'spoiler' role during negotiations in 1996.

As late as February 1996, the London-based newsletter *Focus on Sierra Leone* was criticising the 'diplomatic silence' that was being maintained in the face of violence by government troops, itself part of a more general neglect of the country. Quite apart from condoning the impunity of these troops, this silence was seen as impeding negotiations with the RUF: 'The absence of even-handedness, in apportioning

---

[9] WFP (World Food Programme), *Protracted Emergency Humanitarian Relief Food Aid: Toward 'Productive Relief', Programme Policy Evaluation of the 1990–1995 period of WFP-assisted refugee and displaced persons operations in Liberia, Sierra Leone, Guinea and Cote d'Ivoire*, (Rome, 1996), p. 13.

[10] Marc Sommers, *The Dynamics of Coordination* (Providence, RU: Thomas J. Watson Jr Institute for International Studies, 2000), Occasional Paper No. 40, pp. 23–4.

culpability for these atrocities, by the international community – Amnesty International being the sole exception – is losing the confidence it needs from all sides if it is to play the roles of facilitation and mediation in this conflict'.[11]

In general, emergency aid in Sierra Leone seems to have served as a substitute for effective diplomatic action to address the humanitarian crisis. Relief operations under the NPRC were themselves inhibited by lack of funding from donors (leading to low allocations) and by a variety of distribution problems (including poor security). The potential for remedying these problems (including the possibility of applying pressure on the NPRC to reduce soldiers' attacks on relief trucks) appears to have been reduced by the deference to the military government in Freetown.

Belated international pressures on the NPRC between 1995 and 1996 did play a significant part in its removal. This, however, exposed the failure to apply significant pressure earlier. A peace agreement was eventually reached in Abidjan in November 1996 after civil defence forces and *Executive Outcomes* had turned the tide against rebels and rogue soldiers. But Sierra Leone remained a 'low profile' country for much of the donor community. Foreign diplomats privately reported that their governments did not care a great deal about the implementation of the Abidjan agreement. Crucially, the regional dimension in Sierra Leone's war – especially Taylor's continuing support for the RUF – remained largely un-addressed.[12] DDR (disarmament, demobilisation and reconstruction) was also very poorly funded.

The RUF leader, Foday Sankoh, was allowed to stall the dispatch of UN military observers to support the Abidjan peace process and associated DDR between 1997 and 1998. While a UN plan made provision for 720 troops and 60 military observers at an estimated cost of about $50 million, Sankoh insisted that he could accept just 60 observers. In the end, only 40 observers were deployed. As David Shearer noted: 'The UN's insistence on consent from all parties to a conflict before deploying peacekeepers meant that it was unable to play a key role even with an agreement in place and fighting suspended.'[13] Indeed, rather than spurring the deployment of peacekeepers, violations of Abidjan by government

---

[11] 'It's back to the polls following ... Elections Stalemate As 55% Proves Beyond Reach Of Sierra Leone's Leading Political Parties', *Focus on Sierra Leone*, (February 1996), 16 November 2006, www.focus-on-sierra-leone.co.uk.

[12] See, notably, Hirsch, *Sierra Leone: Diamonds*.

[13] David Shearer argued that UN peacekeepers had rarely, if ever, protected populations with force, that a smaller force would be cheaper and quicker to deploy, and that in any case NGO and UN agencies were already working without 'protection' in areas set aside for demobilisation, David Shearer, *Private Armies and Military Intervention*, Adelphi

soldiers and the RUF were being used as justification for non-deployment.[14] The four moral guarantors of Abidjan – the UN, the Organisation of African Unity (OAU), the Commonwealth and the government of Côte d'Ivoire – did little to induce compliance with the accord.

UN Secretary-General Kofi Annan favoured deployment of peacekeepers to Sierra Leone, but open-ended UN missions were particularly unpopular with the United States and other major powers at this time – a caution that was linked with a desire to save money and an aversion to casualties, especially in the wake of the humiliation experienced by the US-led UN force in Somalia.[15] After the Somalia debacle, Bill Clinton's administration issued a directive tying US participation in UN peacekeeping to finite operations in which US interests or international security were clearly threatened. John Hirsch, the US ambassador to Sierra Leone between 1995 and 1998, later observed: 'The US decision enshrined in Presidential Decision Directive (PDD) 25 to virtually withdraw from United Nations peacekeeping operations had dissipated what little political will there was for US engagement in Africa.'[16] Other UN Security Council members also seem to have seen the Sierra Leone mission as something of a lost cause. One factor may have been the belief that the Clinton administration would be reluctant to embark on a new UN mission while in delicate negotiations with the US Congress on the approximately $1 billion that Washington owed the UN.[17]

Further exacerbating the situation was the fact that lack of RUF demobilisation provided an important argument for those opposing the downsizing or fundamental reform of Sierra Leone's army. There was also insufficient attention to *Kamajor* abuses and to *Kamajor* attacks on rebels, which contravened the Abidjan accord. (The *Kamajors* were not part of the DDR.) The security vacuum created by the departure of *Executive Outcomes* was particularly serious, given the absence of UN peacekeepers and the presence of only 2,000 Nigerian and Ghanaian in the country.[18] In May 1997, a military coup staged by disaffected junior officers was immediately followed by a major influx of RUF

Paper 316 (Oxford: Oxford University Press for International Institute for Strategic Studies, 1998).

[14] William Reno, 'Privatizing War in Sierra Leone', *Current History*, vol. 610 (May 1997), p. 227.

[15] David Shearer, 'Exploring the Limits of Consent: Conflict Resolution in Sierra Leone', *Millennium: Journal of International Studies*, vol. 26, no. 3 (1997), pp. 845–60 and p. 855.

[16] Hirsch, *Sierra Leone: Diamonds*, p. 63.

[17] Mark Tran and Claudia McElroy, 'UN Failure in Sierra Leone Feeds Recriminations', *Guardian*, May 29 1997.

[18] Norrie McQueen, *United Nations Peacekeeping*, p. 184.

fighters into the capital. On the face of it, the sworn enemies of the previous six years were now walking hand in hand into government. In reality, covert collusion 'up-country' had now come to the capital. Sierra Leoneans paid a heavy price for the Security Council's failure to back Annan's earlier call for the provision of more UN peacekeepers.

The regional dimensions of Sierra Leone's civil war, 1997–1998

In order to understand Sierra Leone's crisis, one must examine not only the internal and extra-regional dynamics of this complex war, but also its significant sub-regional dynamics. RUF rebels received military training in Libya (Muammar Qaddafi was an important supporter of Sankoh, Taylor and Blaise Campaoré) and Burkina Faso, and the rebels were assisted by Liberia's Charles Taylor throughout the conflict. Initially, Taylor backed the rebels in order to force the withdrawal of the Sierra Leonean contingent from ECOMOG in Liberia, to help install his RUF allies in power in Freetown, and to profit from the diamond and arms trade between Sierra Leone and Liberia. The RUF invasion led to several hundred Nigerian, Ghanaian and Guinean troops being sent to Sierra Leone to assist the government in Freetown.

Many analysts have erroneously described ECOMOG as simply a vehicle for the pursuit of a *Pax Nigeriana*, the fulfilment of Nigeria's hegemonic ambitions in West Africa.[19] However, several ECOWAS states, particularly Guinea and Liberia (which shared common borders with Sierra Leone) would appear to have far more of an interest in the stability of Sierra Leone than Nigeria. Guinea was flooded by nearly half a million Sierra Leonean and Liberian refugees, and fighting from both countries spilled over sporadically into its territory. Ghana was Nigeria's close ally in the ECOMOG force in Liberia for eight years and saw the importance of providing stability in Sierra Leone by contributing troops to ECOMOG. Côte d'Ivoire, which suffered a military coup in December 1999 and has seen its territory split in two by a rebellion since 2002, also had concrete interests in a stable West Africa, particularly since it was hosting 200,000 refugees from the Liberian civil war. On the other hand, it was strongly influenced by the French government.

After four years of neglect by the international community, significant cooperation between the UN and ECOWAS in Sierra Leone started in March 1995 with the appointment of a UN Special Representative in

---

[19] See Adekeye Adebajo, *Liberia's Civil War: Nigeria, ECOMOG and Regional Security in West Africa* (Boulder, CO and London: Lynne Rienner, 2002), pp. 43–8.

Sierra Leone, Berhanu Dinka. The UN envoy was involved in negotiations between the elected government of Ahmad Tejan Kabbah, a former UN administrator, and RUF rebels in Abidjan in 1996. However, Abidjan proved to be a failure. The negotiations themselves were hampered by profound distrust between Dinka and Côte d'Ivoire, the ECOWAS chair at the time, as well as the pernicious role played by International Alert, which encouraged RUF intransigence during the talks. Subsequently, donors gave very little support to the implementation of Abidjan, either in terms of DDR or the provision of peacekeepers. Discontent among junior ranks in Sierra Leone's army remained unaddressed, and cuts in rice rations combined with growing official favour for the *Kamajors* to create strong grievances within the military.

When a military *junta*, led by Major Johnny Paul Koroma, seized power in May 1997, Nigerian troops stationed in Freetown suffered dozens of casualties. In August 1997, Koroma announced a four-year programme for a return to civilian rule – a leisurely time frame. At this point, ECOWAS officially mandated ECOMOG to enforce sanctions on the *junta* as well as to restore law and order.[20] ECOWAS first attempted to reverse the coup through diplomatic means by convening a series of sub-regional meetings. The most significant of these in Guinea spawned the Conakry agreement, which called for Kabbah's reinstatement by April 1998. In October 1997, the UN Security Council imposed its own mandatory sanctions on Sierra Leone, including an embargo on arms and oil imports. Invoking the UN Charter's Chapter VII (governing enforcement) and Chapter VIII (governing regional arrangements), the Security Council formally empowered ECOWAS to enforce the embargo and to halt ships for inspection.[21] In addition, the Security Council banned members of the military junta and their immediate family from foreign travel.[22] The Security Council, however, did not impose comprehensive trade sanctions; nor did it freeze the financial assets of *junta* members.[23]

In practice, humanitarian aid to Sierra Leone was severely restricted – with damaging consequences. The NGO *Action Internationale Contre la*

---

[20] Jeremy Levitt, 'Pre-Intervention Trust-Building, African States and Enforcing the Peace: The Case of ECOWAS in Liberia and Sierra Leone', *Liberian Studies Journal*, vol. 24, no. 1 (1999), pp. 1–26 and pp. 12–13.

[21] Lansana Gberie, 'The May 25 Coup d'Etat in Sierra Leone: A Militariat Revolt?', *Africa Development*, vol. 22, nos. 2 and 3 (1997), p. 166.

[22] *Ibid.* p. 167.

[23] David Cortright, George A. Lopez and Richard W. Conroy, 'Sierra Leone: The Failure of Regional and National Sanctions', in David Cortright and George A. Lopez (eds.), *The Sanctions Decade: Assessing UN Strategies in the 1990* (Boulder, CO: Lynne Rienner, 2000), p. 171.

Faim noted a large increase in malnutrition in many districts of Sierra Leone.[24] Many aid workers argued that the hostility of foreign donors to the military *junta* was being allowed to undermine the right to humanitarian relief.[25] While the International Committee of the Red Cross (ICRC) and most European NGOs stressed the continuing accessibility of rural areas, the UNDP and the UN secretary-general's Special Representative, Francis Okelo, tended to argue that the country was too dangerous for relief operations.[26]

The military *junta* was eventually overthrown not by sanctions or internal rebellion but by ECOMOG forces, which pushed the rebels out of Freetown in February 1998. Nigeria's unilateral intervention elicited some sharp reactions from neighbours like Burkina Faso, Liberia, Senegal and Ghana amidst traditional fears of the sub-regional Gulliver and a desire by Liberia and Burkina Faso to protect their RUF allies. Côte d'Ivoire was also accused of backing the RUF. A further complication involved diplomatic tensions between Nigeria and Côte d'Ivoire and between Togo and Côte d'Ivoire over leadership of the peace process. In March 1998, Kabbah was restored to the Sierra Leonean presidency. Despite expelling the *junta* from Freetown, ECOMOG's 13,000 ill-equipped peacekeepers – consisting mainly of Nigerians and also of Ghanaians, Guineans and Malians – still lacked adequate logistical support. ECOMOG's funding was erratic and embroiled in the corruption of Nigeria's military *junta*. Nigeria's brutal autocrat, General Sani Abacha, was also keen to ward off the threat of international sanctions against his regime through an implicit threat to withdraw his peacekeepers from Sierra Leone in the full knowledge that the West was unwilling to intervene itself. Relations between Nigerian peacekeepers and Sierra Leonean civilians were ambiguous: while many Sierra Leoneans regarded ECOMOG as heroes who saved their country from ruin, others saw the peacekeepers as an army of occupation.

From ECOMOG to UNAMSIL, 1998–1999

The Security Council established the UN Observer Mission in Sierra Leone (UNOMSIL) in July 1998 under Indian General, Subhash Joshi. UNMOSIL was tasked with: monitoring the military and economic

---

[24] UN Office for the Co-ordination of Humanitarian Affairs (UNOCHA), Claude Bruderlein, *Inter-Agency Assessment Mission to Sierra Leone: Interim Report*, final draft, 10 February 1997, p. 5.
[25] For example, P. Lefort and J. Littell, *Food and Terror in Sierra Leone* (Rome: Action Internationale Contre La Faim, 1998), p. 11.
[26] Sommers, *The Dynamics of Coordination*.

situation in Sierra Leone; monitoring the disarmament and demobilisation of ex-combatants; and observing respect of international humanitarian law.[27] But with only forty observers, UNOMSIL played a very limited role alongside ECOMOG troops. As in Liberia, there was strong resentment among ECOMOG soldiers against the better-paid and better-resourced UN military observers. One ECOMOG officer wryly commented: 'They [UN observers] are here on picnic and holiday. I wish we could open the beaches for them to sun-tan and enjoy their dollars.'[28]

Certainly, the UN was still not providing any significant protection. Plans to provide a substantial UN peacekeeping force in support of the Abidjan agreement were still stalled and as *junta* forces approached Freetown in late December 1998, the UN, other international agencies and foreign governments began withdrawing their staff from the country. The UN observer mission in Sierra Leone completed its evacuation on 6 January 1999,[29] leaving eight military observers behind. Even as foreign staff was being withdrawn, senior UN officials continued to express the damaging over-optimism that had earlier been evident in relation to abuses by government soldiers. Francis Okelo said on 3 January 1999: 'The situation in Sierra Leone is improving steadily, due mainly to the rapid action taken by the Sierra Leone government, ECOMOG and its allies, the CDF, and civilian alertness to reinforce the efforts of the armed forces.'[30]

Three days later, Freetown suffered a devastating attack by ex-Sierra Leone army forces and a minority of RUF fighters. More than 7,000 people were killed. Among the fatalities were many Nigerian civilians and about one hundred Nigerian soldiers. ECOMOG soldiers were themselves responsible for significant abuses against civilians, while the rebels used civilians as 'human shields'. Another factor in the increasing ECOMOG indiscipline at this time was the cumulative effect of poor pay and conditions and a perception of Sierra Leonean civilian 'ingratitude' for ECOMOG's sacrifices.

Dramatic political changes in Nigeria following the sudden death of General Sani Abacha in June 1998 were beginning to have a significant impact on events in Sierra Leone. Olusegun Obasanjo, elected Nigeria's president in May 1999, started almost immediately to withdraw the bulk

---

[27] Clement E. Adibe, 'Muddling Through: An Analysis of the ECOWAS Experience in Conflict Management in West Africa', in Liisa Laakso (ed.), *Regional Integration for Conflict Prevention and Peace Building in Africa: Europe, SADC and ECOWAS* (Helsinki: Ministry for Foreign Affairs, 2002), pp. 145–6.

[28] Personal Interview with an ECOMOG officer, Freetown, July 1999.

[29] Human Rights Watch, *Sierra Leone: Getting Away with Murder, Mutilation, Rape*, Section VII (New York, 1999), p. 2.

[30] http://www.sierra-leone.org., 3 January 1999.

of Nigerian troops from Sierra Leone. With enormous domestic problems, Obasanjo increasingly had to pay attention to Nigeria's parliament, press and public opinion over a profoundly unpopular mission in Sierra Leone. The country could no longer sustain the sacrifices – involving costs of $1 million a day and hundreds of fatalities – which its less accountable military brass hats had accepted.

The security vacuum in Sierra Leone, already highlighted by the January 1999 attack, was growing worse, and with London and Washington joining West African leaders in pressing for an agreement, the Lomé peace accord was signed on 7 July 1999 between Kabbah's government and the RUF. The Inter-Religious Council of Sierra Leone (IRCSL) deserves credit for its facilitation efforts, which helped secure the agreement. Lomé was, however, basically an appeasement of the RUF by West African leaders and an international community that had wearied of a protracted eight-year conflict. As with earlier accords in Abidjan (1996) and Conakry (1997), a controversial amnesty was offered for war crimes. Lomé made RUF leader, Foday Sankoh – after being freed from Nigerian custody – vice-president, and gave him the national 'crown jewels' in the form of the chairmanship of a Commission for the Management of Strategic Resources. Though Lomé proved to be a sumptuous banquet for Sierra Leone's avaricious warlords, there seemed few alternatives left for President Kabbah whose Nigerian protectors were withdrawing amidst lacklustre international support for Sierra Leone. Under the accord, the UN was asked to contribute troops to help oversee disarmament and to provide staff to help conduct elections, while an ECOWAS-chaired Joint Implementation Committee was to meet every three months to oversee the agreement's implementation. This committee was also charged with monitoring the repatriation and resettlement of 500,000 Sierra Leonean refugees from Guinea and Liberia.[31]

There are eerie parallels between the Lomé peace settlement in Sierra Leone and that of Abuja in 1995, which eventually (if temporarily) ended the war in Liberia. Both accords were basically efforts to appease local warlords by giving them political power in exchange for military peace. Both were an open invitation for warlords to enjoy the spoils of office in a giant jumble sale of the national wares. In both cases, few alternatives existed once ECOMOG, and in particular Nigeria, had made it clear that it was no longer willing to continue to sacrifice men and money, particularly with the UN failing to strengthen ECOMOG's

---

[31] See UN Secretary-General, *Seventh Report of the Secretary-General on the UN Observer Mission in Sierra Leone*, S/1999/836, 30 July 1999, p. 2.

peacekeeping capacity. With the military option removed, Liberian and Sierra Leonean politicians were forced to seek a political solution which inevitably left them at the mercy of wealthy, armed warlords (notably Taylor and Sankoh themselves) who had looted their countries' resources. Transitional governments of national unity in both countries were little more than a fractious collection of avaricious warlords and ambitious politicians who used their positions to campaign for national elections.

Within less than a year, Lomé had unravelled and the RUF was once more marching towards Freetown. Five reasons stand out to explain the collapse of Lomé: the continuing, destabilising influence of Liberia; obstructionism by the RUF leadership; the exclusion of the AFRC/SLA from the agreement; the weakness of international support for DDR; and the weak international peacekeeping effort.

Bolstered by Liberian support, Sankoh and other RUF commanders were actually blocking the DDR process, preventing RUF and ex-army combatants from joining the programme,[32] and effectively barring UNAMSIL from Kailahun district in the east.[33] Meanwhile, the access of government soldiers (including rogue soldiers) to the DDR process seems to have been limited – at least initially – to those who had officially been members of the army prior to the 1997 coup.[34] This omission was particularly dangerous in view of the key role played by rogue soldiers throughout most of the war, including during the January 1999 attack on Freetown. Abuses by rogue soldiers abated only when Johnny Paul Koroma was drafted into the power-sharing arrangement in October 1999.[35] Some rogue soldiers were, however, still being marginalised, and the 'West Side Boys' faction – many of them criminals ineligible for integration into the new army – was said to be feeling 'deserted' by Koroma.[36] The 'West Side Boys' were eventually to bring matters to a head by capturing eleven British soldiers in August 2000. A successful British rescue operation, in which

---

[32] UN Secretary-General, *Third Report of the Secretary-General on the United Nations Mission in Sierra Leone*, S/2000/186, 7 March 2000, p. 8.

[33] 'Despite the RUF's immature attitude, UNAMSIL wants a peaceful solution', *Indian Express*, 16 July 2000, www.indian-express.com.

[34] Ricken Patel, *Sierra Leone's Uncivil War and the Unlimited Intervention that Ended it. Case-study for the Carr Centre for Human Rights Policy* (Harvard University, 2002), mimeo, p. 20.

[35] Centre for Democracy and Development (CDD), *Sierra Leone: One Year after Lome*, Conference on the peace process, CDD Strategy Planning Series (London: CDD, 15 September 2000), p. 94.

[36] *Ibid.*; Patel, *Sierra Leone's Uncivil War*, p. 29; Kelvin Lewis, 'UN Acts against Westside Boys', *West Africa*, 21–27 August 2000, p. 22.

several members of the rebel group were killed, sent a powerful message of international resolve.[37]

DDR efforts in Sierra Leone were, however, still being weakly supported. Continued low spending on DDR contrasted sharply with the huge sums (estimated at US$692 million in 2002) that were eventually spent on UN peacekeeping operations, which an adequate DDR might have rendered unnecessary.[38] By December 1999, international donors and multilateral agencies had pledged only half of the $50 million of DDR assistance required, and much of this had not yet reached the field.[39] Kosovo and East Timor were taking a lot more resources and attention.[40] There was a $19 million funding shortfall in Sierra Leone's DDR programme by mid-2000.[41] Critically, the weak international support for DDR reduced the opportunities for weaning Sankoh's increasingly war-weary followers away from violence. There were major problems both with the DDR camps themselves and with the provision made for reintegrating ex-combatants into local communities. Former combatants were also increasingly unhappy about the demobilisation process. Demobilisation centres were slow to be established and insufficient in number. Payments for ex-combatants were delayed and subject to misunderstandings.[42] Significantly, the weakly supported DDR was feeding into the continuing abuse of civilians.[43] Many observers felt that those who had disarmed were mostly abductees and those charged with portering work rather than hard-core combatants.[44]

Compounding the damage caused by weak DDR were the weaknesses of UN peacekeeping – not least because these weaknesses exacerbated the anxieties of combatants about demobilisation. On 19 August 1999, Olusegun Obasanjo wrote to Kofi Annan, informing him of Nigeria's intention to withdraw 2,000 of its peacekeepers from Sierra Leone every month. The Nigerian president, however, offered to subsume some of

---

[37] See Major Phil Ashby, *Unscathed: Escape from Sierra Leone* (London: Macmillan, 2002); and William Fowler, *Operation Barras: The SAS Rescue Mission, Sierra Leone 2000* (London: Weidenfeld and Nicolson, 2004).

[38] Toby Porter, *The Interaction between Political and Humanitarian Action in Sierra Leone, 1995 to 2002* (Geneva: Centre for Humanitarian Dialogue, March 2002), p. 7.

[39] US Committee for Refugees, *Sierra Leone's Path to Peace: Key Issues at Year's End*, press release, 15 December 1999.

[40] Hirsch, *Sierra Leone: Diamonds*, p. 86.

[41] UN Secretary-General, *Fourth Report of the Secretary-General on the United Nations Mission in Sierra Leone*, S/2000/455, 19 May 2000, p. 8.

[42] Christian Aid, *Sierra Leone: What Price Peace? An analysis of the Disarmament, Demobilisation and Reintegration Plan* (London, December 1999).

[43] S/2000/186.

[44] For example, Christian Aid, *Sierra Leone: What Price Peace?*; S/2000/186.

Nigeria's 12,000 troops under a new UN mission.[45] Obasanjo began the phased withdrawal on 31 August and suspended the process only after a plea by Sierra Leonean president, Tejan Kabbah, and Kofi Annan not to leave a security vacuum in Sierra Leone. But with the UN's realisation that Obasanjo was not bluffing when he announced the intention of withdrawing Nigerian troops from Sierra Leone, the UN secretary-general was forced to suggest to the Security Council that a UN peacekeeping mission in Sierra Leone, with a robust enforcement mandate under Chapter VII of the UN Charter, take over from ECOMOG under an Indian Force Commander, General Vijay Jetley.[46]

Obasanjo rejected a UN proposal that ECOMOG continue to protect Freetown and undertake enforcement actions against rogue rebel elements. Nigeria's president realised that ECOMOG, in being saddled with these dangerous tasks, would remain a useful scapegoat if things went wrong in Sierra Leone. The UN had been widely criticised for failing to protect 'safe havens' in Bosnia and civilians in Rwanda, and critics would have been able to blame any failings in Sierra Leone on ECOMOG rather than the UN. Nigeria refused to remain in Sierra Leone in a situation in which there would be two peacekeeping missions with different mandates, commands and conditions of service.[47] The UN secretariat turned down ECOMOG's request for the UN to take over the entire ECOMOG force.[48] Burned by experiences like Sierra Leone, ECOWAS and other sub-regional organisations in Africa continue to question why their peacekeepers should be accountable to a UN Security Council that refuses to finance their missions.[49]

There was also much hostility directed against the presence of Nigerian peacekeepers within the UN secretariat. Many UN officials insisted on a reduced Nigerian role while overselling a new UN mission to Sierra Leoneans, who were misled into believing that the Blue Helmets would be prepared to fight the country's rebels.[50] In order to fill the void left by the departure of Nigerian peacekeepers, a UN mission in Sierra Leone was established, with an eventual strength of

---

[45] UN Secretary-General, *Eighth Report of the Secretary-General on the United Nations Observer Mission in Sierra Leone* S/1999/1003, 23, September 1999, p. 6.

[46] See the *First Report of the Secretary General on the United Nations Mission in Sierra Leone*, S/1999/1223, 6 December 1999, pp. 1–6.

[47] James Jonah, 'The United Nations', in Adekeye Adebajo and Ismail Rashid (eds.), *West Africa's Security Challenges*, p. 330.

[48] *Ibid.*

[49] Funmi Olonisakin and Comfort Ero, 'Africa and the Regionalization of Peace Operations', in Michael Pugh and Waheguru Pal Singh Sidhu (eds.), *The United Nations and Regional Security: Europe and Beyond* (Boulder, CO and London: Lynne Rienner, 2003), p. 246.

[50] Jonah, 'The United Nations', p. 331.

20,000. Oluyemi Adeniji, a Nigerian diplomat who had served as the
UN Special Representative in the Central African Republic (CAR), was
appointed as the UN Special Representative to Sierra Leone, compen-
sating Nigeria for not gaining the Force Commander position, which
Obasanjo had wanted; an appointment that had been strongly resisted
within the UN Secretariat and Security Council.[51] UNAMSIL's
core contingents eventually consisted of Nigerian, Indian, Jordanian,
Kenyan, Bangladeshi, Guinean, Ghanaian and Zambian battalions.[52]

UNAMSIL's baptism of fire: the events of May 2000

The logistically ill-equipped and slowly deploying UN force in Sierra
Leone soon ran into difficulties. The RUF prevented the deployment of
UNAMSIL to the diamond-rich eastern provinces, and, from May
2000, attacked UN peacekeepers, holding 500 of them (mostly from
India, Kenya and Zambia) hostage and seizing their heavy weapons and
vehicles.[53] The rebels were seeking to exploit the vacuum created by the
departure of Nigerian peacekeepers from Sierra Leone.

In February 2000, UNAMSIL's strength was authorised to rise to
11,100 from an initial 6,000, and by the end of April 2000 the number
of UN soldiers had reached 8,700. Yet this UN force was a motley,
multinational army – arriving bit by bit, underfunded and lacking the
necessary equipment. Within the UN peacekeeping force in Bo, for
example, there were twenty-seven different nationalities.[54] As in most
UN peacekeeping operations, those countries contributing troops tended to be those in which the UN pay per soldier was higher than their
own costs per soldier.[55] The lightly armed peacekeepers were out of
their depth in unfamiliar terrain. UNAMSIL's Indian commander, Vijay
Jetley, himself noted that some contingents 'did not come up to the
mark and were an embarrassment both to the countries and to the
UNAMSIL'.[56]

[51] *Ibid.*, p. 330.
[52] For an excellent assessment of UNAMSIL, see John Hirsch, 'Sierra Leone,' in David
    M. Malone (ed.), *The UN Security Council: From the Cold War to the 21st Century*
    (Boulder, CO and London: Lynne Rienner, 2004), pp. 521–35.
[53] S/2000/186, pp. 3–4; *Fifth Report of the Secretary General on the United Nations Mission in
    Sierra Leone*, 31 July 2000, S/2000/751, p. 4.
[54] Ewen McAskill, 'Badly Trained, Ill-defined and Underfunded – UN Peacekeepers
    Endure Humiliations', *Guardian*, 11 May 2000.
[55] Patel, *Sierra Leone's Uncivil War*, p. 21; Linda Polman, 'Blue Helmets as Cannon
    Fodder', *Guardian*, 17 February 2004.
[56] Interviewed in *Indian Express*, 'Despite the RUF's immature attitude, UNAMSIL wants
    a peaceful solution', *Indian Express*, 16 July 2000, www.indian-express.com.

Many observers noted that the deployment of UNAMSIL was far too patchy to be effective; many troops were inexperienced and unmotivated; logistics were poor; and even maps were out-of-date. There was a pressing need for countries with well-equipped and well-trained forces to make contributions to UNAMSIL.[57] With rebels still fearing retaliation by *Kamajors* and government soldiers, it was hard for such a force to reassure RUF combatants that they would not be mistreated after disarming. The *Kamajors* were certainly a growing problem in their own right, a fact very often missed in all the international attention on the RUF. As earlier in the war, a failure to rein in *Kamajor* abuses was helping Sankoh to keep control of his own fighters.

Events in May 2000 exposed the grave weakness of UN peacekeeping. The first trigger came in April 2000, when General Jetley declared that his forces would begin to disarm RUF forces in diamond-rich Kono district in two months.[58] The second came when the Nigerian-led ECOMOG force passed its mantle to the UN troops by the end of April 2000 (though some 3,500 Nigerian ECOMOG soldiers were 're-hatted' as Blue Helmets.)[59] Crucially, the UN's attempt to get tough on demobilisation in Kono more or less coincided with the departure of ECOMOG peacekeepers who had been prepared to use force with more credibility than the UN. At Makeni, RUF fighters demanded the return of ten rebels who had turned in their weapons. When UNAMSIL refused, rebels attacked. Within a week, UNAMSIL was reporting that 500 peacekeepers had been detained by the RUF, including an entire Zambian battalion.[60] After the failings in the run-up to the invasion of Freetown in January 1999, the lack of intelligence capacity of international peacekeepers was again starkly exposed.[61] The RUF may well have calculated that its hostage-taking would get rid of the peacekeeping force altogether – following the inauspicious precedents of Somalia and Rwanda. Sankoh had called the UN peacekeepers 'paper tigers'. There were reports that RUF fighters had began to move towards Freetown.

Having pushed strongly for Lomé within the UN Security Council, Britain, in particular, was on the spot. The British government rejected pleas from Kabbah to commit troops to the UN peacekeeping force.[62]

---

[57] David Usborne and Andrew Marshall, 'UN Vows: 'We Will Not Withdraw as Rebels Circle', *Independent*, 11 May 2000.
[58] *Africa Confidential*, vol. 41, no. 10 (12 May 2000), p. 2.
[59] This raised the question of whether soldiers involved in ECOMOG abuses were now part of UNAMSIL.
[60] *Africa Confidential*, vol. 41, no.10 (12 May 2000).
[61] *Africa Confidential*, vol. 41, no. 12 (9 June 2000), p. 1.
[62] Richard Norton-Taylor and Chris McGreal, 'Sierra Leone Children Carry British Guns', *Guardian*, 11 May 2000.

Instead, Britain sent troops under its own command. The initial aim of the mission was to evacuate British nationals and non-essential staff. The mandate was, however, extended to protecting and bolstering UN troops and providing an extra security apparatus for Sierra Leonean government soldiers.[63] At one point, there were 1,200 British troops in Sierra Leone. British troops helped to protect Freetown and sent a resolute signal to the RUF.[64] However, Britain – which was not prepared to take heavy casualties[65] – largely limited its activities to the Freetown area and was only willing to fight when the position of its military personnel was threatened. Meanwhile, Sankoh was arrested in Freetown in May 2000.

Underlining the new tough international stance, the UN Security Council initiated the establishment of the Sierra Leone Special Court to prosecute war crimes committed during the country's civil war. Subsequently indicted before the war crimes tribunal were Foday Sankoh (who died in detention) and some of his henchmen like Sam Bockarie (assassinated in Liberia under mysterious circumstances). Also indicted were Johnny Paul Koroma (who fled and is suspected to have died) and some other AFRC members as well as Hinga Norman (Sierra Leone's interior minister under the Kabbah administration and a key instigator of the civil defence forces) and Charles Taylor (who fled into exile in Nigeria in August 2003). Taylor was handed over to Sierra Leone's Special Court in March 2006. Sierra Leone's Truth and Reconciliation Commission (TRC), which held hearings across the country, also presented its final report to President Kabbah in October 2004.[66]

UNAMSIL experienced its own internal problems. A UN assessment mission sent to Sierra Leone in June 2000 found serious management problems in UNAMSIL and a lack of common understanding of the mandate and rules of engagement. The assessment mission noted that some of UNAMSIL's military units lacked proper training and equipment.[67] There were constant reports of tension between the UN's

---

[63] Comfort Ero, 'British Foreign Policy and the Conflict in Sierra Leone', in CDD, *Sierra Leone: One Year After* p. 107; Human Rights Watch, *Priorities for the International Community*, (New York, 11 November 2000), p. 6.

[64] Britain agreed to provide 10,000 self-loading rifles to the government army (Richard Norton-Taylor and Chris McGreal, 'Sierra Leone Children'). Some British arms ended up with the West Side Boys; some children in the Sierra Leone army were carrying British-given arms (Alex Renton, 'Our Guns Arm the Children', *Evening Standard*, 24 May 2000).

[65] Ero, 'British Foreign Policy', p. 113.

[66] See, for example, Abdul Rahman Lamin, *The Politics of Reconciliation in the Mano River Union* (Johannesburg: Institute for Global Dialogue, July 2004).

[67] S/2000/751, p. 9.

political and military leadership[68] even before a confidential report written by General Jetley was leaked to the international media in September 2000. In the report, the Indian Force Commander accused senior Nigerian military and political officials of attempting to sabotage the UN mission in Sierra Leone by colluding with RUF rebels to prolong the conflict in order to benefit from the country's illicit diamond trade. No evidence was provided for the allegations in Jetley's report. Nigeria strongly rebutted the allegations of collaboration, and its army chief, General Victor Malu, blamed Jetley for what he described as the 'professional incompetence' characterising UNAMSIL's operations in Sierra Leone.[69] Kabbah backed the Nigerian stance. However, a UN panel of experts report, citing eyewitnesses, noted in 2000: 'There is reason to believe that a certain amount of diamonds have been traded by the RUF with officers of the former West African peacekeeping force in return for cash or supplies.'[70] Furthermore: 'the Panel heard an overwhelming number of reports on Nigerian ECOMOG troops exchanging weapons with the RUF for cash, diamonds, food or other goods'.[71]

Whatever the truth about the diamonds and arms, tremendous political damage was done to UNAMSIL by this incident: Nigeria refused to place its peacekeepers under Jetley's command, and India subsequently announced the withdrawal of its entire 3,000-strong contingent from Sierra Leone in September 2000. India was followed by Jordan, which cited the refusal of Britain to put its own forces under UN command as a reason for its departure.[72] (A small Jordanian medical unit remained behind.) A brief British military intervention outside the UN command had helped to stabilise the situation in Freetown and its environs. Following the difficulties with the RUF, West African leaders also agreed to send a 3,000-strong rapid reaction force, consisting largely of Nigerians, to bolster UNAMSIL: the US trained Nigerian, Ghanaian and Senegalese troops, as part of this force.

---

[68] See Lansana Fofana, 'A Nation Self-destructs', *NewsAfrica*, vol. 1 no. 5 (31 July 2000), pp. 25; Chris McGreal, 'UN to Sack its General in Sierra Leone', *Guardian Weekly*, 29 June–5 July 2000.

[69] Panafrican News Agency, 18 September 2000, Dakar, www.allafrica.com; SLNA, 22 September 2000.

[70] UN Panel of Experts, *Report of the Panel of Experts, Appointed Pursuant to UN Security Council Resolution 1306 (2000), Paragraph 19 in Relation to Sierra Leone*, S/2000/1195, 20 December 2000, p. 30.

[71] S/2000/1195, p. 48. See also International Crisis Group, *Sierra Leone: Time for a New Military and Political Strategy*, 11 April 2001; www.sierra-leone.org, 25 October 1998.

[72] Hirsch, 'Sierra Leone', in Malone (ed.), *The UN Security Council*, p. 528.

Peace breaks out, June 2000–December 2004

It took changes at the domestic, sub-regional and external levels to achieve an end to the conflict in Sierra Leone. There was broad agreement among those consulted – including aid workers, UNAMSIL officials, Sierra Leonean journalists, British officers, ex-combatants, and officials on Sierra Leone's National Commission for Disarmament, Demobilisation and Reintegration (NCDDR) – on six factors that encouraged the softening of the RUF, paving the way for an accelerated peace process and a joint declaration by the government and the RUF in January 2002 that the war was effectively over.

First, and probably most important, was the role of Guinea and fighters based there, which created a willingness within the RUF to accept a UN peacekeeping presence. Guinea made extensive use of gunships bought from Ukraine, inflicting heavy casualties on RUF fighters as well as civilians, including inside Sierra Leone.[73] The Guineans were also reportedly training *Kamajors* among the refugee population who launched attacks back into Sierra Leone – in Kambia and Kono – and reportedly came within three miles of the RUF's main diamond fields in Kono in May 2001. This combined assault from Guinean forces and Sierra Leonean civil defence forces dealt a severe blow to the RUF, encouraging it to welcome UNAMSIL as a buffer against the Guineans.[74]

A second factor weakening the RUF was increased international pressure in regulating Sierra Leone's diamond trade. The UN, led by the United States, Britain, and key donor and ECOWAS states, established an International Contact Group for Sierra Leone. The Group held periodic meetings in order to mobilise funds for Sierra Leone's peace process. In June 2000, the UN Security Council passed a resolution demanding that all states take measures to prohibit the direct or indirect importation of rough diamonds from Sierra Leone, and requiring the government in Freetown to implement a certificate-of-origin system for diamond exports so that diamonds from RUF areas could be distinguished from other diamonds. Official diamond exports from Sierra Leone were suspended (resuming in October 2000) while the certification scheme was put in place. However, smuggling through Liberia was still a major problem; and in practice many diamonds originating from RUF areas were still being certified even after the scheme was put in place.[75]

---

[73] Patel, *Sierra Leone's Uncivil War*, pp. 32–3.

[74] *Ibid.*, pp. 36, 38.

[75] Economist Intelligence Unit, September 2000, p. 37; Greg Campbell, *Blood Diamonds* (Boulder, CO: Westview Press, 2004), pp. 43–4; SLNA, 12 January 2000, citing *New*

Part of the solution to the diamond smuggling came in the form of the third major contributor to peace: the squeeze that donors were putting – belatedly – on Liberia. At the UN in July 2001, Washington and London strongly criticised Charles Taylor and Burkina Faso's President Blaise Compaoré for their role in diamond-smuggling and gun-running in support of RUF rebels in Sierra Leone. Diamond and arms sanctions imposed on Liberia in May 2001 contributed tremendously to halting its support for RUF rebels, weakening Taylor's regime, strengthening his military rivals, and eventually forcing him into exile in Nigeria in August 2003. There was also a travel ban imposed on Liberian government officials. These sanctions were imposed in the face of opposition from several ECOWAS leaders who argued that Taylor's help had been vital in securing the Lomé accord and that such sanctions would be counterproductive. Officials from Sierra Leone's National Commission for Disarmament, Demobilisation and Reintegration who were monitoring Kailahun district, however, reported in September 2001 that rebel supplies from Liberia were drying up,[76] increasing prospects for peace in Sierra Leone.

A fourth factor encouraging a less bellicose RUF was the change in UNAMSIL, with better funding and a clearer enforcement mandate. At the sub-regional level, the diminishing of a preponderant Nigerian role and the establishment of a peacekeeping mission under UN command together made it harder for the rebels to use Nigeria's dominance as an excuse not to surrender their arms to international peacekeepers. The UN's provision of financial support made it easier for ECOMOG states like Nigeria, Ghana, Guinea and Mali to keep their troops in Sierra Leone and for Gambia to contribute troops to the mission. Externally, Britain used its permanent seat on the UN Security Council to convince other members to establish the world's largest peacekeeping mission in Sierra Leone at 20,000 troops. The forceful US permanent representative to the UN, Richard Holbrooke, strongly backed an expanded UN force in Sierra Leone as well as legal and economic sanctions against RUF rebels and Charles Taylor. The arrival of UN reinforcements prepared to respond more robustly to rebel intransigence, coupled with strong Guinean aerial bombardments in 2001, eventually broke the RUF's resolve.

A fifth factor in the softer line of the RUF seems to have been the British intervention – not only the stationing of British forces in Sierra Leone and the September 2000 destruction of the rogue army faction known as the 'West Side Boys' (cited by many RUF fighters as a key

York Times; BBC, 'Correspondent', 21 October 2001, www.news.bbc.co.uk; author's interviews; S/2000/1195, p. 15.
[76] Interview, Freetown, September 2001.

factor in their decisions),[77] but also British (and earlier Nigerian) efforts to reorganise and retrain the Sierra Leonean army (which had done so much to assist the RUF since the war began). The hard-line stance adopted by the British and the Guineans towards the RUF seems to have complemented the trust-building and incentives favoured by the UN.[78] One British official described the arrangement as 'good cop, bad cop', adding: 'The RUF probably thought the UN peace process was more attractive than dealing with British troops and the Sierra Leonean government forces.'[79]

A sixth set of factors encouraging a less belligerent RUF were those internal to the rebel movement. After Sankoh's arrest and incarceration in May 2000, a more moderate RUF leadership emerged under Issa Sesay, which implemented a new peace accord that was crafted in Abuja in November 2000 by the Special Representative of the UN Secretary-General, Olu Adeniji, and ECOWAS leaders. A follow-up meeting in Abuja in May 2001 confirmed RUF cooperation with the peace process, with UNAMSIL having deployed throughout the country, including in diamond-rich areas, two months earlier. There was a growing war-weariness among the RUF rank-and-file – partly the result of the onslaught from Guinea. DDR was still a major problem, however. Many combatants had unrealistically high hopes of the process, and these great expectations ran up against distinctly hard times on the ground. Payments to demobilising fighters had been suspended since the May 2000 demonstration against Sankoh in Freetown and subsequent shootings by Sankoh's men, and the encampment period (already down from ninety days, to six to eight weeks, and then three weeks) was further reduced – in some cases to two to three days. By October 2001, donors had pledged less than half of the government's DDR needs.[80]

Despite these difficulties, the UN's disarmament programme was declared successfully completed on 17 January 2002. Some 33,000 combatants had been expected to go through disarmament and demobilisation. But in the event, more than 72,000 fighters turned up.[81] This stretched already scarce resources even more thinly. Benefits for *Kamajor* fighters (both those registered for DDR and others) were reported to be particularly meagre. However, elections in May 2002,

---

[77] Patel, *Sierra Leone's Uncivil War*, p. 30.
[78] Patel points out, there was considerable tension between the British and UNAMSIL (Patel, *Sierra Leone's Uncivil War*).
[79] Patel, *Sierra Leone's Uncivil War*.
[80] International Crisis Group, *Sierra Leone: Managing Uncertainty*, 24 October 2001, p. 15.
[81] Women's Commission for Refugee Women and Children, *Precious Resources: Participatory Research Study with Adolescents and Youths in Sierra Leone*, April–July 2002, www.womenscommission.org.

monitored by the UN, saw Kabbah re-elected in a landslide victory and the RUF Party (RUFP) failing to win a single seat. The brutal, decade-long war in Sierra Leone was finally over. In September 2004, UNAMSIL completed the transfer of primary responsibility for maintaining peace and security to the government of Sierra Leone. By the end of December 2004, the UN had about 4,000 peacekeepers in Sierra Leone, and its last troops left in 2005.[82] The Blue Helmets had somehow contrived a rare peacekeeping success in a thoroughly improvised mission, which had been on the brink of collapse. UNAMSIL had muddled through with a combination of West African diplomacy and military muscle, Guinean bombardment, British military force and diplomatic guile, and American political pressure and financial support.

Learning Lessons

The history of UN involvement in Sierra Leone explored in this chapter provides four major lessons. These are

- the need to define and implement an effective relationship between the UN and regional organisations like ECOWAS;
- the need for external actors to play a significant political, military and financial role in peacekeeping efforts;
- the importance of devising effective strategies to deal with 'spoilers' who are determined to wreck peace processes and;
- finally, the need for international actors to contribute significantly to post-conflict peace building efforts to ensure that war does not return.

The United Nations and ECOWAS: from burden shedding to burden sharing

In discussing the lessons of UN peacekeeping in Sierra Leone, it is important to emphasise that the UN Security Council has primary responsibility for international peace and security and simply shifted its responsibilities to ECOWAS due to the reluctance of the Council to sanction UN missions in Africa after debacles in Somalia (1993) and Rwanda (1994).[83] As James Jonah, a former UN under secretary-general for political affairs and former Sierra Leonean finance minister

---

[82] 'First Report of the Secretary-General on the UN Integrated Office in Sierra Leone', S/2006/269, 28 April, 2006.

[83] For interesting African perspectives on this issue, see International Peace Academy/ Center on International Cooperation, *Refashioning the Dialogue: Regional Perspectives on*

noted: 'It is of vital importance that the UN work closely with regional forces at the operational level. Such cooperation provides credibility and can inspire confidence in local populations that the international community cares about peace in the country.'[84]

The ECOMOG interventions in Liberia and Sierra Leone underlined the importance of an active UN role in sub-regional peacekeeping efforts. In Sierra Leone, the UN played a military monitoring role, with about 50 military observers, in support of ECOMOG, as it had done in Liberia, until it took over ECOMOG's peacekeeping duties and sub-sumed some of its troops under UN command in 2000. The August 2000 Brahimi report on peacekeeping disappointingly neglected to define in detail effective relations between the UN and regional orga-nisations.[85] The UN High-level Panel on Threats, Challenges and Change which submitted its report to Kofi Annan in December 2004 went somewhat further in recommending that the UN Security Council consider funding regional organisations, but even this report failed to devote enough attention to this critical area.[86]

The UN peace-building office in Sierra Leone will have to be sub-stantially bolstered with stronger mandates and greater staff, and its cooperation with ECOWAS and civil society groups will have to be better defined. The UN peace-building office in Liberia, established in 1997, was the first-ever such office established by the UN. However, as an internal UN report of July 2001 admitted, the UN peace-building office was poorly resourced and its mandate was weak and not politically intrusive (in the sense of getting involved in internal affairs) due to the initial reluctance of the UN Security Council to establish the office.[87] These offices have been mandated to perform such tasks as providing electoral assistance; promoting human rights and the rule of law by working through both governments and civil society actors; mobilising donor support for disarmament, demobilisation and the reintegration of ex-combatants into local communities; supporting the rebuilding of administrative capacity; and rehabilitating local infrastructure.

Many of these goals have often not been met in fragile situations in which donors repeatedly fail to deliver on their pledges. Following the recommendations of the UN's Inter-Agency Task Force on West Africa

---

the Brahimi Report on UN Peace Operations, Regional Meetings, February–March 2001, pp. 6–11.

[84] Jonah, 'The United Nations', p. 343.

[85] See *Report of the Panel on United Nations Peace Operations*, S/2000/809, 21 August 2000.

[86] See *A More Secure World: Our Shared Responsibility*, Report of the UN Secretary-General's High-Level Panel on Threats, Challenges and Change, (New York: United Nations, 2004.)

[87] IPA/CIC, *Refashioning the Dialogue*, p. 11.

of May 2001, the decision to establish a UN office in West Africa and to appoint a Special Representative of the UN secretary-general, Ahmedou Ould-Abdallah, to head this office represented positive steps for UN/ECOWAS cooperation. The UN was asked to help strengthen ECOWAS' peacekeeping and electoral capacities and to work with civil society groups in West Africa. The UN office in West Africa was also tasked with performing the following specific tasks: assist the UN and its sub-regional offices to coordinate strategies in West Africa; monitor and report on political, humanitarian and human rights developments; harmonise UN activities with those of ECOWAS; monitor ECOWAS' decisions and activities; and support national and sub-regional peace-building efforts.[88] This office has, however, been short-staffed and has not been able to fulfil much of its mandate. Only belatedly did it start consulting closely with ECOWAS.

External friends and foes

The second important lesson for future UN missions based on our Sierra Leone case is the need to encourage external actors to contribute positively and substantially to peacemaking efforts. While external actors like the United States, the Soviet Union and France often fuelled conflicts and/or supported autocrats in Africa during the Cold War era; external actors have sometimes played a positive role in peacemaking efforts in post-Cold War West Africa. Washington's provision of logistical assistance to ECOMOG in Liberia before disarmament and its contributions to elections together helped put a temporary stop to the war in 1997. The European Union and UN agencies also provided vital financial, logistical and humanitarian support, which assisted peacemaking efforts in Liberia. In Sierra Leone, Britain led international efforts to mobilise donor support and used its permanent seat on the UN Security Council to help establish the largest peacekeeping mission in the world at the time and to impose sanctions (with the support of the United States) against Charles Taylor. The United Kingdom also made a useful contribution to security sector reform, addressing some of the poor conditions that had helped make *sobel* violence such a prominent feature of this war.

The current UN mission in Liberia was established with strong US support. In February 2004, the UN also established a 6,240-strong

---

[88] Security Council, *Report of the Inter-Agency Mission to West Africa: 'Towards a Comprehensive Approach to Durable and Sustainable Solutions to Priority Needs and Challenges in West Africa'*, S/2001/434, 2 May 2001, p. 15.

mission in Côte d'Ivoire (MINUCI) to work alongside 4,600 French troops who are currently separating the government and rebels. A 1,478-strong ECOWAS peacekeeping force in Côte d'Ivoire (ECOMICI) from Senegal, Ghana, Niger, Togo and Benin was subsumed under this new UN mission.[89] Significantly, it took the support of Britain, the United States and France – three Western 'godfathers' and all permanent members of the UN Security Council – to establish a UN presence in their former 'spheres of influence.' The decision by Britain and France – to deploy troops outside the UN chain of command, could, however, set bad precedents for future UN missions.

Western support for peace-building activities in Africa has been derisory compared to similar efforts in the Balkans and East Timor. Even in countries like Sierra Leone where donors understandably have doubts about political stability and democratic rule, they must find creative ways of channelling resources to affected communities – through the UN and international and local NGOs – to disarm fighters, rebuild state institutions, restore judiciaries and police forces, and consolidate democracy. Such a conflict-prevention strategy is crucial in ensuring that conflicts do not erupt again in these countries (at greater cost to the international community) and that long-suffering populations are not punished for the excesses of their unaccountable leaders.

Spoilers and sanctions

The Sierra Leone case, thirdly, underlines the importance of developing effective strategies and sanctions to deal with sub-regional 'spoilers' like Foday Sankoh and Charles Taylor.[90] In Sierra Leone, warring factions killed and kidnapped ECOMOG and UN peacekeepers and stole their weapons and vehicles. The RUF insisted that ECOMOG troops depart as a condition for signing the Abidjan accord of 1996. The economic, political and legal sanctions of the sort that were applied to the RUF in Sierra Leone and Charles Taylor in Liberia would seem appropriate in these cases. Qaddafi and Compaoré were also sources of support for the RUF, as were mercenaries from Ukraine. Foreign firms played a

---

[89] See the *Second Report of the Secretary-General on the United Nations Mission in Côte d'Ivoire*, S/2003/1069, 4 November 2003; and the *Report of the Secretary-General on the United Nations Mission in Côte d'Ivoire*, S/2004/3, 6 January 2004, pp. 15–17, submitted pursuant to Security Council Resolution 1514, 13 November 2003.

[90] See, for example, David Cortright and George A. Lopez (eds.), *The Sanctions Decade*; and Stephen Stedman, 'Spoiler Problems in Peace Processes', *International Security*, vol. 22, no. 2 (Fall 1997), pp. 5–53.

negative role in supporting Sierra Leonean warlords through the illicit export of natural resources and minerals. In devising sanctions against factions or sub-regional states, the actions of these firms will need to be carefully scrutinised by their governments, and, if necessary, punished. The UN Security Council imposed economic and travel sanctions, as well as an arms embargo, on Charles Taylor's regime in 2001. Though ECOWAS leaders opposed these sanctions at the time, the punitive measures appear to have had a major impact in ending the arms-for-diamond trade between Taylor and the RUF. They weakened his regime tremendously and helped to end the wars in Liberia and Sierra Leone.

The case of Sierra Leone also demonstrates the importance of remembering that actors within government structures may be important promoters of abuse and spoilers of peace. Throughout the 1990s, donors tended to underestimate abuses by government actors (notably disgruntled soldiers) and to focus almost exclusively on the RUF. The nadir of this approach was when the abusive NPRC military government was praised for financial orthodoxy while Sierra Leone was devastated by rebels and *sobels*. UN agencies did very little to remedy this impasse.

Post-conflict peace building

The final lesson from the Sierra Leone case is the crucial importance of post-conflict peace building. As civil administration and social services collapsed and the economy declined during Sierra Leone's civil war, the country depended on the UN and various NGOs to provide humanitarian assistance. These international actors provided humanitarian relief and socio-economic support. Any successful post-conflict strategy must, however, be sub-regional and take into account the interconnectedness of the conflicts in West Africa. Liberia's civil war spilled into Sierra Leone, Côte d'Ivoire and Guinea; sub-regional governments backed various warring factions; and most significantly, warlords in Liberia and Sierra Leone assisted each other through supplying fighters, trafficking arms and smuggling diamonds. The UN must find ways to support ECOWAS – an economic institution which strives to promote regional integration through the creation of a free trade zone – to channel resources to joint commercial and infrastructural projects which can link countries together to promote peaceful cooperation rather than violent confrontation.

The various donor conferences, which provided crucial electoral and post-conflict assistance in Sierra Leone, must continue to mobilise resources to support peace building. As a UN Security Council mission, which visited West Africa in June 2004, clearly recognised, funding must be provided to create a viable army loyal to the civilian government, to rebuild moribund national institutions and to revive mineral production.[91] Rebuilding the state must involve ensuring proper salaries for state officials, without which it will be impossible to rein in smuggling and to harness Sierra Leone's natural and human resources for development. Though programmes have been developed in Sierra Leone to provide jobs for demobilised fighters and to reintegrate them into local communities, these have been mostly short term and have not been well funded. A major reason why Sierra Leone's war persisted for so long was the consistent under-funding of DDR programmes. Harnessing the creative energy of ex-combatants will be crucial, as will avoiding the temptation to reinforce traditional structures that helped fuel the war in the first place.[92] It is also important that donors show more understanding for the plight of cash-strapped governments in countries devastated by civil wars like Sierra Leone. Debts will have to be forgiven or substantially reduced – as is already occurring in some cases – while borrowing restrictions and stringent aid conditionalities must be eased on these countries until they have recovered sufficiently from the ravages of war. More, not less, resources must still be found to nurse these international patients back to health.

Acknowledgements

The authors would like to thank John Hirsch and Dawn Alley for their comments on an earlier version of this chapter. David Keen would also like to thank James Vincent for his research assistance in Sierra Leone.

---

[91] See the *Report of the Security Council Mission to West Africa, 20–29 June* 2004, S/2004/525, 2 July 2004, pp. 10–11.

[92] See, for example, Caspar Fithen and Paul Richards, 'Making War, Crafting Peace: Militia Solidarities and Demobilisation in Sierra Leone', in Paul Richards (ed.), *No War, No Peace: An Anthropology of Contemporary Armed Conflicts* (Oxford: James Currey; Athens: Ohio University Press, 2005).

References

Abdullah, Ibrahim and Patrick Muana, 'The Revolutionary United Front of Sierra Leone: A Revolt of the Lumpenproletariat', in Christopher Clapham (ed.), *African Guerrillas*, Oxford, Kampala and Bloomington, IN: James Currey, Fountain Publishers and Indiana University Press, 1998.

Abdullah, Ibrahim and Yusuf Bangura (eds.), 'Lumpen Youth Culture and Political Violence: The Sierra Leone Civil War', *African Development*, special issue, 22(2 and 3), 1997.

Adebajo, Adekeye, *Building Peace in West Africa: Liberia, Sierra Leone and Guinea-Bissau*, Boulder CO and London: Lynne Rienner, 2002.

Adebajo, Adekeye, 'From Congo to Congo: United Nations Peacekeeping in Africa after the Cold War,' in Ian Taylor and Paul Williams (eds.), *Africa in International Politics: External Involvement on the Continent*, London: Routledge, 2004.

Adebajo, Adekeye, *Liberia's Civil War: Nigeria, ECOMOG and Regional Security in West Africa*, Boulder, CO and London: Lynne Rienner, 2002.

Adebajo, Adekeye and David Keen, 'Banquet for Warlords', *The World Today*, 56(7), July 2000, 8–10

Adebajo, Adekeye and Ismail Rashid (eds.), *West Africa's Security Challenges: Building Peace in a Troubled Region*, Boulder, CO and London: Lynne Rienner, 2004.

Adelman, Howard, Astri Suhrke and Bruce Jones, *Early Warning and Conflict Management: Study II of the Joint Evaluation of the Emergency Assistance in Rwanda*, Copenhagen: DANIDA, 1996.

Adibe, Clement E., 'Muddling Through: An Analysis of the ECOWAS Experience in Conflict Management in West Africa', in Liisa Laakso (ed.), *Regional Integration for Conflict Prevention and Peace Building in Africa: Europe, SADC and ECOWAS*, Helsinki: Ministry for Foreign Affairs, 2002.

Africa Confidential, 41(10), 12 May 2000.

Africa Confidential, 41(12), 9 June 2000.

Africa Rights, *Somalia – Operation Restore Hope: A Preliminary Assessment*, Occasional Report, May, London, 1993.

Akashi, Yasushi, 'The Challenges Faced by UNTAC', *Japan Review of International Affairs*, 7(3), Summer 1993.

Amnesty International, 'Haiti,' in *Amnesty International Annual Report 2001*.

Annan, Kofi A., 'Foreword by the United Nations Secretary-General', in United Nations Secretary-General, *A More Secure World: Our Shared Responsibility*.

Report of the Secretary-General's High-Level Panel on Threats, Challenges and Change, New York, United Nations, 2004.

Annan, Kofi A., *Speech Given at Banqueting House*, Whitehall, London, 10 February 2005, available at http://www.globalpolicy.org/reform/papers/annanspeech.htm.

Atkinson, Rick, 'For UN Force in Mogadishu, the Comforts of Home', *International Herald Tribune*, 25 March 1994.

Australian Department of Foreign Affairs and Trade, *East Timor in Transition 1998–2000: An Australian Policy Challenge*, Canberra: Brown and Wilton, 2000.

Barnett, Michael, *Eyewitness to a Genocide: The United Nations and Rwanda*, Ithaca, NY: Cornell University Press, 2002.

Barnett, Michael, *The Politics of Indifference: The Professionalisation of Peacekeeping and the Toleration of Genocide*, unpublished paper, December 1995.

Bauduy, Jennifer, 'US Forces UN to Reduce Haiti Human Rights Mission,' *Reuters*, 16 June 1999.

BBC, 'Correspondent', 21 October 2001 available at http://www.news.bbc.co.uk.

Beauvais, Joel C., 'Benevolent Despotism: A Critique of UN State-Building in East Timor', *New York University Journal of International Law and Politics*, 33(4), 2001, 1101–78

Bellamy, Alex J., *Kosovo and International Society*, Basingstoke: Palgrave, 2002.

Berdal, Mats, *Whither UN Peacekeeping?*, Adelphi Paper no. 281, London: Brassey's, for the International Institute for Strategic Studies, October 1993.

Bogumil, W. Andrzejewski and Ioan M. Lewis, *Somali Poetry*, Oxford: Oxford University Press, 1964.

Bogumil, W. Andrzejewski and Sheila Andrzejewski, *Somali Poetry*, Bloomington, IN: Indiana University Press, 1993.

Borton, John, Emery Brusset, and Alistair Hallam (core team) *et al.*, *Humanitarian Aid and Effects: International response to Conflict and Genocide: Lessons from the Rwanda Experience – Study III*, London/Brussels: Steering Committee of the Joint Evaluation of Emergency Assistance to Rwanda, 1996.

Bose, Sumantra, *Bosnia after Dayton: Nationalist Partition and International Prevention*, London: Hurst & Company, 2002.

Boutros-Ghali, Boutros, *Agenda for Peace: Preventive Diplomacy, Peacemaking and Peacekeeping. Report of the Secretary-General Pursuant to the Statement Adopted by the Summit Meeting of the Security Council on 31 January 1992*, New York: United Nations, 1992.

Brown, Colin, 'British Troops Will Protect Aid Convoys', *The Independent*, 19 August 1922.

Brownlie, Ian (ed.), *Basic Documents in African Affairs*, Oxford: Clarendon Press, 1971.

Bruderlein, Claude, *Inter-agency Assessment Mission to Sierra Leone: Interim Report*, United Nations Office for the Co-ordination of Humanitarian Affairs (UNOCHA), Final Draft, 10 February 1997.

Bull, Hedley, *The Anarchical Society*, London: Macmillan, 1977.

Business Times, 'Khmer Rouge Bogey Gets Cut Down to Size', 16 April 1993.

Cambodia Times (Phnom Penh), 31 October –7 November 1993.

Campbell, Greg, *Blood Diamonds*, Boulder, CO: Westview Press, 2004.

Caplan, Richard, 'International Diplomacy and the Crisis in Kosovo', *International Affairs*, (74) 4, 1998, 745–61.

Caplan, Richard, *A New Trusteeship? The International Administration of War-Torn Territories*, Adelphi Paper no. 341, Oxford: Oxford University Press, 2002.

Cassanelli, Lee V., 'Qat: Changes in the Production and Consumption of a Quasilegal Commodity', in Arjun Appadurai (ed.), *The Social Life of Things*, Cambridge: Cambridge University Press, 1986.

Cassese, Antonio, *Self-Determination of Peoples: A Legal Reappraisal, Hersch Lauterpacht Memorial Lectures*, Cambridge: Cambridge University Press, 1995.

Centre for Democracy and Development (CDD), *Sierra Leone: One Year After Lome*, Conference on the peace process, CDD Strategy Planning Series, London: CDD, 15 September 2000.

Chanda, Nayan, *Brother Enemy: The War After the War*, San Diego, CA: Harcourt Brace Jovanovich, 1986.

Chandler, David, *Bosnia: Faking Democracy After Dayton*, London: Pluto Press, 1999.

Chesterman, Simon, *You, the People: The United Nations, Transitional Administration, and State-Building*, Oxford: Oxford University Press, 2004.

Chopra, Jarat, 'Building State Failure in East Timor', *Development and Change*, 33(5), 2002, 979–1000.

Chopra, Jarat, 'The UN's Kingdom of East Timor', *Survival*, 42(3), 2000, 27–39.

Chopra, Jarat, John Mackinlay and Larry Minear, *Report on the Cambodian Peace Process*, Oslo: Norwegian Institute of International Affairs, February 1993.

Christian Aid, *Sierra Leone: What Price Peace? An Analysis of the Disarmament, Demobilisation and Reintegration Plan*, London, December 1999.

Clark, Wesley K., *Waging Modern War: Bosnia, Kosovo and the Future of Combat*, New York: Public Affairs, 2001.

Clarke, Warren and Jeffry Herbst, 'Somalia and the Future of Humanitarian Intervention', *Foreign Affairs*, 75(2), 1996, 70–85.

Cloud, David, 'Haiti to Delay Vote Until Next Year,' *Wall Street Journal*, 6 April 2004.

Commission of the European Communities on behalf of the Commission for Yugoslavia, *Press Release*, CEECAN 270066DGO8 and 09, February–March 1992 (various).

Compagnon, Daniel, 'Somaliland, un ordre politique en gestation?', *Politique Africaine*, 50, June 1993, 9–20.

Compagnon, Daniel, 'The Somali Opposition Fronts', *Horn of Africa*, 13(1/2), 1990, 29–54.

Conselho Nacional da Resistancia Timorense (National Council of Timorese Resistance – CNRT) 2000, *Report on Outcomes of theCNRTNational Congress, 21–30 August* 2000 (English Version).

Cortright, David and George A. Lopez (eds.), *The Sanctions Decade: Assessing UN Strategies in the 1990*, Boulder, CO: Lynne Rienner, 2000.

Cortright, David, George A. Lopez and Richard W. Conroy, 'Sierra Leone: The Failure of Regional and National Sanctions', in David Cortright and George A. Lopez (eds.), *The Sanctions Decade: Assessing UN Strategies in the 1990*, Boulder, CO: Lynne Rienner, 2000.

Crossette, Barbara, 'UN Diplomats Search for Ways to Avoid Violence in Haiti', *New York Times*, 27 August 1999.

Dailey, Peter, 'Haiti: The Fall of the House of Aristide', *New York Review of Books*, 50(4), 13 March 2003, 41–7.

Daily Telegraph, 'Cambodian Peace Plan "Threatened" by UN Delay', 14 January 1992.

de Cordoba, Jose, 'Haiti Seeks its Fortune in a Nineteenth Century Pact with the French: Impoverished Country Demands Restitution for Gunboat Diplomacy', *Wall Street Journal Europe*, 2–4 January 2004.

des Forges, Alison, *Leave None to Tell the Story: Genocide in Rwanda*, New York: Human Rights Watch, 1999.

Dodd, Mark, 'Give Us a Free Hand or We Quit, Leaders Say', *Sydney Morning Herald*, 5 December 2000.

Dodd, Mark, 'Give Us a Say, Urges Gusmao', *The Age* (Melbourne), 10 October 2000.

Dodd, Mark, 'UN Peace Mission at War with Itself', *Sydney Morning Herald*, 13 May 2000.

Dodd, Mark, 'UN Staff Battle over Independence Policy', *Sydney Morning Herald*, 13 March 2000.

Donelan, Michael, *Elements of International Theory*, Oxford: Oxford University Press, 1991.

Doyle, Michael and Nishtala Suntharalingam, 'The UN in Cambodia: Lesson for Complex Peacekeeping', *International Peacekeeping*, 1(2), 1994, 117–47.

Doyle, Michael, Ian Johnstone and Robert Orr (eds.), *Keeping the Peace: Multidimensional UN Operations in Cambodia and El Salvador*, Cambridge: Cambridge University Press, 1997.

Durch, William J., Victoria K. Holt, Caroline E. Earle and Moira K. Shanahan, *The Brahimi Report and the Future of Peace Operations*, The Henry L. Stimson Center, December 2003.

Economides, Spyros, 'Balkan Security: What Security? Whose Security?', *Journal of Southeast European and Black Sea Studies*, 3(3), 2003.

Economist Intelligence Unit, September 2000, 105–29.

Edwards, Geoffrey and Chris Hill, 'European Political Co-operation, 1989–1991', in Ami Barav and Derrick A. Wyatt (eds.), *Yearbook of European Law 1991*, Oxford: Clarendon Press, 1992.

Elliot, David W. P (ed.), *The Third Indochina Conflict*, Boulder, CO: Westview Press, 1981.

Ero, Comfort, 'British Foreign Policy and the Conflict in Sierra Leone', in Centre for Democracy and Development (CDD), *Sierra Leone: One Year After Lome*, Conference on the peace process, CDD Strategy Planning Series, London: CDD, 15 September 2000.

Etcheson, Craig 'The "Peace" in Cambodia', *Current History*, 91(569), December 1992, 413–17.

Evans, Grant and Kevin Rowley, *Red Brotherhood at War*, London: Verso Books, 1984.

Far Eastern Economic Review, 'I Want to Retake Power', 4 February 1993.

Farah, Ahmed Y. and Ioan M. Lewis, *Somalia: The Roots of Reconciliations* London: Actionaid, 1993.

Farah, Douglas, 'General Calls for Pullout from Haiti; Region's Commander Says Instability Threatens Safety of US Troops on Island,' *The Washington Post*, 13 March 1999.

Feil, Scott, *Preventing Genocide: How the Early Use of Force might have Succeeded in Rwanda*, Washington DC: Carnegie Commission on Preventing Deadly Conflict, 1998.

Financial Times, 'UN Representative Sounds Cambodia Warning', 16 March 1992.

Findlay, Trevor, *Cambodia: The Legacy and Lessons of UNTAC*, SIPRI Research Report, no. 9, Oxford: Oxford University Press, 1995.

Fithen, Caspar and Paul Richards, 'Making War, Crafting Peace: Militia Solidarities and Demobilisation in Sierra Leone', in Paul Richards (ed.) *No War, No Peace: An Anthropology of Contemporary Armed Conflicts*, Oxford: James Currey; Athens, OH: Ohio University Press, 2005.

Focus on Sierra Leone, February 1996, available at http://www.focus-on-sierra-leone.co.uk.

Fofana, Lansana, 'A Nation Self-destructs', *NewsAfrica*, 1(5), 31 July 2000.

Fowler, William, *Operation Barras: The SAS Rescue Mission, Sierra Leone 2000*, London: Weidenfeld and Nicolson, 2004.

Frankfürter Allgemeine Zeitung, 'Die Kambodschaner sterben still', 1 June 1993.

Frankfürter Allgemeine Zeitung, 'Leichtsinnig, schwerfällig, teuer – Die UN-Operation in Kambodscha: Kein Modell für Afghanistan', 3 July 1993.

French, Howard, *New York Times*, 12 October 1993.

Furley, Oliver and Roy May (eds.), *Peacekeeping in Africa*, Aldershot and Vermont: Ashgate, 1998.

Gambari, Ibrahim 'The United Nations', in Mwesiga Baregu and Christopher Landsberg (eds.), *From Cape to Congo: Southern Africa's Evolving Security Challenges*, Boulder, CO and London: Lynne Rienner, 2003.

Garfield, Richard, *The Impact of Economic Sanctions on Health and Well-being*, Relief and Rehabilitation Network Paper, no. 31, London: Overseas Development Institute, November 1999.

Gberie, Lansana, 'The May 25 Coup d'Etat in Sierra Leone: A Militariat Revolt?', *Africa Development*, 22(2&3), 1997, 149–70.

General Dallaire, Romeo, *Force Directive No. 01: Rules of Engagement*, United Nations Assistance Mission for Rwanda (UNAMIR), October 1993.

General Dallaire, Romeo, *Shake Hands with the Devil: The Failure of Humanity in Rwanda*, New York: Avalon Publishing Group, 2004.

General Sir Rose, Michael, *Fighting for Peace: Bosnia 1994*, London: The Harvill Press, 1998.

Gonzalez, David, 'Civilian Police Force Brings New Problems to Haiti', *The New York Times*, 26 November 1999.

Goulding, Marrack, 'The United Nations and Conflict in Africa since the Cold War', *African Affairs*, 98(391), April 1999, 155–66.

Gow, James, 'Deconstructing Yugoslavia', *Survival*, 33(3), 1991, 291–311.

Gow, James, *The Serbian Project and its Adversaries: A Strategy of War Crimes*, London: Hurst & Company, 2003.

Gow, James, *Triumph of the Lack of Will: International Diplomacy and the Yugoslav War*, London: Hurst & Company, 1997.

Gow, James, *Yugoslav Endgames: Civil Strife and Inter-State Conflict*, London Defence Studies no. 5, London: Brassey's, for the Centre for Defence Studies, June 1991.

Gow, James and James D. D. Smith, *Peace-Making, Peace-Keeping: European Security and the Yugoslav Wars*, London Defence Studies no. 11, London: Brassey's, for the Centre for Defence Studies, May 1992.

Greenwood, Christopher, 'Yes, But is the War Legal', *The Observer*, 28 March 1999.

Guicherd, Catherine, 'International Law and the War in Kosovo', *Survival*, 41(2), 1999, 19–34.

Gusmão, Xanana, *New Year's Message*, 31 December 2000.

Hagman, Lotta, 'Haiti's Betrayal', *New York Review of Books*, 50(5), 27 March 2003.

Hagman, Lotta 2002, 'Lessons Learned: Peacebuilding in Haiti,' in *International Peace Academy Conference Report*, New York: IPA, 23–24 January.

Hainsworth, Paul and Stephen McCloskey (eds.), *The East Timor Question: The Struggle for Independence from Indonesia*, London: I.B. Tauris, 2000.

Halperin, Alex, 'Haiti Wins Donors' Help With Reconstruction Plans', *Financial Times*, 21 July 2004.

Heinl, Robert Debs Jr. and Nancy Gordon Heinl, *Written in Blood: The Story of the Haitian People 1492–1971*, Boston, MA: Houghton Mifflin, 1978.

Higgins, Rosalyn, 'The New United Nations and Former Yugoslavia', *International Affairs*, 69 (3) July 1993, 465–83.

Hirsch, John, 'Sierra Leone,' in David M. Malone (ed.), *The UN Security Council: From the Cold War to the 21st Century*, Boulder, CO: and London: Lynne Rienner, 2004.

Hirsch, John, *Sierra Leone: Diamonds and the Struggle for Democracy*, Boulder, CO: Lynne Rienner, 2001.

Hohe, Tanja, 'Totem Polls: Indigenous Concepts and "Free and Fair" Elections in East Timor', *International Peacekeeping*, 9(4), 2002, 69–88.

Holbrooke, Richard, *To End a War*, New York: Modern Library, 1999.

House of Commons Select Committee on Foreign Affairs, *Fourth Report*, 1999, www.publications.parliament.uk/pa/cm199900/cmselect/cmfaff/28/2813.htm.

Human Rights Watch, *The Lost Agenda: Human Rights and UN Field Operations*, New York: Human Rights Watch, June 1993.

Human Rights Watch, *Priorities for the International Community*, New York, 11 November 2000.

Human Rights Watch, *Sierra Leone: Getting Away with Murder, Mutilation, Rape*, Section VII, New York, 1999.

Human Rights Watch, *Unfinished Business: Justice for East Timor*, Press Backgrounder, August 2000, www.hrw.org/backgrounder/asia/timor/etimor-back0829.htm.

Human Rights Watch Africa, *Somalia Beyond the Warlords*, Occasional Report, Washington DC: News from Africa Watch, 7 March, 5(2), 1993.

Human Rights Watch Asia, *Political Control, Human Rights and the UN Missions in Cambodia*, New York: Asia Watch, September 1992.

Ifill, Gwen, *New York Times*, 6 January 1994.

Indian Express, 'Despite the RUF's Immature Attitude, UNAMSIL Wants a Peaceful Solution', 16 July 2000, www.indian-express.com.

International Bank for Reconstruction and Development, *Haiti Assistance Strategy Document 15945-HA*, 13 August 1996.

International Commission on the Balkans, 'The Balkans in Europe's Future', April 2005, www.balkan-commission.org.

International Crisis Group, 'Collapse in Kosovo', ICG Europe Report no. 155 Brussels: ICG, 22 April 2004.

International Crisis Group, 'Kosovo: Towards Final Status', ICG Europe Report no. 161, Brussels: ICG, 24 January 2005.

International Crisis Group, 'A New Chance For Haiti?', in *ICG Latin America/Caribbean Report*, no. 10, Brussels: ICG, 18 November 2004.

International Crisis Group, *Sierra Leone: Managing Uncertainty*, 24 October 2001.

International Crisis Group, *Sierra Leone: Time for a New Military and Political Strategy*, 11 April 2001, 25 October 1998.

International Herald,'Renewed Fighting in Cambodia Places UN Truce in Peril, *Tribune*, 17 June 1993.

International Herald Tribune, 4 August 1992.

International Herald Tribune, 'Khmer Rouge Reported to Grab for Territory', 14–15 March 1992.

International Herald Tribune, 'Khmer Rouge Widens Its Attacks ... Ceasefire at Risk Nationwide', 16 July 1992.

International Herald Tribune, 'UN Cambodian Force Is Malfunctioning', 5 October 1992.

International Herald Tribune, 'UN to Halt Cambodian Disarmament', 22 October 1992.

International Herald Tribune, 'With the UN in Town, Phnom Penh Booms – Is This a Good Thing?', 23 June 1992.

International Peace Academy/Center on International Cooperation, *Refashioning the Dialogue: Regional Perspectives on the Brahimi Report on UN Peace Operations*, Regional Meetings, February–March 2001.

Jackson, Robert, *Quasi-States: Sovereignty, International Relations and the Third World*, Cambridge: Cambridge University Press, 1991.

Jenkins, Simon, 'Out of the Valley of Death', *The Times*, 20 April 1994.

Jolliffe, Jill, 'Jail Breakout over Delays', *The Age* (Melbourne), 17 August 2002.

Jonah, James, 'The United Nations', in Adekeye Adebajo and Ismail Rashid (eds.), *West Africa's Security Challenges: Building Peace in A Troubled Region*, Boulder, CO and London: Lynne Rienner, 2004.

Jones, Bruce, *The Arusha Peace Process*, Background Paper for Study II of the Joint Evaluation, London, 1995.

Jones, Bruce D., *Peacemaking in Rwanda: The Dynamics of Failure*, Boulder, CO: Lynne Reinner, 2001.

Jones, Bruce and Astri Suhrke, 'Preventive Diplomacy in Rwanda: Failure to Act, or Failure of Actions Taken?', in Bruce Jentleson (ed.), *Opportunities Missed, Opportunities Seized: Preventive Diplomacy in the Post-Cold World*, New York: Carnegie Commission on Preventing Deadly Conflict, 1999.

Judah, Tim, *Kosovo: War and Revenge*, New Haven, CT: Yale University Press, 2000.

Judah, Tim, *The Serbs: History, Myth and the Destruction of Yugoslavia*, New Haven, CT: Yale University Press, 1997.

Jusu-Sheriff, Yasmin, 'Civil Society', in Adekeye Adebajo and Ismail Rashid (eds.), *West Africa's Security Challenges: Building Peace in a Troubled Region*, Boulder, CO: and London: Lynne Rienner, 2004.

Kamber, Michael, 'A Troubled Haiti Struggles to Find its Political Balance', *The New York Times*, 3 January 2005.

Keen, David, *Conflict and Collusion in Sierra Leone*, Oxford: James Currey/ Palgrave Macmillan/International Peace Academy, 2005.

Khouri-Padova, Lama, *Haiti: Lessons Learned*, UN Department of Peacekeeping Operations, Best Practices Unit Discussion Paper, March 2004, http:// pbpu.unlb.org/pbpu/library/Haiti per cent20lessons per cent20learned per cent2030 per cent20March per cent202004 per cent20final.pdf.

Kingsbury, Damien (ed.), *Guns and Ballot Boxes: East Timor's Vote for Independence*, Clayton, Australia: Monash Asia Institute, 2000.

Kingsbury, Damien, 'The New Timor: A Xanana Republic?' *Jakarta Post*, 16 December 2000.

Knaus, Gerald and Felix Martin, 'Travails of the European Raj', *Journal of Democracy*, 14(3), 2003, 60–74.

Koch, George, 'The Cross', *Saturday Night*, 1 September 1996.

Kola, Paulin, *The Search for Greater Albania*, London: Hurst & Company, 2003.

Kovalski, Serge, 'Haitian Police Tinged by Thin Blue Line', *The Washington Post*, 23 October 1999.

Kumar, Chetan, ' Sustainable Peace as Sustainable Democracy: The Experience of Haiti,' *Politik und Gesellschaft*, April 1999, www.fes.de/ipg/ipg4_99/ artkumar.htm.

Kuperman, Alan, 'Rwanda is Retrospect', *Foreign Affairs*, 79(1), January/ February 2000, 94–118.

La Rose-Edwards, Paul, *The Rwandan Crisis of April 1994: The Lessons Learned*, Report for Regional Security and Peacekeeping Division (IDC), International Security, Arms Control, and CSCE Affairs Bureau, Ottawa: Department of Foreign Affairs and International Trade, November 1994.

Lawson, George, 'A Conversation with Michael Mann', *Millenium, Journal of International Studies* 34(2), 2006, 477–85.

Le Monde, 3 January 2004.

Ledgerwood, Judy L., 'UN Peacekeeping Mission: The Lessons of Cambodia', *Asia-Pacific Issues* (East–West Center), 11 March 1994.

Lefort, Pascal and Jonathan Littell, *Food and Terror in Sierra Leone*, Rome: Action Internationale Contre La Faim, 1998.

Leifer, Michael, 'The Indochina Problem', in Thomas Bruce Millar and James Walter (eds.), *Asian-Pacific Security After the Cold War*, Canberra: Allen and Unwin, 1993.

Leifer, Michael, 'The International Representation of Kampuchea', *Southeast Asian Affairs 1982*, Singapore: Heinemann Asia for Institute of Southeast Asian Studies, 1982.

Levitt, Jeremy, 'Pre-Intervention Trust-Building, African States and Enforcing the Peace: The Case of ECOWAS in Liberia and Sierra Leone', *Liberian Studies Journal*, 24(1), 1999.

Lewis, Ioan M., 'Ambush in Somalia', *The Guardian*, 7 October 1993.

Lewis, Ioan M., *Blood and Bone*, Trenton, NJ: Red Sea Press, 1993.

Lewis, Ioan M. (ed.), *Blueprint for a Socio-Demographic Survey and Reenumeration of the Refugee Camp Population in the Somali Democratic Republic*, Geneva: UNHCR, 1986.

Lewis, Ioan M., *Making History in Somalia: Humanitarian Intervention in a Stateless Society*, Discussion Paper no. 6, London: The Centre for the Study of Global Governance, LSE, 1993.

Lewis, Ioan M., 'Misunderstanding the Somali Crisis', *Anthropology Today*, 9(4), 1993, 1–3.

Lewis, Ioan M., *A Modern History of Somalia: Nation and State in the Horn of Africa*, Boulder, CO: Westview Press, 1988.

Lewis, Ioan M., *A Pastoral Democracy* New York: Afrikana Press, 1982.

Lewis, Ioan M., 'Restoring Hope in a Future of Peace', *Cooperazione*, Rome, March 1993.

Lewis, Kelvin, 'UN acts against Westside Boys', *West Africa*, 21–27 August 2000.

Los Angeles Times, 'UN to Combat Political Murders in Cambodia', 8 January 1993.

Macdonald, David Bruce, *Balkan Holocausts? Serbian and Croatian Victim-centred Propaganda and the War in Yugoslavia*, Manchester: Manchester University Press, 2002.

Major Ashby, Phil, *Unscathed: Escape From Sierra Leone*, London: Macmillan, 2002.

Malan, Mark, Phenyo Rakate and Angela McIntyre, *Peacekeeping in Sierra Leone: UNAMSIL Hits the Home Straight*. Pretoria: Institute for Security Studies, 2002.

Malcolm, Noel, *Kosovo: A Short History*, London: Macmillan, 1998.

Mango, Anthony, 'Finance and Administration', in *A Global Agenda: Issues Before the 49th General Assembly of the United Nations*, New York: United Nations, 1994.

Marcella, Gabriel, 'Protectorate may be Haiti's only Alternative', *The Miami Herald*, 2 January 2005.

Marchal, Roland, 'Le *mooryaan* de Mogadiscio. Formes de la violence et de son contrôle dans un espèce urbain en guerre', *Cahiers d'Etudes Africaines*, 130(33), 1993.

Martin, Ian, 'No Justice in Jakarta', *Washington Post*, 27 August 2002.

Martin, Ian, *Self-Determination in East Timor: The United Nations, the Ballot, and International Intervention, International Peace Academy Occasional Paper Series*, Boulder, CO: Lynne Rienner, 2001.

Mayall, James, 'The Battle for the Horn: Somali Irredentism and International Diplomacy', *The World Today*, 34(9), September 1978, 336–45.

Mayall, James, *Nationalism and International Society*, Cambridge: Cambridge University Press, 1990.

Mayall, James, 'Self-Determination and the OAU', in Ioan M. Lewis (ed.), *Nationalism and Self-Determination in the Horn of Africa*, London: Ithaca Press, 1983.

McAskill, Ewen, 'Badly trained, ill defined and under funded – UN peacekeepers endure humiliation', *The Guardian*, 11 May 2000.

McGreal, Chris, 'UN to sack its general in Sierra Leone', *The Guardian Weekly*, 29 June – 5 July 2000.

McQueen, Norrie, *United Nations Peacekeeping in Africa since 1960*, Harlow: Pearson Education Limited, 2002.

Menkhaus, Ken, 'Getting Out v. Getting Through: US and UN Policies in Somalia', *Middle East Policy*, 3(1), 1994, 146–62.

Mersiades, Michael, 'Peacekeeping and Legitimacy: Lessons from Cambodia and Somalia,' *International Peacekeeping*, 12(2), Summer 2005, 205–21.

Mission of the Netherlands to the United Nations, 'No Exit Without Strategy', by the Security Council, New York, October 2000.

Mobbekk, Eirin, 'Enforcement of Democracy in Haiti', Paper for the Political Studies Association; UK Fiftieth Annual Conference, London, 10–13 April 2000.

Mohammed, Sahnoun, *Somalia: The Missed Opportunities*, Washington, DC: United States Institute of Peace, 1994.

National Democratic Institute and the Faculty of Social and Political Science of the University of East Timor, *Carrying the People's Aspirations: A Report on Focus Group Discussions in East Timor*, Dili, East Timor: NDI, February 2002.

NATO, *Military Technical Agreement between the International Security Force ('KFOR') and the Governments of the Federal Republic of Yugoslavia and the Republic of Serbia*, 9 June 1999, available at http://www.nato.int/kosovo/docu/a990609a.htm.

New York Times, 11 September 1992.

New York Times, 'UN Bosnian Commander Wants More Troops, Fewer Resolutions', 31 December 1993.

Newbury, Catherine, *The Cohesion of Oppression: Clientship and Ethnicity in Rwanda, 1860–1960*, New York: Columbia University Press, 1988.

Norton-Taylor, Richard and Chris McGreal, 'Sierra Leone Children Carry British Guns', *The Guardian*, 11 May 2000.

Observer, 3 January 1993.

Olonisakin, Funmi and Comfort Ero, 'Africa and the Regionalization of Peace Operations', in Michael Pugh and Waheguru Pal Singh Sidhu (eds.), *The United Nations and Regional Security: Europe and Beyond*, Boulder, CO and London: Lynne Rienner, 2003.

O'Neill, William G., *Kosovo: An Unfinished Peace*, Boulder, CO: Lynne Rienner, 2002.

Orenstein, Catherine, 'The Roads Built in Haiti Only Go So Far', *The Washington Post*, 30 January 2000.

Organisation of American States Permanent Council, Resolution 862, CP/Res. 862 (1401/04), 26 February 2004.

Organisation of American States, Resolution MRE/Res. 6/94, 9 June 1994.

Organisation of American States, *Representative Democracy*, Resolution 1080 AG/Res. 1080 (XXI-0/91), 5 June 1991.

Organisation of American States, *Support for Democracy in Haiti*, Resolution MRE/Res. 2/91, 8 October 1991.

Owen, David, *Balkan Odyssey*, New York: Harcourt Brace and Company, 1995.

Panafrican News Agency, Dakar, 18 September 2000.

Parsons, Anthony, 'The UN and the National Interests of States', in Adam Roberts and Benedict Kingsbury, (eds.), *United Nations, Divided World: The UN's Role in International Relations*, Oxford: Clarendon Press, 1988.

Pastor, Robert A., 'The Clinton Administration and the Americas: The Postwar Rhythm and Blues', *Journal of Interamerican Studies and World Affairs* 38(4), Winter 1996, 99–128.

Patel, Ricken, *Sierra Leone's Uncivil War and the Unlimited Intervention that Ended It. Case-study for the Carr Centre for Human Rights Policy*, Harvard University, mimeo, 2002.

Patman, Robert G., *The Soviet Union in the Horn of Africa*, Cambridge: Cambridge University Press, 1990.

Patman, Robert G., 'The UN Operation in Somalia', in Ramesh Thakur and Carlyle Thayer (eds.), *UN Peacekeeping in the 1990s*, Boulder, CO: Westview Press, 1995.

Pick, Hella, *The Guardian*, 29 October 1993.

Polman, Linda, 'Blue Helmets as Cannon Fodder', *The Guardian*, 17 February 2004.

Porter, Toby, *The Interaction Between Political and Humanitarian Action in Sierra Leone, 1995 to 2002*, Geneva: Centre for Humanitarian Dialogue, March 2002.

Powell, Colin, *My American Journey*, New York: Random House, 1995.

'Pre-Poll Violence Overwhelms UN in Cambodia', *Independent*, 6 April 1993.

President of the United States, *Blocking Property of Certain Haitian Nationals*, Executive Order 12922, 22 June 1994, available at http://www.archives.gov/federal_register/executive_orders/pdf/12922.pdf.

President of the United States, *Prohibiting Certain Transactions with Respect to Haiti*, Executive Order 12920, 10 June 1994, available at http://www.archives.gov/federal_register/executive_orders/pdf/12920.pdf.

Prunier, Gérard, 'A Candid View of the Somali National Movement', *Horn of Africa*, 13/14(3/4), 1992, 107–20.

Prunier, Gérard, *The Rwanda Crisis: History of a Genocide*, Rwanda, New York: Columbia University Press, 1997.

Rahman Lamin, Abdul, *The Politics of Reconciliation in the Mano River Union*, Johannesburg: Institute for Global Dialogue, July 2004.

Ratner, Steven, 'The United Nations in Cambodia: A Model for Resolution of Internal Conflicts?', in Lori F. Damrosch (ed.), *Enforcing Restraint: Collective Intervention in Internal Conflicts*, New York: Council on Foreign Relations Press, 1993.

Rawski, Frederick, 'Truth-Seeking and Local Histories in East Timor', *Asia-Pacific Journal on Human Rights and the Law*, 3(1), 2002.

Reno, William, 'Privatizing War in Sierra Leone', *Current History*, no. 610, May 1997.

Reno, William, *Warlord Politics and African States*, Boulder, CO: and London: Lynne Rienner Publishers, 1998.

Renton, Alex, 'Our Guns Arm the Children', *Evening Standard*, 24 May 2000.

Reyntjens, Filip, *L'Afrique des Grands Lacs: Rwanda et Burundi, 1990–1994* Paris: Khartala, 1994.

Reyntjens, Filip, *Rwanda. Trois jours qui ont fait basculer l'histoire*, Bruxelles et Paris: Institut Africain-L'Harmattan, Cahiers Africains, 1996.

Richards, Paul, *Fighting for the Rainforest: War, Youth and Resources in Sierra Leone*, Oxford and New Hampshire: James Currey and Heinemann, 1996.

Roberts, Adam, 'NATO's "Humanitarian War" over Kosovo', *Survival*, 41(3), 1999, 102–23.

Roberts, Adam and Benedict Kingsbury, 'The UN's Role in International Society', in Adam Roberts and Benedict Kingsbury (eds.), *United Nations, Divided World: The UN's Role in International Relations*, Oxford: Clarendon Press, 1988.

Rohter, Larry, 'Political Feuds Rack Haiti: So Much for its High Hopes,' *The New York Times*, 18 October 1998.

Said, Samatar S., *Oral Poetry and Somali Nationalism*, Cambridge: Cambridge University Press, 1982.

Sanderson, John M., 'UNTAC: Successes and Failures', in Smith Hugh (ed.), *International Peacekeeping: Building on the Cambodian Experience*, Canberra: Australian Defence Studies Centre, 1994.

Schulz, Dennis, 'East Timor's Land Rights Mess', *The Age* (Melbourne), 23 December 2000.

Sealy, Sally, 'The Changing Idiom of Self-determination in the Horn of Africa', in Ioan M. Lewis (ed.), *Nationalism and Self-Determination in the Horn of Africa*, London: Ithaca Press, 1983.

Shawcross, William, *Cambodia's New Deal*, Washington, DC: Carnegie Endowment for International Peace, 1994.

Shearer, David, 'Exploring the Limits of Consent: Conflict Resolution in Sierra Leone', *Millennium: Journal of International Studies*, 26(3), 1997, 845–60.

Shearer, David, *Private Armies and Military Intervention*, Adelphi Paper no. 316, Oxford: Oxford University Press for International Institute for Strategic Studies, 1998.

Sierra Leone News Agency (SLNA), 12 January 2000.
Sierra Leone News Agency (SLNA), 22 September 2000.
Silber, Laura and Allan Little, *The Death of Yugoslavia*, London: Penguin/BBC Books, 1996.
Smith, Hugh (ed.), *International Peacekeeping: Building on the Cambodian Experience*, Canberra: Australian Defence Studies Centre, 1994.
Smith, Michael G., *Peacekeeping in East Timor, International Peace Academy Occasional Paper Series*, Boulder, CO: Lynne Rienner, 2003.
Somalia News Update, Uppsala, 2(12), 1993.
Sommer, John G., *Hope Restored? Humanitarian Aid in Somalia 1990–1994*, Washington, DC: Refugee Policy Group, Center for Policy Analysis and Research on Refugee Issues, November 1994.
Sommers, Marc, *The Dynamics of Coordination*, Providence, RU: Thomas J. Watson Jr Institute for International Studies, Occasional Paper no. 40, 2000.
Stedman, Stephen J. and Fred Tanner, *Refugee Manipulation: War, Politics, and the Abuse of Human Suffering*, Washington, DC: The Brookings Institution, 2003.
Stedman Stephen, 'Spoiler Problems in Peace Processes', *International Security*, 22(2), Fall 1997, 5–53.
Stohl, Rachel, 'Haiti's Big Threat: Small Arms,' Christian Science Monitor, 23 March 2004, available at http://www.csmonitor.com/2004/0323/p09s02-coop.html.
Strohmeyer, Hansjoerg, 'Building a New Judiciary for East Timor: Challenges of a Fledgling Nation', *Criminal Law Forum*, 11(3), 2000, 259–85.
Strohmeyer, Hansjoerg, 'Collapse and Reconstruction of a Judicial System: The United Nations Missions in Kosovo and East Timor', *American Journal of International Law*, 95(1), 2001, 46–63.
Taylor, Paul, 'The Role of the United Nations in the Provision of Humanitarian Assistance: New Problems and New Responses', in James T. H. Tang (ed.), *Human Rights and International Relations in the Asia Pacific*, London and New York: Pinter, 1995.
Taylor, Paul, 'The United Nations System Under Stress: Financial Pressures and Their Consequences', in Paul Taylor (ed.), *International Organization in the Modern World*, London: Pinter, 1993.
Taylor, Paul and Arthur J. R. Groom, *The United Nations and the Gulf War: Back to the Future*, Discussion Paper no. 38, London: Royal Institute of International Affairs, February 1992.
The Economist, 'Getting Ready for Statehood', 13 April 2002.
The Economist, 'Help Wanted: One Government,' 25 July 1998.
The Economist, 'Operation deep Pockets', 18 December 2004.
The Guardian, 'Child Sex Boom Blamed on UN', 4 November 1993.
The Guardian, 'UN Blamed for Delay in Clearing Mines', 22 November 1991.
The Independent, 3 July 1992.
The Independent, 6 April 1993.
The Independent, 'Cambodians Fall out with UN Peacekeepers', 26 January 1993.

The Independent, 'Phnom Penh Offensive Threatens Peace Plan', 2 February 1993.

The International Commission on Intervention and State Sovereignty, *The Responsibility to Protect,* Ottawa, ON: International Development Research Centre, 2001.

The Times, 24 April 1993.

The Times, 23 April 1993.

The Times, 21 April 1993.

The Times, 11 February 1993.

The Times, 'Sex and Inflation End the UN Honeymoon in Cambodia', 26 November 1992.

The Times, 2 October 1992.

The Times, 3 September 1992.

The Times, 29 August 1992.

The Times, 28 August 1992.

The World Bank Group, *Haiti: The Challenges of Poverty Reduction,* Washington DC: *World Bank Group,* August 1998.

Tran, Mark and McElroy Claudia, 'UN failure in Sierra Leone feeds recriminations', *The Guardian,* 29 May 1997.

United Nations, *Agreement on a Comprehensive Political Settlement of the Cambodia Conflict,* London: HMSO, 23 October 1991.

United Nations, *Charter of the United Nations,* New York: United Nations, 26 June 1945.

United Nations, 'Document 68', in *Haiti,* 23 June 1993.

United Nations, *Eleventh Report of the Multinational Force in Haiti,* S/1995/149, 21 February 1995.

United Nations, *First Periodic Report on the Operations of the Multinational Force in East Timor,* S/1999/1025, 4 October 1999.

United Nations, *Letter from the Permanent Representative of the United States of America to the President of the Security Council,* S/1994/1148, 10 October 1994.

United Nations, *Letter by Representatives of Countries Participating in the Multinational Force to the President of the Security Council,* S/1995/55, 19 January 1995.

United Nations, *Press Release,* UN Doc GA/AB/3570, 4 June 2003.

United Nations, *Press Release,* UN Doc SC/6882, 27 June 2000.

United Nations, *Report of the Independent Inquiry into the Actions of the United Nations during the 1994 Genocide in Rwanda,* 15 December 1999.

United Nations, *Report of the International Commission of Inquiry on East Timor to the Secretary-General,* A/54/726-S/2000/59, 31 January 2000.

United Nations, *Report of the Panel on United Nations Peace Operations* (Brahimi Report), A/55/305–S/2000/809, 21 August 2000, available at http://www.un.org/peace/reports/peace_operations.

United Nations, *Security Council Briefed by Sergio Vieira de Mello, Special Representative for East Timor,* SC/6882, 27 June 2000.

United Nations, *Statement by the Director of UNTAC Human Rights Component on Political Violence,* 23 May 1993.

United Nations, *The United Nations and East Timor: Self-Determination Through Popular Consultation*, New York: UN Department of Public Information, 2000.

United Nations, *The United Nations and Rwanda, 1993–1996*, DPI/1768, New York: Department of Public Information UN, 1996.

United Nations, *Yearbook of the United Nations 1994*, The Hague: Martinus Nijhoff, 1995.

United Nations Chronicle, 'Cambodia Election Results', UN DPI/1389, June 1993.

United Nations Daily Highlights, 25 November 1998, available at http://www.hri.org/news/world/undh/1998/98–11–25.undh.html

United Nations Department of Political Affairs, *Report of the Reconnaissance Mission*, New York: United Nations, 21 March 1993.

United Nations Economic and Social Council, *Report of the Ad-hoc Advisory Group on Haiti*, E/1999/103, 2 July 1999.

United Nations General Assembly, *Report of the Panel on United Nations Peace Operations*, A/55/305, 21 August 2000.

United Nations General-Assembly, Resolution 54/193, A/RES/54/193, 18 February 2000.

United Nations General Assembly, *Report of the Secretary General pursuant to General Assembly Resolution 53/35*, A/54/549, 15 November 1999.

United Nations General Assembly, Resolution 46/7, 11 October 1991.

United Nations Interim Administration Mission in Kosovo, *Standards Implementation Plan*, 31 March 2004.

United Nations Panel of Experts, *Report of the Panel of Experts, Appointed Pursuant to UN Security Council Resolution 1306 (2000) Paragraph 19 in Relation to Sierra Leone*, S/2000/1195, 20 December 2000.

United Nations Secretary-General, *A More Secure World: our shared responsibility*, A/59/565, 2 December 2004.

United Nations Secretary-General, *Agenda for Peace: Preventive Diplomacy, Peacemaking and Peacekeeping. Report of the Secretary-General Pursuant to the Statement Adopted by the Summit Meeting of the Security Council on 31 January 1992*, New York: United Nations.

United Nations Secretary-General, *Eighth Report of the Secretary-General on the United Nations Observer Mission in Sierra Leone*, S/1999/1003, 23 September 1999.

United Nations Secretary-General, *Electoral Assistance to Haiti: Note by the Secretary-General*, A/45/870/Add.1, 22 February 1991.

United Nations Secretary-General, *Fifth Report of the Secretary General on the United Nations Mission in Sierra Leone*, S/2000/751, 31 July 2000.

United Nations Secretary-General, *First Report of the Secretary General on the United Nations Mission in Sierra Leone*, S/1999/1223, 6 December 1999.

United Nations Secretary-General, *Fourth Progress Report of the Secretary- General on the United Nations Transitional Authority in Cambodia*, S/25719, 3 May 1993.

United Nations Secretary-General, *Fourth Report of the Secretary-General on the United Nations Mission in Sierra Leone*, S/2000/455, 19 May 2000.

United Nations Secretary-General, *No Exit Without Strategy: Security Council Decision-making and the Closure or Transition of United Nations Peacekeeping Operations*, S/2001/394, 20 April 2001.

United Nations Secretary-General, *Question of East Timor: Report of the Secretary-General*, S/1999/862, 9 August 1999.

United Nations Secretary-General, *Renewing the United Nations: A Program for Reform*, A/51/950, 14 July 1997.

United Nations Secretary-General, 'Report by the Secretary-General Concerning the Situation in Somalia', S/1994/1968, 17 September 1994.

United Nations Secretary-General, *Report of the Secretary General*, A/53/951-S/1999/513, 5 May 1999.

United Nations Secretary-General, *Report of the Secretary-General to the Committee on Peacekeeping*, A/59/___, January 2005.

United Nations Secretary-General, *Report of the Secretary-General on the United Nations Mission in Côte d'Ivoire*, S/2004/3, 6 January 2004.

United Nations Secretary-General, *Report of the Secretary-General on the United Nations Transitional Administration in East Timor (for the period 27 July 2000 to 16 January 2001)*, S/2001/42, 16 January 2001.

United Nations Secretary-General, *Report of the Secretary-General on the Implementation of the Report of the Panel on United Nations Peace Operations*, A/55/502, 20 October 2000.

United Nations Secretary-General, *Report of the Secretary-General on the United Nations Transitional Administration in East Timor (for the period 27 January to 26 July 2000)*, S/2000/738, 26 July 2000.

United Nations Secretary-General, *Report of the Secretary-General on the United Nations Transitional Administration in East Timor*, S/2000/53, 26 January 2000.

United Nations Secretary-General, *Report of the Secretary-General on the Situation in East Timor*, S/1999/1024, 4 October 1999.

United Nations Secretary-General, *Report of the Secretary-General on the United Nations Civilian Police Mission in Haiti*, S/1999/579, 18 May 1999.

United Nations Secretary-General, *Report of the Secretary-General on the Implementation of Security Council Resolution 792 (1992)*, S/25289, 13 February 1993.

United Nations Secretary-General, *Report of the Secretary-General Pursuant to Security Council Resolution 757 (1992)*, S/ 24075, 6 June 1992.

United Nations Secretary-General, *Report of the Secretary-General on Cambodia*, S/23613, 19 February 1992.

United Nations Secretary-General, *Report on Haiti*, S/2004/300, 16 April 2004.

United Nations Secretary-General, *Report on Haiti*, S/2004/698, 30 August 2004.

United Nations Secretary-General, *Report on the UN Stabilization Mission in Haiti*, UN Doc, S/2004/908, 18 November 2004.

United Nations Secretary-General, *Report on the United Nations Civilian Police Mission in Haiti to the Security Council and the General Assembly* A/55/154, 17 July 2000.

United Nations Secretary-General, *Report on the United Nations Civilian Police Mission in Haiti to the Security Council and the General Assembly*, S/1999/908, 24 August 1999.

United Nations Secretary-General, *Report on the United Nations Civilian Police Mission in Haiti*, S/1998/144, 20 February 1998.

United Nations Secretary-General, *Report on the United Nations Civilian Police Mission in Haiti*, S/1998/434, 28 May 1998.

United Nations Secretary-General, *Report on the United Nations Civilian Police Mission in Haiti*, S/1998/796, 24 August 1998.

United Nations Secretary-General, *Report on the United Nations Civilian Police Mission in Haiti*, S/1998/1064, 11 November 1998.

United Nations Secretary-General, *Report on the United Nations Civilian Police Mission in Haiti*, S/1999/181, 19 February 1999.

United Nations Secretary-General, *Reports on the Question Concerning Haiti*, S/1994/1143, 28 September 1994.

United Nations Secretary-General, *Reports on the Question Concerning Haiti*, S/1994/1180, 18 October 1994.

United Nations Secretary-General, *Reports on the Question Concerning Haiti*, S/1995/46, 17 January 1995.

United Nations Secretary-General, *Reports on the Question Concerning Haiti*, S/1995/305, 13 April 1995.

United Nations Secretary-General, *Second Report of the Secretary-General on the United Nations Mission in Côte d'Ivoire*, S/2003/1069, 4 November 2003.

United Nations Secretary-General, *Seventh Report of the Secretary-General on the UN Observer Mission in Sierra Leone*, S/1999/836, 30 July 1999.

United Nations Secretary-General, *Statement by the UN Secretary-General*, SG/SM4627 HI/4, 1 October 1990.

United Nations Secretary-General, *Supplement to an Agenda for Peace: Position Paper of the Secretary-General on the Occasion of the Fiftieth Anniversary of the United Nations*, A/50/60, S/1995/1, 3 January 1995.

United Nations Secretary-General, *Third Report of the Secretary-General on the United Nations Mission in Sierra Leone*, S/2000/186, 7 March 2000.

United Nations Secretary-General, *Twenty-Fourth Report of the Secretary- General on the UN Mission in Sierra Leone*, S/2004/965, 21 June 2004.

United Nations Secretary-General, *UN Secretary-General, Report on the International Civilian Support Mission in Haiti*, A/55/154, 17 July 2000.

United Nations Secretary-General's High-level Panel on Threats, Challenges and Change, *A More Secure World: Our Shared Responsibility*, New York: United Nations, 2004.

United Nations Security Council, *Agreement on the Kosovo Verification Mission of the Organization for Security and Cooperation in Europe*, S/1998/978, 20 October 1998.

United Nations Security Council, *Kosovo Verification Mission Agreement between the North Atlantic Treaty Organization and the Federal Republic of Yugoslavia*, S/1998/991, 23 October 1998.

United Nations Security Council, *Report of the Security Council Mission to West Africa, 20–29 June 2004*, S/2004/525, 2 July 2004.

United Nations Security Council, *Report of the Inter-Agency Mission to West Africa: 'Towards a Comprehensive Approach to Durable and Sustainable Solutions to Priority Needs and Challenges in West Africa*, S/2001/434, 2 May 2001.

United Nations Security Council, *Report of the Security Council Mission to East Timor and Indonesia*, S/2000/1105, 20 November 2000.

United Nations Security Council, *Report of the Security Council Mission to Jakarta and Dili, 8 to 12 September 1999*, S/1999/976, 14 September 1999.

United Nations Security Council, *Rambouillet Accords: Interim Agreement for Peace and Self-Government in Kosovo*, S/1999/648, 7 June 1999.

United Nations Security Council, Draft Resolution, S/1999/328, 26 March 1999.

United Nations Security Council, *Statement by the Contact Group Issued in London*, S/1999/96, 29 January 1999.

United Nations Security Council, *Report of the Commission of Inquiry Established Pursuant to Security Council Resolution 885 (1993) to Investigate Attacks on UNOSOMII Personnel Which Led to Casualties Among Them*, New York: United Nations, 24 February 1994.

United Nations Security Council, *Report of the Secretary-General pursuant to Security Council Resolution 752 (1992)*, S/24000, 26 May 1992.

United Nations Security Council, Resolution 713, 25 September 1991.

United Nations Security Council, Resolution 745, 28 February 1992.

United Nations Security Council, Resolution 770, 13 August 1992.

United Nations Security Council, Resolution 757, 30 May 1992.

United Nations Security Council, Resolution 771, 13 August 1992.

United Nations Security Council, Resolution 795, 11 December 1992.

United Nations Security Council, Resolution 814, 26 March 1993.

United Nations Security Council, Resolution 872, 5 October 1993.

United Nations Security Council, Resolution 948, 15 October 1994.

United Nations Security Council, Resolution 953, 31 October 1994.

United Nations Security Council, Resolution 975, 30 January 1995.

United Nations Security Council, Resolution 1063, 28 June 1996.

United Nations Security Council, Resolution, 1160, 31 March 1998.

United Nations Security Council, Resolution 1199, 23 September 1998.

United Nations Security Council, Resolution 1244, 10 June 1999.

United Nations Security Council, Resolution 1246, 11 June 1999.

United Nations Security Council, Resolution 1264, 15 September 1999.

United Nations Security Council, Resolution 1272, 25 October 1999.

United Nations Security Council, Resolution 1514, 13 November 2003.

United Nations Transitional Administration at East Timor (UNTAET), Daily Briefing, 8 August 2000.

United Nations Transitional Administration at East Timor (UNTAET), *On the Establishment of a National Council*, Regulation 2000/24, 14 July 2000.

United Nations Transitional Administration at East Timor (UNTAET), *On the Establishment of the Cabinet of the Transitional Government in East Timor*, Regulation 2000/23, 14 July 2000.

United Nations Transitional Administration at East Timor (UNTAET), Regulation 1999/2, 2 December 1999.

United Nations Transitional Administration at East Timor (UNTAET), Regulation 1999/3, 3 December 1999.

United Nations Transitional Administration at East Timor (UNTAET), Regulation 2000/11, 6 March 2000.

United Nations Transitional Administration at East Timor (UNTAET), Regulation 2000/24, 14 July 2000.

United Nations Transitional Administration at East Timor (UNTAET), Regulation 2001/10, 13 July 2001.

United States Army Peacekeeping Institute, *Success in Peacekeeping: United Nations Mission in Haiti–The Military Perspective*, Carlisle Barracks, Pennsilvania PA: US Army Peacekeeping Institute, 1996.

United States Committee for Refugees, *Sierra Leone's Path to Peace: Key Issues at Year's End*, press release, 15 December 1999.

United States Department of State, *International Narcotics Strategy Reports, 2003*, 1 March 2004.

United States Department of States, *Clinton Administration Policy on Reforming Multilateral Peace Operations (Presidential Division Directive – PDD 25)*, 22 February 1996.

United States Department of Transportation, Order 94–6–28, 17 June 1994.

United States General Accounting Office, *UN Peacekeeping: Lessons Learned in Managing Recent Missions: Report to Congressional Requesters*, Washington, DC: General Accounting Office, December 1993.

Usborne, David and Andrew Marshall, 'UN Vows: 'We Will Not Withdraw' as Rebels Circle', *Independent*, 11 May 2000.

Uvin, Peter, *Aiding Violence: The Development Enterprise in Rwanda*, West Hartford CT: Kumarian Press, 1998.

Vaccaro, Matthew J., 'The Politics of Genocide: Peacekeeping and Disaster Relief in Rwanda', in William J. Durch (ed.), *UN Peacekeeping, American Politics, and the Uncivil Wars of the 1990s*, first edition, New York: St. Martin's Press, 1996.

Valpy, Edmund and Knox FitzGerald, 'The Economic Dimension of the Peace Process in Cambodia', in Peter Utting (ed.), *Between Hope and Insecurity: The Social Consequences of the Cambodian Peace Process*, Geneva: UNRISD Report, 1994.

van Meurs, Wim, 'Kosovo's Fifth Anniversary – On the Road to Nowhere?' Munich: Centre for Applied Policy, Working Paper, 2004, available at http://www.cap.lmu.de/download/2004/2004_Kosovo.pdf.

Varner, Bill and Glenn Hall, 'UN Peacekeepers Should Stay in Haiti for 20 Years, Envoy Says', *Bloomberg*, 30 March 2004.

Vickers, Miranda, *Between Serb and Albanian: A History of Kosovo*, London: Hurst & Company, 1998.

Ware, Michael, 'Murder Charge Bolsters INTERFET Get-Tough Policy', *The Australian* (Sydney), 17 December 1999.

Washington Post, 13 May 1994.

Weiner, Tim and Lydia Polgreen, 'Facing New Crisis, Haiti Again Relies on US Military to Keep Order,' *The New York Times*, 7 March 2004.

Weller, Marc, 'The Rambouillet Conference on Kosovo', *International Affairs*, 75(2), 1999, 211–51.

Wheeler, Nicholas J., 'Humanitarian Intervention after Kosovo: emergent norm, moral duty or the coming anarchy?', *International Affairs*, 77(1), 2001, 113–28.

Wheeler, Nicholas J., *Saving Strangers: Humanitarian Intervention in International Society*, Oxford: Oxford University Press, 2000.

Wight, Gabrielle and Brian Porter eds., *International Theory: the three traditions*, Leicester: Leicester University Press, for the Royal Institute of International Affairs, 1991.

Wight, Martin, *International Theory: The Three Traditions*, London: Leicester University Press, 1991.

Williams, Carol, 'Road to Democracy in Haiti Hits an Impasse', *Los Angeles Times*, 26 June 2003.

Women's Commission for Refugee Women and Children, *Precious Resources: Participatory Research Study with Adolescents and Youths in Sierra Leone*, April–July 2002, available at http://www.allafrica.com

World Bank, *Report of the Joint Assessment Mission to East Timor*, 8 December 1999, available at http://www.worldbank.org.

World Food Programme (WFP), *Protracted Emergency Humanitarian Relief Food Aid: Toward 'Productive Relief', Programme Policy Evaluation of the 1990–1995 period of WFP-assisted refugee and displaced persons operations in Liberia, Sierra Leone, Guinea and Cote d'Ivoire*, Mission Report, Rome, October 1996.

Yannis, Alexandros, 'Kosovo Under International Administration: An unfinished conflict', Athens: Hellenic Foundation for European and Foreign Policy, 2001.

Zacarias, Agostinho, *The United Nations and International Peacekeeping*, London: I.B. Tauris and Co, 1996.

Zametica, John, *The Yugoslav Conflict*, Adelphi Paper No. 270, London: Brassey's, for the International Institute for Strategic Studies, May 1992.

www.allafrica.com
www.focus-on-sierra-leone.co.uk
www.indian-express.com
www.kosovo.com
www.parliament.the-stationery-office.co.uk/pa/cm19990/cmselect/cmfaff/28/28a.
www.sierra-leone.org
www.un.org/News/ossg/rwanda_report.htm.
www.unmikonline.org/archives/news04_02full.htm.
www.unmikonline.org/pub/misc/ksip_eng.pdf
www.yayasanhak.minihub.org.

Index

United Nations
intervenionism,
1991-2004.

DATE			